COMPARATIVE POLITICS

COMPARATIVE POLITICS
An Introduction

Sam C. Sarkesian
Loyola University of Chicago

James H. Buck
University of Georgia

Alfred Publishing Co., Inc.
Sherman Oaks, California 91403

   Alfred Publishing Co., Inc.
   15335 Morrison Street,
   Sherman Oaks, California 91403

Printing (last digit)
10   9   8   7   6   5   4   3   2   1

Library of Congress Cataloging in Publication Data

Sarkesian, Sam Charles.
   Comparative politics.

   Includes bibliographical references and index.
   1. Comparative government.   2. United States -
Politics and government.   3. Russia - Politics and
government.   4. China - Politics and government.
5. Japan - Politics and government.   I. Buck,
James Harold, joint author.   II. Title.
JF51.S28   320.3   78-12083
ISBN 0-88284-067-3

Cover design by Bill Conte

CONTENTS

PREFACE

This book is about comparing political systems. While there are many reasons for undertaking a comparative study of political systems, three are particularly important. First, comparing political systems provides us with knowledge about the world we live in. We have gone beyond the period in which individual nation-states can isolate themselves from others and expect to enjoy a safe and secure existence sheltered from the problems of the world. Through a comparative study of politics, we can learn about other systems, ideologies, and cultures. In this way, we can gain the kind of understanding necessary to maintain some reasonable order in the world. Second, by studying other systems, we can develop a better understanding of our own political system. A comparative examination can reveal characteristics of our own system which might otherwise be difficult to identify. In addition, comparative studies broaden our perspective on our own system. Third, the comparative study of political systems helps us to conceptualize about political life. By identifying political phenomena common to various political systems, we are able to assess how these differ or are alike and thus to sharpen our analytical ability and reasoning processes.

To accomplish these various purposes, we have used a comparative approach based on four concepts. First, we examine political systems rather than states. *Political system* is more encompassing than *state* and directs the attention of the student to the informal dynamics of the system as well as to its formal institutions. Moreover, such an approach gives an important place to the interdependency of the parts of the system, their relationships, and their interactions.

Second, rather than limit our perspective to the formal institutions of government, we use the concept of *political actor* to study the functioning of political systems. Political systems do not perform functions. It is the institutions within these systems that perform functions. In the aggregate, their functions determine the shape and character of the systems. The political actor concept encompasses not only formal institutions, but a variety of other important political groups and individuals as well. Using this concept allows us to also consider the many informal political processes and activities that affect political systems.

Third, we examine *ideology* as an organizing concept. In other words, we use the concept of ideology to organize our information about the political system. Ideology establishes the accepted patterns of political behavior, determines the relationship between the ruled and the rulers, and is the philosophical source of political power. Moreover, studying ideology allows us to develop an understanding of the values and purposes of the political system and establishes a reference point for determining the character of the system.

Finally, we use the concept of *power* to link the other three concepts. Political actors seek to achieve certain goals. In this pursuit, they use power. Power is a factor in virtually every political relationship. Thus power is an important concept in our comparative approach.

Using these concepts we identify political actors, describe the political system in which they operate and its basic ideology, and analyze how these actors affect the system. The final step is to assess the results of this study and ascertain how well the system performs. To do so, we examine the policy process and output. This final step allows us to see the results of the interactions of political actors, the application of power, and the degree to which ideological principles are applied and pursued. We seek to answer the question: How well does the system perform in terms of its own ideology?

One of the major issues facing students of comparative politics is what political systems to study. In this book we examine four systems, those of the United States, the Soviet Union, China, and Japan. There are important reasons for this kind of selection. Along with the United States, the Soviet Union and Japan are the world's largest economic entities, while China has the world's largest

population and high economic potential. The United States and the Soviet Union represent contending superpowers and ideological centers of Western thought. Moreover, they provide relatively clear contrasts between major political systems. China and Japan represent similar contrasts in Asia. Both have been influenced by Western thought (i.e., China by the Soviet Union and Marxism-Leninism; Japan by the United States). Moreover, China is a Maoist system falling on one end of the ideological spectrum, while modern Japan represents a political system oriented in the opposite direction. Finally, these four countries are important influences on developing societies.

We begin by studying the United States. Such a beginning takes advantage of prior student knowledge and provides a familiar landmark for comparison. The material included is not intended to repeat what is covered in American government courses, but rather to introduce new perspectives and a comparative approach to the study of American government. Equally important, studying the American political system first gives us an opportunity to go into more detail in explaining the scheme and approach of this book. Using a familiar political system, we can better grasp the analytical discussion of the role and purpose of political parties, for example, or of the classification of interest groups and political actors. As a result, the student will find the chapters on the American political system somewhat more detailed and descriptive than those on other systems.

While we have focused on identical concepts in each country, we have attempted to avoid a rigid format. That is, we have tried to allow flexibility within chapters by not forcing our examination into artificial categories. For example, in the examination of the Chinese system, much time is spent on Mao and the Maoist philosophy, because these are fundamental considerations in the study of the modern Chinese system. In the study of the Japanese system, attention is focused not only on the Buddhist doctrines, but on Shintoism, on the Chinese influence, as well as on the ideological impact of the American occupation. Similarly, much time is spent on the United States legislative process and the role of Congress in the decision-making process; whereas, in examining the Soviet system, little time is spent on the Soviet legislative process. The reasons for this are clear. The Soviet legislature is of relatively minor importance in that country's policy-making process. Indeed, the Soviet legislature is, at best, a minor political actor. In the final analysis, our concern with political actors within each system invariably leads to varying emphases; the nature of power and political actors in each system required such an approach.

Yet we know that it is difficult to get the same kind of reliable information about each of the systems discussed here. For example, while there are various behavioral analyses of the American political system, similar analyses are generally scarce for other political systems. To provide an "even" assessment, therefore, we have used information from different but comparable sources. We have consulted the experts on each concept and system. Doing so has enabled us to avoid distorting the realities of the political process and has reinforced the relevance of the comparative method.

Our approach is at once historical, descriptive, and analytical. First we develop a historical foundation of the evolution and interpretations of a system's ideology, giving some attention to the historical events and forces that have shaped the ideology and to the relationships between this ideology and the development of the political system.

Second, this study is descriptive. That is, the political environment that has fostered and is fostered by the various systems is described. Moreover, analysis generally evolves from descriptive studies, particularly on an introductory level. It is quite difficult to analyze political systems, ideologies, political actors, and power without describing what they are—their characteristics and their relationships. To study, for example, the executive office in the United States without first describing the office and its roles, identifying its sources of power, studying the character of its incumbents, and becoming aware of the relationship of this office to other parts of the political system is to ignore the basis of the analytical process.

Our approach is also analytical. That is, we examine major parts of the various political systems according to our concepts to understand their nature, function, and relationship. From our examination, we draw conclusions regarding similarities, differences, and impact on the political system. This perspective is reflected not only in the approach, but in the comparative chapters, in our assessments of the power of political actors, the nature of the ideology, and the performance of the system.

In the final analysis, we have been guided by the recognition that this is an introductory study in comparative politics. Thus we have made little attempt to develop theoretical constructs, synthesize theories, or discuss the various elements of comparative theory. We have based our approach primarily on country case studies, but have integrated these into a particular conceptual framework which we feel can be the basis for the development of a comparative model. While our perspective may therefore be termed configurative, it is more. It is an attempt to integrate and interpret case studies by organizing them around specific concepts and comparing the performance of systems in accordance with these concepts. We feel, therefore, that this textbook stands somewhere between the two extremes represented by existing textbooks on comparative politics, between those that are primarily single-country monographs or multicountry case studies, and those that are more theoretical and functionally oriented cross-national examinations of system elements (for example, political parties). We have attempted to provide a conceptual and descriptive clarity, even at the expense of more intellectually complex but easily misunderstood explanations.

We have tried to be objective in our assessments, but we are aware that few, if any, authors are completely objective, regardless of their efforts. Thus at the outset, we would like to make it clear that our scholarly objectivity has been muted somewhat by our convictions that a democratic system, whose concern is the individual, political justice, human rights, and a government based on the consent of the governed, is morally and ethically superior to other forms. We have, however, tried to avoid making moral and ethical judgments about political systems. This does not necessarily mean that we accept the moral and ethical superiority of the American democratic system above all others—our own system has much to achieve in terms of its own ideology—but it has come a long way, committed to the values of democracy. We also recognize that systems continually evolve; that democracy cannot be achieved overnight; that there are many forms of democracy; and that at some stage in the evolution of political systems, order, stability, and growth may be more compelling than the niceties of parliamentary democracy.

On the other hand, our own experience in a variety of foreign countries leads us to believe that those systems committed to democratic values do provide an environment that is sensitive to the individual, to political justice, and to human rights. Our biases compel us to regard such values as morally and ethically superior and a just goal for all systems.

Sam C. Sarkesian
James N. Buck

PART 1

Introduction

CHAPTER 1

THE COMPARATIVE METHOD

Some three hundred years before the time of Christ, Aristotle was completing his famous analysis of the constitutions of various Greek city-states. Comparing and analyzing these constitutions, he developed a procedure that has become the basis for the comparative method. Today, scholars have developed sophisticated schemes and employ complex computer technology in comparing political phenomena. However, Aristotle's method of description, analysis, and identification of similarities and differences remains at the heart of the comparative method.

Of course, the study of comparative politics has become more complicated since the time of Aristotle. Both the limited number of formal political entities of the Greek city-state period and the limited range of scholarship have been replaced by a complex world structure and greatly expanded human knowledge. This has led to vast changes in the field of comparative politics, particularly over the past three decades. For example, the breakdown of the European order and the proliferation of new states in Africa and Asia have made the study of non-

European systems essential. Additionally, all kinds of political phenomena, such as corruption, crime, and educational policies, are now studied on a comparative basis. Finally, the burst of intellectual activity in developing new comparative perspectives has added a great many new words, phrases, and concepts to the literature. Consequently, the study of comparative politics may now include a variety of models and approaches, as well as a variety of structures, processes, and activities. It is no wonder that political scientists have been unable to agree on *one* acceptable comparative model!

The first order of business, therefore, is to outline the comparative approach used in this book and to explain why we chose it, how the various parts of the approach are related, and what they are intended to show about the systems we study. It may be useful at the outset, however, to point out what this book is *not* about. It is not a book on comparative theory, nor is it a synthesis of various comparative approaches. Our primary concern is to introduce *one* comparative approach, integrating it with case studies of four different

2

political systems. While this is not "theory," it is a necessary first step in the development of theory and in developing sophisticated comparative assessments.

As used here, the *comparative approach* is "a predisposition to adopt a particular conceptual framework . . . [it] is the particular orientation that one adopts when addressing a subject or issue."[1] In this respect, we seek to analyze four political systems on a case study basis from a traditional descriptive perspective. Doing so allows us to synthesize a great deal of information about the systems. We seek, however, to go beyond this traditional perspective by adopting a conceptual framework that enables us to generalize on a comparative basis across the four political systems.

Political Actors and Power: A Systems Perspective

Our comparative approach rests on four concepts: political system, political actors, ideology, and power. We intend to define each of these terms, discuss their relationships, and apply them to the study of four political systems. While the first three concepts provide the general perspective to study four different systems, the concept of power provides the integrative thread that connects political system, ideology, and political actors. In brief our comparative approach asks the question: How is power acquired, maintained, and used by political actors to affect the performance of the political system? In this context, performance means the degree to which the political system is able to satisfy the expectations of the most powerful groups in society, and most members of society. Thus, to examine performance, we need to identify and study the elements of each system's ideology. (See Figure 1-1 for an overview of the systems perspective used here.)

POLITICAL SYSTEM

A political system is a mechanism for making decisions. In the words of one authoritative source, a political system consists of "persisting patterns of human relationships through which authoritative decisions are made and carried out for a society."[2] Therefore, to perform its function properly, the political system must have direct links with, and be sensitive to, social needs and demands. The political system does not exist in isolation from the society it must serve.

Generally speaking, the definition of system suggests an interdependence of parts, a beginning and an end. For example, the human body can be conceived of as a system. It has a visible form, it begins and ends somewhere, the parts are interdependent, and there are specific functions associated with it. If your fingers touch a hot object, signals are immediately sent to your brain causing a response—you quickly withdraw your finger. These general considerations apply to a political system. All of the parts of a political system are interdependent. Change taking place in any one particular part has an effect on all others. Where the political system begins and ends is not clear, however. Similarly, its "physical" form—if indeed there is such a thing—is difficult to envision. As in any system, the political system consists of many parts formed into a unified whole. Each of the parts of the system performs specific functions which, in turn, make the system work.

All members of society are included in the political system and are affected by its operation. However, what makes the political system unique from all other systems, such as the social system or the religious system, is that it alone has the authority to make legitimate decisions affecting everyone.[3] This includes using legitimate physical coercion to ensure that people abide by its decisions.

It becomes clear, therefore, that the defini-

Figure 1-1: Political Actors and Power, a Systems Perspective*

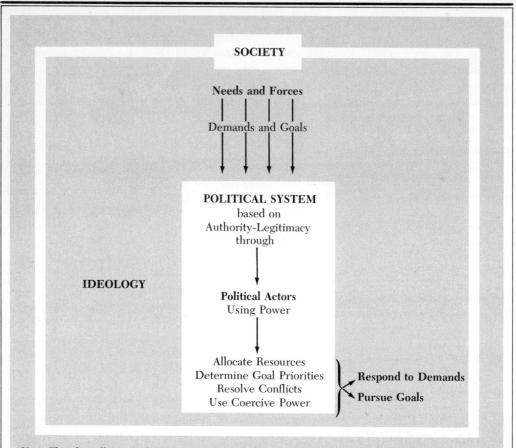

SOCIETY

Needs and Forces

Demands and Goals

POLITICAL SYSTEM
based on
Authority-Legitimacy
through

IDEOLOGY

Political Actors
Using Power

Allocate Resources
Determine Goal Priorities
Resolve Conflicts
Use Coercive Power

Respond to Demands

Pursue Goals

Note: This chart illustrates the conceptual framework used in this book and discussed in the first chapter. In brief, *power* is used by *political actors* to perform the functions of the *political system*. These functions are determined primarily by societal demands and goals. To remain legitimate, the functions and the use of power must be within the general principles of the system's *ideology*. Ideology not only is the basis for system legitimacy, but is also the determinant of the individual's own value judgments on the political environment and his own role in the system.

tion of a political system needs to go beyond a "mechanism for making decisions." For example, we can reasonably ask: Making decisions for what purpose? The political system must make decisions on how to achieve the goals of society, involving the allocation of resources and the establishment of priorities.

Obviously these are not the kinds of issues on which all major groups in society will agree. There is bound to be conflict—not necessarily bloody street battles, but disagreement, often violent—on what goals should be pursued and how the nation's money should be spent. In providing a mechanism for making decisions, therefore, the political system must also be able to anticipate and identify the conflicts that are bound to arise and must establish a mechanism for resolving these conflicts. And we need to note that all political systems have conflict, even the most authoritarian, if only among the ruling elite.

In light of these considerations, we need to expand our definition of political system even further. It is not only a mechanism for making legitimate decisions, but also one that allocates resources, determines the priority of goals, and anticipates, identifies, and resolves conflicts that may arise. No political system can do all of these things perfectly. Nevertheless, the stability of the system is, in large part, determined by its effectiveness in performing such functions.

POLITICAL ACTORS

The concept of political system, however, is an abstraction. As we suggested earlier, one cannot see a political system, nor can one identify its form. What gives substance to the system and what actually does all of these things a system is supposed to do are its institutions, which, in the aggregate, make up the system. In addition, the processes used by these institutions to make laws and to adjudicate and implement them are also parts of the political system.

If, however, we limit our study only to the formal institutions and processes, we are likely to overlook very important parts of the political system, such as interest groups, political parties, and even individuals. Equally important, we may overlook the interaction and processes that take place among a host of important political actors outside government. Thus, we use the concept *political actor*, which simply means those groups, institutions, and individuals who have an important impact (or potential impact) on the politi-

cal system. It is the action of such actors that determines the actions of the state and shapes the character of the political system.

The kinds of political actors and their relative power is determined by the type of political system, more specifically, by the ideology of the system. The degree of political power and where such power rests, therefore, differs in every political system. In the Soviet Union, for example, political power resides, generally, in the Communist party, and more specifically in a small group (elite) within the party. In the United States, power resides not only in groups and institutions within the government, but in political influentials and public interest groups. Indeed, in the Soviet Union, political actors are generally limited to a small sector of Soviet society; in the United States, political actors encompass a much larger segment of society. Thus, one can make distinctions between Soviet and American systems by studying such indicators. Similar comparisons can be made between Japanese and Chinese systems.

All political actors are not struggling for power with the same intensity and scope over all issues at all times. Where the issues are not of great concern, only a few participants will be involved in the power equation. As the issues become more important, they touch a greater number of participants. In addition, the composition of the participants and the kinds of roles they play are likely to change depending on the issues involved. Regardless of who is involved in the power equation, the essential factor is that a relatively stable system is maintained by satisfied groups, even though they may not achieve all of their goals in the power struggle. This satisfaction comes from the realization that, within the system, they can play the power game and will have continuing opportunities to achieve their goals.

To help us in studying political actors and their power, we.have placed them into five major categories. These political actors, however, do not operate in isolated compartments: their boundary lines are not sharply drawn. They are inexplicably intermeshed with one another.

Institutions: the formal institutions that are primarily involved in implementing policy and whose functions have an impact on the political system. This category would include subinstitutions, such as the military and various bureaucracies within formal institutions, and might also encompass semiofficial groups, such as government-appointed task forces or committees.

Decision makers: those persons who have an official position within the political system and are high enough on the responsibility scale to be able to make important decisions regarding the values, resources, and operations of the political system.

Groups: those interest groups whose main operational environment is or can be the political process and who are specifically organized for political participation, for example, political parties, labor unions, and professional associations.

Potential influentials: those persons who generally do not have official decision-making positions in the political system but, by virtue of their status and resources, can have important impact on the operation of the political system, for example, rich contributors to financial campaigns or the board chairmen of large corporations.

Individuals: although this category is included here, we will generally find that only in certain instances are individuals important political actors. Very little can be accomplished by average individuals working by themselves to influence the political system, although there are some exceptions; however, at times of crisis or when issues are more clear and of major proportion, individuals are important. They form a national constituency and a public that can

exert power on the political system. In democratic systems, elected officials also desire to maintain the proper image with the people. It is through such indirect linkages that individuals have an impact on the political system. The collective term *people* does perhaps have some substance but very little identity. It covers all sections of the country, all ethnic groups, all socio-economic levels, and a multitude of political attitudes.

IDEOLOGY

The activities of political actors and their particular function in the political system are generally determined by ideology. Recalling the definition of legitimacy and authority, we note that "the right to make rules" is justified in the political system when these directly reflect the ideological principles and interpretations of the political system. Equally important, ideology not only provides a criterion by which to judge the character of the political system, but also is important in the individual's own role in the political system.

Briefly, *ideology* is "an interrelated, persisting set of beliefs that predisposes a person to respond in a particular way to some object or situation."[4] Thus, ideology provides an individual with a set of coherent reference points by which he judges his environment, other men, and the functioning of the political system. For the political system, ideology provides a coherent set of reference points around which its functioning and the functioning of political actors can proceed systematically. Without a relevant ideology, not only would an unpredictable and ultimately chaotic environment develop within the political system, but anarchy could develop, with every political actor claiming that it alone was the source of all authority and it alone was legitimate, that is, acting according to "rightful" authority.

The same is true for the individual's own immediate environment and his role in the system. In this respect, ideology of the system is reflected in the law, the rules and regulations of society, and the general political style at all levels within the system. For the individual, as well as the system, ideology reflects the general values of society and provides the proper roads by which the goals of the individual and society are to be pursued. To be sure, few systems function in perfect accord with proclaimed ideological principles, nevertheless, it is the ideology that provides the reference points by which the system is ultimately legitimized, the actions of political actors are judged, and the roles of individuals are determined.

POWER

What links these concepts together is the concept of power. We recognize that there may be some problems in using power as an integrating concept. Some scholars hesitate to use power because it is difficult to define and even more difficult to apply in the study of political systems. Yet, we are convinced that power can be used as an integrative concept and can be usefully examined on a comparative basis, as long as we recognize the methodological difficulties. What is more important, however, is that power is the "energy source" for the functioning of the entire political system.

Briefly, political actors use power to obtain their particular goals. Equally important, the interaction and relationships among political actors, society, and the political system as a whole are determined by power, who has it and how it is used. *Power* is an "ability to get what one wants by whatever means—by eloquence, reasoned argument, bluff, trade, threat, or coercion, but also by arousing pity, annoying others, or making them uneasy."[5] In the words of another scholar,

No society in recorded history has ever been able to dispense with political power. This is as true of liberalism as of absolutism, as true of laissez-faire as of an interventionist state. . . . But the methods applied by those who wield power and the scope of its application vary, of course. And it is precisely this problem that is of major significance for the political scientist. . . . Three basic methods are at the disposal of the power group: persuasion, benefits, violence, are always present in all forms of government.[6]

Power is difficult to measure, however. Many times power is used in subtle and complex ways. Other times it is applied quite visibly. It is not difficult, for example, to see the power of the state when its police or military forces go into action against dissidents or mobs. On the other hand, power is a more subtle factor when the government bureaucracy selects a person for a tax audit, or an individual is asked to serve on a jury. While the state is not threatening the person with coercive action in such cases, there is no doubt that the individual should comply. Similarly, it is difficult to measure power in many situations where nongovernmental groups are involved. In the American political system, for example, it would be difficult for a local community organization to challenge the American Bar Association. The power of the community organization is quite limited and its focus, primarily on the immediate local area. The American Bar Association, representing lawyers from all over the country, has the skills, resources, and a national focus to successfully counter challenges from lesser groups.

With respect to these examples, in a democratic system, we assume that the individual accepts the tax audit and complies with a jury call because he feels it is a legitimate function of government, not necessarily because he will be physically coerced if he does not comply. Similarly, the local community organization may accept its subordination to the American Bar Association because it may perceive that the Bar Association is a legitimate group in society and operates according to the rules of the game.

In a broad sense, therefore, power has two faces: coercive and consensual. These are interconnected and interdependent, and it is difficult to conceive of coercive power without consensual power in some degree. As a matter of fact, some part of consensus develops out of the recognition that the political system does have a physical coercive capability. That is, most people recognize that a political system needs to maintain some kind of order and stability, using coercion at times, if necessary.

Yet, the relationship between coercion and consensus is delicate, particularly in a democratic society, where we would expect that power is based primarily on consensus. If a democratic system increasingly uses physical coercion, it undermines the democratic basis of the system. In a totalitarian system, on the other hand, the use of physical coercion and the pervasive threat regarding its use are a dominant feature. Yet, even in a totalitarian system, there must be some kind of consensus, if only among the ruling elite.

We can see that it is difficult to conceive of many situations where consensus can be completely separated from coercion. Rather, it is the balancing or mixing of these two that distinguishes various types of political systems. Figure 1-2 illustrates these relationships. No system operates on absolute consensus, just as no system operates on absolute coercion. In democratic systems, there is a major reliance on consensus; in totalitarian systems, on coercion. Thus we expect that democratic systems are generally on one end of the line (continuum) and totalitarian systems, on the other.

We must also develop some idea of how power is used among political actors. In a democratic political system whose ideology restrains considerably the use of force and

thrives on individual liberty and freedom, we would not expect political actors to use force or the threat of force against one another, except that physical force exercised legitimately and sparingly through the state, that is, the police. The fact that political actors are not limited to the official sphere of government means that few political actors have direct access to legitimate physical force. We would expect, therefore, that political actors in a democracy would engage in a variety of "peaceful" activities to develop consensus for a particular policy or activity without fearing the use of force by other political actors, particularly those actors having access to state machinery.

In an authoritarian system, whose ideology is primarily concerned with the state and society as a collectivity, the use of force against domestic opposition to protect the state is thought to be legitimate and is frequent. Moreover, in such a setting, a highly select and small group of political actors controls and uses the power of the state. The use or threat of force is ever present. Fear of the state compels most people to comply with even the most arbitrary rules. The narrow range of political activities limits the impact of political actors on the system. This greatly circumscribed range of activities in an authoritarian system, with its limited number of political actors, is maintained by the coercive instruments of the state. Such coercion is legitimized by the ideology. Therefore, the way power is used by political actors controlling the state machinery and among political actors themselves is an important indicator of the nature of the system.

One of the basic problems in any political system is that power is easily misused. In a democratic political system, in which there is a vast arena replete with negotiations, bargaining, discussions, shifting power alignments, and a variety of power holders, the boundaries of power and the interpretation of the rules of the game create a great deal of

Figure 1-2: The Power Scale as an Indicator of Types of Political Systems

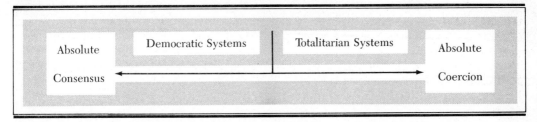

ambiguity regarding the limits of power. Thus is created an environment in which power holders are enticed to seek more power rather than to use the power they have to achieve legitimate goals within the rules of the game. Nevertheless, in nondemocratic systems, the power struggle is no less intense and is, perhaps, more deadly.

Systems Performance

If we are to complete our investigation into comparative politics using the comparative approach developed here, we must finally answer two questions: How well does each of the systems perform? How do these performances compare? As we noted earlier, performance is the degree to which the political system meets the expectations of the most powerful groups in society and of society as a whole. In examining performance we need to study the results of three separate, but interrelated dimensions: the product of the system (output), the process by which political actors pursue their goals (process), and the ideological relevance of the output and process (ideology). (See Figure 1-3.) In simple terms, if we examine the performance of the Soviet system, for example, it should be done according to Soviet Communist ideology, not democratic ideology. By doing so, we may be able to avoid ethnocentric judgments, judgments that presume that one system's ideology is necessarily better than another.

OUTPUT

One method of assessing the system output is to study how and to what groups resources are allocated, that is, how the nation's wealth is spent. For example, if the political system is based on a democratic ideology, we would expect that resources would generally be allocated to a vast range of social groups in an attempt to narrow gaps between the haves and have-nots. If we find, however, that resources are allocated on a fairly consistent basis to the highest socioeconomic groups in society, then we could reasonably conclude that the performance is contrary to its ideology and indeed is an indicator of dysfunction or improper functioning of the system. In addition, such a condition would also indicate that political actors favoring the higher socioeconomic groups dominate the system.

PROCESS

Similarly, the process can be studied by identifying the political actors involved and the extent to which they are successful in achieving their particular goals. For example, in the United States policy outputs on fiscal and monetary matters generally reflect the strength of business groups, labor organizations, and the power of the presidency. These political actors exercising power, interacting with one another, aligning with one then the other political actor, determine the kind of economic policy that is to be followed in any

Figure 1-3: Systems Performance

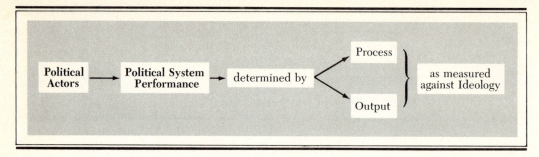

given administration. In authoritarian systems, such as those of the Soviet Union and China, the top echelons of the party attempt to control the entire policy process, favoring a small elite in control of the party. In the United States and, to a lesser degree, in Japan, the policy process is less amenable to the control of *one set* of political actors. Power and policy are thus closely intertwined in determining what the system has accomplished, reflecting the exercise of power within the system.

IDEOLOGY AND PERFORMANCE

As we can see, for the political system to remain legitimate, the process and output must be in accord with ideological principles. At least the most powerful groups in society must perceive the process and output to be ideologically acceptable. For example, it would do little good for the political system in the United States to try to eradicate political apathy and develop a high degree of individual political participation if this required arresting all those who did not vote on election day. Similarly, conducting a criminal trial in the United States by threatening bodily harm to the defendant might uncover the truth or result in a confession but would, at the same time, ignore one of the fundamental principles of democratic ideology: the rights of the individual.

In a system whose ideology is communistic, one would expect that the major concern is the rights of the collectivity, and that individual rights are subordinated to social justice. Thus the accumulation of wealth by one individual or the rise of a middle class may be considered contrary to such ideologies, regardless of the benefits that may result to society as a whole.

To be sure, assessing ideological principles with process and output is not an easy task. Ideology has a way of being interpreted differently by political actors in any one system. In addition, there is a difference between ideological proclamations and implementation. Nevertheless, if we understand the essence of ideologies, whether they are democratic, socialistic, or communistic, we can describe and analyze the general thrust of the process and output, and are able to make generalizations regarding the performance of the political system. From these generalizations we can also develop a comparative perspective.

PROCESS AND OUTPUT PHASES

To study performance, we have developed five phases of process and output. These are:
Emergence: identification of policy needs, response to pressures of society and political actors; generally unsystematized and unorganized.

Figure 1-4: Policy Process and Output

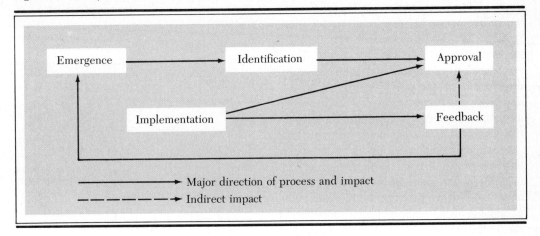

Identification: emerge of a policy proposal, coalescing of supporters, organization of opponents, application of power to win support or obstruct the policy; revision of the policy.

Approval: formal approval process, coalescence of supporters; opponents bringing power to bear on other political actors involved in the formal approval process.

Implementation: development of programs and commitment of resources to apply policy; reaction of bureaucrats; agencies involved in implementation, carrying out the policy; application of power by both supporters and opponents to affect policy implementation; policy revision.

Feedback: the response and reaction by political actors to the output of policy; revisions of policy in response to exercise of power; re-entry of the policy into the policy process.

Process and output in most political systems, however, is never as clearly delineated as these phases might suggest. More often than not, each of these phases overlaps and blends in with other phases, defying neat analytical categories. Yet, it does assist our study if we use these phases as an organizing device to examine political actors and systems

performance. Figure 1-4 shows the general outlines and relationships of these phases.

In the final analysis, the real measure of a political system is its ability to maintain a balance between stability and change while making decisions that are generally accepted by political actors. Thus the political system must respond to conflicting demands by various actors by applying power in accordance with the beliefs and values that are the ideology of the system. If the system is unable to operate effectively, it will be susceptible to revolutionary movements based on an ideology that purports to resolve conflicts in legitimate ways.

In examining process output, therefore, our primary concerns are the kinds of political actors involved in the various phases and how they use power in each phase.

Summary

The comparative approach used in this book integrates four concepts: political system, political actors, ideology, and power. Each of these concepts is defined, and their relationships are analyzed. The conceptual framework formed by these concepts is used to study four political systems. While these systems are treated on a country-by-country basis, the comparative approach used here attempts to generalize and integrate the various concepts across the country studies. Thus, our approach presumes that there are common factors among political actors in all systems that lend themselves to a comparative examination. We are not concerned here with the relationship, for example, between local groups and local elections. Rather, our focus is on those political phenomena that directly affect the performance of the political system and the political actors that are relevant at the national level. Our concern, therefore, is not the political environment of the individual (micropolitics), but the political environment and functioning of the system (macropolitics). Finally, the purpose of this study is to assess how well political systems perform in terms of their own ideology. This is reflected not only in the use of the four concepts but also in our assessment of the policy output and process of the systems.

NOTES

1. James A. Bill and Robert L. Hardgrave, Jr., *Comparative Politics; The Quest Theory* (Columbus, Ohio: Charles E. Merrill, 1973), p. 25.
2. Jack C. Plano and Robert E. Riggs, *Dictionary of Political Analysis* (Hinsdale, Ill.: Dryden Press, 1973), p. 69.
3. To provide a generally acceptable definition of various terms used in this book, we have borrowed liberally from Jack C. Plano and Robert E. Riggs, *Dictionary of Political Analysis* (Hinsdale, Ill.: Dryden Press, 1973). According to the authors, *authority*, to be legitimate, must come from "willing acceptance by others of one's right to make rules or issue commands and to expect compliance with them [p. b]." Similarly, *legitimacy* is "the quality of being justified or willingly accepted by subordinates that converts the exercise of political power into 'rightful' authority [p. 45]."
4. Ibid, p. 5.
5. Louis J. Halle as quoted in Ivo D. Duchacek, *Nations and Men: An Introduction to International Politics*, 3rd ed. (Hinsdale, Illinois: Dryden Press, 1975), p. 140.
6. Franz L. Neumann, "Approaches to the Study of Political Power," p. 51 in Roy Macridis and Bernard Brown, eds., *Comparative Politics: Notes and Reading*, 4th ed. (Homewood, Ill.: Dorsey Press, 1972).

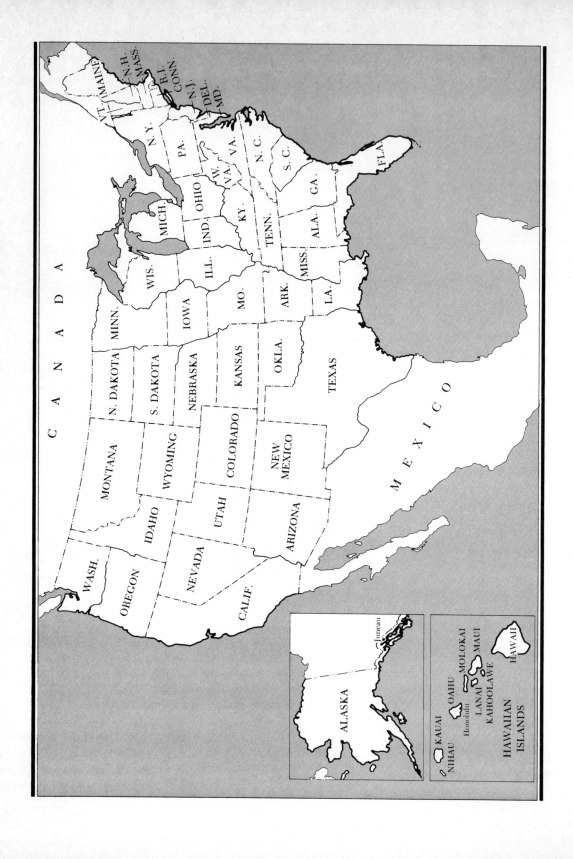

PART 2 The American Political System

CHAPTER 2

AMERICAN TRADITION AND IDEOLOGY

When American farmers challenged British regulars at Concord Bridge in 1776, few could have foreseen its result. Not only did this spark the American Revolution leading to independence from British rule, but it was a harbinger of a political system unique in Western civilization, a system based on responsibility and accountability to the people. Indeed, Americans are likely to look back over their experience during the past 200 years and logically conclude that the American democratic system is a hallmark of Western civilization and a great contributor to Western intellectual tradition.

This view is based not only on the American Revolution and its colonial past, but also on the principles of the American political system as expressed in the Declaration of Independence and the U.S. Constitution—one, an expression of revolution and ideals of government; the other, an instrument for the establishment of government. To understand the basis for the modern American political system and ideology, therefore, we need to study not only these two documents, but also the heritage of the colonial relationship and revolution, and the political philosophy of the American experiment.

The Colonial Experience

The colonies were not all established at the same time. Rather, there was an almost hodgepodge approach to the colonial system. "At no time did the British develop an effective, centralized government for the colonies." While ". . . the particular circumstances, that led to its [the particular colony's] founding determined the specific form of each colony's government and degree of local independence permitted it," there was a general pattern to all colonial governments.[1] Thus, the English political and legal tradition became a part of the colonists' political tradition. A variety of practices found a common linkage from the English system, through the colonial period, to modern America.

In the main, the colonial governments were organized around a governor chosen by the king for royal colonies and by the founding companies for Maryland, Delaware, and Pennsylvania. The powers of the governors were similar to the power of the king in England. Most colonial legislatures had two houses. Members of the lower house were elected by a limited male suffrage and members of the upper house were appointed by the king. Similarly, judges were appointed by the king. In theory then, the American colonies were organized like most other English colonial possessions. They were governed by an executive appointed by the king and by bicameral legislatures with very limited power.

However, the character of the colonists, who after all were basically Englishmen, and the nature of the colonial environment did not make of the colonists subservient subjects. Indeed, the governors and the king's appointees were really prisoners of the people they ruled. Thousands of miles separated the governor from England, and the colonists themselves were well versed both in the notion of individual rights and responsibility of government.

The first cautious movements toward revolution came because the colonists considered themselves entitled to the traditional rights of Englishmen and could therefore satisfy themselves that they were upholding the English constitution by defying the English government when in their opinion it denied them their rights.[2]

Moreover, members of the legislatures were concerned with perpetuating their own interests in a realistic way. The "fine" theories of colonial government gave way to the political realities and power of the colonists. The colonial legislators "extended their influence by slow accretion. Governors came and went but the lawmakers remained, accumulating experience, building upon precedent, widening decade by decade their control over colonial affairs."[3]

While the colonists were increasing their power within the colonial government, England began to impose a series of regulations to make the colonies self-sufficient economically. Guided by the concept of mercantilism, England intended that the colonies should support the mother country. It was presumed that colonies were important economic assets. Moreover, the French-Indian Wars led to a further tightening of controls over the colonies. Thus, while the colonists were developing increasing power and control over the colonial government, England was attempting to centralize its rule from London. Beginning with the Navigation Acts, extending through the Stamp Act, then the Townshend Acts, and finally the Tea Act, the English attempted to monopolize trade, while taxing the colonists. At the Boston Tea Party the colonists expressed their outrage and defiance. England responded with parliamentary "Coercive Acts" and the Boston Port Act, which closed the port of Boston. The colonists called these the "Intolerable Acts." The British responded with coercion, and colonists came together to declare their independence from Great Britain.

The Revolution

Regardless of how one views the American Revolution (some scholars even deny that it was a revolution), the fact remains that it shifted the legal basis of power from England to America. For all practical purposes, the Revolution was the culmination of the increasing power of Americans as reflected in the colonial government and in the struggle against the economic impositions of England. Moreover, the Revolution required a central form of authority, both to direct the military struggles against the British and to mobilize resources in colonial America. It became clear that a government based on the power of colonies would be inadequate to deal with the problems of the new country.

Equally important, Americans had been exposed to the idea of natural rights and illegal government. As one scholar notes,

By the time of the American Revolution, and considerably before, the New England clergy had turned from their preoccupation with the duty to obey and concerned themselves with topics that have a familiar ring today. They were preaching that the people had natural rights, that a government existed to preserve those rights, and that a government that fails to do this not only could be but should be overthrown by the people.[4]

The Revolution also legitimized the concept of militia in defense of the state. Indeed, the idea that every able-bodied citizen with his own weapon would come to defense of the state became a basic premise of the American tradition. Moreover, it re-emphasized the status of the individual and the individual's relationship to government. Thus, even in time of war, the fear of an overpowering central authority gave particular credence to individual rights and freedoms.

Moreover, the Revolution took its own peculiar American twist. It was not a revolution bringing with it idealistic expectations or revolutionary rhetoric. It was not a revolution that was intended to wash away the vestiges of the old in one cataclysmic sweep. As de Tocqueville wrote, the revolution in America "was caused by a mature and thoughtful taste for freedom not by some vague, undefined instinct for independence [that is, for absence of order and constraint]. No disorderly passion drove it on; on the contrary, it proceeded hand in hand with a love of order and legality."[5]

In 18th-century America, the Revolution provided not only the "myth" but the "hardening" process through which the colonists developed a system of government that continues today. As Garraty states, ". . . events had forced the colonists to think out their relation to Great Britain, and they had decided overwhelmingly that drastic changes must be made. Fumblingly but inexorably, they were also becoming aware of their common interests, their Americanism. . . . A nation was being born."[6]

Independence from Great Britain brought with it a new and more difficult problem. It was one thing to fight a war, another to govern a new nation at peace. How were the colonists to incorporate their experience and ideas into a system of government? How could the people be sovereign, yet be governed? Could people both govern and be governed? Some of the wisest men in America came together in Philadelphia in 1787 to try to answer these questions.

American Political Thought

While it is true that there was a commitment to liberal traditions of democracy in the founding of the American Republic, it was also true that there were deep divisions regarding the role of the people and their right to rule. As a result of the contradictory themes in American political tradition—suspicions of the people and the fear of irresponsible government—there has developed an ambiguity and an unstructured character to American ideology and its cultural tradition. Nevertheless, the American political system rests on specific principles and beliefs that have had a relatively long history. These have been conditioned by the uniqueness of the American experience, particularly the unusual set of circumstances evolving out of the American Revolution, a revolution fought by the colonists to retain what they had already achieved as British subjects.

The revolutionary purposes and goals were articulated in the Declaration of Independence and detailed in the Constitution. While the first document expressed the ideals of American society, the second established the framework for a system of government manifesting these ideals. Many of the issues of modern American culture and ideology stem from the various and sometimes conflicting interpretations of these documents. Indeed, one can also argue that present-day cultural issues stem from the perceived differences between the ideals expressed in these documents and the realities of American political life.

To understand the principles expressed in the Declaration of Independence and in the concepts underlying the framework of government in the Constitution, we need to look back to the 17th- and 18th-century political theorists. For not only were the Founding Fathers practical men experienced in colonial practice and in revolutionary struggle, they were also well-read men familiar with the writings of John Locke, John Stuart Mill, Baron de Montesquieu, and Thomas Hobbes.[7]

DISTRUST OF DEMOCRACY

Most scholars would agree that the Founding Fathers had little faith in the ability of the people to rule themselves. Indeed, they felt that man was primarily concerned about his own self-interest and the great danger to government was democracy. As one authoritative source notes, the Founding Fathers "did not believe in man, but they did believe in the power of a good constitution to control him."[8] On the other hand, the Founding Fathers "were intellectual heirs of seventeenth century English republicanism with its opposition to arbitrary rule and faith in popular sovereignty."[9] In this respect, one of the great achievements of the Constitution was the integrating of democracy with balanced government: the fears of democracy were countered by the fears of arbitrary government. How this was done is the primary focus of this chapter.

The Founding Fathers' view of the people derives from the Hobbesian concept of man. According to Hobbes, the natural state of mankind is war and the natural drive of man is self-interest. As a matter of protection and survival, therefore, man exercises his natural right to establish government based on mutual contract. Thus man is prior to any political organization. A sovereign must be given the power to rule other men to keep man from exercising his passions in a brutal way. As Hobbes wrote:

The final cause, end, or design of men . . . is the foresight of their preservation and of a more contented life thereby—that is to say of getting themselves out from that miserable condition of war which is necessarily consequent . . . to the natural passions of men when there is no visible power to keep them in awe and tie them by fear of punishment to the performance of their covenants and observation of these laws of nature.[10]

Hobbes's view of natural right is not based on the concept of right reason or natural law conceived of in the classic sense, but on man's legal right to use his own strength to secure his own survival: "Therefore, notwithstanding the laws of nature . . . if there be no power erected or not great enough for our security, every man will—and may lawfully—rely on his own strength and art for caution against all other men."[11] Hence, Hobbesian man is basically a man of passion bent on grasping power to control other men—all because of man's natural right.

THE GOODNESS OF PROPERTIED MEN

Although all of these threads were woven into the tapestry of early American political thought, it is the view of John Locke that is most pronounced. Locke viewed man as a reasonable being whose actions are a result of the autonomy of the individual. Pragmatic and empirical premises underlie the development of a political system whose main purpose is to protect the individual's natural right to include life, liberty, and property.

These individual rights of man can never be granted away, and government is specifically limited to their protection. In accomplishing these purposes, government must act strictly according to law and systematized procedures. All individuals must be treated equally while the primary purpose of laws is to achieve the good for the people. From these precepts developed the idea of laissez-faire economics and the concept that government is best when specifically limited to the protection of property. According to Locke:

Men being, as has been said, by nature all free, equal, and independent, no one can be put out of this estate and subjected to the political power of another without his own consent. The only way whereby any one divests himself of his natural liberty and puts on the bonds of civil society is by agreeing with other men to join and unite into a community for their comfortable, safe, and peaceable living one amongst another, in a secure enjoyment of their properties and a greater security against any that are not of it. . . . When any number of men have so consented to make one community or government, they are thereby presently incorporated and make one body political wherein the majority have a right to act and conclude the rest.[12]

Locke is quite emphatic in his view regarding the rights of and the state of nature: "Men living together according to reason, without a common superior on earth with authority to judge between them is properly the state of nature. . . . The natural liberty of man is to be free from any superior power on earth and not under the will or legislative authority of man, but to have only the law of nature for his rule."[13]

Contrary to the Hobbesian view, therefore, Locke viewed government as a device established by men of property to ensure the continued enjoyment of life, liberty, and property. Government was established by consent of the majority of men, but more important, to

"secure enjoyment of their properties and a greater security against any that are not of it." In other words, the goodness of man was primarily assigned to those who were propertied. The Founding Fathers could find no basic contradiction between Hobbesian and Lockean man: the one referred to the masses; the other, to these propertied groups or men of substance like the Founding Fathers. As Hofstadter notes, "Government, thought the Fathers, is based on property. Men who have no property lack the necessary stake in an orderly society to make stable or reliable citizens. Dread of the propertyless masses of the towns was all but universal."[14] In sum, the two perspectives had to be synthesized into a workable form of government. The writings of other political theorists of the 17th century and earlier provided some idea of how this could be done. The political system required a commitment to the idea of liberty and equality for all; the actual government, while perpetuating this ideal, had to function well enough to ensure that it remained in the hands of the enlightened and responsible classes who would reasonably weigh and respond to the demands of the masses. Or, in the words of Jeremy Belknap, a New England clergyman, "Let it stand as a principle that government originates from the people; but let the people be taught . . . that they are not able to govern themselves."[15]

GOVERNMENT AND LIBERTY

Regardless of the fear of the unpropertied masses, the Founding Fathers were aware that government had to provide an environment for liberty and, equally important, had to be limited in its powers and constitutionally mandated. This was necessary if arbitrary and tyrannical rule was to be avoided, something the colonists had become acutely aware of in their struggle against what they considered the arbitrary rule of the English monarch.

The Constitution of the United States was based upon a pessimistic view of human nature but an optimistic assessment of the potential of institutions to control human tendency toward corruption. The Founding Fathers were individualists and firmly believed, however skeptical they were of democracy and the capabilities of the masses, that the only true justification for political authority was the consent of the governed and that the only purpose of government was to operate in the interests of the people.[16]

The ideas of John Stuart Mill best expressed this concern of the Founding Fathers. According to Mill, "Liberty is not only an individual good but a social one . . . freedom is the proper condition of a responsible human being . . . the function of a liberal state in a free society is not negative but positive." Indeed, Mill argued that freedom is necessary to produce a high type of moral character.

Mill saw a positive role for government in perpetuating liberty.

A government cannot have too much of the kind of activity which does not impede, but aids and stimulates, individual exertion and development. The mischief begins when, instead of calling forth the activity and powers of individuals and bodies, it substitutes its own activity for theirs; when instead of informing, advising, and, upon occasion, denouncing, it makes them work in fetters, or bids them stand aside and does their work instead of them. The worth of a State in the long run, is the worth of the individuals composing it . . . a State which dwarfs its men, in order that they may be more docile instruments in its hands even for beneficial purposes—will find that with small men no great things can really be accomplished.[17]

He goes on to say,

The first element of good government, therefore, being the virtue and intelligence of the human beings composing the community, the most important point of excellence which any form of government can possess is to promote the virtue and intelligence of the people themselves . . . as one criterion of the goodness of government is the degree in which it tends to increase the sum of good qualities in the governed, collectively and individually.

. . . A representative constitution is a means of bringing the general standard of intelligence and honesty existing in the community, and the individual intellect and virtue of its wisest members, more directly to bear upon the government, and investing them with greater influence in it than they would in general have under any other mode of organization."[18]

Although there is much criticism of the logic of Mill's arguments and some of his basic premises, he does supply a basic theme for American political thought. With his emphasis on individuality and private judgment, toleration and freedom of thought and discussion, he reinforced the basic principles of the Constitution and the Declaration, and provided a new argument for the meaning of democracy.

MIXED GOVERNMENT AND SEPARATION OF POWERS

These theoretical perceptions did not, however, blind the Founding Fathers to the need of developing a workable government. Moreover, being practical men, they knew that government could not operate on the niceties of political theory. Applying their own hardheaded view of government to the views of Montesquieu, the Founding Fathers determined that the best government was one based on a mix of aristocratic and democratic elements, one in which power would counterbalance power.

The idea of mixed government was not new, having been expressed by philosophers and political theorists such as Aristotle and Polybius. According to Aristotle, what made a constitution good and a government stable was a mix that allowed all of the various elements of a society to have some power within the government. To ensure, however, that such power remained for the good of the constitution, the state had to be governed —according to law and justice.

> . . . there is a rule of another kind, which is exercised over freemen and equals by birth—a constitutional rule, which the ruler must learn by obeying. . . . the conclusion is evident; that governments which have a regard to the common interest are constituted in accordance with strict principles of justice, and are therefore true forms.[19]

One of Montesquieu's major concerns in the *Spirit of the Laws* (1784) was separation of powers. Analyzing the British government, Montesquieu concluded that separation of powers provided stability and freedom. Although Montesquieu's assessment regarding separation of powers in the British government was incorrect, he did put forth the theoretical perspective that separating powers between various branches of government provided a check within government, preventing domination by one branch or authority. Moreover, he noted that laws made in such a system of government were likely to protect the individual and provide an environment fostering liberty.

> When the legislative and executive powers are united in the same person, or in the same body of magistrates, there can be no liberty. . . . Again there is no liberty, if the judiciary power be not separated from the legislative and executive. . . . There would be an end to everything, were the same man or the same body, whether of the nobles or of the people, to exercise these three powers, that of enacting laws, that of executing the public resolutions, and of trying the causes of individuals.[20]

Not only did the Founding Fathers incorporate separation of powers into the Constitu-

tion, but they took this concept a step further by integrating it with mixed government.

In this brief review of some of the major political theories that were expressed in the Constitution and became part of American political thought, one fact is clear: there existed a fundamental contradiction between the desire to foster liberty and freedom and the need for a strong and effective government, one that could not be dominated by any individual or group.

LIBERTY AND EQUALITY

This contradiction was further complicated by the apparent tensions between liberty and equality. On the one hand, liberty requires an environment in which the individual can develop his talents and accomplishments to the fullest. On the other hand, equality necessitates rules and regulations to reduce the differences between people regardless of individual talents.

Major elements of these views are reflected in the writings of Jefferson and Hamilton. According to Jefferson, the basis for democratic systems rests on equality that is best manifested in a nation of self-sufficient, landowning farmers. It is through such a system that the differences between men are minimized. Moreover, the virtues developed in men who are attached to the land reinforce the stability of the system.

On the other hand, Hamilton, who was concerned primarily with the prosperity of the new nation, advocated the establishment of a commercial state whose desire to acquire property and wealth would allow the talents of individuals to develop a strong democratic nation. His primary concern was liberty. He wanted to create an environment that would allow each man to develop his own individual talents. It was through this maximization of liberty, according to Hamilton, that democratic society could become strong, self-sufficient, and stable.[21]

While both Hamilton and Jefferson sought strong government, they differed as to how it would be accomplished. Hamilton felt a strong national government that would allow each man to develop his own talents within a commercial economy was the best means of achieving a strong and stable government. Jefferson, on the other hand, felt that an agrarian society based on sturdy, landowning farmers would develop the necessary virtues and loyalty to maintain a stable system. Moreover, Jefferson assumed that the best government would be one concentrated at the local and state levels, with minimum government at the national level. He felt that the closer the government was to the people, the more effectively it could rule and be controlled.

The debates at the Constitutional Convention regarding representation and the powers of the central government reflected these differing interpretations. Yet, the fact remains that, when Jefferson became president of the United States, he was no less concerned about a strong central government than Hamilton.

Regardless of these differences, however, American political thought and the principles established in the Constitution rest on generally accepted ideas about government and the character of the political system. This is well summed up by Hofstadter, who writes:

> However much at odds on specific issues, the major political traditions have shared a belief in the rights of property, the philosophy of economic individualism, the value of competition; they have accepted the economic virtues of capitalistic culture as necessary qualities of man. . . . The sanctity of private property, the right of the individual to dispose of and invest it, the value of opportunity, and the natural evolution of self-interest and self-assertion, within broad legal limits, into a beneficent social order have been staple tenets of the central faith in American political ideologies.[22]

SUMMARY

In the main, the major principles of political thought underlying the American perspective during the founding of the Republic evolved from Locke and, somewhat later, from Mill. It is the intermingling of concepts expressed by Locke and Mill which is fundamental to understanding the American political evolution.

> . . . whereas for Locke, because of the equality and freedom of the mental substances, government, even the minimum government, is an evil, and something to which the individual contributes only grudgingly in order to preserve his private property, for Mill government is not merely a positive good to which the individual makes his unique contribution and in return for which he receives the unique contributions of his fellow citizens, but also a necessary instrument for achieving the greatest happiness for the greatest number.[23]

Whether one agrees with Hobbesian or Lockean man, the concept of natural right was characteristic of both theorists. Yet, in the Founding Fathers' view, man was basically Hobbesian; that is, man's nature was one of self-interest which created a constant state of tension. Thus government was necessary to control the people. However, the Founding Fathers accepted the Lockean view that government, in turn, must be responsible to the people, but protect property, as well as life and liberty.[24]

Throughout the evolution of the American political system, the dilemma between "free" people and the necessities of government has been the fundamental issue. The arguments of Hamilton and Jefferson, as well as those of Locke and Mill, are attempts to resolve this dilemma. How can one achieve a democratic society, maximizing freedom while ensuring a stable and effective government? Indeed, creating an environment for liberty in which each man could pursue his wants based on his own talents could ultimately give rise to a situation in which the most talented individuals control the system. On the other hand, stressing equality would require a government to actively pursue the general welfare, subordinating the individual for the sake of all, a condition that could easily lead to conformity and "heavy-handed government." These two concepts have been at the root of struggles between liberals and conservatives, and between order and liberty. Throughout the years, positions may have changed on specific issues, but the fundamental dilemma remains.

The Declaration of Independence

The Declaration of Independence was a formal statement reflecting causes of the American Revolution and embodying the grievances of the colonists. Eloquently written, this document outlined the basic principles upon which all government should be based, and the rights of all men to change their form of government if that government did not secure certain inalienable rights. The Declaration states, in part,

> We hold these truths to be self-evident, that all Men are created equal, that they are endowed by their Creator with certain unalienable Rights, that among these are Life, Liberty, and the pursuit of Happiness—That to secure these Rights, Governments are instituted among Men, deriving their just Powers from the consent of the governed, that whenever any Form of Government becomes destructive of these Ends, it is the Right of the People to alter or to abolish it, and to institute new Government, laying its Foundation on such Principles, and organizing its Powers in such Form, as to them shall seem most likely to effect their Safety and Happiness.

While not establishing any particular form of government, it enunciated the power of the people, the concept of justice, and the principles of rule, reflecting the power of the people as expressed by Locke and man's natural right and reason as expressed by a number of theorists throughout the 17th and the 18th centuries.

Moreover, according to the Declaration, the basis upon which the government is instituted must be popular consent. Simply stated, men had the right to establish by popular consent any form of government that among other things secures protection of life, liberty, and property. When a government fails to do this, it must be changed.

> . . . the Declaration, strictly speaking, is neutral on the question of forms of government: any form is legitimate provided it secures equal freedom and is instituted by popular consent. . . . As to those democratic institutions, the Declaration says no more than this: If you choose the democratic form, rather than the aristocratic or monarchic or any mixture thereof, it must be a democratic government which secures to all people their unalienable rights. But how to do that? The Declaration is silent.[25]

The Declaration written by Jefferson is also an ardent expression of the colonists' outrage against the monarchical government of Great Britain—not because it was a monarchy, but because it failed to secure and protect the unalienable rights of the colonists and had destroyed the basis of popular consent. In brief, the British government had lost its legitimacy in the eyes of the colonists.

While the Declaration expressed the sentiments of the colonists, it was left to James Madison, who wrote the Constitution, to provide a system of government that put these sentiments into practice. As Skidmore notes,

> The subsequent development of American politics indicates that the Constitution was a splendid

reflection of the basic assumptions of mainstream American political thought. In terms of the presuppositions of the American people, it is probably true that the Constitution was the best possible codification of the principles and rhetoric of the Declaration that could survive in this society. It would have been difficult, therefore, and probably impossible, for the founders or any other group to have produced anything superior to it; the United States Constitution appears most fully to represent the political spirit that has motivated this special branch of Western civilization, America.[26]

The Constitutional Convention

Most Americans look back at the Constitutional Convention of 1787 with reverence and view the Constitution it produced as the work of heroes, divinely ordained and inspired. During the convention and the subsequent period of ratification, however, a number of people opposed the Philadelphia gathering. While Thomas Jefferson and others could look upon their works as masterpieces of political genius, others would say,

These lawyers and men of learning, and monied men that talk so finely, and gloss over matters so smoothly, to make us poor illiterate people swallow down the pill, expect to get in the Congress themselves . . . get all the power . . . and then they will swallow up us little fellows, just as the whale swallowed up Jonah.[27]

Patrick Henry, who did not attend the Convention, bluntly stated, "I smelt a rat." Moreover, there were a number of notable Americans who, for a variety of reasons, were absent, including John Adams, Sam Adams, John Hancock, Tom Paine, and Thomas Jefferson. Thus from the outset controversy surrounded the Convention.

The fifty-five delegates to the Convention were men of property and wealth represent-

ing a wide range of political views. Their average age was 40, yet these men were accomplished lawyers, bankers, merchants, and congressmen. In the main, the delegates were familiar with the theories of Locke, Mill, and Montesquieu. Yet, they were practical men who were aware of the problems faced by a new nation. Although the delegates were initially called to revise the Articles of Confederation, they were aware of the need to establish an effective government with powers of its own, not dependent upon individual states.

In 1787, the Founding Fathers were faced with a number of important issues. First, they were aware of the weaknesses in the Articles of Confederation under which the colonists gained their independence. A government with a strong central executive which could take positive measures in emergencies was needed. The Hamiltonians, in particular, never again wanted a government in which the central authority had to go begging to the states for money and men to fight a war. Second, the framers were concerned about the tyranny that could develop from power granted to a strong central government. They wanted to ensure that one part of the government could not control other parts. They spoke in terms of a balanced government, one in which there would exist countervailing powers to any attempt by one branch to gain control over others, and a government that could exercise only that power expressly given to it by the people. Admittedly, there were many disagreements, selfish sectional interests, and conflicts over economic issues at the Constitutional Convention. Yet, nearly all of the delegates agreed on the basic issues:

That there should be a federal system, with sovereignty somehow divided between the states and central government, was accepted by all but one or two of them. Republican government drawing its authority from the people and eventually responsible to them, was also a universal assumption. A measure of democracy followed inevitably from this principle, for even the most aristocratic delegates agreed that the ordinary citizen should share in the process of selecting those who were to make and execute the laws. All also agreed, however, that no group within society, no matter how numerous should have unrestricted authority.[28]

Constitutional Principles

What finally evolved was a short compromise document based on five fundamental principles: power of the people; federalism; separation of powers and checks and balances; limited government; and judicial supremacy. Each of these has been interpreted and reinterpreted over the past 200 years in response to the requirements of the particular age; nevertheless, the substance remains as the framers had envisioned. Although much was left unsaid, these principles established the basis for, limits to, and constraints on power to be exercised by the political actors within the political system. Moreover, they embody the core values of the American ideology. And as we discussed earlier, these reflect a synthesis of 17th- and 18th-century political thought and the realities of the American experience.

THE POWER OF THE PEOPLE

The most basic principle underlying the Constitution is that the people are sovereign and that all power granted to any form of government emanates from them, reflecting the principles found not only in the writings of Locke and Mill, but in the Americans' grievances against England as well. Popular sovereignty is clearly the intent of the Preamble of the Constitution, which states, "We, the People of the United States . . . do ordain and establish this Constitution for the United States of America." And it is from this Con-

stitution that the major political actors in the American political system acquire power. Throughout the Constitution, there are references to the power of government not only being limited by the rights and power of the people but clearly subordinate to the people. The First, Ninth, and Tenth Amendments, for example, are particularly clear on the subject of rights and power of the people. While the First Amendment prohibits government from infringing upon basic individual rights, the Ninth and Tenth Amendments make it clear that power ultimately rests with the people.

The Ninth Amendment states, "The enumeration in the Constitution, of certain rights, shall not be construed to deny or disparage others retained by the people." The Tenth Amendment particularly makes it clear where power resides: "The Powers not delegated to the United States by the Constitution, not prohibited by it to the States, are reserved to the States respectively, or to the people."

As one might expect, however, proclaiming power to the people is one matter, and its practical application another. A complex system of representation, voting, and laws was intended to provide realistic application of power to the people; however, the individual in the American system is completely overshadowed by the modern American state.

Yet, power emanates from the people. No major political actor can remain legitimate without making some response to the people. Elected officials, from members of school boards to the president of the United States, must take their case to the people to win elections and retain their offices.

Moreover, the Founding Fathers, as we noted earlier, were concerned about the irrationality and self-interest of the people. Fear of the tyranny of the majority and of the rebellious mobs in the cities was reflected in the attempt to control the passions of the people through a series of checks and balances in government. Elected assemblies would be checked by a more "orderly" process of government. Thus the Founding Fathers were faced with a dilemma: they needed to reconcile their view that man was basically selfish with their desire to create a "free" society and responsible government.

From a humanistic standpoint there is a serious dilemma in the philosophy of the Fathers which derives from their conception of man. They thought man was a creature of rapacious self-interest, and yet they wanted him to be free—free in essence, to contend, to engage in an umpired strife, to use property to get property. They accepted the mercantile image of life as an eternal battleground, and assumed the Hobbesian war of each against all; they did not propose to put an end to this war, but merely to stabilize it and make it less murderous. They had no hope and they offered none for any ultimate organic change in the way men conducted themselves. The result was while they thought self-interest the most dangerous and unbrookable quality of man, they necessarily underwrote it in trying to control it. They succeeded in both respects. . . .[29]

In any event, the "sovereign people" is a basic part of the United States Constitution. More realistically, however, the people hold all of the power to control the "governors," but it was thought that the people are not in a position to govern themselves.

FEDERALISM: DUAL POLITICAL SYSTEMS

Political systems can be organized in one of three ways: federal, unitary, or confederation.[30] In a federal system, power from the people is delegated to two political systems, the central authority and the states. Each authority has autonomous powers in its own sphere. Certain powers are shared while others are exclusive. In a unitary system, powers are delegated from the people solely to the central authority. The central authority, in turn, may delegate some of its power to subordinate government units. For example, the state system within the United States is based on a unitary system; that is, the states establish local governments and delegate varying degrees of authority to them. Similarly, in England, the Parliament is supreme over all other governmental units. In a confederation, such as the American Confederation of 1775, power of the people is given to the states, which in turn may delegate certain powers to a central authority. The central authority does not derive its power directly from the people—the states are clearly superior to the central authority. The power patterns in each of these systems becomes clearer when viewed as a schematic (Figure 2-1).

The constitution establishes a federal system in the United States by creating two political systems with authority divided between the two. Paragraph 2 of Article VI explicitly provides for national supremacy or more pointedly constitutional supremacy:

This Constitution, and the laws of the United States which shall be made in pursuance thereof; and all treaties made, or which shall be made under the authority of the United States, shall be the supreme law of the land; and the judges in every State shall be bound thereby, any thing in the Constitution or laws of any State to the contrary notwithstanding.

Thus, although a federal system is established, when there is conflict between the laws of the state and the laws of the national government, the national government prevails.

The Tenth Amendment to the Constitution provides another element of federalism:

The powers not delegated to the United States by the Constitution nor prohibited by it to the States, are reserved to the States respectively, or to the people.

Figure 2-1: Three Basic Political Systems

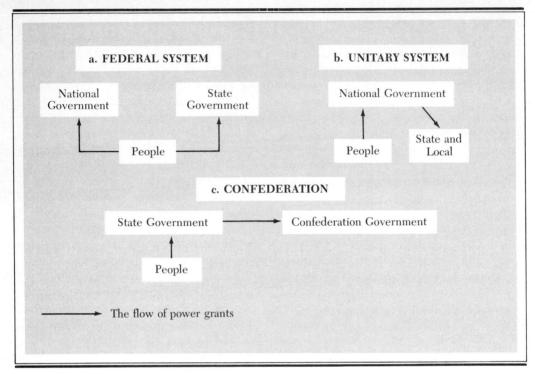

This doctrine of "reserve" powers or "state's rights" has been the basis for limiting the power of the federal government in areas not expressly stated in the Constitution. However, attempts to limit federal power under this amendment have met with only limited success, because the provisions of Article I, section 8 establish the concept of necessary and proper powers, implied powers:

The Congress shall have power . . .

To make all laws which shall be necessary and proper in carrying into Execution the foregoing Powers, and all other powers vested by this Constitution in the Government of the United States, or in any Department or Officer thereof.

In the American political system, therefore, power is shared between the states and the federal government, while certain powers are exercised exclusively by each. There is established a state political system and a federal political system, with each American being a member of both systems.

SEPARATION OF POWER AND CHECKS AND BALANCES

In addition to power distributed among the states and the national government, the Constitution distributes power among the various branches of government. Concerned over the possibility of tyrannical government, the framers established a balanced government, in which each of the branches would share a degree of power with one another. Article I states: "All legislative powers herein granted shall be vested in a Congress of the United States, which shall consist of a Senate and House of Representatives." Article III states: "The executive power shall be vested in a President of the United States of America." Finally, Article III gives power to the judiciary: "The Judicial power of the United States shall be vested in one Supreme Court, and in such inferior Courts as the Congress may from time to time ordain and establish."

While these articles appear to provide exclusive powers to each of the three branches of government, in reality there are provisions within the Constitution for the sharing or checking of power. For example, the president takes part in the legislative process by his power to call special sessions of Congress, veto bills, and decide aspects of policy directly affecting the legislative process. The Congress becomes involved in the executive office by its power to approve ambassadorial appointments, and hold hearings on many aspects of the executive office, and by its power in financial matters and impeachment. The Judiciary, by virtue of its power to invalidate legislation and rule on the extent of executive power, provides a check on the powers of the other branches.

These considerations obviously do not exhaust the list of shared powers. As a matter of fact, beyond the legal provisions, there are many informal means by which power can be checked between the branches. The web of personal relationships and the exercise of power by individuals in each of the branches through the use of mass media, personal contacts, and "behind-the-door" pressures provide many substantial checks on power between the various branches. For example, President Lyndon Johnson's close friendships with many of the senior senators were important sources of power in proposing and supporting legislative programs. He was able to go beyond the formalities of executive-legislative relationships to take advantage of his friendship with key members of the senate. On the other hand, the lack of these close relationships tends to isolate the presi-

dent and diminish his influence on the legislative process. This isolation was apparent during the last days of the Nixon administration. Cut off from any enduring relationships with senior congressmen and operating within a staff system which was inclined to protect the president from the "outside," Richard Nixon was increasingly isolated in office. With this isolation came diminished power. The concept of shared power and exclusive powers, therefore, has both legal and extralegal connotations.

LIMITED GOVERNMENT

Constitutionalism and limited government go hand in hand. A constitution grants power to government; at the same time, it limits government. It is also an instrument embodying the principles of government authority, the philosophy of the political system, and the rules of public debate regarding the aims of government and restraints on the exercise of power. In such an environment, government can never be an ultimate authority unto itself, but is limited by the grants of power it receives from the people. Popular sovereignty—the idea that the ultimate authority rests with the people—is basic to the concept of limited government.

Limited government is also based on the idea that the people have basic rights and freedoms that cannot be taken away without due process of law. These were originally spelled out in the first ten amendments to the Constitution—the Bill of Rights—and later in the Fourteenth Amendment. Since the passage of these amendments, a number of court decisions and additional amendments have expanded the rights and freedoms of citizens.

Furthermore, limited government is associated with the pluralistic concept of politics. This means that a variety of ethnic, economic, religious, and cultural groups in

American society are political actors and share power in the system. They not only act as a countervailing power to each other, but they also can counter the power of formal government institutions. Pluralism also stimulates "participatory democracy," encouraging involvement in politics by groups and individuals in order to gain some share of the "pie," further increasing the number and activity of political actors.

JUDICIAL SUPREMACY

The concept of judicial supremacy is one of the most important characteristics of the American system. It is based on the idea that the judiciary is the final authority in interpreting the meaning of the Constitution. The highest court in the land, the Supreme Court, thus becomes the final authority in any constitutional or legal conflict brought before it.

The Founding Fathers had not intended for the Supreme Court to be "democratic," in the sense of having its member judges be elected or accountable to the people. The Court was established to check and control the representative institutions and reflected the Founding Fathers' concern over the inability of people to rule themselves.

Judicial supremacy is not explicitly granted in the Constitution; however, Article III, section 2, states: "The Judicial Power shall extend to all Cases, in Law and Equity, arising under this Constitution, the Laws of the United States, and Treaties made, or which shall be made, under their authority." It was the famous case of *Marbury* v. *Madison* (1803) which clearly established the principle of judicial supremacy. Chief Justice John Marshall held that the Supreme Court had the power to invalidate federal laws also when they conflicted with the Constitution. Judicial supremacy, however, does not mean that the Supreme Court is supreme over all other branches as such, rather that the Supreme Court has the authority of judicial review. This judicial review simply means that the Supreme Court is indeed supreme when it comes to interpreting the Constitution and reviewing the constitutionality of actions taken by other branches of government. All political actors in the system are legally bound by the decisions of the Court.

The Changing Constitution

Since the Constitutional Convention, many complex social, economic, and political issues have plagued the American political system, issues that could not have been envisioned by the Founding Fathers. These have resulted in a number of amendments to the Constitution, many judicial interpretations, and continually changing constitutional practices. For example, the growth and development of a strong political party system has worked against the separation of powers and federal structure. When the President, the Congress, and many state executives come from the same political party, the tendency may be to act in concert rather than to limit or restrain power.

Similarly, the rise of the presidency to a dominating office in the political system may have circumvented some of the countervailing power concepts envisioned by the Founding Fathers. The establishment of a large and efficient bureaucracy, which remains outside the electoral process, cuts across constitutional and party lines. These and other factors must be considered as qualifications to the original concepts envisioned by the Founding Fathers.

The Constitution should not be viewed as a rigid answer to all men for all times. It was not intended to be a document in which all the answers are found for all the problems. What the Founding Fathers intended was a document capable of establishing a stable democratic government, yet one that would be flexible enough to respond to changing times and demands.

Democratic Ideology

In the American political system, the concept and practice of democracy is based on the five constitutional principles. It is presumed that these principles are the most effective way to achieve the goals of democracy. But what are the goals of democracy? How are they to be achieved? Indeed, what is meant by democratic ideology? In this section we will explore these questions in more detail.

The constitutional principles, the Bill of Rights (the first ten amendments), and later amendments (for example, the Fourteenth Amendment) provide the essential features of American democratic government. Limited government provides the fundamental basis, while a number of other features protect the individual from invasion of his rights while maximizing his freedom. Thus, to properly understand the operation of the political system, one must have some idea not only of the power vested in the Constitution, but also of how this power is to be exercised and for what purpose. Not only is power to be exercised according to the constitutional principles, but it must also be used in accord with the principles of democracy, to achieve the goals of democracy. The ends of government are important, but so also are the means. That is, to achieve peace, one is not supposed to kill all those who disagree. In the name of freedom of speech, one cannot scream "Fire!" in a crowded theater when there is no fire.

The United States political system rests on a set of core values based on the concept of democracy. We will speak more of the meaning of democracy later. At the minimum, *democracy* means the political importance of the individual and accountability of those in power. As long as there is a high degree of commitment to these core political values by the society, the political system is likely to remain relatively strong and effective.

Although the concept of democratic ideology is basic to the American political system, many persons, scholars and students alike, have difficulty identifying the specific elements of democratic ideology. Here again, the problem arises not only because of varying perceptions, but also as a result of the perspective used in defining democracy. In simple terms, if one is an idealist, the concept of democratic ideology is tied in closely with the Declaration of Independence, the Constitution, and the Bill of Rights. Moreover, the nature of man is viewed as being basically "good" and capable of the highest moral behavior. On the other hand, the realist would probably accept the Declaration of Independence, the Constitution, and the Bill of Rights as the working basis for democracy. He would, however, acknowledge that these idealistic documents do not realistically reflect and cannot realistically reflect human nature and the workings of political systems. Therefore, the realist would stress that there is no such thing as a perfectly working democracy. Rather, democratic ideology should be based on the reasonably adequate operations of a political system striving to achieve the best for the most. Needless to say, the idealist and the realist have been arguing since the time of Socrates and no end is in sight.

The Meaning of Democracy: An American View

While it is difficult to define democracy to the satisfaction of all democrats, its meaning is tied closely to the manner in which decisions are made. Briefly, democracy is a form of decision making which provides for a wide range of political decisions to be made by the people. Equally important, the decisions must include a concern for certain kinds of values and social environment.

Democracy presumes that the machinery of the political system provides, protects, or supports: (1) a regularized system of periodic elections which, in turn, gives rise to representative government; (2) public access to facts upon which to base political decisions; (3) the basic right of the people to criticize the operations of the political system; (4) the right of the people to participate in all aspects of the political system and to organize for political purposes; (5) rule by the majority with basic safeguards for minorities; and (6) equal voting power for all qualified people, as individuals.

Democratic ideology is based on certain values, including the legal equality of human beings; emphasis on the individual, that is, individual worth; the supremacy of the people over their officials, in other words, all elected officials are ultimately responsible and accountable to the people; the derivation of authority from the people; and perhaps, the basic value of maximum freedom and dignity in order to foster all other democratic values, the individual's need to be free if, in fact, the democratic political system is to operate. This does not mean unrestrained freedom and liberty. Even in a democratic society, all of this must be consistent with maintaining a relatively balanced and stable society.

Democracy is based on the assumption that a certain type of social environment must exist if democratic machinery is to operate and democratic values are to prevail. Democracy cannot be established in the political sphere unless the rest of society is in harmony with democratic ideology. In short, certain social and economic conditions must exist to further democratic practices and values. There must be reasonable opportunity for social mobility, the opportunity to advance from a lower socioeconomic grouping to a higher one. Similarly, there must be a reasonable opportunity

within the political and social system for individuals to acquire a share in the economic wealth. The political system must provide for channels and opportunities for individuals to better themselves politically, socially, and economically, if in fact, democratic machinery and values are to operate.

In the late 1960s and lingering on into the 1970s, the social principle of democracy within the American political system has been particularly susceptible to criticism. Unemployment and poverty have been acute among black Americans. Similarly, Spanish-speaking Americans and Indian-Americans have been vocal in their criticisms regarding social and economic opportunities. However, we ought to note also the observations of de Tocqueville, a Frenchman who visited America in the early 1800s, who stated that "the advantage of democracy does not consist, therefore, as has sometimes been asserted, in giving prosperity to all, but simply in contributing to the well-being of the greatest number."[31]

How to Achieve Democracy

If one is to have "democracy," then all three of these principles—democratic political machinery, democratic values, and democratic environment—need to be embodied in the framework of government and work reasonably well. While it is clear that none of these premises will work perfectly in any system, regardless of how democratic it is, at a minimum, one should expect that the political system is actively pursuing these premises and relatively effective in maximizing all three. More important, the people must perceive that the political system is, in fact, working in accord with these three principles.

As was suggested earlier, ideology is supposed to provide some plan of action to change the real world into something that ought to be. A democratic ideology is likely to have many routes by which the "is" can be changed to "ought to be." A totalitarian system, on the other hand, is likely to have a specific route. Therefore, most totalitarian systems are preoccupied with the relevance of their ideology and can provide a coherent explanation of it while democratic systems have difficulty explaining theirs. For example, democratic countries include the United States, England, Sweden, Canada, France, Japan, and Norway, to mention a few. Yet in each country democracy has a different meaning while operating within a different political system. In communist countries, there is an ideological cohesion based on a strong central party structure and dominance of the individual by the state. Moreover, in such authoritarian countries, the ideology spells out programs to be achieved and goals to be accomplished in specific terms. Democratic ideology does not presuppose a party system; it does not require two, three, or more parties. Indeed, one can argue that democracy does not require any particular form of government so long as the three principles outlined above are the basis for establishing the government and the political system is acting on them to promote democracy.

The very nature of a democratic political system militates against a clearly articulated program for the achievement of specific goals. Indeed, one of the essential features of a democratic system is the "openness" of debate and the variety of views regarding the purpose and operation of the political system. Concerning this seeming lack of direction, one scholar writes:

Turning from communism to democracy is like finding oneself moved from a lightly wooded hillside with a clear path to the middle of the jungle with no beaten track in sight. With Marxism it was possible to go directly to certain writers and certain key topics, without any hesitancy. With democ-

racy, there are no specific writers, and there is not even much agreement on what topics must be considered. . . . All of this is not too surprising because democracy is not, and never has been, a clearly defined political theory.[32]

To achieve democracy, then, the American political system must be organized according to the principles of power to the people; separation of powers and checks and balances; federalism; limited government; and judicial supremacy. In addition, the political system must function to ensure the pursuit of the principles of democracy associated with democratic political machinery, democratic values, and social democracy.

Democratic Liberalism and Conservatism

In addition to the ambiguous nature of democratic theory and the variety of views of how the American political system whould operate, there is a distinction between conservative and liberal sentiments, sentiments that have been a distinguishing characteristic of America. In modern-day America, it is not clear at times who is a conservative and who is a liberal; nevertheless, there are clear conservative and liberal positions on a variety of issues. For example, liberals would probably applaud America's accomplishments in détente with the Soviet Union and closer relationship with China. Conservatives, on the other hand, would probably warn against these policies while demanding more support for the military establishment. Similarly, in domestic policies a liberal views welfare programs and increased protection of individual rights against the establishment as a necessary condition for democracy. The conservative, however, would caution against large welfare programs, claiming they undermine the concept of individual worth. Likewise, conservatives argue that eroding institutional control for the sake of individuality may lead to anarchy. Yet both liberal and conservative sentiments fall within the democratic fold.

From a more philosophical perspective, liberals are likely to accept the view that man by nature is a rational being who, through the free flow of ideas and information, will engage in rational debate. Through such debate man can determine an objective moral order and identify values worth pursuing. Moreover, individuals have certain inalienable rights that transcend political institutions. These rights must be protected under any circumstance. Thus, the best approach to democracy is a free flow of ideas and information and maximum individual involvement in the political process. To achieve these ends, the political institutions must, under all circumstances, protect the individual's right to freedom and political involvement. Instruments of government are merely a means of fulfilling social desires. Moreover, as man interacts with his environment, he gains additional knowledge and has new experiences. Instruments of government must be responsive to resulting changes in his demands.

Conservatives, on the other hand, would argue that man's ability to submit to reason and rational discussion is limited. It is more likely that man is moved by passion and self-interest. Therefore, an environment must be created which provides controlled and restrained involvement in the political process. It logically follows that those of greatest talent must use their talents for the good of all. Moreover, to ensure that there is no dominance of one faction by another (since people tend to be factious), government must be balanced and rule must be by a limited aristocracy.

Conservatives feel that civilized society requires order and a class structure. Moreover, conservatives would argue that change and reform are not identical. Thus, there must be order and stability in political institutions and

some continuity reflected in tradition, if, indeed, there is going to be true equality and democracy.

Obviously, there is much overlap in the views of liberals and conservatives, particularly those whose convictions are not on the extreme ends of the political continuum. Hence, most American political leaders are difficult to categorize as purely conservative or liberal. Yet, when one views these perspectives from extreme liberal or conservative positions, one can identify clear positions and political officials who are closely identified with each sentiment. Equally important, the range of these sentiments is part and parcel of democratic political systems.

Summary

The American perspective on man and his government and the nature of authority has emphasized the individuality and autonomy of man. Government is thought to be limited only to those things that maximize individual, freedom and opportunity—freedom in the sense described by Mill. Yet the acceptance of freedom of the individual has been tempered by the recognition that government must be orderly, indeed, that people cannot govern themselves. These philosophical principles, which were present in 17th- and 18th-century political thought in the writings of such philosophers as Hobbes, Locke, Mill, and Montesquieu, formed the basis for the U.S. Constitution. While the Declaration of Independence proclaimed them, the Constitution provided a system of government embodying them. They are reflected in the five major principles in the Constitution: power of the people, separation of powers and checks and balances, federalism, limited government, and judicial supremacy.

The actual operation of the American political system, however, is a reflection of the differing interpretations of the Constitution. Indeed, the American ideology is a diversity of subideologies. Rather than a specific program and agreed-upon goals, democratic ideology may be best served by a continually changing, dynamic, and responsive system attuned to political participation by the people. In other words, the people should be able to participate realistically in making decisions regarding their own lives.

The American political system is ideally based on this premise. That the system works imperfectly is recognized by many people. Thus, in recent years, there has been significant criticism of the American political system and its inability to achieve stated goals of democracy. Some of this criticism stems from what some critics feel was intended by the Founding Fathers. They see the colonial experience and the Revolution as embodying the best of democracy. Others glorify the relative freedom and individuality of the late 1800s and early 1900s, particularly as reflected in agrarian America. Many feel that, with urbanization and industrialization, came changes in values that have resulted in the sacrifice of individuality to bureaucratic control and centralized government. Thus, in the past decade, there has been increasing antagonism between the role of the individual and government control. As early as 1948, Hofstadter expressed this concern:

Above and beyond temporary and local conflicts there has been a common ground, a unity of cultural and political tradition, upon which American civilization has stood. That culture has been intensely nationalistic and for the most part isolationist; it has been fiercely individualistic and capitalistic. In a corporate and consolidated society demanding international responsibility, cohesion, centralization, and planning, the traditional ground is shifting under our feet. It is imperative in time of cultural crisis to gain fresh perspectives on the past.[33]

The basic contradictions among the ideas expressed by Locke, Mill, and Hobbes are manifested in these dynamics of the American society. While many Americans view these contradictions with some alarm, others look upon them as a reflection of the "dynamic" nature of American society. Without elaborating on the major historical periods in American society since the promulgation of the Constitution, one can argue that the dramatic experiences of America leading to the Civil War, industrial revolution, economic depression, and development into a modern industrial democratic state are, in one major sense, reflections of the continuing struggle between the rights and freedoms of the individual and the response and reaction of community institutions and structures. While the purpose of the struggles may vary from issues of slavery to economic justice, the substance remains basically the same: the quality of freedom and the limits and purpose of government. Equally important, the constant interaction, conflicts, and compromises have generally perpetuated an unstructured view of politics, restraining any significant movements toward dogmatic interpretations of democratic ideology. The intent of the Founding Fathers in balancing interests and in resting the power of government on the people has, in the past, served as a resilient and adaptable arrangement for the functioning of the American political system. Nevertheless, many questions remain unanswered regarding the ability of the American political system and its democratic credo to adapt to the postindustrial, bureaucratic, and managerial environment of the 1980s.

NOTES

1. John A. Garraty, *The American Nation: A History of the United States* (New York: Harper & Row, 1966), p. 63. The remainder of this section is based on the discussion presented in Garraty, pp. 63–88.

2. Max J. Skidmore, *American Political Thought* (New York: St. Martin's Press, 1978), p. 33.
3. Garraty, op. cit., p. 64.
4. Skidmore, op. cit., p. 48.
5. J. P. Mayer, ed., *Alexis de Tocqueville, Democracy in America,* translated by George Laurence (New York: Anchor Books, 1969), p. 72.
6. Garraty, op. cit., p. 64.
7. For a detailed discussion, see A. J. Beitzinger, *A History of American Political Thought* (New York: Dodd, Mead, 1972), pp. 3–30.
8. Richard Hofstadter, *The American Political Tradition and the Men Who Made It* (New York: Vintage Books, 1974), p. 4.
9. Ibid., p. 6.
10. Thomas Hobbes, *Leviathan, Parts One and Two* (New York: Liberal Arts Press, 1938), p. 139.
11. Ibid.
12. John Locke, *The Second Treatise of Government* (New York: Liberal Arts Press, 1952), pp. 54–55.
13. Ibid., pp. 13 and 15.
14. Hofstadter, op. cit., p. 16.
15. Ibid., p. 8.
16. Skidmore, op. cit., p. 64.
17. John Stuart Mill, *Considerations of Representative Government* (New York: Liberal Arts Press, 1958), pp. 25–27.
18. Ibid., pp. 170–171.
19. Leonard Dalton Abbott, *Masterworks of Government,* vol. 1 (New York: McGraw-Hill, 1973), pp. 93 and 96.
20. Ibid., vol. 2, p. 150.
21. The case for the Hamiltonians was argued in the Federalist Papers. Written by Hamilton, Madison, and Jay before and after the writing of the U.S. Constitution, these papers argued the need for a strong republican form of government based on separation of powers and a strong and energetic executive. The general outline of government parallels what eventually evolved from the U.S. Constitution. See for example, Ray P. Fairfield, ed., *The Federalist Papers,* 2nd ed. (Garden City, N.Y.: Anchor Books, 1966).
22. Hofstadter, op. cit., p. xxxvii.
23. F. S. C. Northrop, *The Meeting of East and West* (New York: Macmillan, 1960), p. 124. See pages 124–126 for a more detailed explanation of these matters.
24. Donald J. Devine, *The Political Culture of the United States* (Boston: Little, Brown, 1972). The author uses survey data to examine a number of Lockean principles in contemporary America. He finds that, in the main, Lockean principles remain a basic part of the American ideology.
25. Martin Diamond, "The Revolution of Sober Expectation," in *The American Revolution: Three Views* (New York: American Brands, 1975), p. 68.
26. Skidmore, op. cit., p. 67.
27. Richard A. Watson, *Promise and Performance of American Democracy* (New York: John Wiley, 1972), p. 33.
28. Garraty, op. cit., p. 147.
29. Hofstadter, op. cit., p. 20.
30. This and the following four sections follow closely the discussions in Sam C. Sarkesian and Krish Nanda, *Politics and Power in American Government* (New York: Alfred, 1975), pp. 77–87.
31. Mayer, op. cit., p. 233.
32. L. T. Sargent, *Contemporary Political Ideologies,* rev. ed. (Homewood, Ill.: Dorsey Press, 1972), p. 66.
33. Hofstadter, op. cit., p. xxxix.

CHAPTER 3

AMERICAN POLITICAL ACTORS: POWER AND LEGITIMACY

As we saw in the previous chapter, there are fundamental principles in the American ideology that serve as guidelines for the use of power by political actors. These ideological guidelines are quite broad and provide a wide area for political actor activity. Nevertheless, to be legitimate, such activity must generally adhere to the basic ideological principles and also to the rules of the game, which determine specific criteria for legitimacy. For example, it is quite legitimate for the American Medical Association to spend thousands of dollars lobbying in Congress to defeat a medical welfare bill; but if the American Medical Association were to publicly announce a policy of refusing to treat medical welfare patients, serious questions would be raised regarding the legitimacy of its actions, not only within the association but by other political actors as well.

Sensitive to legitimacy, political actors in the American system, as in any democratic system, attempt to justify their actions by linking them to concern for the public welfare and the rights of individuals. Moreover, it is not uncommon for political actors to rely on the Founding Fathers as a justification for political activities. Yet, in light of the character of the American political system—its pluralistic and heterogeneous nature—boundaries fixing the extent of political power and its proper use are themselves unclear and can be interpreted differently. Indeed, it would appear that, as long as political activities are perceived generally to adhere to principles of American ideology, the power holder is relatively free to use all kinds of techniques to acquire, maintain, and use power.

Who are these political actors? How do they use power? What legitimate activities and procedures do they engage in? As we learned earlier, political actors can be categorized into institutions, decision makers, groups, influentials, and individuals.[1] Let us examine how they function in the American system, keeping in mind several important features.

Some political actors achieve power by virtue of their wealth and ability to influence decision makers. Others achieve power because of their official position in government. Still others develop a power base because of their business interests or organization associations. Yet, the most basic means of attaining power is through the ballot box, via election to some position, whether it be city alderman or president of the United States. In any event, all must operate within the limits established by the Constitution.

Institutions

Earlier, we included within our definition of *institutions* only those officially connected with the government. In the American political system, the Constitution identifies and grants powers to three separate institutions: the legislature, the executive, and the judiciary. Obviously, most systems have similar official institutions. In the American political system, as in many democratic systems, these institutions realistically exercise power. That is, they are the focal point from which power emanates and around which other political actors function. We also include the federal bureaucracy in this category.

The uses of power, the character of the institution, and its procedures develop from those individuals in positions of authority in the institution. Yet the character of the institution is not necessarily the sum total of the individuals within it. The institution represents the heritage of the past, expectations for the future, and a continuity that goes beyond the individual. The executive office of the United States, for example, is much more than the individual in the office of the president. The executive office is the embodiment of the heritage of America and symbolic of the country. It has a character and power of its own, beyond that of the incumbent president. In examining institutions, therefore, we must be careful not to equate the power of the institution *solely* with the men and women who happen to be in office.

To gain a proper picture of institutional power in the United States, we also must recognize that there are many groups outside the institutional framework that are important political actors influencing institutional power. For example, anyone familiar with the American political system knows that labor unions have an important role in determining economic policies. Similarly, the mass media play a significant role in the American system, influencing the uses of power and the activities of political actors.

Assessments by politically influential Americans appear to support these observations on institutional power. For example, a leading national news magazine surveyed over 1,000 influential Americans to determine the power of institutions in the United States.[2] The results are as follows:

1. The White House
2. Television
3. Labor unions
4. Supreme Court
5. Big business
6. U.S. Senate
7. Federal bureaucracy
8. U.S. House of Representatives
9. Banks
10. Newspapers
11. Lobbies and pressure groups
12. Cabinet
13. Wall Street
14. Democratic party
15. Educational institutions
16. Public opinion polls
17. Family
18. Legal profession
19. Radio
20. Advertising agencies
21. State and local government
22. Magazines
23. Civil rights organizations
24. Military
25. Medical profession
26. Organized religion
27. Cinema
28. Small business
29. Republican party

As we can see, five of the top ten are government institutions, two are part of the mass media, and three have important economic roles. (According to our categorization, only the branches of government and the bureaucracy are institutions, while labor unions, big business, banking, and mass media are groups. Also note that the five major institutions we will discuss as political actors (the White House, the Supreme Court, the U.S. Senate, the federal bureaucracy, and the U.S. House of Representatives) are in the first ten.

THE PRESIDENTIAL OFFICE

The presidency is a special creation and invention of the American political system. There is no other executive in the world that has developed into such a unique, pervasive, powerful, and yet often misunderstood office.

It is paradoxical that, although it was fashioned by men who had a deep mistrust of executive power, the office has become the apex of national politics, and the *one* office with which most Americans can identify.

Views of the Presidency   There is much disagreement among scholars and serious students regarding the limits of the office and its influence on the American political system. Most scholars agree on the more clearly identifiable roles and functions of the presidency. Nevertheless, how these roles are to be performed, the extent to which the incumbent can expand these roles, and the constitutional and practical restrictions on the office remain matters of study and serious debate.

Studies of the American presidency have attempted to provide some focus by developing models and identifying specific functions of the office. For example, some scholars regard the president as primarily a manager of the bureaucracy and a legislative leader: he establishes priorities and goals for the nation,

and subsequently uses his office to shape the bureaucracy and the legislative program to reach these goals.

Others view the president as an absolute monarch with all the trappings of divine majesty. Indeed, some suggest that the presidency is the most powerful office in the world, limited only by the perceptions and personality of the incumbent. Some scholars argue that the president is a pawn of entrenched bureaucrats, that he can in fact produce no change while in office, and that he is bound by existing procedures, policies, and constitutional safeguards against making any dramatic changes. Between these two positions lies a variety of concepts of the presidency.

The power of the presidential office comes from the Constitution and from the roles that have evolved as a result of the changing interpretation of the powers it grants. Equally important, the character of the incumbents has done much to expand presidential power. Reinforcing this is the fact that there has been a significant growth in the functions of the federal government and a parallel growth in the functions of the presidential office (see Figure 3-1).

From the grants of constitutional power, specific roles have evolved in the presidential office (for example, chief of state and commander-in-chief). In addition, the president enjoys informal roles evolving from his position. These include leader of his party and protector of the welfare of the nation. In many ways, the president combines powers of a monarch with those of a prime minister. Very little of importance takes place in the federal government without some linkage to the presidency, whether it be a discussion of taxes or foreign policy in the Middle East. As we noted earlier, this exercise of power has led some scholars to conclude that the presidency has grown too powerful and is distorting its relationship to other political actors.

Most students of American government learn about the president through a study of

Figure 3-1: The Government of the United States

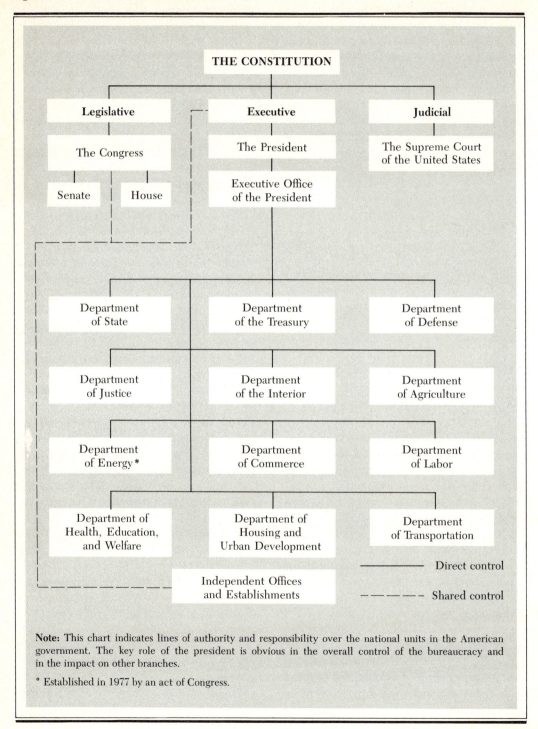

THE CONSTITUTION

Legislative — Executive — Judicial

The Congress — The President — The Supreme Court of the United States

Senate | House — Executive Office of the President

Department of State — Department of the Treasury — Department of Defense

Department of Justice — Department of the Interior — Department of Agriculture

Department of Energy* — Department of Commerce — Department of Labor

Department of Health, Education, and Welfare — Department of Housing and Urban Development — Department of Transportation

Independent Offices and Establishments

————— Direct control

— — — — — Shared control

Note: This chart indicates lines of authority and responsibility over the national units in the American government. The key role of the president is obvious in the overall control of the bureaucracy and in the impact on other branches.

* Established in 1977 by an act of Congress.

his various roles. Unfortunately, it is difficult to know what role is being played at what time. As one British observer has stated, "Whenever there has been a national crisis . . . I have found myself worried by the interventions and appearances of the President. Who, I always want to know, is speaking? The Head of the State? The Commander-in-Chief? The head of the temporary administration? The temporary head of a political party? It is never quite clear. . . . All right: 'Hail to the Chief!' But, what chief, I ask, and chief of what?"[3]

Basis of Power　As a result of the confusion and disagreement regarding the roles and power of the president, it may be useful to view the president as the focus of legal, political, administrative, and symbolic power of the American political system. Doing so will allow us to look at general areas of presidential power regardless of roles and functions. In brief, the president has specifically defined legal powers, such as those of chief executive and commander-in-chief, granted by the Constitution; but the way that this power is exercised has much to do with the president's ability as a political leader. A president who is able to develop consensus on major issues, who is able to reduce the differences within his own administration, who is able to provide a sense of direction, commitment, and loyalty, is in essence providing leadership to the nation and the various constituencies. An incumbent who is able to do all of these things can use the legal role to maximum advantage.

Presidents who are "active-positive," that is, who see politics and the presidency as a positive force in American politics, who are confident of their own abilities, and who are able to project their own personalities in a positive way, are likely to be "strong" presidents.[4] There are some factors, of course, that the incumbent must adjust to, such as the temper of the times and the international environment. In assessing the personality of incumbents, one observer of presidential politics concludes, "The ego element of presidential personalities does more than self-impose a duty to protect the office they hold and inspire their will to win. It maintains their acute self-consciousness of the supremacy of the office they hold. Presidents do not regard the legislative and judicial branches as equal; separate sometimes, but never equal."[5]

Part of a president's power arises because of his control over vast administrative machinery. This machinery, if controlled and supervised properly, provides information, extends the executive presence throughout the country, and allows the executive to direct and implement the policies as he interprets them. Obviously, this is a difficult task because the bureaucracy is a political actor in its own right. Nonetheless, there are few other political actors who have at their disposal anything comparable to the administrative machinery available to the president.

Equally important, the symbolism inherent in the presidential role can do much to expand the incumbent's base of power. By this we mean that the president's image and his general demeanor are at the root of his constituency's trust and confidence in the office. By projecting an image of concern for the "average" man, courage, strength, and compassion, the incumbent can take forward-looking and imaginative stands on policy positions knowing he can mobilize constituency support.

Moreover, whatever he does, wherever he goes, the president symbolizes the United States. This symbolic role need not be limited to the formal ceremonials of office. It can be used to expand the president's power to achieve the policy he desires.

Every incumbent begins his term with generally the same bases of power: legal, political, administrative, and symbolic. Yet it is clear that incumbents differ in their ability to integrate these, in their ability to provide

President Jimmy Carter shown in a variety of roles including holding a press conference, working in the Oval Office, meeting with Cabinet members and advisors, and meeting with congressmen and others concerned with legislative action. (Official White House photos)

the leadership to develop a coherent policy, and in their ability to "move" the nation. It is the degree of ability in this respect that distinguishes strong from average presidents. In the final analysis, the president's personality and his own perception of the presidential office determine the quality of his leadership.

Power in Domestic and Foreign Affairs   The powers of the presidential office differ in the domestic and foreign areas. As unbelievable as it may seem, the president may find it easier to engulf the United States in nuclear war than to get congressional approval for a domestic spending program. In domestic policies, a greater number of political actors are involved, and the president's domestic power is more limited than the power he exercises over foreign policy. Moreover, Supreme Court decisions have made it clear that the presidential office is virtually supreme in the foreign field. This is not to suggest that there are no countervailing powers to the presidential office, but in contrast to those operating in the domestic field, the countervailing powers are limited. Indeed, it is probably best to view the power of the presidential office on a continuum (Figure 3-2). There is an inseparable link between domestic and foreign affairs. At the very least, there must be a strong domestic base for the success of any foreign policy.

Moreover, three of the most powerful subinstitutions within the federal government are primarily concerned with foreign policy. These subinstitutions are the Department of State, Department of Defense, and the National Security Council (and intelligence agencies). Each of these institutions plays a significant part in supporting the roles assigned to the presidential office (for example, those of commander-in-chief and chief diplomat). Thus, they complement the presidential office and, in this sense, are an extension of that office. In terms of their bureaucratic

nature, these subinstitutions may well develop their own bases of power, as will be discussed in the section on the bureaucracy.

Although there are a number of ways that a president can be checked in exercising his power in the domestic field, most scholars agree that there are few such restraints on his power in foreign affairs. He can call upon a vast bureaucracy, intelligence service, military establishment, and other resources to carry out foreign policy with little reference to Congress, the judiciary, or the people. Indeed, some argue that the most effective countervailing power in foreign policy has been the mass media.

The Crucial Office   Major political actors in the American system focus much of their effort on either capturing or influencing the presidency. Every four years, the vast election machinery of every state focuses on the election of a president. This is the most important event in the political process and best epitomizes the nature of the American political system. The events leading to the selection of a candidate and the election of a president make visible all of the decentralized and diffused power bases, the many forces at work, and the vast array of political actors involved. The president is the most powerful political actor in the American system. Power emanating from this office affects all other political actors.

THE EXECUTIVE OFFICE AND
WHITE HOUSE STAFF

The executive office of the United States consists, in its widest and simplest sense, of the president, his staff, the departments and independent offices, and establishments of the federal government (see Figure 3-1). In a more realistic sense, however, the executive office is the president, the executive office,

Figure 3-2: Presidential Power in Domestic and Foreign Spheres

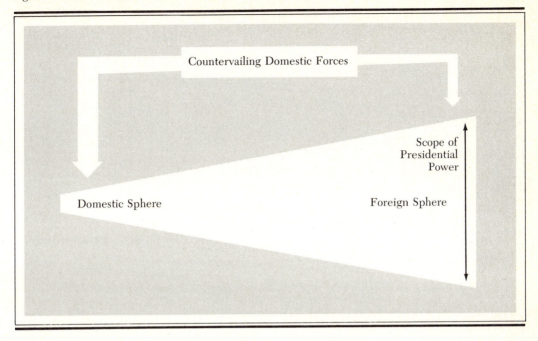

Countervailing Domestic Forces

Scope of
Presidential
Power

Domestic Sphere

Foreign Sphere

and the White House staff (see Figure 3-3). These offices are more properly called the presidential office. Those who occupy them are the "president's men." They are appointed by him and are presumed to work directly for him, with little congressional control and few external pressures. The federal departments and the independent offices and establishments, more realistically, are the major part of the federal bureaucracy. Moreover, these offices are most susceptible to congressional influence and interest group activity, and are prone to develop their own power bases, resistant to executive control.

Operating within the executive office is the White House staff. Considered the president's own staff, it exercises the strongest influence on his policies. This staff and its functions vary according to the needs, desires, and personality of the incumbent. The range of tasks of members of the White House staff is as varied and broad as the president's own responsibilities.

The functioning of the White House staff is quite visible in domestic affairs, generally more so than in foreign affairs. It is on the home front that this staff has the greatest impact on presidential power and image, primarily because of the many other political actors involved in domestic politics. Moreover, much of the activity in the foreign field takes place outside congressional control and public scrutiny. Only when there are clear and major issues in foreign affairs do members of the White House staff gain widespread public prominence.

One of the major dangers of the staff system is the likelihood that the president will be cut off from the public by inner counselors who filter out much information and many contacts they feel should not reach the president. The president, therefore, must be careful not to

Figure 3-3: The Executive Office of the President

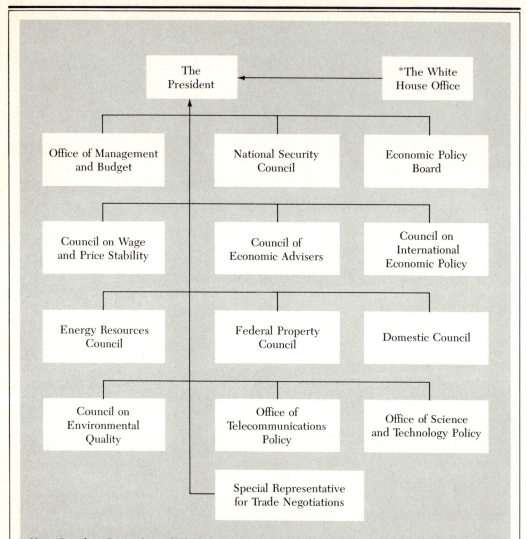

Note: President Roosevelt established the Executive Office of the President in order to provide him with assistants that he could personally control and direct in carrying out executive policy. Since that time it has grown significantly to what it is today.

° The White House Office, or the White House Staff as it is often called, is the president's personal staff. They are directly and personally responsible to him and can be appointed or dismissed at the president's pleasure. Normally, the staff numbers from 15 to 20 persons (not including secretaries) including such positions as Press Secretary and the Presidential Advisor on National Security.

Source: Adapted from U.S. Bureau of the Census, *Statistical Abstracts of the United States: 1976.* (Washington, D.C., 1976) 97th Edition and *The United States Budget in Brief, Fiscal Year 1977* (Washington, D.C.: U.S. Government Printing Office, 1976).

surround himself with unyieldingly loyal yes-men who would disregard any responsibility or accountability to other constituencies, or he will receive advice based on unrepresentative views and lacking in feasible alternatives. There is also a danger that the president may eventually feel that the White House staff represents the public and that they are presenting him with widely expressed public views. One of the most frequent criticisms of President Nixon in the Watergate affair, for example, was that not only did he seek isolation but his staff perpetuated it.

The White House staff, in many respects, is viewed as an extension of presidential power and style of politics. As such, this staff can reinforce the president's power or diminish it, depending on how they view and respond to other political actors. Because of this relationship, the staff is usually subject to criticism. One observer writes,

The strangest and most questionable feature of the government of the United States is the President's political family. The President, after his election, appoints a band of personal aides and advisers. . . . The electorate has no say in this. Yet some of the President's personal minions have greater power de facto than any officer of the United States government who has been appointed by constitutionally established procedures.[6]

THE CONGRESS

Congress is the elected representative institution that is supposed to reflect the people's will. It is the body upon which the Constitution confers legislative power. Consisting of two houses, the Senate and the House of Representatives, it was originally conceived as a device to both represent and check the irrational passion of the masses. That is, the Senate, consisting of men elected for a six-year term, was to act as a "rationalizing" body for the House, whose membership was elected for two-year terms, based on population, and more reflective of popular passions.

Both houses have power bases that are unique. The Senate, by virtue of its size (100 members, two from each state) and its term of office, represents an exclusive club. As an institution, it is perceived by many to be the more sedate and powerful body. The House, with 435 members representing various districts (based on population) throughout the country, has more difficulty in conducting its business and is constantly involved in electioneering because members are elected for two-year terms. Moreover, there is a closer linkage between members of the House and local political officeholders than one finds in the Senate.

While the presidential office may be at the center of the political process, it is Congress that is viewed as the direct link between the people and their government. The presidential office is often viewed as a lofty office, out of reach of the average person. Senators and, more often, members of the House are seen as the links between the people and Washington. Thus as institutions, both houses rest their fundamental power on their role as the "voice of the people." Because the Constitution specifically grants each house important legislative power, it is these institutions that give legitimacy and authority to the laws of the land. Even when the presidential office is the initiator, it is Congress that must give its seal of approval in order for legislation to become a legal part of the policy and laws of the country. Moreover, Congress serves as the national public forum, where all major issues are debated, made public, and acted upon. Contrary to the British system of Parliament, however, much of the political maneuvering and many of the important political decisions are made in committees, and through the formal and informal network of friends and colleagues established by various congressmen.

Both houses of Congress are organized on a committee system. And it is in these committees that most of the important legislative work is done. Procedure of both houses for passing legislation is complicated, yet susceptible to influence by other political actors. Briefly, both houses must pass legislation before it can become law. Normally, this requires a bill to be initiated by a member or members of a particular house and then passed through the legislative process, which is rooted primarily in the committee system. That is, the committees of each house are organized on the basis of special subjects. Any bill dealing with that particular subject must be referred to that particular committee. Whether the bill is approved or not depends heavily upon the views of the committee.

As an institution, Congress is expected to inquire into the activities of the various parts of the federal government (congressional oversight) to ensure that the public is made aware of the operations of the various agencies. Moreover, it is Congress, and only Congress, that can make laws to raise money and direct how that money should be spent. Indeed, Congress is the focal point for the "democratic process." That is, it is Congress that formally receives most of the major inputs for the political system, whether they be from constituencies, interest groups, or other political actors.

In sum, most of the power of Congress as an institution rests in its representative function and its oversight responsibility. Not only is Congress presumed to express the "will" of the people, but it represents the focal point of the democratic function: the legislative process. Moreover, the actual powers granted to Congress give it final authority in budgetary matters and in supervision of the federal government. How these powers are used, of course, depends to a great extent on the individual members of Congress, the personality of the president, and the resulting presidential-congressional relationships. Not the least of the powers of Congress also stem from the fact that many congressmen are political leaders in their own right. They have their own power base which gives them flexibility and freedom from presidential and congressional dictates.

Congress versus the President   Commentators agree that over the years the power of Congress has diminished. Today it no longer effectively checks the president. It no longer is the originator of domestic programs. It does not have its own list of national priorities but merely reacts to the legislative measures recommended by the president. In foreign affairs, it has almost completely surrendered its role to the president. Whereas Congress once determined, item by item, how much money the government should spend and for what purpose, today it rarely alters the administration's budget by more than 5 percent. Although Congress has responsibility for appropriating funds, the president himself can impound them, as Nixon did with some $11 billion in water pollution control and highway money.

But while it is true that the power of Congress has diminished, it is also true that the president is not the master of all he surveys. Much of the congressional session may be taken up by the president's legislative programs, but he does not monopolize the legislative agenda, nor can he legislate without Congress. Congress may have little power in foreign policy decision making, but it still must be called upon to legitimize or support the president's decisions. And while Congress may have lost the initiative in policy formulation, it still retains the crucial function of oversight, which is an important component of the policy-making process.

Moreover, during the final days of the

Nixon presidency (1974), Congress started to reassert itself in the legislative and policy process. It passed the War Powers Act (1973), passed bills to limit the president's power to impound funds (1973), established its own Congressional Budget Office (1974), and took steps to provide a closer oversight of intelligence activities. Indeed, in 1978 members of President Carter's staff complained about congressional interference in functions of the executive office.

The Presidential Veto   There are a number of powers given to the president by the Constitution which, in their aggregate, are formidable in circumscribing Congress. In addition to the power to call Congress into special session, to report to the Senate and the House on the state of the Union, and to recommend national programs, the president has the power to veto legislation. This alone is an important legislative weapon. The threat of presidential veto may be enough to prevent Congress from passing a particular piece of legislation. To override the veto requires a two-thirds vote of Congress. Thus a successful veto, with all of its accompanying publicity, tends to diminish the power of Congress in the eyes of the people. Rather than expose Congress to this possibility, many congressmen are reluctant to support legislation that is likely to be vetoed by the President. Moreover, the president's threat of veto indicates the presidential sentiment on a piece of legislation and is a "cue" to many congressmen sympathetic to the president or to the presidential party.

Obviously, when Congress is unified on a particular bill—that is, when there is a decisive commitment by many to support legislation—it does not fear a presidential veto. Indeed, in such circumstances, it is the president who must be wary of vetoing a bill because of the possibility that Congress will override the veto. This would tend to di-minish presidential power vis-à-vis Congress. Equally important, Congress may enact a stronger bill (one that is less desirable) in reaction to the veto.

THE JUDICIARY

The role of the courts in the modern American political system involves them deeply in national and local decision-making processes and in shaping the political environment. The tone is set primarily by the Supreme Court. Indeed, over the past twenty years the Supreme Court has played an important role in shaping the public policy of the nation. This power stems from the Court's role in questions of constitutionality with respect not only to decisions of government, but to the rights and freedoms of individuals, to conflicts between national and state governments, and to the interpretation of powers for other branches of government. In fulfilling its role, the Court implicitly provides guidelines as to the directions of national policy. This has been particularly true since the era of the New Deal in the 1930s.

Court Structure   The court structure in the United States is a complicated and complex one. We have already noted that the American political system consists of a national system and a state system. Each one of these has its own executive, legislature, bureaucracy, judiciary, and laws. In addition to the federal system, which has as its pinnacle the Supreme Court, there is a state judicial system, which has as its pinnacle the state supreme court. Theoretically, the state supreme court holds a position in the state structure similar to that held by the Supreme Court in the federal structure, but it is not as simple as that. The Supreme Court in certain cases has authority over the state judiciary in determining constitutionality. In this sense, the Supreme

Court straddles both national and state systems. For example, the constitutionality of state laws may be challenged through the state legal system. But in such cases, the state supreme court need not be the final authority. Decisions of state supreme courts can be appealed to the Supreme Court of the United States when the constitutionality of state laws is questioned. Similarly, in cases where the defendant's rights under the federal Constitution are involved, the ruling of the state courts can be overturned by the U.S. Supreme Court.

Power of the Court   Although the power of judicial review is inherent in the role of the Court, how it is used by the Court depends on a number of other considerations. Like all officials of government and political actors, the members of the Supreme Court are human. They see their positions on the Court according to their own perceptions and preconceived ideas about how the American political system should operate. The Court as an institution also has an impact on the individual judge. Because appointments to the Supreme Court are for life, the judges are freed from the requirements of catering to political forces. Furthermore, sitting in the lofty chambers of the Supreme Court does create new perspectives and attitudes on issues of constitutionality and the workings of the political system.

A great deal of judicial power and effective enforcement of its decisions rests on consensus within society regarding the role of the Supreme Court and the individual justices. In every case, the Court must depend on other branches of government to implement its orders. Political actors are likely to accept the Court's decisions enthusiastically when there is a consensus that these decisions are just and correct. But resistance to the Court occurs when political actors disagree over decisions.

The Court's power can also be expanded or

diminished as a consequence of the impact of judicial decisions on other institutions of government. As suggested above, enforcement of judicial decisions depends largely on the acceptance of their legitimacy and consensus within the bureaucratic structure. Enforcement depends also on acceptance by elected officials and society as a whole.

Finally, the relationships within the judicial system can also add to or diminish the power of the Court. The judiciary is not a monolithic structure in which the "robed" hierarchy has absolute and unquestioned support. There is a continual struggle within the judiciary not only as to the role of judges, but also as to interpretations of judicial decisions and their impact on society. More often than not, there are strong dissenting opinions.

Restraints and Limitations   There are a number of restraints on the power of the Court. Some of these have already been mentioned. The Court cannot act until an actual case comes before it. It cannot initiate policy until the proper question has arisen. In some cases, it may take years for such issues to be resolved. In addition, the Court does not have built-in machinery to enforce or supervise the enforcement of its decisions. It must rely on the executive branch and on a vast array of local officers to enforce its decisions. Obviously, this presents a number of problems. It is conceivable that local officers executing the Court's decisions may interpret them differently and with varying degrees of enthusiasm. By the time the Court's decisions reach the lower rungs of the political system, they may be considerably diluted.

The members of the Supreme Court are not democratically elected; they are not held responsible to the electorate. Political decisions arising out of judicial interpretations are not controlled by other branches and are not necessarily accountable to popular will; therefore, it is very difficult for the Court to develop any kind of mandate for directing public policy.

The Court and the Democratic Society In this brief overview of the Court, one can see that political and social environment is an important determinant of its decisions. Moreover, it is clear that the Court's power over the other institutions of government is quite broad, and its impact on the political system, society, and the economy can be of major importance. Finally, the personalities in the Court, particularly the chief justice, are important factors in the power and nature of the decisions. Strong chief justices inevitably dominate the Court and give it a broad and very visible impact on the politics of the country. Similarly, the composition of the Court—the attitudes of the individual justices—has significant influence on judicial decisions and perceptions regarding the proper role of the Court.

The basic dilemma faced by a democratic society with respect to its laws is to reconcile stability with the need for change. Because of its flexibility, the Constitution has provided the basis for stability and also the basis for change. Through custom and usage, judicial interpretation, legislative acts, and constitutional amendment, the system of laws has remained relatively responsive and flexible.

The role of the Supreme Court has been harshly criticized. Its critics question whether its nine justices should be the moral and legal guides to society, or whether they should be in a position to make national policy. They point out that the justices are not elected or accountable: their political decisions are not under the control of popularly elected representatives or of the popular will. For proponents of popular will, such power seems elitist and arrogant. Some suggest that the popularly elected legislature should be the final determinant of constitutionality, as it is in England where the laws of Parliament are supreme.

Critics also point out the fact that, in a number of instances, presidents who have long departed still have an impact on national policy through their lifetime appointments of judges to the Court. Scholars still debate whether Supreme Court judges should serve for only ten years, or be elected by popular vote. However, the American political system has built into it so much diffusion and decentralization, so many checks and balances, that Court decisions require the cooperation and consensus of various political actors within the system to be effective. If the Court gets too far ahead of the times, that is, goes beyond the political and social climate as perceived by the political actors, it will diminish its credibility. Its decisions would then have no real authority behind them.

THE FOURTH BRANCH OF GOVERNMENT: THE FEDERAL BUREAUCRACY

Bureaucracies have become a fourth branch of government. Bureaucratic agencies come into existence by virtue of legislation by Congress, which places them under control of the executive. Inherently this creates congressional-executive conflict over the boundaries of bureaucratic responsibilities and their management. It creates a vast gray area, where there are no clear-cut responsibilities regarding issues of control and management. Bureaucrats are prone to exploit this ambiguity to provide the bureaucracy with greater flexibility and a greater base of power.

In reviewing the major characteristics of the bureaucracy, we can see its tremendous potential and actual power as an institution. The dangers are obvious. The bureaucracy is not accountable to the public at large. It is in a position to regulate itself as an autonomous institution. There is ambiguity of responsibility regarding its control. The entrenched institutional interests of the bureaucracy threaten any political system that prides itself on responsiveness to, and control by, the people.

In the American system, the power of the bureaucracy has been limited and controlled primarily by the pluralistic nature of politics, which is reflected in the bureaucratic structure. Thus, the tendency for a monolithic structure to develop has been counterbalanced by a general diffusion and decentralization of power. Moreover, the prerogatives of various political actors are jealously guarded, creating additional countervailing forces to the expansion and exercise of bureaucratic power.

It should be noted that bureaucracies exist in practically every economic enterprise and administrative agency, both public and private. Some are large; others are small. They are concerned with economics, research, education, and a host of other activities. Indeed, bureaucracies are not only a dominant administrative institution in American society, but also a dominant form of social organization. Our concern here is with public bureaucracy and public administration. And we will focus on these primarily at the national level, although a vast number of bureaucracies exist also at state and local levels.

Roles and Functions   It is the bureaucracy that links the passage of laws and the pronouncements of directives with the day-to-day lives of the people. In the main, it is the bureaucracy that assesses and applies the spirit of the laws in the daily operation of the government. For this reason, the bureaucracy is an important and powerful institution in our political system.

At best, laws and policy pronouncements provide only general guidelines. The bureaucracy or the individual bureaucrat is thus given a wide range of discretionary power regarding the interpretation and application of rules. Not only does the bureaucrat inter-pret and give substance to laws and policies, but he can, in a sense, make decisions, identifying individuals and groups to which these are applicable. Moreover, he has a degree of discretion, allowing him to apply the letter of the laws with varying degrees of impact. This then is the first element of bureaucratic power: the opportunity to exercise choice and discretion in administering policy. From this stem a number of other related characteristics that reinforce and expand the power of the individual bureaucrat and of the bureaucratic institution. Bureaucrats are a major factor in the policy process: they initiate policy proposals, have a voice in considering various alternatives, and have a significant impact on the final policy and its implementation.

Knowledge and Power   It is more than likely that individual officeholders in the administrative structure have developed a particular expertise or skill in their assignments. In addition, they have probably developed the political and social astuteness to operate in a highly complex institution. This expertise, both in the technicalities of their jobs and in their relationships within the institution, provides a source of power in dealing with the public and with elected government officials. It is unlikely that either the public or the elected officials have the information and access needed to properly assess the inner workings of the bureaucracy. Hence, there is a quasi-confidentiality that nurtures the power in the bureaucracy. In discussing this important characteristic, one scholar observes:

Every bureaucracy seeks to increase the superiority of the professionally informed by keeping their knowledge and intentions secret. Bureaucratic administration always tends to be an administration of "secret sessions"; insofar as it can, it hides its knowledge and action from criticism. . . . The absolute monarch is powerless opposite the superior knowledge of the bureaucratic expert.[7]

Other Bases of Power The bureaucracy develops an entrenched interest in protecting itself and its individual members from outside interference and regulation. Bureaucratic procedure, areas of responsibility, and internal social relationships are viewed as the exclusive domain of the bureaucracy. This fosters autonomy and the self-regulating capacity in which the bureaucrats tend to determine values, rules, and regulations by which individual bureaucrats must operate. Thus the bureaucracy acquires a formidable institutional power in dealing with other political actors. In simple terms, bureaucracies try to rule themselves and, in many instances, succeed.

The governmental bureaucracy is vested with authority by law. Aside from cloaking bureaucratic activities with legality, this provides the initial grant of power to the highest bureaucrat from whom power flows to subordinates, right down to the file clerks in a local office.

Most members of the bureaucracy retain their offices by virtue of tenure or seniority. In accordance with civil service regulations, officeholders cannot be dismissed after a certain period in office unless they are convicted of malfeasance, incompetence, or criminal or immoral acts. Mediocrity is not sufficient cause for firing the bureaucrat. Even the highest political appointees and elected political officials have limited leverage in dealing with this situation. In this sense, bureaucratic power is enhanced by tenure.

Bureaucratic Clientele On the other hand, no bureaucracy can exist without support from its clientele. To further its power and to protect its domain, the bureaucracy solicits support from congressmen and congressional committees and subcommittees, as well as from interest groups. It is probably this characteristic that prevents the bureaucracy from becoming a totally autonomous, dictatorial system. To maintain and expand its power, the bureaucracy must adapt itself to the pluralistic and decentralized system in American society. Thus, disagreements, conflicts, and varying political views and styles are likely to be reflected within the bureaucratic structure.

If the bureaucracy can succeed in developing support from Congress, as well as particular interest groups, it enhances its power to deal with other political actors. For example, the departments of Agriculture, Labor, and Commerce realistically represent the special concerns and interests of the farmer, the laborer, and the businessman, respectively. Special interests represented by such organizations as the American Farm Bureau Federation and the National Rural Elected Cooperative Association have a direct channel to the Department of Agriculture. Similarly, the AFL-CIO labor union closely watches the activities of the Labor Department, as a number of business organizations watch the Department of Commerce.

This close association between particular bureaucratic departments and their clientele gives rise to criticism. Some critics claim that this association provides interest groups with a direct, official link to the decision-making bodies of government. According to another observer:

The bureaucracy is recognized by all interested groups as a major channel of representation to such an extent that Congress rightly feels the competition of a rival. . . . Agencies and bureaus more or less perforce are in the business of building, maintaining, and increasing their political support. They lead and in large part are led by the diverse groups whose influence sustains them.[8]

Types of Government Bureaucracies There are a number of types of bureaucracies within the federal structure. Initially, the bureaucracy consisted of a small group of people directly controlled by the executive and organized into the departments of War, State, and Treasury, but over the years it has expanded tremendously in a number of directions.

The *first* type of federal bureaucracy is the presidential bureaucracy, which consists primarily of the president's own staff as shown in the Figure 3-3. Appointments to this bureaucracy are primarily controlled by the president, with little involvement from other branches of government. This bureaucracy, the president's own, generally consists of individuals with a special commitment and loyalty to the president. They are the president's personal staff.

The *second* type of bureaucracy at the federal level is that associated with each of the executive departments (see Figure 3-1). This bureaucracy publicly links the decisions and policies made at the highest level with the people. It is this bureaucracy that has the greatest numbers and the most pervasive structure of all the federal bureaucracies. Theoretically, it is controlled by the cabinet members appointed by the president, but because of its vastness and the importance of its functions, it is subject to tremendous political pressures from other political actors. It is improbable that one man could control the day-to-day operations of this complex bureaucracy.

A *third* type of bureaucracy is that composed of administrators and staff associated with congressmen. Its main functions include linking the individual congressman with his constituency, establishing communications with other political actors, maintaining the proper congressional image, and in general, ensuring that the congressman and his constituents get a fair share of the resources. In addition, members of the congressional staff review the actions of the federal bureaucracy.

The *fourth* type of federal bureaucracy is the independent regulatory commission.

Each commission is under the direction of a board of commissioners that functions independently, outside the executive. They are responsible for establishing regulations or standards with respect to certain operations in the private sector of the economy. The president cannot remove any of the commissioners although they perform functions crucial to executive control of policy. These independent regulatory commissions actually perform executive, quasi-legislative, and quasi-judicial functions in establishing rules and regulations, executing them, and punishing offenders. There is little question of the necessity for such independent regulatory commissions, in view of the need for some type of government regulation of the vast range of economic activity in America. Each of these commissions has its own autonomous bureaucratic structure, and each seems to be particularly responsive to interest group activities. Thus, this type of bureaucracy appears to serve a particular clientele, with little possibility of direction and supervision at the presidential level.

The Bureaucracy, Congress, and Interest Groups The bureaucracy, congressional committees, and interest groups may become partners in tripartite alliances of power which can frustrate attempts to override bureaucratic interests. When the three partners are in agreement regarding policy, they reinforce each other's powers, collaborating to protect their respective interests and thus epitomizing quid pro quo political gamesmanship. If the president or other political actors are to influence and manage the bureaucracy, they must prevent the coalescence of this "iron triangle." Commenting on the issues of Nixon's first term, Theodore White notes:

Political Scientists identify in Washington examples of what they call an "Iron Triangle"—an interlocking three-way association between a well-financed lobby (whether it be mining, education, highways, oil or other areas), the Congressional committee or subcommittee that makes laws on such subjects, and the bureaucracy in Washington which applies these laws. When these three—the committee, the lobby and the bureaucracy—in any given area all agree, and wash each other's hands with influence, information and favors, they are almost impervious to any executive or outside pressures. Within their jurisdictions, they control national power.[9]

Problems in a Democracy   Bureaucratic control has expanded with the expansion of federal power and the proliferation of independent regulatory agencies. To be sure, as the people demand more and more support and services from governments at all levels, the bureaucratic structures become even more pervasive in democratic society. The fundamental problem resulting from this is the question of responsibility and accountability of the bureaucracy. Not elected, most bureaucrats owe their responsibility and accountability to an organizational hierarchy. Moreover, the complexity of the bureaucracy and the plethora of power centers within it make it difficult to pinpoint responsibility for actions or decisions. It is relatively easy for a bureaucrat to obscure the point of decision making and to elude responsibility for decisions, whether good or bad. Finally, the American people elect the president and give him power, among other things, to control the federal bureaucracy. This is an almost impossible task. No one individual, no matter how excellent a president, can control a structure numbering in the hundreds of thousands, replete with centers of power and susceptible to the power of other political actors.

The persistent question revolving around the bureaucracy in a democratic system is: To whom does the bureaucrat owe his responsibility and accountability? Equally important, Can a bureaucracy function democratically?

And finally, Are bureaucratic purposes compatible with democratic ideology? While some answers may be self-evident, in actuality the existence of a bureaucracy creates tensions between bureaucratic efficiency and the democratic stress on individuality. In any event, there is much to be said for the view that America is, in part, a bureaucratic state, because nothing of importance can be accomplished without the existence and cooperation of the bureaucracy.

Decision Makers

Decision makers are individuals who, by virtue of their position in the official institutions of government, can make decisions regarding resource allocation and policy goals affecting the political system. While it may be difficult in this context to clearly separate the president as an individual from the institution of the presidency, it is less difficult to do so when examining lesser officials, such as the secretary of state or the secretary of defense. While the decision maker as a political actor is closely wedded to his particular position within an institution, it is clear that the individual's own perceptions of his position and those of others, his style of operation, and his personality have much to do with how far he can expand his own power and affect others.

The fact that the American political system is decentralized with power diffused at a number of levels makes it difficult to specifically identify all of the important decision makers. In addition, all decision makers as important political actors do not exercise power equally on every political problem at any given time. Nevertheless, there are clusters of decision makers who can be identified and studied in this power political actor model.

Our concern is not necessarily the entire bureaucratic structure or all of the politically elected officials, but rather those in these categories who are the centers of power among their colleagues and in performing institutional roles. In the bureaucracy, most of the important decision makers are the top management people, such as assistant secretaries and political appointees at the highest levels. The top management is generally a "different breed" from the rest of the bureaucracy. Some persons in this category may be politically powerful in their own right, even before assuming office; some move into public service directly from high-paying and important business positions. Most are highly educated and experienced administrators or politicians.

Generally speaking, we can categorize decision makers into two groups: elected and appointed officials (this includes bureaucrats). We should note that in the United States the federal government employs about 2.5 million persons (not including the armed forces); state and local governments employ about 10 million persons. These figures should provide some idea of the extent of the bureaucratic structure and some appreciation of its complexity and the internal politics generated within it.

ELECTED OFFICIALS

There are 537 elected officials at the national level. This includes the president, vice-president, and the members of Congress. Obviously, this does not include all of the elected officials in the American system. Because our concern is primarily with the national level, we do not include the 521,000 elected officials at the state and local levels. (There are about 78,000 state and local governments.) In any event, the 537 elected officials have important, but varying roles in decision making.

The president is the chief decision maker.

Policy decisions are ultimately his responsibility, although in reality many decisions are made in his name without his specific knowledge. The fact remains, however, that the execution of the laws and the symbol of the United States culminate in one man: the president. In this sense, the president as decision maker is essentially chief bureaucrat "writ large." Even if the president does nothing but sit in the oval office, he has an impact on the political system.

All members of Congress are elected, although some may be appointed to fill terms of congressmen who have resigned, retired, or passed away. While all congressmen do not have equally important roles in the decision-making process, all are involved in one form or another in legislative programs and in serving their own constituencies. The Speaker of the House and those congressmen who are committee chairmen have particularly important roles in the decision-making process. Twenty-one members of the House and 16 members of the Senate fall in this category. In light of our earlier discussion on Congress as an institution, it can be seen that these individual congressmen exercise individual power by virtue of their decision-making role in the legislative process.

The major point is that the president and other holders of key offices make decisions using their office as the basis of authority. These decisions shape and influence the policy process and affect other political actors.

The president as an individual is at the center of the policy process. In the final analysis, therefore, the policy decisions rest with him. Regardless of the pressures for and against certain policies and the power exerted by other political actors, the president can simply say, "I want it done this way." That is the culmination of the policy process. Yet it is clear that a president who does not attempt to balance the various inputs in determining policy will have untold obstacles in developing support for and implementing policy. Countervailing powers of other actors can do much to frustrate policy implementation.

APPOINTED OFFICIALS

In the category of appointed officials who are major decision makers, we include certain members of the presidential staff, as well as federal department heads. Figure 3-4 shows the relationship of a number of appointed officials to the presidential decision-making role. We can see that, at the highest levels of the administration, there are identifiable clusters of decision makers who are political actors. Generally, it is at the assistant secretary level that major policy decision making begins. Appointees below this level are primarily engaged in carrying out policies rather than making them.

Groups

POLITICAL PARTIES

The main purpose of political parties is to gain sufficient power to control government. In democratic societies they do so primarily by winning elections. In simple terms, a political party is a group that wants power to run a government. To succeed, a party must have good leadership, efficient organization, and sufficient financial and manpower resources, and must develop programs that appeal to the voters. The need for efficiency would seem to dictate a somewhat rigid organization. Yet, in a democratic society it is unlikely that one will find a monolithic party structure. The very basis for democratic political party activity militates against a closed, rigid, hierarchical system. Nevertheless, party organization requires, at the minimum, a structure through which the party can systematically recruit people for campaigns, provide party literature, attract resources, and allocate resources to party loyalists and sympathizers.

Major Characteristics   One major characteristic of the American political system is its two-party tradition. Although there have been a number of parties throughout American history, the Democratic and Republican parties have dominated the political scene since the Civil War.

The American political system began with no party structure; however, members of the first Congress quickly coalesced around the personalities of Hamilton and Jefferson. The Hamiltonians were committed to a strong national legislative program, such as the National Bank and strong centralized government. The Hamiltonians also represented shipping and building interests, as well as the banker and commercial classes. In 1793, there developed the nucleus of a party system around Hamilton consisting of a strong coalition of officeholders, party activists, and supporters. This became the Federalist party. The Jeffersonians, on the other hand, following the Jeffersonian concept of government, developed a much wider appeal to the masses of people while stressing the need for strong states and grass roots government. The Jeffersonians, organized into the Republican party, appealed primarily to agricultural interests, initially from the South and mid-Atlantic states. From this evolved the Democratic and Republican parties and two-party system that is now a tradition in the United States.

In discussing the two-party tradition, a number of qualifications need to be made. There is no question that the Democratic and Republican parties have been the main competitors for power at the national level. At the state and local levels, however, both one-party and multiparty systems are in operation. Again, this is a reflection of the dual American

Figure 3-4: The President and Power Relationships with Appointed Officials

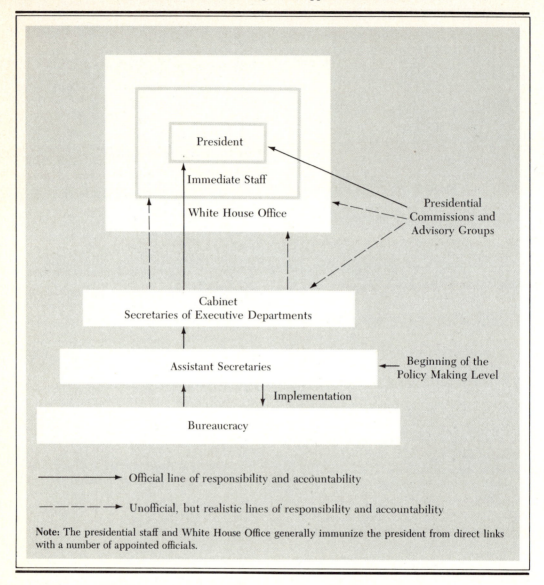

President

Immediate Staff

White House Office

Presidential
Commissions and
Advisory Groups

Cabinet
Secretaries of Executive Departments

Assistant Secretaries

Beginning of the
Policy Making Level

Implementation

Bureaucracy

—————————▶ Official line of responsibility and accountability

— — — — —▶ Unofficial, but realistic lines of responsibility and accountability

Note: The presidential staff and White House Office generally immunize the president from direct links with a number of appointed officials.

political system: a national and a state system. For example, in the states of South Carolina, Georgia, and Louisiana, the Democratic party has had consistent control, and at present, these states are run by one-party systems. In Kansas, Vermont, and New Hampshire, there is more or less a one-party system dominated by the Republicans. Moreover, throughout American history there have been "third parties"—parties such as the Socialist party, Communist party, the Prohibition party, the Bull Moose party, and so on.

An effective two-party system presumes that only the two major parties are likely to gain national power. Thus, a system may have more than two parties and still be categorized as a two-party system if there is little likelihood that third parties can realistically achieve national power. In the American system, any third party would need to win some congressional offices to be considered a major party. The inability of third parties to gain national office is in no small way a result of the pragmatism and flexibility of the two major parties. They have co-opted most third party programs which appealed to American voters, thereby diminishing the attraction of third parties.

Categorizing Party Systems Attempting to classify the American party system, therefore, can cause some confusion and misunderstanding. To help us study party structures, it is best to use a simple, yet useful categorization. We use four categories based on the number of parties realistically involved in the political system. The categories are: authoritarian one-party system; dominant, nonauthoritarian one-party system; two-party system; and multiparty system.

A democratic ideology is usually compatible with any party system except the authoritarian one-party system. Under this system, one party is in power with little if any provision for any other parties to exist legally. Under the dominant, nonauthoritarian one-party system, while one party dominates, opposition parties continue to exist legally. Given the nature of the political system, however, the dominant party is unlikely to forfeit or lose power. A two-party system presumes that one party is not isolated from power for any great length of time, that the power pendulum swings from one party to the other. In multiparty systems, a number of parties exist, each exercising enough power to effectively prevent the concentration of power in one or two parties. Rarely can one or two parties muster enough power to dominate the political system.

Table 3-1 shows the relative strengths of the Democratic and Republican political parties in attracting voters. Even during times of turmoil when neither party seems to be offering clear policies, American voters tend to coalesce around one or the other party (i.e., 1968 and 1972—major problems associated with United States involvement in Vietnam). In brief, the two-party tradition is strong and remains a basic characteristic of the American political system.

Changing Party System In the 1970s the American party system appeared to be undergoing some changes. While there was not a significant departure from the two-party system, fewer people were voting strictly along party lines. An increasing number of voters considered themselves to be "independent." They asserted their prerogative to vote for a Republican candidate in one race and a Democrat in another. They wanted a certain freedom to, as they said, vote the issues, not the personalities. They refused to accept, unexamined, entire party platforms and chose to look instead at the stand individual candidates took with regard to separate planks.

What they found when they looked was that the sharp delineation between parties had faded. By adopting popular stances, parties had lost their distinction. Nevertheless, it is generally recognized that the Democratic party has a "liberal" political orientation while the Republican party has a "conservative" one. In simple terms, the Democratic party has traditionally stood for the rights of workers and has advocated government intervention to protect the individual and to stimulate the economy. In general, the Republican party has supported business interests and has favored limited government intervention in the

Table 3–1: Voter Participation in Presidential Elections by Political Party

Political Party	1960		1964		1968		1972		1976	
	Number of Votes Cast (millions)	Percent of Votes Cast/ Received	Number of Votes Cast (millions)	Percent of Votes Cast/ Received	Number of Votes Cast (millions)	Percent of Votes Cast/ Received	Number of Votes Cast (millions)	Percent of Votes Cast/ Received	Number of Votes Cast (millions)	Percent of Votes Cast/ Received
Democratic	34.2	49.7	43.1	61.1	31.2	42.7	29.1	37.5	40.2	50.6
Republican	34.1	49.5	27.1	38.5	31.7	43.4	47.1	60.7	38.5	48.4
Other	.5	.8	.4	.4	10.3	13.9	1.5	1.8	.9	1.0
Total Vote	68.8	100	70.6	100	73.2	100	77.7	100	79.6	100

Source: U.S. Bureau of the Census, *Statistical Abstracts of the United States: 1976*, 97th ed. (Washington, D.C.), p. 52.

social sphere and limited government control in the economic one.

Because of these characteristics, each major party attracts support from certain segments of the population. For example, to be a Democrat normally means that one is from the lower socioeconomic groups in the country and is a city dweller. Blacks, labor unions, and Catholics generally support the Democratic party. The Republican party draws much of its support from the higher socioeconomic groups: business, Protestants, the better educated, and suburbanites. While both parties received support from all sectors of society, the general tendency is for particular groups to support the party they feel has their best interests at heart.

The Party and the Political System   Parties in the American political system are channels through which major offices at the national, state, and local levels are sought. They recruit leaders and mobilize the public to participate in the political system. It is unlikely that any individual can achieve an elected office without support of a political party. Moreover, parties are the basis for organizing the national government. Thus the party that gains the most seats in Congress controls the committee structure. And the party in power determines, to a large extent, the nature and direction of the national government.

INTEREST GROUPS

An interest group is an association of like-minded people who have organized to bring political power to bear on political actors in order to achieve their goals. It has a formal structure, a plan of action, and a focus on specific actors within the political system.

Fundamental to this interest group concept in a democracy is the premise that large numbers of people are willing to support active efforts to influence political actors. This premise does not necessarily mean that a large number of people must, in fact, actively participate, but at least they must lend their support to the active core group if anything is going to be accomplished. In most interest groups, a rather small minority speaks in the name of the group.

Some interest groups prefer to remain hidden from public view and to operate without soliciting public support. They are powerful because of their access to money and because of their particular influence over economic (and other) activities. While managing to conceal their special interests, they effectively influence decision makers and the policy process.

There are a variety of interest groups in the American political system, many of whom are important political actors. The list includes, for example, business groups, such as the National Association of Manufacturers, American Trucking Association, and Society of American Florists; employee and labor groups, such as the AFL-CIO Maritime Committee, the United Mine Workers of America, and a host of labor unions; professional groups, such as the American Bar Association, American Medical Association, American Sociological Association, and the American Political Science Association; and citizens' groups, such as Common Cause, the Navajo tribe, and Retired Persons, Inc. As a matter of fact, in 1977 it was estimated that there existed about 12,000 national associations. The number of groups is much greater if we include state and local associations.

Such organizations differ widely with respect to both interests and organization. They can be small or large, permanent or temporary, rich or poor, racial or geographic, economic or social, powerful or weak. It is virtually impossible to determine their exact number, the sources of their strength, or their specific interests. Moreover, groups are not always involved in trying to influence political decisions, but they become interest groups per se when they do try to do so.

Official Functions   Whereas political parties have a broad function and purpose, interest groups have a more limited one and focus on specific interests, specific issues, and specific groups of people. This relationship is shown in Figure 3-5, which is a simple representation of the operation and role of interest groups in the political system.

Certain groups of people have their economic interests represented by labor unions (for example, the AFL-CIO). Labor unions attempt to place pressure on political parties (historically, the Democratic party) to work for legislation and policies favoring labor and the workingman. Similarly, the NAACP represents the interests of many segments of the black population. It has worked mainly through the Democratic party (the Republican party has only a small black following) to bring about legislation and policies supporting the black people's drive for equality. The National Association of Manufacturers (NAM), primarily a business-oriented association, focuses much of its effort through the Republican party to gain favorable policies toward business. The American Chambers of Commerce operate in the same manner. It should be made clear, however, that a number of groups operate through both political parties, attempting to influence legislation and policies regardless of what party is in power.

Semiofficial Functions   Interest groups also perform semiofficial functions. That is, they provide government with a particular expertise in special areas, such as medicine, dentistry, law, and labor. The American Medical Association (AMA), for example, is directly involved in licensing physicians in the various states. No doctor can practice in a state without first passing the state medical examinations, which must meet the approval of the AMA. The same is true of the American Bar Association and its role in licensing lawyers

Figure 3-5: Interest Groups and Their Role in the American Political System

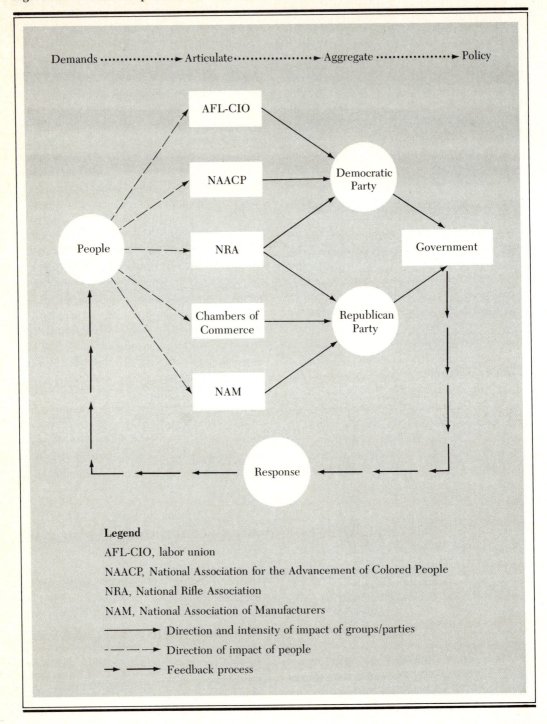

and passing judgment on qualifications for judgeships.

Interest groups also provide a vast amount of information to Congress and to administrative agencies. For example, during the oil crisis in 1974, most of the information on oil production, storage, and pricing was available only through the petroleum industry. Congressional and presidential action was based on this information. Thus, the industry provided the information necessary for government action.

Regulatory Agencies and Groups Regulatory agencies play a role in the economy of the nation and in establishing rules and regulations for industry. Interest groups realize that such agencies are critical points in the government power structure; therefore, much of the effort of interest groups is directed at influencing administrative agencies to ensure favorable decisions. Industrial associations, labor unions, farmers' groups, and citizens' groups are all directly involved in attempts to influence administrative agencies. The power theme is clear in these interactions. Administrative agencies have important power affecting many groups; therefore, the groups exert their own power to ensure favorable policies. In the words of a noted scholar:

With the growing complexity of government, legislative bodies have had to delegate authority to administrative agencies to make rules and regulations. Administrators become legislators, and pressure groups inevitably direct their activities to the point at which authority to make decisions is lodged. Where power rests, there influence will be brought to bear.[10]

Categorizing Interest Groups Groups can be studied in terms of their special interest, organization, the types of power they exert, the composition of their membership, or the main focus of their activities. We place in-

terest groups into four categories, according to formal and informal affiliations and interests. Using the American political system as examples, these are as follows:

1. *Institutional:* legislative groups, civil servant associations, policeman's unions.
2. *Voluntary:* political parties, labor unions, professional and cultural associations.
3. *Nonvoluntary:* racial and ethnic groups and associations, religious groups (in many instances).
4. *Spontaneous:* riots, demonstrations, street mobs.

Institutional interest groups are made up of individuals holding official positions within governmental structures. These individuals come together to act in concert to achieve certain goals. For example, scholars have clearly identified various groupings of congressmen, outside political party identification, who generally act in unison on various legislative matters and policies. A recent example of this is the Black Caucus, an organization of black congressmen. Similarly, there are individuals within government bureaucracy who form subgroups to pursue certain values by placing pressure on other political actors. Institutional interest groups have a built-in power base, due to their positions in formal governmental institutions.

Voluntary interest groups are made up of individuals who come together of their own free will for a particular economic or social reason, and who are not necessarily in official governmental positions. For example, all of the labor unions would be considered voluntary interest groups, although a number of critics would argue that, due to the pressures sometimes applied, there is nothing voluntary about labor union membership. Other examples of voluntary interest groups are Veterans of Foreign Wars, the American Legion, and Common Cause.

Nonvoluntary interest groups are formed along ethnic, racial, religious, or geographic lines. They are labeled nonvoluntary because membership is determined by birth or other circumstances over which people have very little control. Generally, such groups are latent or potential interest groups. For example, it is unlikely that *all* blacks would act as a unified interest group except in extreme circumstances where blacks as a group were threatened and this threat was clearly perceived and articulated.

Spontaneous interest groups evolve almost overnight in response to events or to actions of other political actors and exist for a very short period of time. They include those anomic groups associated with demonstrations and riots. A spontaneous group can arise, for example, from an incident involving police brutality when crowds gather immediately in response to the event and demonstrate their disapproval. In other words, an event precipitates the temporary sharing of values, crossing other organizational lines, and brings together a group of people for a short-term association.

Each of these types of groups either exerts power, or rests on a latent (potential) power base, and influences to varying degrees other political actors and the performance of the political system. It should be clear that these categorizations are not mutually exclusive or clearly delineated, one from another. There are interrelationships and complex organizational patterns among all of the categories.

Interest Groups and Power   The power of interest groups is directly related to their size, leadership, composition, cohesiveness, and resources. Interest groups must be large enough in size to be worthy of some political consideration. A few hundred people would probably not make a great impact; on the other hand, a few thousand or few hundred thousand could constitute a powerful interest group. We should not assume, however, that

size alone gives power to an interest group. The millions of persons who are members of the Parent-Teacher Association, for example, do not wield a fraction of the power of the American Medical Association, whose members number in the thousands.

The question of size must be qualified by a number of other factors. The political astuteness of the leaders and their ability to articulate their group's values have much to do with the image of the group as perceived by other political actors and groups. For example, the leadership of Martin Luther King, Jr., in propelling the Southern Christian Leadership Conference to the forefront of the Black rights movement in America has not been matched since his death. Indeed, one can argue that the SCLC has been considerably diminished in its power as a result.

The composition of an interest group likewise is an important factor in determining the group's power. Obviously, an interest group such as the American Medical Association, composed of doctors who enjoy great prestige in society and are also probably in the high income bracket, has greater power than a local sanitation workers' union. In the former, an intelligent, politically astute leadership and an educated, respected, wealthy membership combine to make the group powerful.

The cohesiveness of the group is another factor that helps determine its power. Group members who agree on specific goals and tactics are likely to remain unaffected by pressures from other political actors and are likely to support the group's activities. Labor unions are a good example of group cohesiveness, particularly when they become involved in wage disputes with various industries. Generally speaking, in such circumstances union members support their leadership. Indeed, it is likely that other unions will conduct sympathetic strikes or not cross picket lines, jeopardizing the operations of an entire industry. On the other hand, the heterogeneous nature of the Parent-Teacher Association of

America makes it difficult for that organization to develop a cohesive structure.

A major problem regarding interest groups as a political actor is their composition and leadership. While proclaiming to represent thousands of people, in a number of instances, leaders of interest groups (the elite) tend to deal only with each other, justifying their actions on the basis of their leadership position. In a democratic society, therefore, one can reasonably ask: To whom does the leadership of interest groups owe responsibility? Can a member of an interest group have an impact on its own leadership? Equally important, many thousands of people are not members of any interest group; and indeed, an argument can be made that they are underrepresented in the American political system. For example, the membership of labor unions is less than 30 percent of the work force in the United States, yet there is a popular tendency to assume that labor unions speak for labor!

Interest Groups, Lobbying the Public
Among the major concerns of any group are the attitudes of its membership and the images of the group as perceived by the public. Therefore, the leadership of an interest group has at least two major targets in an effort to mold opinions: its own membership and the public.

Considerable resources are expended by major groups on the mass media in attempts to convince the public of the righteousness and legitimacy of their points of view and objectives. The presumption is that if public opinion is made receptive and supportive of the group's point of view, other political actors will be more likely to be influenced by group power. In addition, every group tries to indoctrinate its own membership regarding its purposes in the hopes of developing or maintaining cohesiveness. Groups also try to place into public office those persons who are favorably disposed toward their interests, and persuade public officials to adopt and enforce

policies that the group thinks will be beneficial to its own interests. Lobbying is one of the primary ways that this is accomplished. Lobbying is an attempt by a person or small groups of persons representing a particular interest group to bring about defeat or passage of legislative bills or to influence their contents. Usually the lobbyist is a lawyer retained by an interest group, who operates in Washington, D.C. He knows the intricacies of the legislative process and who the key members of Congress are with respect to any particular legislation. As John F. Kennedy wrote in 1955 when he was still a senator:

> Lobbyists are in many cases expert technicians and capable of explaining complex and difficult subjects in a clear, understandable fashion. They engage in personal discussion with members of Congress in which they can explain in detail the reason for positions they advocate.[11]

Lobbying is a legal activity as long as it conforms to the rules established in the Federal Regulation of Lobbying Act of 1946. This act requires that all lobbyists register; give their expenditures, salary, and name of employer; and, quarterly, give full information of their activities for publication in the Congressional Record. Lobbying and the Lobbying Act have been criticized by a number of people as giving an advantage to those groups who can afford high-priced talent in Washington. Moreover, the Lobbying Act is said to be vague and with little enforcement power.

Interest groups also engage in indirect lobbying. In trying to persuade public officials, representatives of interest groups periodically testify at public hearings, write letters to officials, provide them with information, and generally try to convince them to take a certain course of action.

Additionally, a number of interest groups contribute sizable sums of money to various candidates running for office. While new campaign financing laws are designed to limit such contributions, the fact remains that it is difficult to control interest group activities in election campaigns. Figure 3-6 shows the connection between interest groups, campaign financing, and members of various committees in the House of Representatives. By such involvement, interest groups hope to influence election outcomes and bring pressure to bear on those whom they supported.

Political Influentials

Political influentials are persons who, by virtue of their status and resources, can have important impact on the political system. For example, a number of academicians and scholars in the United States are respected experts on various areas of the political system, such as the presidency, or are economists of repute. Thus, individuals such as Milton Friedman and Paul Samuelson will have some impact on other political actors because of their recognized expertise on economic matters. Similarly, John Kenneth Galbraith has an impact on other political actors not only because of his prestige but also because of his ability to develop insights into the political system and to articulate these in understandable terms.

Nationally known commentators and newspaper columnists can also be political influentials. Commentary by television personalities, such as Howard K. Smith, John Chancellor, and Walter Cronkite, has an impact on public opinion and on other political actors. The initial revelations of Watergate by the *Washington Post* are an example of the mass media performing a role as a political actor countering the power of other political actors: President Nixon and his immediate staff.

It is not always easy to identify political influentials. Some are not clearly visible to the public and operate in a quiet fashion. Others may also be decision makers and representatives of powerful institutions. Thus, the roles are intermixed. Nevertheless, there are some political influentials who can be readily identified. In an annual survey, "Who Runs America," a national news magazine identified a number of influential Americans.[12] In 1977, the top ten were:

Jimmy Carter, president of the United States
Arthur F. Burns, chairman of the Federal Reserve Board
Warren E. Burger, chief justice, U.S. Supreme Court
George Meany, president, AFL-CIO
Thomas P. O'Neill, Speaker of the House
Bert Lance, director of the office of management and budget
Cyrus Vance, secretary of state
Robert C. Byrd, Senate majority leader
Walter Cronkite, television news correspondent
W. Michael Blumenthal, secretary of the treasury

While most of the top ten are in government, it is instructive to note the range of government activities they represent. Equally important, the list also includes a labor leader and a television commentator. A list of the next twenty most influential Americans includes two publishers (Katherine Graham and Arthur Sulzberger), a banker (David Rockefeller), a consumer advocate (Ralph Nader), the president's wife (Rosalynn Carter), a former president (Gerald Ford), a preacher (Billy Graham), and a corporate chairman (Thomas Murphy, General Motors). Also included are the vice-president of the United States and the U.S. Ambassador to the United Nations.

While these ratings change from year to year, it is important to note that they usually

Figure 3-6: Interest Groups as Political Actors

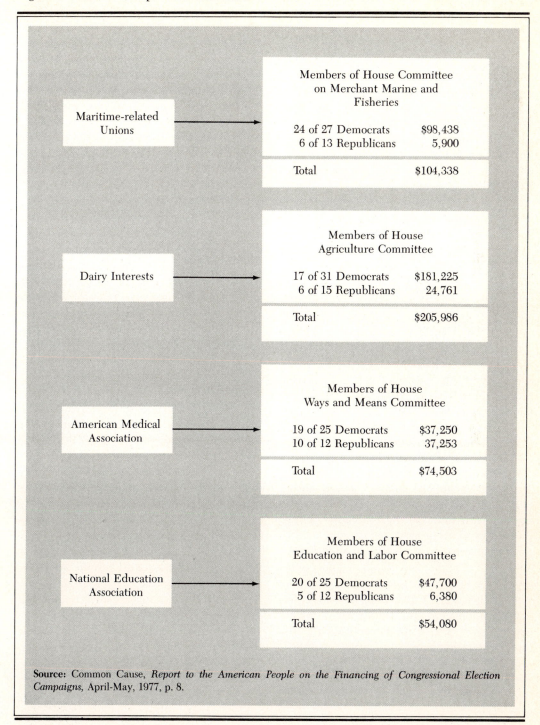

Maritime-related Unions →

Members of House Committee
on Merchant Marine and
Fisheries

24 of 27 Democrats $98,438
6 of 13 Republicans   5,900

Total $104,338

Dairy Interests →

Members of House
Agriculture Committee

17 of 31 Democrats $181,225
6 of 15 Republicans   24,761

Total $205,986

American Medical Association →

Members of House
Ways and Means Committee

19 of 25 Democrats $37,250
10 of 12 Republicans   37,253

Total $74,503

National Education Association →

Members of House
Education and Labor Committee

20 of 25 Democrats $47,700
5 of 12 Republicans   6,380

Total $54,080

Source: Common Cause, *Report to the American People on the Financing of Congressional Election Campaigns,* April-May, 1977, p. 8.

include a variety of persons representing a number of groups and government institutions. The fact that some can be placed in more than one political actor category—for example, the president is a decision maker, a leader of the most powerful institution in government, and an individual political influential—makes them even more powerful than the ratings suggest.

The American ideology perpetuates the rise of political influentials by its emphasis on opportunity, freedom of speech and assembly, individual worth, and a host of other ideological principles, including those associated with private enterprise. The major point is that, in a democratic system such as the United States, political influentials exist in virtually all sectors of society. Equally important, there are channels and opportunities for such persons to exert power on the political system. Obviously, where political systems are closed and access to mass media is strictly controlled, political influentials do not exist or have only limited power.

Individuals

As stated earlier in this chapter, very little can be accomplished by individuals working by themselves. Given the nature of the American political system, individuals become meaningful only in groups and in their official capacities within the governmental structure, or by virtue of status and prestige. In the main, individuals have a "latent" importance and are indirectly and implicitly linked to political actors.

During times of crisis, when issues can be clearly articulated, the individual becomes important as part of the "mass public." His opinion is a component of "public opinion." Also, the individual, as part of the voting public, helps officials from national president to local alderman. His role as a voter is the most

important in the American political system—indeed, in any democracy. In addition, individuals participate in many nonelectoral activities. They involve themselves in community organizations, write letters to officials, participate in demonstrations, and petition the government at all levels.

The individual appears to have little to say, however, about the specific operation of the political system. As a part of a larger voting public, the individual legitimizes the power of political actors, who then operate the political system with relative freedom from public control. Thus, in the American political system, the individual is important as part of "the people," but the system operates on the pressures exerted by other political actors, which do not include most of "the people." This kind of relationship and function can continue only if "the people" perceive political actors as operating within the rules of the game and with some concern for the interests of "the people."

Summary

In our assessment of political actors in the American political system, we see that formal institutions of government and organized interests are major actors. Moreover, the nature of the political system provides the environment in which political actors can seek their interests relatively unrestricted. The focus of these political actors is on the decision-making process and on other actors who can either assist or who are likely to prevent a particular actor from achieving its goals. It is important to understand that these political actor relationships and the exercise of power take place within the context of democratic ideology, qualifying to a great degree the arbitrary exercise of power.

We also note that the formal institutions of government as political actors cannot exercise unlimited power. Other political actors exercise their own power to influence governmental institutions. Moreover, within most formal structures of government there are a number of subinstitutions with their own politics and power. These characteristics, combined with the democratic nature of the system and American ideology, create an "open" system, which is susceptible to a variety of influences and political actors, both public and private. While the individual has an important place in this democratic system, he can exercise very little power over the day-to-day operation of the system. Indeed, the individual has little impact except as a member of the "public" or of an organized group.

As we saw in this chapter, the interaction between a variety of political actors and the dynamics of the system are important to an understanding of the American political system. We identified the basis of power of political actors, some of the major relationships, and the resulting power positions. Finally, we examined these matters in some detail, not because of our concern with the basics of American government, but rather to provide a broader dimension to the understanding of the approach of this book. These perspectives should assist in analyzing other political systems.

NOTES

1. The discussion on political actors is adapted from Sam C. Sarkesian and Krish Nanda, *Politics and Power in American Government* (New York: Alfred, 1975), pp. 56–59.
2. Adapted from the *U.S. News and World Report*, April 18, 1977, p. 36. The survey participants were given a list of 29 leading institutions and asked to rate each one "according to the amount of influence it has on decisions or actions affecting the nation as a whole."
3. Henry Fairlie, "Thoughts on the Presidency," *The Public Interest*, no. 9 (Fall 1967), p. 29.
4. For a discussion of presidential performance using various political-psychological categories, see James Barber, *The Presidential Character: Predicting Performance in the White House* (Englewood Cliffs, N.J.: Prentice-Hall, 1972).
5. Joseph A. Califano, Jr., *A Presidential Nation* (New York: W. W. Norton, 1975), p. 226.
6. As quoted in the *Alabama Journal*, July 19, 1973, p. 4.
7. Max Weber, "Essay on Bureaucracy," in Francis E. Rourke, ed., *Bureaucratic Power in National Politics* (Boston: Little, Brown, 1973), pp. 61–62.
8. Norton E. Long, "Power and Administration," in Rourke, ibid., pp. 8–9.
9. Theodore H. White, *The Making of the President 1972* (New York: Bantam, 1973), pp. 71–72.
10. V. O. Key, Jr., *Politics, Parties, and Pressure Groups* (New York: Thomas Y. Crowell, 1960), p. 154.
11. As quoted in *The Washington Lobby* (Washington, D.C.: Congressional Quarterly, 1971), p. 6.
12. *U.S. News and World Report*, April 18, 1977, pp. 28–36.

CHAPTER 4

AMERICAN POWER AND POLICY

Policy is a course of action, usually a long-term commitment, by government to achieve a particular purpose. To be effective, policy must include a commitment of resources and a mobilization of agencies to implement a plan of action. But policy decisions do not necessarily evolve from weighing alternatives and objectively selecting what is best. In most instances, policy is determined by political actors who use power to affect other political actors. In short, application of power is the main determinant of policy. The nature of this policy process and the outcome are also a reflection of the nature of the political system, whether it be democratic or totalitarian. A serious study of political systems should include, therefore, some attention to what the system attempts to achieve, its actual accomplishments, and its impact on political actors.

Policy is, in itself, worthy of lengthy and intensive study. A number of scholars have devoted considerable attention to this subject. As one would expect, the scholarship reflects a variety of views and approaches. Nevertheless, there are two basic approaches to studying policy: the elitist and the pluralist approach.

The *elitist approach* is best understood and persuasively argued by C. Wright Mills in his book *The Power Elite*. According to Mills, policy is essentially in the hands of an identifiable elite whose policy is primarily self-centered and antithetical to the public interest. On the other hand, Robert Dahl argues that, although policy is made primarily by an elite group, rarely are the same groups involved with the same degree of intensity in making all policy. One can argue, therefore, that policy is made by a shifting number of elite groups, which exert varying amounts of pressure on the policy process. In such a process, policy is the outcome of a contest to decide who gets what, when, where, and how.

This process is characteristic of a pluralistic system. American society is made up of a variety of heterogeneous institutions, organizations, and groups representing diversified religious, ethnic, economic, and cultural interests. In a pluralistic democratic system, it is presumed that elites representing these diversities compete with one another and attempt to influence the political system. As a result there is usually a shifting alliance of elites competing and exercising their power according to the issues involved and the degree to which these issues touch the various groups in society.

Somewhere between the view that a small elite at the top makes and controls policy and the view that "the people" are in control lies a more realistic assessment. At times a small elite does make decisions, and at other times the voice of the people comes through loud and clear. But in the main, most policy emerges somewhere above the people and below the highest levels of officialdom. Given the pluralistic nature of American society and the diffusion of power, the points of policy emergence are many. We are inclined to agree with Donovan that

Anyone bold enough to undertake a serious analysis of how policy is made in the American political system must begin with the realization that he is examining one of the most complex structures ever contrived by man. He must also realize that the "system" under examination has been evolving over at least two centuries—all while subject to an inexorable process of change—and that he is studying American political development at a time when the process of change seems to be more relentlessly driven than ever before in American experience.[1]

Recalling the discussion in Chapter 1 regarding the policy phases, the American political system is characterized by a relatively "open" policy process. Political actors enter into the policy process for three reasons: to achieve more power, to achieve political goals, and to support the system. They pursue these purposes through a variety of channels, the major one being the policy process. Figure 4-1 shows a simplified overview of the policy process, one that will be used in this chapter to study power and policy.

Emergence Phase

The emergence phase of the policy-making process is the most difficult phase to identify and study. In many instances, policy is not recognized for what it is until it becomes associated with an institution or is being clearly articulated by a number of political actors. While it is much easier for social scientists to identify a policy at the later phase, to develop data regarding its directions, and to examine the process, a more realistic veiw of the policy field must consider emergence.

UNSTRUCTURED PROCESS

Pinpointing the time that policy emerges is a difficult task. Yet there are general criteria. As increasing attention is given a particular issue by the mass media or other publicity channels, awareness of the issue increases. At some stage, the issue becomes compelling enough to require official response. The emergence phase is that period during which issues become public, but before they are officially recognized as policy issues.

Policy issues seem to be floating around in the political system waiting to be identified, perceived, and injected into the policy-making process. During the emergence phase, a variety of political actors (depending on the type of political system we are examining) may become involved in publicizing an issue, that is, in making an unpublicized problem into an issue. At this point, positions have not become fixed, nor are policy battle lines drawn. Through a process of information sharing and increasing awareness, political actors develop positions on a particular issue.

In the American political system, policy may emerge from a variety of sources. Yet there are those who presume an ideal view of policy emergence; that is, that major policy alternatives are developed by the highest

Figure 4-1: An Overview of the Policy Process

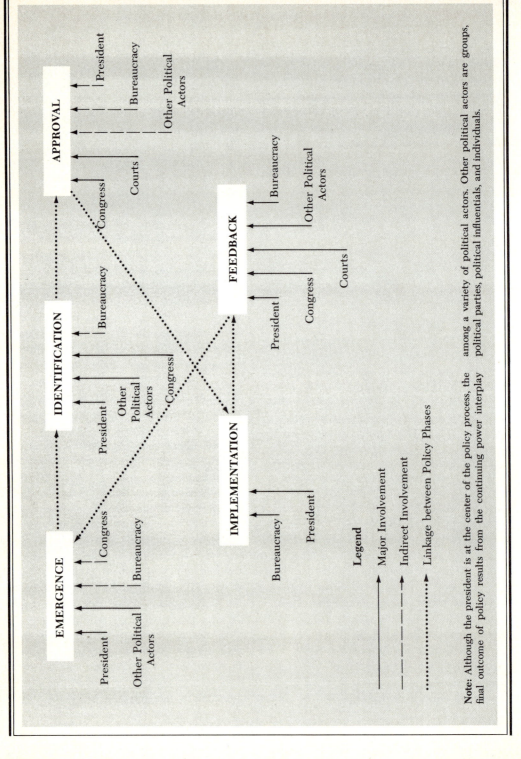

Note: Although the president is at the center of the policy process, the final outcome of policy results from the continuing power interplay among a variety of political actors. Other political actors are groups, political parties, political influentials, and individuals.

levels of government and bureaucracy, and that in a rational manner, these alternatives are identified and perceived from a common point of view. While some policies may emerge from public bureaucracies, most stem from political actors outside government. Bureaucrats tend to accept what is and to routinize all actions, shying away from making changes or developing initiatives.

Members of Congress may become involved in policy emergence, but their main role is in the policy approval phase. In the course of debates and discussions, congressmen may stimulate the emergence of policy that is separate from the specific issues at hand. For example, a debate over the defense budget may give rise to a new initiative for United States policy in Asia. Yet, most would agree that Congress is primarily a reactive body, responding to issues raised by other political actors.

THE MASS MEDIA

The mass media play an important role in the emergence phase. Acting as an informal channel for communications with all elements of society, the mass media can give publicity and exposure to policy initiatives. By bringing matters to the attention of a wide reading or viewing public, the mass media move policy from emergence to identification and finally, approval. The media also play an important role in the implementation and feedback phases. In light of the emphasis on freedom of the press in the American political system, the media have an almost absolute right to delve into matters of policy at all levels and during all phases of the policy process.

Press conferences have also become an institutionalized part of the political process. The president uses the press conference as a major instrument for publicizing policy. Candidates for office continually seek press cover-

age for policy statements and responses to various aspects of the political system. Most politicians seek publicity, particularly television coverage, when an event can lead to positive exposure. On the other hand, many bureaucrats and other political actors fear the mass media because of possible adverse publicity. Bureaucrats prefer to maintain an aura of mystery around their activities.

FOREIGN POLICY

With regard to foreign policy, initiatives come primarily from government agencies or the executive office. Rarely does one find such proposals coming from political actors outside government. The reason seems clear: most information on foreign policy is funneled into the executive office. More important, the president has traditionally been the key, not only in implementing foreign policy, but also in the policy formulation process. The involvement of other political actors has, in the main, been reactive, consisting of criticism of an existing policy.

The primary agencies involved in the foreign policy process are the National Security Council and a number of interdepartmental committees. Originating generally in the bureaucracy, policy proposals emanate from originating agencies and flow to other interested agencies. The purpose is to develop a broad consensus upon which the president can act. On the other hand, agencies opposing the policy will attempt to develop enough resistance to prevent the president from implementing the policy.

Identification

When issues generate sufficient pressures to require official response, they enter into the identification phase, one that involves defining the issue, establishing a policy position, and formulating a plan of action for support or resistance to the emerging policy. Political actors, both in and out of government, attempt to develop coherent policy positions to attract other political actors as allies for one position or the other.

VARIETY OF POLITICAL ACTORS

Clearly there is much disagreement over who makes policy. It is probably safe to say that "bits and pieces" of a general policy are identified by political actors in every area. That is, groups, institutions, political influentials, and even individuals may play some role in policy identification. Although interest groups, parties, and institutions have a greater role in policy initiatives, other political actors do contribute, depending on the type of policy involved.

This particular point of view is reinforced by the observations of Dean Acheson, former secretary of state, who stated, "It should be clear to anyone with experience in Government [United States] that the springs of policy bubble up; they do not trickle down."[2]

In any one particular policy, such as the American decision to enter the Vietnam War in 1965, one can identify a specific group or elite body from the emergence phase through the entire range of policy phases. In the case of Medicare legislation of 1965, however, a variety of groups were involved, including labor unions, professions, and a combination of political actors. Increased medical competence raised consumer expectations and utilization, and rising costs laid the groundwork for Medicare policy.

In still another instance, an individual can be the basis for policy identification. For example, most students of American politics are familiar with *Baker* v. *Carr* (1964), in which the Supreme Court decided that "un-

equal citizen participation in the selection of lawmakers, leading directly to legislative under-representation for others, was held to be a denial of equal protection of the laws."[3] This case led to the reapportionment in the lower houses of state legislatures and in the House of Representatives in Congress.

In this instance, the wellsprings of policy identification can be traced directly to Charles W. Baker, a resident of Memphis, Tennessee, who had been active in local politics and had been chairman of the governing board of Shelby County, the most populous county in the state. Baker's concern was over the basis of representation. His county, with over 300,000 voters, could elect one state representative while Moore County, Tennessee, with 2,340 voters, could also elect one state representative.

Baker challenged the legality of the election laws and the representative system. The case eventually was heard by the Supreme Court. With the decision on *Baker* v. *Carr*, the Supreme Court gave approval for a change in policy regarding elections and representation which now governs state legislatures and the House of Representatives.

As demonstrated in this case, the representative system and election laws at the local level provided an environment in which an individual, a political influential, initiated a policy change. Ultimately, one of the three major branches of government became the instrument for this change.

THE IDENTIFICATION PROCESS

The competitive political process in the American political system is clearly visible during the identification process. The initiative in policy identification, as we suggested earlier, is taken primarily by interest groups or government agencies (see Chapter 3). The political actors actively pursuing certain policies attempt to build support for the proposal among a large number of political actors. Coalitions are formed among political actors, and attempts are made to identify officials of government, particularly in Congress, who may be sympathetic. An effort is made to enlist an active core of congressmen and other government officials.

Simultaneously, opposition to the proposal develops as other political actors seek to develop coalitions against the policy. Thus, at least two competing coalitions normally develop on policy proposals, each taking its strength from political actors within similar areas, that is, interest groups, government agencies, political parties. For example, while political actors within the Department of Health, Education, and Welfare may be fostering a particular policy, other political actors within the Department of Defense may be developing coalitions to resist such a policy because of its possible negative impact on the defense budget. During this process, the original proposals of the emergence phase are modified not only in content but even in objective to broaden the base of support.

In the final analysis, political maneuvers and alliance building are aimed at those who must eventually make a decision on policy. On domestic matters, the focal point for many policy initiatives is Congress. On a number of issues, however, it is the presidential office, because many measures require presidential support to pass through Congress.

Proponents and opponents of a particular policy often attempt to convince the public at large of the impact of that policy. Using the mass media and a variety of other techniques (for example, letters to influential individuals, members of the academic community, etc.), each side tries to convince others of the propriety of its position. For example, during the public debate over Medicare, members of the American Medical Association provided credence for their opposition to the policy by playing on the fear that socialized medicine would bring lowered medical standards.

Policy proposals may, of course, never get beyond the identification phase. The nature of the public debate may simply provide an impasse. On the other hand, compromise, accommodations, and exercise of power may prevent the policy proposal from actually being placed in policy decision-making channels. Thus, political actors who have seen the need for certain policy initiatives may simply not have enough power to ensure that the policy becomes identified in the fashion necessary to develop into the approval stage. On the other hand, political actors, opposing or supporting a particular policy, may make accommodations in interpretations and procedures that satisfy both groups and make it unnecessary to proceed further.

THE CONGRESSIONAL ROLE

Congressional support is sought for obvious reasons: every policy normally requires budgetary support. In addition, Congress has oversight responsibility in many areas. In 1975 and 1976, for example, Congress conducted hearings on the activities of the Central Intelligence Agency and submitted a report on its findings. The Central Intelligence Agency is the primary agency for foreign intelligence gathering and as such is the direct and important instrument to foreign policy decision making. Thus, although the role of Congress is subordinate to that of the president in foreign policy, Congress can directly influence the conduct of foreign policy, as well as the goals of policy, by its budgetary controls and oversight responsibility (see Chapter 2). A more clearly visible example is congressional reaction to United States activities in Angola in late 1975 and early 1976. Fearing a Vietnam-type involvement and reluctant to have the United States again committed to unstable political factions, Congress rejected the president's request for economic and military aid to pro-Western factions in the Angola struggle.

Approval Phase

CONGRESS: THE MAJOR ACTOR

Major policy initiatives must ultimately be approved by Congress through a tortuous legislative process. This is particularly true of domestic policy. As a matter of fact, it is probably correct to say that major policy initiatives may be easier to implement in foreign policy than in domestic policy. Congress is not a monolithic body: there are many groups and subsystems within it, any of which could effectively kill policy proposals. Additionally, for policy to succeed, support must be given by top officials of government. They must convince Congress not only of their support, but that they are actively pursuing the passage of such legislation. Lack of enthusiasm or silence by government officials on policy proposals, even if they are proposed by the president, is not likely to develop congressional enthusiasm for passage. It is the convergence of these dynamics of the policy process in Congress that makes this phase and the congressional role so important in policy.

The Legislative Process The complicated and lengthy policy approval phase is shown in Fig. 4-2. We should note that this is a simplified version. In reality the process is even more difficult and complicated than that shown here.

The intricacies and complexities of the legislative process test even the most committed and skilled congressman. Not only must he develop his knowledge of the legislative procedures and rules of order within the Congress, he must establish a complicated web of personal relationships with his colleagues, interest groups, the presidential of-

fice, the bureaucracy, and his own constituency. At the same time, the congressman must always be sensitive to the impact of the mass media and his image. How the congressman views his role in Congress will, in many ways, determine the kinds of relationships he will establish with the individuals and groups that have an influence on his office. How well the congressman can develop and maintain a working relationship with his colleagues will determine his effectiveness. Most important, his ability to balance his obligations to colleagues with those to his constituency will significantly affect his ability to win in the next election.

At the heart of the legislative process lie the committees. These committees were set up to handle the enormous volume of bills and resolutions introduced in each legislative session. While all the standing committees of Congress have authority and expertise in their own policy areas, not all of them are equally prestigious nor are they of equal concern to a congressman.

Immediately following the initial reading of a bill before Congress, it is sent to the standing committee under whose jurisdiction it seems to fall. Committee jurisdictions occasionally overlap; this increases the discretion of party leaders in assigning bills to committees thought to be favorable or unfavorable to a particular proposal. Once the bill is in committee, the committee is free to act upon it in any way it wants to: it may or may not report the bill for House or Senate consideration. Most bills are simply pigeonholed by the committees. The committee can speed a bill through, that is, send it back to the Congress for a quick vote, or it can sit on a bill until late in the session. Committees can kill a bill by failing to act upon it. If they do present it to the floor, they determine the form in which it will be considered by the House or Senate, and can exercise great control over the floor decision. Clearly, then, committees are little legislatures with big powers in themselves. As

Figure 4-2: The Policy Approval Phase

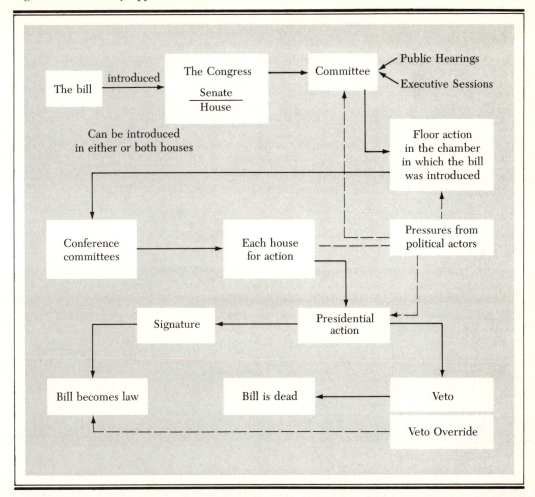

Woodrow Wilson observed in 1885, "Congress in session is Congress on public exhibition, while Congress in its committee-rooms is Congress at work." The two large houses sit to sanction the conclusions of their committees.

Characteristics of the Legislative Process
Two basic characteristics determine the general direction of the legislative process. One is that there are many committees and subcommittees. The second is that these

committees are bipartisan in composition, with the two parties represented in proportion to their total strength in the respective chamber. They are not working instruments of the majority party. The committees have become the instruments for resolution of conflicting policy views because of their bipartisan composition, their expertise in handling complex legislation, their domination of the legislative process, and the relationships of their members to constituents and key interest groups.

The leaders of the House and Senate are, in fact, the chairmen of the standing committees, and there are as many of them as there are subjects of legislation. These chairmen do not constitute a cooperative body: each committee goes its own way, at its own pace. The Speaker is a "great party chief," but at bottom, the committees and the chairmen, because of their experience and seniority, shape, control, and present legislation.

The bipartisan composition of the committees also has its consequences. Woodrow Wilson observed that it is the representation of both parties on the committees that makes party responsibility indistinct and organized party action almost impossible. If the committees were composed entirely of majority party members, committee reports would be taken to represent the views of the party in power. The work of the committees makes it possible for a great many bills to be passed by bipartisan majorities in both the House and Senate. This helps Congress run smoothly and effectively, because such bills are passed not along strict party lines, but with basic consensus.

THE EXECUTIVE AND THE BUREAUCRACY

While Congress has the chief role in approving policy through the legislative process, the roles of the executive and bureaucracy are also important. The power exerted by the president on congressional proceedings, in many instances, can determine the outcome of legislation. Moreover, as we learned earlier, presidential-congressional relationships during the early phases of the policy process are crucial in affecting congressional attitudes. Of course, we are speaking not only of the president, but of the entire executive office. Not only do many in the executive office become directly involved with key congressmen, but they may contact other political actors both in and out of government for support of the president's position.

As we noted earlier, the bureaucracy plays an important part in all phases of the policy process. This is true in the approval phase, but is probably less explicit or visible than in other phases. Congress often has direct links with bureaucrats from whom it receives information, reports, and support. In turn, bureaucratic attitudes on legislation are conveyed to Congress through such channels, as well as through a number of informal links. Large-scale resistance to certain legislation, regardless of presidential attitudes, can create serious doubts about its passage.

THE COURTS

Perhaps one of the most unique aspects of the policy process in the American political system is the policy-making role (approval) of the courts, specifically the Supreme Court. Based on the concept of judicial supremacy established by the landmark case of *Marbury* v. *Madison* (1803), the Court has been placed in a position to decide the constitutionality of cases brought before it. Moreover, in many respects, it not only makes decisions on major constitutional cases, but in its written opinion interprets and provides guidelines for policy to achieve the desired goal of the Court decision.

Equally important, the power of the Court is based on the very nature of the American democratic system. Established as one of the three separate but equal branches of government, the Court's power is buttressed by democratic ideology that holds that conflicts should be resolved peacefully.

Alexis de Tocqueville made the succinct observation in 1835 that "hardly any question arises in the United States that is not resolved sooner or later into a judicial question."[4] Combining this observation with that of Chief Justice Charles Evans Hughes (1907), "We are under a Constitution, but the Constitution is what the judges say it is," one can readily understand the basis of judicial power and appreciate the Court's role in the policy process.

The role of the courts in policy making with respect to the legislatures has already been noted *(Baker* v. *Carr).* To point out examples of the Court's role, one need but briefly view the Warren Court (Chief Justice Earl Warren, 1953–1969). That Court's work began with its monumental decision in the *Brown* v. *Board of Education* (1954) school desegregation case. The decision overturned the long-standing policy of "separate but equal" educational facilities established by the Supreme Court in *Plessy* v. *Ferguson* (1894). Since 1954, school districts throughout the United States have taken major steps to comply with this decision. Needless to say, this school desegregation decision established the guidelines of federal educational policy. Since that time

. . . the Court has declared Bible reading and all other religious exercises in public schools unconstitutional; it has ordered the reapportionment of the national House of Representatives, of both Houses of state legislatures, and of local government bodies on a one-man, one-vote basis; it has reformed numerous aspects of state and federal criminal procedure, significantly enhancing the rights of the accused, including juvenile offenders; it has laid down a whole set of new rules governing the admissibility of confessions evidence, and in effect, the conduct of police throughout the country toward persons arrested on suspicion of crime; and it has held that wiretapping and eavesdropping are subject to the Fourth Amendment's prohibition against unreasonable searches and seizures. The Court has also enlarged its own jurisdiction to hear cases challenging federal expenditures . . . [it] has limited the power of state and local governments . . .[5]

Whether or not one agrees with the decisions of the Warren Court, this brief cataloging of the Court's actions shows its direct involvement in policy approval.

Implementation

While Congress passes legislation that establishes broad purposes of policy, it is the president, through the bureaucracy, who implements the policy. Once a law is passed or directive issued by the president, most people assume that a goal has been reached or a policy established; however, nothing really happens until basic provisions, rules, and regulations are devised and used to administer the law and to apply the directive to the day-to-day lives of the people. In the main, it is the bureaucracy that assesses and applies the spirit of the laws in the daily operation of the government. For this reason, the bureaucracy is an important and powerful institution in any political system.

BUREAUCRACY: THE MAJOR ACTOR

Given the various structures of bureaucracy at the federal level and the vast number of state and local bureaucracies with their own particular bases, we can see that the term *bureaucracy* certainly does not mean a monolithic structure in the American system of government. Indeed, one can argue that bureaucracies act similarly to interest groups, in certain instances providing opposition to other bureaucracies, in other instances joining together to perform some particular task.

The involvement of the bureaucracy in policy implementation can better be appreciated by taking a look at bureaucratic growth. In 1792, there were about 300 federal employees; by 1900, there were 300,000. In 1976, there were an estimated 2.8 million. State and local governments employ over 12 million persons. Thus, out of a total labor force of about 90 million people, one out of every seven persons in the work force works for a government bureaucracy. In addition, federal departments, commissions, and agencies oversee virtually every conceivable kind of activity, from the placement of fire extinguishers in industrial plants to the establishment of air fares for all airlines.

If one adds the variety of state and local agencies, a picture emerges of a vast conglomerate of interlocking, counterbalancing, and competing governmental agencies, from the small urban area to the national government in Washington. Thus, not only does the bureaucracy have a web of channels at all levels in society to identify policy, but the same web becomes an instrument of policy implementation. Indeed, as most presidents learn rather quickly, the bureaucracy can be moved only by firm, persistent, and pervasive pressure. And even then, the ability of the president to give the bureaucracy specific policy directions is counterbalanced by bureaucratic inertia and reaction. In such an environment, key implementers of policy are not only the highest level bureaucrats, but also the middle range managers, in many cases, the local office chief.

Pluralistic Structure While the bureaucracy may appear to be monolithic, in reality it is a porous and amorphous social mass, susceptible to external power and internal manipulation. Thus, in almost all phases of policy, but particularly in the emergence and implementation phases, the bureaucracy is exposed to power pressures from a variety of interest groups and other political actors at virtually all levels, from the local bureaucrat to the highest placed bureaucrats seating in Washington. This manipulation by a variety of political actors may be one important countervailing force to bureaucratic power. As one expert has observed: "The basic issues of federal organization and administration relate to power: who shall control it and to what ends?"[6] Here is what Henry Kissinger, secretary of state under the Nixon and Ford administrations, had to say about the power of the bureaucracy:

When I first started advising at high levels of the government in the early days of the Kennedy Administration, I had the illusion that all I had to do was walk into the President's office, convince him I was right, and he would then naturally do what I had recommended. There were a number of things wrong with this view. . . . There is only so much that even a President can do against the wishes of the bureaucracy, not because the bureaucracy would deliberately sabotage him, but because every difficult issue is a closed one. The easy decisions are made at subordinate levels. A closed issue is characterized by the fact that the pros and cons seem fairly evenly divided and/or because the execution really depends on certain nuances of application. Unless you can get the willing support of your subordinates, simply giving an order does not get very far.[7]

Bureaucratic Power At best, laws and policy pronouncements provide only general guidelines. The bureaucracy or the individual bureaucrat is thus given a wide range of discretionary power regarding their interpretation and application. Not only does the bureaucrat interpret and give substance to laws and policies, but he can, in a sense, make decisions identifying individuals and groups to which these are applicable. Moreover, he has a degree of discretion, allowing him to apply the letter of the laws with varying degrees of impact. This then is the first element of bureaucratic power: the opportunity to exercise choice and discretion in administering policy. From this stem a number of other related characteristics that reinforce and expand the power of the individual bureaucrat and of the bureaucratic institution. Bureaucrats are a major factor in the policy process. They initiate policy proposals, have a voice in considering various alternatives, and they have a significant impact on the final policy and its implementation.

Feedback

As with the emergence phase, during feedback, virtually all elements of the American political system are involved. Indeed, when comparing all of the phases of the policy process, the emergence and feedback phases are more clearly alike in the scope of political actor involvement. During the intermediate phases, certain sections of the American political system are involved (that is, a relatively narrow group of political actors), but during the emergence and feedback phases, many more political actors are involved.

UNPREDICTABILITY OF POLICY IMPACT

Feedback deals primarily with the impact of policy, the support or resistance it generates, and the pressures exerted on the system to respond. Most scholars and those in government would agree that the impact of policy cannot be completely anticipated. There are a number of imponderables in a policy process. Thus, the policy of school desegregation combined with school busing has stimulated a flight to the suburbs and has even resulted in increased school segregation. Similarly, the establishment of Medicare, while providing significant support to the elderly and relieving burdensome health care bills for younger members of the population, has also created a medical benefit for a number of doctors, namely, those who thrive on Medicare patients and are able to amass a great deal of wealth in practices based solely on Medicare patients.

One of the earlier examples of feedback is the repeal of Prohibition. Congress proposed the Eighteenth Amendment in 1917, and it was ratified in January 1919. This national liquor prohibition created an environment for the mass smuggling of liquor and helped swell the coffers of the criminal elements in society. The resistance of the American people to the amendment increased until Congress finally proposed a repeal, the Twenty-First Amendment, which was ratified in December 1933. The essential factor in this repeal was feedback from many groups within the populace, including law enforcement officials and special liquor interests.

A more current example of feedback was the United States involvement in the Vietnam War. Initially, both Congress and the public at large felt that the United States should assist South Vietnam. As the war progressed and results became increasingly ambiguous, the American people became disillusioned. Demonstrations, riots, and campus unrest indicated that the United States policy in Vietnam had lost its consensus; indeed, large segments of the populace were actively resisting it. These moods were reflected in Congress and in no small measure were responsible for Lyndon Johnson's decision not to run for re-election in 1968.

The Vietnam War aso provides an example of feedback from other political actors. Journalists such as David Halberstam reported early in the war some basic weaknesses in American policy. A few individuals in the military publicly expressed reservations about United States policy. A few congressmen, contrary to the general mood in Congress during the early years of the war, also expressed doubts about United States involvement. Thus, while the public response to the war was becoming increasingly negative during 1967 and 1968, feedback of a similar nature was producing questions and suspicions of United States policy in the intellectual community, as well as in Congress and in the bureaucracy.

One of the examples of continuing feedback on policy is the activity associated with the defense budget. Passage of the defense budget involves a multitude of actors, ranging from labor unions and industrial interests to congressmen. After passage, there is continuing debate on the nature of weaponry, amounts of money involved, corruption, inefficiency, and waste. Money spent on any major weapon or other hardware invariably creates significant feedback. The attempt to build antiballistic missiles, for example, almost immediately involved communities in which sites were planned, scientists who disagreed with the technical performance of the ABMs, and congressmen who were opposed to the potential costs of the ABM. The amount of pressure placed on the defense establishment and Congress by disgruntled communities, congressmen, and bureaucrats significantly limited the number of ABM sites and restricted the scope of the program.

NEVER-ENDING PROCESS

Feedback is a continuing characteristic of the American political system. The policy process never ends. There is a continuing interplay of forces, those opposed, those for, and those seeking revision. Feedback is not limited to any particular sector of American society or to any particular institution in the political system. A variety of political actors from all levels of American society are involved in feedback. The ultimate revision, reinforcement, or repeal of policy is a result of the power exercised by political actors.

It is important to note that, once policy is approved, it is quite difficult to change or revise it: political actors tend to coalesce around such policy, and it becomes entrenched. Nevertheless, as we can see from history, policy changes have been numerous, particularly in those areas where policy has

been perceived by important groups in American society as directly affecting them.

Policy feedback may eventually lead to the reinstitution of the entire policy process. Reaction to policy will emerge, be identified, and proceed through the various phases and again develop feedback which may again initiate the never-ending process.

Accomplishments and Prospects

No modern political system remains unchanged. Some changes are imperceptible, others quite visible. Changes are brought about by strong pressure from the people, by the working of the political institutions, and by the processes of politics itself. For a political system to function effectively, it must be able to incorporate these changes while remaining relatively stable and operating according to the basic rules of the game. In a democratic society we assume that the political system remains open to a variety of pressures and thus is susceptible to a numer of changes.

In the 1970s the American political system is faced with a number of dilemmas, stemming from a need to incorporate change while trying to maintain a democratic social and political base. The autonomy and power of the individual have diminished in contrast to the power of other political actors. Yet, if the democratic condition is to be maintained, this power equation must be reversed.

At this point, the conventional approach would be to list a number of major issues faced by the American political system and then to discuss them and offer solutions. For example, some attention would be given to such issues as energy, environment, employment, welfare, economy, equality, individual rights and freedom, the nature of political leadership, and so on. There is no question that

these are major issues and they do need resolution in the immediate future. Our concern,
however, is with the more fundamental issues
that are the basis of the political system itself.
Therefore, rather than turning our attention
to all these specific questions, discussions of
which are available in many magazines and
newspapers, we will concern ourselves with
the basic issues of individual autonomy and
power and their relationship to political actors
and the political system as a whole. These
are the fundamental issues in any political
system.

Four Themes of American Politics

There are four major themes influencing
the direction in which American politics and
society are moving: integration and centralization, decentralization and diffusion,
social and psychological changes, and political
skepticism.

INCREASING INTEGRATION AND CENTRALIZATION

Increasing integration and centralization is
likely because the continued industrialization
of American society motivates increasing integration of American life. As new sources of
political power are sought, economic institutions and processes will continue to move toward a more centralized system which is presumed to be more efficient. Simultaneously,
there will be a movement toward a more unified and integrated society paralleling the
economic system. The close interrelationship
between society and economy will increasingly demand central planning and integration of various sectors of society.

Closely related to this is the extent and
scope of governmental authority at all levels.
As the economic power of large corporations
and institutions expands, individuals and
groups will be less able to cope with the system. In American society, where economic
power easily leads to political power, individuals and groups will tend to turn more and
more toward government to regulate and control the economic system. In matters of social
security, housing, welfare, and a host of other
issues, governmental institutions will emerge
as the only agencies able to cope with the vast
conglomerate economic power. In turn, government will have to expand its authority at all
levels to deal properly with the economic and
social structure. The growth of administrative
agencies will probably continue and with it,
the extension of bureaucratic control. Scholars who have in the past characterized the
American system as a bureaucratic state were
probably not far wrong. There are no indications that suggest the lessening of bureaucratic control in the future.

One should not necessarily envision conspiracy on the part of those operating the
political system. In a number of instances, the
demands of the people and the inability of
local government are the real causes of the
expansion of governmental authority on the
higher level. The Jeffersonian ideal of a nation
of stout, hardworking farmers and strong local
and state governments has been clearly replaced by the Hamiltonian concept of a strong
centralized national government.

DECENTRALIZATION AND DIFFUSION OF POWER

The second theme, decentralization and diffusion of power, may appear contradictory to
the first. Even though there is a definite
movement toward centralization and expansion of governmental authority, there are also

definite pressures for decentralization and diffusion of power within the political system. Local and state governments, political parties, and a number of political actors reflect the heterogeneous nature of American society. This diversity provides a varied power base within the national system. Such power bases, stemming from local and regional constituencies, provide countervailing pressures and resistance to the centralizing trend at the national level.

Local governments and political actors who must operate at the grass roots level are much more sensitive to grievances and pressures of the people. The existing power base at the local level will be reinforced, as people and groups turn more and more to governmental authority to cope with the increasing problems of society. Thus, while the extent of national power will expand, it will be countered by increasing power at the local levels.

Closely related to the theme of decentralization and diffusion is political participation. The phenomenon of populist politics that first emerged in 19th-century America had its modern counterparts in the presidential campaigns of Senator Eugene McCarthy and Senator George McGovern. Although neither man was able to reach the presidency, they provided a spark that may have rekindled the concept of individual participation in politics. Coming after the significant accomplishments of the civil rights movement and the involvement of individuals in this movement, the 1972 campaign of Senator George McGovern provided a populist model at the national level. Jimmy Carter's election as president in 1977 was a reflection of this phenomenon. Perhaps more important for immediate individual impact is the expansion of this populist model at the community level. Over the past ten years there has been a proliferation of community action groups and community organizations. The civil rights groups perhaps provided the first visible method by which

individuals at the local level could make some impact on the establishment.

Suspicion of political actors and general distrust of the workings of the American political system have created a high degree of political skepticism within the body politic and have caused community organizations and action groups to proliferate. It is as if a number of people are saying, "We have to do it ourselves." For example, in the city of Chicago alone in 1977 there were over eighty major community organizations, that is, organizations with an office and a staff of one or more persons. If one were to include all of the community organizations within the city (even those without office space and staff), the number would go well into the hundreds. All of these organizations attempt to scrutinize some governmental action and bring pressure to bear on some aspects of government. This relatively new phenomenon of community organization has provided new channels for the individual. It gives him a sense of power that is difficult to achieve in official institutions or political parties. Nevertheless, effective political power continues to elude the individual.

Whether this phenomenon of participatory politics will overcome the sense of skepticism and apathy is open to question. Much depends on the ability of community organizations to achieve some of their professed goals and the degree to which political leaders respond to community problems. If nothing else, participatory politics diffuses the power of other political actors.

While conditions have motivated some to move toward active involvement, they have also turned off a number of people—youths, people whose high hopes were dashed in the 1972 elections, and those who are convinced that "you can't fight city hall." Thus we see developing a unique and contradictory phenomenon: participation existing side by side with apathy and alienation.

CONTINUED SOCIAL AND PSYCHOLOGICAL CHANGE

The third theme, social and psychological change, is directly related to the political system and the attitudes and values associated with it. Most scholars seem to agree that basic changes are taking place in the social pattern. As a result of the impact of a generation of highly industrialized society, the civil rights movements, and the movement toward equality in all facets of our life, the social basis of society is shifting to a more egalitarian structure. The concept of middle class, for example, appears to be an increasingly vague one. Although poor and less privileged groups still exist, the increasing impetus toward an egalitarian society, buttressed by welfare assistance, social security, and a host of other programs, has obscured, for example, the distinction between the lower middle class and the lower class.

Indeed, the American social structure is more realistically characterized in terms of ethnic groups, racial groups, youth groups, sex groups, citizens' groups, and the like. Whereas not too many years ago one would speak of the vast middle class in terms of mainstream politics, the infusion of new groups into the traditional middle class has produced pockets of political awareness and political activity. Thus, the basic apathy of the vast number of American people is counterbalanced by a political awareness and involvement on the part of new middle class groups.

POLITICAL SKEPTICISM

Last, the American people are liable to be quite suspicious of policies committing the United States to foreign ventures. Americans are developing an increasing introspection, although not necessarily isolationism, that will affect the future amount of United States involvement in foreign problems. Because of the fear of more Vietnams, disillusionment with the United Nations, and a general frustration with the issues associated with developing nations, the American people are likely in the future to take a more selfish attitude on the use of American resources in the international field. The problems of poverty, inflation, unemployment, responsiveness of government, urban development, and a host of other economic and social issues will undoubtedly get most of the attention of the American people.

Obviously there is danger in this, because introspection breeds isolationism, and isolationism in a world in which nation-states are becoming increasingly interdependent may lead to policies that are contradictory to the national interest of the United States. A recognition that the world is interdependent and that there are limits to resources and to the power of the United States may be the first step toward developing a policy that is free of cold war rhetoric and is responsive to the interests of the United States without violating the sensitivities of the rest of the world.

Need for Balance

For the American political system to operate effectively while emphasizing the democratic condition, there must be some reconciliation of these four themes, as well as a balancing of their power and resolution of the conflicts inherent within each. This reconciliation and balance must take place at all levels of governmental authority and between the major political actors. In the main, the American people expect their leaders to provide the key to this reconciliation and balance. In a study of public opinion, two scholars concluded:

Because of the pragmatic, humanitarian value system that characterizes the American political credo, the conflict between conservative ideologies and the liberal programs most people favor is understandable; but this divergence between theory and practice certainly spells caution, patience, and tact for any leader who counts, as he must count on continual popular support for legislation he believes will promote the public welfare. The effective leader in American Democracy must of course formulate and communicate overall goals. But he must do more; he must plausibly demonstrate to a majority of citizens that the means by which he proposes to attain the goals are realistic, at the same time he must try to persuade them that the means are inconsistent with their basic ideological assumptions.[8]

Political leaders, whether they be elected or appointed, are focal points or reference points from which many individuals and groups develop perceptions and attitudes on the nature of the political system.

As suggested earlier, conflict and confrontation are an inherent part of democratic political systems. Through such means, issues are identified, voices heard, positions taken, and resolutions achieved. Therefore, we should not assume that in a democratic system conflict is evil; on the contrary, it is necessary. Obviously, we are not speaking about armed conflict or bloodshed, but that conflict and confrontation that evolve between reasonable human beings, responsive institutions, and wise political actors.

In our discussion so far, we have identified the general political, social, and psychological environment within which the American political system is operating. In essence what we have been suggesting is that there has been an ongoing conflict, at times implicit and at other times quite explicit, between the power of the individual and that of corporate organizations and the establishment. Moreover, there is a continuous movement in society to make official institutions responsive to individual grievances, to recognize that the fundamental premise of democracy is individual worth and involvement. Hence, the basic issue has been and remains a struggle for power.

Psychologically the struggle for power is reflected in a restiveness within the general mass of people, stemming from unfulfilled promises and dreams. The decline in the legitimacy of our political system and in the credibility of its leaders is at the base of this social and political restiveness. People are searching for some meaning in the chaos of our times. Their search for the realization of unfulfilled dreams focuses mainly on the operation of the political system and on its leaders.

The major political result is the increasing use of power by individuals to influence the political system. This has led to individual and community search for power to use on the establishment. More and more, the institutions of our government will be assessed in terms of how responsive they are to the public and how effectively they articulate the power of the people. Corporations and individual political actors possessing economic power will continue to be viewed by many with suspicion. Such political actors will gain credibility mainly through an image of service to the public.

The System Continues

Peering into the future, based on our assessment to this point, we see no dramatic changes in the principles of power to the people, federalism, separation of powers and checks and balances, judicial review, and limited government. While there may be varying interpretations, we seen no dramatic changes in the acceptance of democratic ideology. Rather we see increasing pressure on the entire American political system to recapture the traditions and operations of the past while recruiting committed, loyal, and trustworthy political leaders to deal with the problems of the future. A political premise of a democratic system is that, when the inherent flexibility and divergency are stretched to the maximum, forces will be exerted to restore the proper balance or equilibrium between contending groups and actors. This simply means that the power base of the people must be restored to maintain a balance in the democratic condition.

It would appear that individuals and communities are still committed to existing institutions, but not necessarily to the way the political process has operated in the immediate past. To restore the democratic condition, institutional operations must be based on an effective accountability and responsibility to the people. This can only be done by an intensive and extensive system of public scrutiny of institutional operations, political actors, and the policy process. Moreover, although political parties and traditional groups must play a role in such an operation, community organizations and new channels of expressing individual power may well become important ingredients in the American political system.

Groups and individuals in a democratic society will rarely ever achieve all that they desire. For a democratic system to work, there must be reasonable and rational men who understand the process of compromise. They must understand that not all goals will be achieved but that individuals and groups must have the opportunity to struggle for their goals with a reasonable chance of success.

More important, opportunities must exist for an individual to acquire and maintain the power he needs to make his voice heard and felt in the political system. Undoubtedly there are those even in a democratic society who question whether one person has any real impact on the operations of the political system. It is our contention that power *is* mean-

ingful in individual terms. Individual rights and power are the foundation of the American political system. Almost two decades ago, Eleanor Roosevelt touched upon this issue when she stated:

> Where, after all, do universal human rights begin? In small places, close to home—so close and so small that they cannot be seen on any maps of the world. Yet they are in the world of the individual person; the neighborhood; the school or college he attends; the factory, farm or office where he works. Such are the places where every man, woman or child seeks equal justice, equal opportunity, equal dignity without discrimination. Unless their rights have meaning there, they have little meaning anywhere. Without concerned citizen action to uphold them close to home, we shall look in vain for progress in the larger world.[9]

The proper operation of a democratic political system begins in the world of the individual person, his neighborhood, and his community. The individual must perceive that he has power to influence his own political system. Without this perception, the democratic political system will soon decay into one in which the individual not only loses all power, but his autonomy as well.

Summary

In retrospect, the American political system has achieved much operating according to democratic principles. To be sure, corporate interests, organized groups, and the political elite still dominate politics and the making of policy choices. Yet, the American system shows an increasing concern for the individual and for social justice. Moreover, the opportunities for minorities and women have been expanded considerably, particularly over the past decade. Thus, if we presume that democracy means, among other things, sensitivity to the individual, the creation of social environment conducive to freedom, and a political system accountable and responsible to the people, we can argue that the American political system is performing reasonably well in terms of its own ideology.

American ideology, with its emphasis on liberty and equality, has given rise to the contradictory concepts of elitism and pluralism. These concepts have directly affected the kinds of political actors and the political process. On the one hand, there has developed a pride in individual accomplishment and competition. On the other, there is expressed a concern for the welfare of the less fortunate, a concern that appears to be reflected in governmental action. The individual is constantly being confronted by the group, the society, and the state. The ideals of the laissez-faire spirit are matched by the self-sufficient individual in the political sphere. In turn, this is countered by the organizational structures that have evolved to spread the wealth of America more equitably, reflecting the concern for equality. Corporate structures epitomizing the individual competitiveness of the American experience have evolved and with them, a denigration of the ability of the individual to compete in the business world.

These contradictory themes, directly linked to American ideology, have created a political system in which a variety of political actors have emerged. Taking their cue from American ideology, particularly from the principles of limited government and increased liberty, these political actors struggle over a share in governing America. The tensions evolving from their interaction arise out of the contradictions between elitism and pluralism, between liberty and equality, between the right to govern and the rights of the governed. All of these, in turn, are issues arising from the basic problem of a democratic society, well stated at the Constitutional Convention: "Let it stand as a principle that government originates from the people; but let the people be taught . . . that they are not able to govern themselves."

NOTES

1. John C. Donovan, *The Policy Makers* (New York: Pegasus, 1970), p. 19.
2. Dean Acheson, "Thoughts about Thought in High Places," *New York Times Magazine*, October 11, 1959, p. 20.
3. Andrew Hacker, "The Supreme Court: Entering the 'Political Thicket' of Reapportionment," in Allan P. Sindler, *American Political Institutions and Public Policy: Five Contemporary Studies* (Boston: Little, Brown, 1969), pp. 230–246.
4. J. P. Mayer, ed., *Alexis de Tocqueville in America*, translated by George Lawrence (Garden City, N.Y.: Doubleday, Anchor Books, 1969), p. 270.
5. Alexander M. Bickel, "Close of Warren Era," *The New Republic*, July 12, 1969.
6. Harold Seidman, *Politics, Position, and Power: The Dynamics of Federal Organization* (New York: Oxford University Press, 1970), p. 27.
7. Henry A. Kissinger, "Bureaucracy and Policymaking: The Effect of Insiders and Outsiders on the Policy Process," in Morton H. Halperin and Arnold Kanter, eds., *Readings in American Foreign Policy: A Bureaucratic Perspective* (Boston: Little, Brown, 1973), p. 86.
8. Lloyd A. Free and Hadley Cantril, *The Political Beliefs of Americans* (New Brunswick, N.J.: Rutgers University Press, 1967), pp. 179–180.
9. As quoted in Joseph P. Lash, *Eleanor: The Years Alone* (New York: Signet Books, 1973), p. 72.

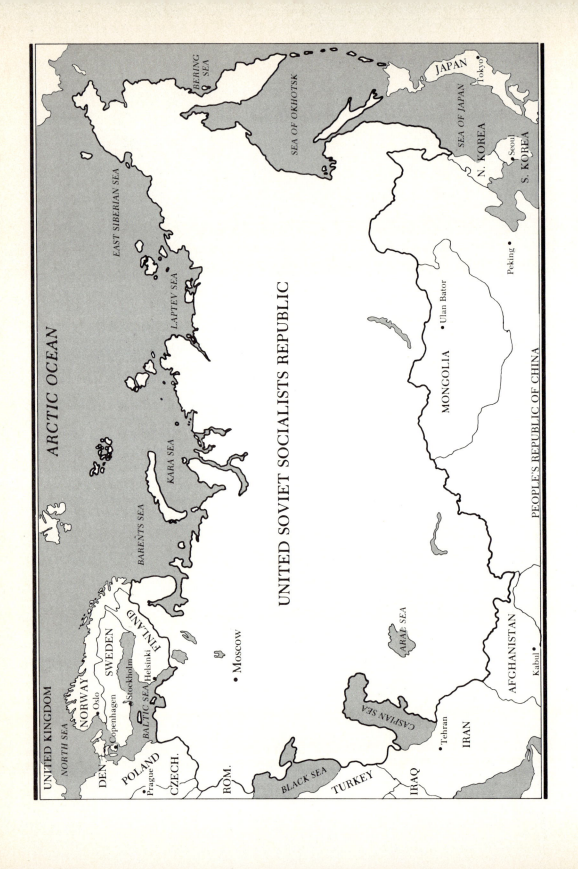

PART 3 The Soviet Political System

CHAPTER 5

SOVIET COMMUNIST IDEOLOGY

In 1977, the Soviet Union celebrated its sixtieth anniversary as a communist state, indeed, the first communist state. Ten years earlier, on the occasion of its fiftieth anniversary, Nikita Khrushchev had stated, "The very history of our Soviet State and the victory of our Communist Party are sufficient testimony to our virtues and our achievements. If we look down the road of the past fifty years, we can see where we started and how far we have come. We have astonished even our enemies."[1] Ten years later, there is still cause to wonder at the Soviet achievement. A country of over 240 million people ranking second in power only to the United States, the Soviet Union has survived civil war, famine, purges, terror, assassination, and a world war. She has entered into the nuclear era and now challenges the United States as a superpower— and all of this within two generations!

Yet there are important contradictions. The superpower status of the Russian state must be qualified by the traditional character of society. A Pulitzer-prize-winning journalist with years of experience in the Soviet Union writes,

I also had to unlearn the notion that Russia had become a modern industrial state on a par with the advanced West, for that concept obscures as much as it reveals. Behind the mask of modernism, of missiles, jets and industrial technology, is concealed the imprint of centuries of Russian history on the structure of Soviet society and the habits and character of the Russian people.[2]

A number of scholars tend to compare the expansion of the Soviet state and the accompanying problems with the early struggles of the United States. Admittedly, there are a number of similarities, particularly in the 1970s climate of détente. But upon closer examination, one finds that similarities are superficial at best, and cultural differences are quite pronounced. An examination of the revolutionary heritage and prevailing ideologies in the United States and the Soviet Union reveals sharp contrasts. Indeed, these distinctions lead directly to major differences in the political rules of the game and in the resulting political structure and processes.

To understand the basis of the Soviet political system, one must develop some insights into the nature of the Revolution of 1917, the evolution and implementation of Marxist-Leninist ideology, and the subsequent development of the political system.

There is general agreement among scholars that Russian involvement in World War I was the catalyst for the Bolshevik Revolution. The war exposed the weaknesses of the tsarist regime and created problems of organization, order, and legitimacy which the autocratic ruler of Russia and his ruling elite could not overcome. After disastrous defeats on the battlefield and the general breakdown of the entire war effort, the tsarist regime was replaced in February 1917 by a moderate revolutionary group headed by Kerensky. Given a few more months, the Kerensky regime might have survived and established a Soviet Union considerably different from the one we know today. But the Bolsheviks under Lenin, aware of the instability of the regime and attuned to the attitudes of the Russian masses, quickly moved to place themselves in power. Thus, the November 1917 Revolution, the second in the same year, became the "real" revolution and led to significant changes in the Russian political system.

Reflecting on the November Revolution, Louis Fischer writes,

When those at the peak are as inept as the last Tsar, as conniving as the last Tsarina, as corrupt as Rasputin, or as decent but indecisive as Kerensky, a Lenin has only to cough, or to laugh, and the walls of Jericho come tumbling down.[3]

Russian history is primarily the story of an autocracy striving for absolute control, struggling against external forces and trying to establish internal order. Its methods included despotic rule, the suppression of dissent and opposition in the name of the state, and the expansion of Russian hegemony into Asia and Europe. The autocratic structure was also able to maintain enough stability and power to provide a brief period in which Tsarist Russia played a major role in the balance of power in Europe (from the end of the 18th century through the Napoleonic period). Thus, the history of Russia is at times that of Europe, at other times that of Asia, and most of all that of a society struggling to maintain its traditional structure against the inroads of modernity. Russians as a society were conscious of their own uniqueness, ambivalent about Western culture, and proud of their presumed superior qualities of spirit. During the period of the tsars, the Russian people found themselves enveloped in a culture that was part Eastern and part Western. Russian political institutions reflect this paradox. Throughout Russian history run the contradictory themes of an autocratic tradition and anarchism.

The Birth of Modern Russia

The Mongol Tartar domination of what is now Russia lasted for about 200 years. Not only did this domination bring an Eastern flavor to Russian culture, but it also isolated the Russian people from European influence, namely, the Reformation and the Renaissance. Some scholars argue that this isolation is responsible for the uniqueness of modern Russia.

More important, the Mongol domination sowed the seeds of Russian unity. While the princes of the various Russian states paid tribute to the Khan, they strove to develop some unity to regain their freedom.

Before the Mongol domination, the forerunners of the modern tsarist system proclaimed themselves bearers of the Byzantine legacy and founders of the Third Rome. Indeed, tsar is a corruption of the imperial title caesar. While Rome and Constantinople fell by the historical wayside, the tsars of Russia were thought to represent a new power. Defenders of the Orthodox Church, the tsars proclaimed themselves descendants and inheritors of the God-Emperor role. Thus at an early stage in Russian history the tsar as a secular ruler was identified with the tsar as the defender of the faith. The Mongol domination only served to strengthen the idea of the tsar as absolute ruler and symbol of the unity of secular with religious power.

Modern Russia was born with the reign of Ivan III. Uniting various princes, he defeated the Mongols and established the Grand Duchy of Muscovy as the most powerful princely state. Not only did Ivan struggle against the Mongols, but also he fought against Poland and Lithuania, and against the Eastern Slavs. By winning the independence of Moscow, Ivan demonstrated that independence and survival could be achieved only by authoritarian rule and thus established a heritage that continues today in modern Russia.

Ivan III became known as Ivan the Great, not only because of his struggles against the Mongols and external powers, but also because of his attempts to unify the Russian people, institutionalize a central authority, and stimulate Russian cultural development and administrative coherency. The centralization of authority based on the Byzantine ideas of government not only enhanced the aristocratic nature of his rule but laid the foundations for the development of a modern Russian state. It was through his efforts that there occurred the first stirrings of Russian nationalism.

From this period until World War I, the tsars continued the autocratic tradition buttressed by religious authority. While there were periods of relatively moderate rule, most periods were characterized by harsh rule in which the tsars manifested their divine right to rule with a tradition completely divorced from more enlightened political development in Europe. Indeed, even when changes beneficial to the masses were made, they came from above, by authority of the tsar. Students of modern Russia can recognize identical patterns of political rule in present-day Russia.

Through a succession of tsars from Ivan the Great to Nicholas II, the Russian political system continued its autocratic character and centralizing focus. In the main, the system reflected the personality of the rulers. Even an enigmatic and erratic ruler such as Paul (1796–1801) had a major impact on the system, trying to undo much of what his mother Catherine had done.

AUTOCRACY AND SOCIETY

During the rule of Ivan the Terrible in the 16th century, the Russian peasant, whose lot was already difficult, was reduced to serfdom. The terror and fear upon which Ivan the Terrible built his reign, combined with the external struggles against traditional enemies, required increased taxes and produced a growing debt. The great mass of Russian peasants were small farmers who rented the land they tilled from the gentry, the church, or the state. They had the right to end their tenancy and to move to another landowner's estate. But under the increasing burden of taxes and mounting debts, peasants found themselves bound to a specific landowner. For all practical purposes, the relatively free movement of peasants was replaced by a system in which the peasant was bound to the landowner. Similar to the feudal system in Europe, Russian serfdom deprived the peasant of all rights and bound him to the soil to be sold with the land if the landlord so desired.

Under Peter the Great, Russian society underwent forced "westernization," and an eroding of the traditional social structure. Enamored with the West, Peter borrowed freely to modernize the military and the government. Although thought by many to be the period of flowering in Russian cultural history, the years of Peter's reign were characterized by autocratic and centralized rule.

As always, changes in Russian society were forced from the top.

The state became the main planner and executor of economic and social policy, a characteristic of the Russian state that continues today. The attempted reforms and modernization of the Russian state did not result in an integrated society. Increasingly, gaps appeared between intellectuals, the aristocracy, and the masses. The intellectuals, imbued with Western ideas of liberal democracy, became alienated from the tsarist government. The aristocrats, seeing their position in society eroded by the policies of Peter the Great, blamed not only the peasants, but the intellectuals and the tsar for their declining power and prestige. In essence, these major groups in society became alienated from the tsarist regime. One scholar calls Peter the Great's impact on Russia "cataclysmic":

The impact of Peter the Great upon Russia was cataclysmic. The effect of the reign was no less than to divide ancient Russia from modern Russia. Russian society remained for two and a half centuries essentially in the form in which Peter molded it. To the end of the monarchy the governmental structure of the state remained fundamentally what Peter had made it. He brought Russia out of oriental barbarism into contact with Western civilization. The fact that the transformation was not complete left the nation half Eastern and half Western, half medieval and half modern, half superstitious and half enlightened. From the reign of Peter I on, Russia as a nation and the Russians as a people seemed to Westerners full of contradictions and paradoxes.[4]

Catherine the Great (1762-1796) attempted to follow through on the reforms begun by Peter. By the end of her reign, Russian linkage with the European civilization had become increasingly important. The upper elements of Russian society became "civilized" in a European way: the languages of the West were spoken, arts and letters were imitations of the West, and even Russian dress gave way to Western clothes. Nevertheless, the great masses in Russia were still widely separated from the aristocracy. Indeed, the masses counted hardly at all. The serfs were in worse condition than before, while the gentry and landlords virtually dominated Russian society.

By the time of Alexander III, the Russian system had liberated the serfs—more in name than in fact—the tsarist system had consolidated its hold on the government structure, and a number of problems with neighbors had been settled. Indeed the reign of Alexander III was called the era of peace. Never in Russian history had there been a span of so many years in which no major wars were fought by the Russian state. With the passing of Alexander and the ascension of Nicholas I in 1825, antagonisms appeared between the masses and the ruling elite. Westernization had brought with it an "awareness" of the relative conditions of the ruled and the rulers. Moreover, the passing of the tsar left the Russian government in disarray. Court intrigues and pressures brought to bear by the church and the aristocracy led to political manipulation regarding the line of succession.

The Revolutionary Environment

During the reign of Nicholas I, the Russian state faced its first modern revolutionary attempt. The Decembrist movement of 1825 was an army putsch that failed. Led by young aristocrats and army officers, it was an attempt to install some constitutional and reform ideas borrowed from the West. Although the putsch failed, it set a precedent. Throughout the 19th century, revolutionary plots and uprisings were common.

Nicholas II, the last tsar, reigned over a Russian state that was characterized by increasing unrest among the masses, a state embroiled in intense political maneuvering in Europe (which eventually led to World War I), and a state that was the first major modern European power to be defeated by an Eastern power. The Russo-Japanese War of 1905 was indeed a humiliation to the Russians. Equally important, the defeat exposed the increasingly fragile power structure of the tsarist system.

During the 19th century the tsars paid little heed to the social and political changes and demands from within Russian society. Industrialization, albeit agonizingly slow, brought with it the beginnings of a working class. Peasants were increasingly being made aware of the disparities between their lot and that of the aristocracy. While the tsars were being isolated from the masses by the ruling circles, court pomp and ceremony, and the Russian Orthodox Church, various conspiratorial groups within society were plotting ways to oppose the government. Given the nature of the tsarist bureaucracy, the police state system, and the absolutism of the tsar, dissenters had few alternatives but to organize into conspiratorial groups. Thus the immediate pre–World War I period in Russia was characterized by the rise of a variety of secret groups and by assassinations, plots, and counterplots.

By the early 1900s, mutinies in the military and the defeat in the Russo-Japanese War marked the beginning of the end of the reign of Nicholas II. In an attempt to ease the revolutionary situation, a Duma (Congress) was created. For the first time in their history, Russians were able to elect a representative assembly with limited powers. The experiment was short-lived, however, as the tsar quickly reasserted his absolute power.

As we noted earlier, involvement in World War I, although initially hailed as a struggle for Mother Russia, led to disillusionment and to the collapse of the tsarist regime. The period of the tsars through World War I is summarized by one scholar who concludes:

Through century after century, from Kievan to Communist times, the course of Russian history has been set by its strong rulers. The story of the nation's past often seems to be simply the history of the state. The history of the Russian people is elusive. For years and decades on end they go unnoticed, serving the needs of the state anonymously, working and dying without identity. Occasionally, however, the people rise up and dominate the story, pushing the state into the background. Momentarily the observer's attention focuses upon the Russian masses and upon the leaders who arise from their midst to lead them. Such moments would come with the rising of Stenka Razin in the seventeenth century and with that of Pugachov in the eighteenth. Such a moment would come in the twentieth century with the overthrow of the monarchy.[5]

Conclusions: The Tsarist System

As we noted, in Tsarist Russia, the rule of the tsar was considered to be the fundamental basis for achieving unity and stability. Tsarist rule was based on a long tradition of autocratic rule, which emphasized political centralization and the exercise of absolute power. Belief in the absolutism of the tsar went hand-in-hand with fear of anarchy. Any decrease in the authority of the tsar generally resulted in war, invasion, or internal conflict. Moreover, this fear tended to reinforce and legitimize the tsar's absolute power as the only means of maintaining unity and stability within the state. The position of the tsar was further reinforced by the Russian Orthodox Church.

These prevailing traditions prevented any changes from "below" (from the peasant and working class). Demands for such changes always raised the fear of anarchy and were suppressed by the ruling class. As a result, any political activity not sanctioned by the tsar found its outlet in conspiratorial or revolutionary organizations. Reforms that did not come from "above" (from the ruling class) could be made only by revolution. Parenthetically, reforms from above were rare.

These were the general political characteristics of Tsarist Russia at the turn of the 19th century. Immediately before World War I, certain social and economic reforms were initiated. Although Tsarist Russia was making some progress as an industrialized society, it remained largely an agrarian one.

When the old political, social, and economic traditions combined with the new emerging industrial base, the stage was set for the impact of Marxist ideology. Marxist groups began to form in the 1880s and 1890s in urban Russia, but it was not until 1903 that Lenin's Bolsheviks emerged as an organized group.

At the turn of the century, Tsarist Russia had experienced economic crisis, worker repression, and peasant rebellion. At the same time, the power of the nobles had declined while the power of the intelligentsia had increased. Indeed, it was the alienation of the intelligentsia that was the harbinger of revolution.

In this situation, Marxist ideology found a sympathetic audience not only among Lenin's Bolsheviks, but also among the intelligentsia and other liberal groups. It offered them a framework in which to consolidate their ideas and a rationale for instituting much-needed social reforms.

In addition, Marxist ideology appealed to the peasants because it spoke out against those who owned property and against the exploitation of the landless. The Marxist concept of mass ownership of property was particularly appealing to the peasants because it implied the destruction of the landlord class, which had been exploiting them.

Moreover, the Russian army, a pillar of the tsarist state, was composed largely of peasants and workers. Permeated by peasant and worker grievances, it was vulnerable to the appeals of Marxist ideology.

All these factors made Russia ripe for revolution in 1905. Fortunately for the tsar, the army did not disintegrate but remained loyal and suppressed the revolt.

Meanwhile, between 1900 and 1917, the tsarist state, largely in panic, attempted to enact reforms with the one hand while trying to root out revolutionaries with the other. With Tsarist Russia on the edge of defeat in 1917 and the Russian masses war-weary and disillusioned, Lenin urged, "We must not wait. We may lose everything." And indeed, the Bolsheviks did not wait. With a few hundred marines and soldiers, they seized Petrograd, and the Bolshevik revolution became a reality.

Marxism, Leninism, and Stalinism

Since the appearance of the *Communist Manifesto* in 1848 and the subsequent writings of Karl Marx, Communist leaders and scholars from various parts of the world have attempted to interpret and assess political, social, and economic conditions in terms of Marxian ideology.[6] In the Soviet Union, Marxian ideology has been interpreted and applied by Lenin, by Stalin, and by more modern Russian leaders, such as Khrushchev and Brezhnev. Marx's theories have also been Sinocized by Mao Tse-tung, Africanized by African leaders, and Latinized by Castro and Allende.

The ideological descendants of Marx have revised and reinterpreted Marx's theories to apply to their own particular power position and to the conditions prevailing within their respective countries. This preoccupation with ideological relevance is one of the major characteristics of the communist states. Concomitantly, Marxian ideology has provided the vehicle by which power has been attained and maintained by a small elite. All of this has been done in the name of the people, the proletariat.

To understand the ideas of Karl Marx and Nikolai Lenin, one must be cognizant of some of the major distinctions in the experiences and perceptions of these two men. Marx was the theoretician. Writing during a period of revolutionary ferment throughout Europe, he was concerned with the working class, the proletariat as a whole, and thus perceived the revolutionary processes in universalistic terms spelled out in an apparent systematic assessment of world history. Marx was concerned with establishing a philosophical rationale for the legitimate fight of the proletariat to rule.

Lenin was the "operator," that is, he was the first leader of a Marxist state. His concern was not primarily with rigid adherence to the philosophical precepts of Marxian theory, but rather with the best methods by which the Bolshevik party could attain power and expand to control the Russian state. From this initial phase, Lenin hoped to develop Russia into a socialist state. Lenin was concerned initially with retaining party power and developing a proletariat revolution within Russia. "Give me an organization of revolutionists," he boasted, "and we shall overturn the whole of Russia."[7] Later, he asserted that "politics cannot but have precedence over economics. To argue differently means forgetting the ABC of Marxism."[8] In so doing, he revised Marxian theory to justify its relevance to the conditions within the Soviet Union during the period between 1917 and 1924. He retained the goal of Marxian orthodoxy but was willing to use virtually any tactic he found useful to achieve it.

THE STATE AND CLASS STRUCTURE

Lenin, for example, adhered to Marx's views on the nature of the state; that is, all states are class states, instruments of the ruling classes.

Capitalistic states reflect the laws, morality, and politics of the capitalistic classes. For Marx, it is ownership of the means of production that distinguishes classes and determines the nature and shape of the state. Thus the proletariat is completely dominated and subdued in a capitalistic state. It is from this condition that the proletariat ultimately develops the revolutionary mentality and recognizes that its mission is to seize state power.

"Society is based on the antagonism of oppressing and oppressed classes," according to Marx, who predicted that the proletariat would ultimately triumph.[9] The capitalists would get wealthier and smaller in number, while the proletariat would become more impoverished and larger in number. Eventually, the proletariat would be the vast majority and would become conscious of its condition and historical mission. It was only in the advanced stages of an industrial society that the proletariat would develop the revolutionary mentality and consciousness needed to rise up in revolution and seize the state. For Marx, the proletariat class was not only the instrument but also the precipitator of the revolution. As Friedrich Engels noted,

While the capitalist mode of production more and more completely transforms the great majority of the population into proletarians, it creates the power which under penalty of its own destruction, is forced to accomplish this revolution. While it forces on more and more the transformation of the vast means of production already socialized, into state property, it shows itself the way to accomplish this revolution. The proletariat seizes political power and turns the means of production into state property.[10]

According to Marx, there was no need of any elite or organization to accomplish the proletariat revolution. He wrote,

The communists do not form a separate party opposed to other working-class parties. They have no interest separate and apart from those of the proletariat as a whole. . . . The Communists, therefore, are on the one hand, practically, the most advanced and resolute section of the working-class parties of every country . . . on the other hand, theoretically, they have over the great mass of the proletariat the advantage of clearly understanding the line of march, the conditions, and the ultimate general results of the proletariat movement.[11]

MARXIST HUMANISM

Marxist ideology was particularly relevant to the Russian situation because it combined both humanistic and revolutionary elements; that is, it promised a revolutionary attack upon the poverty of the masses and granted human dignity to the disaffected. Marxist humanism stressed the importance of free, creative self-development, a value much lacking in the ideology of Tsarist Russia. In addition, it provided the scientific rationale and the revolutionary process by which to achieve a better life on earth.

In its simplest form, humanism can best be explained as opposing alienation. That is, the worker in a capitalistic society does not realize his natural capacity. The economic system, based on limited ownership of the means of production, requires him to use his labor, not to further his own interests, but to further those of others. Thus the worker alienates his own labor and himself from his natural capacities and interests. In *Capital* Marx writes:

Manufacture . . . seizes labor power by its very roots. It converts the laborer into a crippled monstrosity, by forcing his detail dexterity at the expense of a world of productive capabilities and instincts; just as in the states of La Plata they butcher a whole beast for the sake of his hide or his tallow. Not only is the detail work distributed to the different individuals, but also the individual him-

self is made the automatic motor of a fractional operation. . . . In manufacture, in order to make the collective laborer and through him capital, rich in social productive power, each laborer must be made poor in individual productive powers.[12]

To destroy this system, the working class, the proletariats, must organize a revolutionary movement. In the *Communist Manifesto* Marx writes that Communists representing the proletariat

openly declare that their ends can be attained only by forcible overthrow of all existing social conditions. Let the ruling classes tremble at a communist revolution. The proletariats have nothing to lose but their chains. They have a world to win. Working men of all countries unite.[13]

THE PROLETARIAT AND REVOLUTION

Revolution in a capitalistic society would occur with the emergence and organization of the proletariat and the development of contradictions within the capitalistic society. Capitalistic society is made up of two classes, the bourgeoisie and the proletariat. Marx observes,

The history of all hitherto existing society is the history of class struggles. By bourgeoisie is meant the class of modern Capitalists, owners of the means of social production and employers of wage-labor. By proletariat, the class of modern wage-laborers who, having no means of production of their own, are reduced to selling their labor-power in order to live.[14]

Hence, to correct the repressive actions of the bourgeoisie, the proletariat must overthrow them so that the interests of all classes may be realized.

Contradictions within capitalism will give rise to the clear and antagonistic distinction between the bourgeoisie and the proletariat, which can result only in conflict. Further-more, the increasing oppression of the work-ing class by fewer and fewer capitalists will deepen the antagonism between the bour-geoisie and the proletariat and eventually cre-ate a revolutionary environment. Finally, there will be economic crisis within capital-ism, according to Marx, which will create ad-ditional misery among the working class and act as the catalyst to revolution.

MARXISM AND REVOLUTIONARY RUSSIA

Lenin, although adopting the universalistic appeals of Marxian theory, revised the basic premises regarding the revolutionary process and the role of the party. To reiterate, given the historical conditions of the Russian state during the period between 1917 and 1924, one can readily appreciate the major prob-lems the new Communist government faced. Immediately after the overthrow of the Kerensky government in 1917, Lenin was faced with a Russian state torn apart by separatist movements, civil war, foreign in-tervention, and the harsh dictates of the Brest-Litovsk Treaty of 1918. More impor-tant, Lenin needed to consolidate his power throughout Russia. Consequently, Lenin and the Bolsheviks were not necessarily inclined to adhere to the ideological "nicety" of Marx-ian theory. This is not to suggest that they did not attempt to follow Marxian theory. Rather, the historical realities of ruling forced them to revise Marxian theory to make it relevant to the situation in Russia. Indeed, Lenin was determined to demonstrate that the Russian Revolution was a legitimate expression of Marxian theory.

Lenin reaffirmed the historical dialecticism of Marx and Engels and accepted the inevita-bility of the proletariat state; however, he ar-gues that, since the revolution was inevitable, it was not necessary to wait for a mature

capitalistic state. With respect to this aspect of Lenin's idea, Stalin wrote,

Where will the revolution begin? Where, in what country, can the front of capital be pierced first? Where industry is more developed, where the proletariat constitutes the majority, where there is more culture, where there is more democracy—that was the reply usually given for-merly. No, objects the Leninist theory of revolu-tion, not necessarily where industry is more de-veloped, and so forth. The front of capital will be pierced where the chain of imperialism is the weakest, for the proletarian revolution is the result of the breaking of the chain of the world imperialist front at its weakest link; . . .[15]

The proletariat, even though a minority, could make an alliance with the peasants in the name of democracy and seize state power.

According to Lenin, the proletariat must carry to completion the democratic revolution by allying itself with the mass of the peasantry to crush by force the resistance of the autoc-racy and to paralyze the instability of the bourgeoisie.[16] This statement was obviously an attempt to rationalize the Bolshevik Rev-olution of 1917. Russia was not a mature capitalistic state. Indeed, at the time of the revolution, Russia had only begun to develop some signs of capitalism. The downfall of the tsar and short-lived Kerensky government, however, presented the kind of power vac-uum Lenin and the Bolsheviks were quick to exploit, justifying it in the name of Marxian theory.

It should be noted that the implementation of the New Economic Policy in 1921 was also a reflection of the pragmatic and opportunistic view of Lenin. To maintain power, Lenin adapted state policy temporarily to react to conditions of economic breakdown and mass starvation. He even called on the capitalistic states for assistance.

Marxian theory was also revised to rationalize the role of the Bolshevik party in the Russian Revolution. Although the proletariat as a minority could seize power in the state, Lenin argued that they could only succeed if they were led by a dedicated group, that is, by the Bolshevik party. Lenin wrote,

> . . . forward development i.e., towards communism, proceeds through the dictatorship of the proletariat . . . and the dictatorship of the proletariat, i.e., the organization of the vanguard of the oppressed as the ruling class for the purpose of suppressing the oppressors. . . . The role of the vanguard fighter can be fulfilled only by a party that is guided by the most advanced theory.[17]

Acting in the name of the proletariat, the party leads in the revolutionary process, guiding the proletariat in its historical mission. According to Lenin, a proletariat revolution was not likely to develop by spontaneous actions of the proletariat. Rather, revolution had to be planned, implemented, and accomplished by a dedicated group of professional revolutionaries acting in the name of the proletariat. For all practical purposes, under Lenin, the dictatorship of the proletariat was changed to the dictatorship of the party.

STALINISM

In the postrevolutionary period, the dictatorship of the party gave way to personal dictatorship under Stalin. Faced with major problems within Russia after 1917, Lenin increasingly relied on a highly unified and committed group who would respond directly to his orders. Lenin felt that only with such a dedicated organization led personally by him could the Russian state be reconstituted and the Communist party retain power. In doing so, however, he set a precedent for one-man rule.

Following a period of collective leadership, Stalin became the leader of the Russian state in 1929. He used the Leninist version of Marxian theory as the basis for industrialization and modernization of Russia. The revolutionary process was complete in the Soviet state, according to Stalin. That is, exploiting classes had been abolished and there were no longer any hostile classes in the country. In 1939, Stalin wrote, "We have abolished the exploiting classes; there are no longer any hostile classes in the country; there is nobody to suppress.[18] Thus, there was no serious preoccupation with the revolutionary process within the Soviet Union, but rather an outward view of revolution in the world. Stalin insisted that the Soviet state, rather than withering away, must develop a strong political and military base in order to assist the world revolutionary forces. From this there developed the Stalinist concept of socialism in one country. Only after the Soviet state has developed into a powerful country could the revolutionary forces in the world be assisted. Stalin wrote,

> Commenced after the October Revolution. Objective: to consolidate the dictatorship of the proletariat in one country using it as a base for the overthrow of imperialism in all countries. The revolution is spreading beyond the confines of one country; the period of world revolution has commenced.[19]

The concept of a monolithic and dedicated party continued under Stalin but under a more personalistic rule. While he continually stressed collective leadership, he increasingly practiced personal dictatorship. In his famous secret speech, Khrushchev stated,

> Stalin originated the concept "enemy of the people." This term automatically rendered it unnecessary that the ideological errors of a man or men engaged in a controversy be proven; this term made possible the usage of revolutionary legality, against anyone who in any way disagreed with Stalin.[20]

By labeling anyone who opposed him as "enemy of the people," Stalin was able to charge him with treason and execute or banish him without a trial. The same method enabled Stalin to strengthen his power within the party and to rid it of those who resisted the harsh industrialization he imposed on Russia.

From 1924 until the beginning of World War II, Stalin and the Communist party were faced with the problem of developing an industrialized nation-state.[21] To most Russian Communists, this was an essential goal in the face of what they considered a hostile world environment, that is, encirclement by the capitalistic camp. Perhaps one of the most difficult tasks of the revolution was to ferret out and neutralize resistance and counter-revolutionary activities. For Stalin this meant not only cleansing the party but also the state bureaucracy and the military as well. Stalin wrote, "Proletarian parties develop and become strong by purging themselves of opportunists and reformists, social-imperialists and social-chauvinists, social-patriots and social-pacifists. The party becomes strong by purging itself of opportunist elements."[22]

Faced with all of the problems of social, political, and economic change, Stalin, even more so than Lenin, recognized the need for internal discipline, political monopoly, and absolute power. In his determination to build a Marxist state, Stalin blended Marxist philosophy into the traditional Russian culture. At the same time, Marxism was altered by the Russian environment. Ultimately Marxism and Russia became virtually synonymous to much of the world.

THE COMMUNIST PARTY

From this brief assessment of Marxian ideology and its implementation in Russia by Lenin and Stalin, one can see how Marxism combines a long-range goal with short-range flexibility. The role of the proletariat was revised by Lenin to include a specific role for the Bolshevik party. Stalin, using Leninist interpretation of Marxian theory, rationalized the need for a strong monolithic party to build a personal dictatorship. Thus the Marxist emphasis on the dictatorship of the proletariat became the dictatorship of the party and ultimately the dictatorship of one. Similarly, the revolutionary process developed by Marx was revised by Lenin to focus on the revolutionary role of the party. This idea was used by Stalin to rationalize in Marxist terms the strong socialist state he was building in Russia. It provided the guideline to focus on world revolution when Stalin concluded that the revolution in the Soviet Union was virtually complete. The flexibility of Marxist ideology and its presumed scientific assessment provided a philosophical rationale for the seizure of power by a small elite and universalistic guidelines to legitimate the continual expansion of power by the Communist party. And as the following sections will point out, the Communist leaders of the Soviet Union from Stalin to Brezhnev have established their power on the ideology of Marxist-Leninism.

Revolutionary Russia and the Communist State

The history of Communist Russia is tied directly to its strong rulers, as was that of Tsarist Russia. Lenin, Stalin, Khrushchev, and Brezhnev—these are the four principal Communist leaders who have shaped the Russian communist state. Indeed, these men are modern versions of the tsar. Basing their power primarily on their role as leaders of the Communist party, they have exercised rule through a vast hierarchy of party officials and bureaucracy and a vast state machinery. They have created an absolutism that would make any tsar green with envy. They have established a bureaucratic structure that not only reinforces the power of the Communist leaders, but also provides a network of control and information that makes the tsarist police state appear moderate by comparison. Yet, the loyalty of the Russian people, their commitment to the communist state, and their pride in the Russian heritage appear strong. Their loyalty and commitment cannot, however, be attributed solely to the system of government: credit must be given to the relative advances made in the standard of living, to the strong attachment of the people to Mother Russia, to the general improvement of the quality of life over the past two decades, and to pride in the fact that the Soviet Union has emerged as one of the superpowers.

The evolution of the communist political system in Russia can be divided into five periods: Civil War and War Communism, the New Economic Policy, Stalinist Revolution, Khrushchev and de-Stalinization, and Brezhnev and Détente. An examination of each of these periods will provide insights regarding the continuity of the tsarist tradition and the unique contributions of Communist ideology and practices to the growth of the Russian state.

In each of these periods, struggles continued over the control of the party and, ultimately, the state machinery. The process of change from one leader to another continued in unpredictable patterns, reminiscent of the tsarist period. Significant changes took place in the Soviet Union, shifting the economic forces from agriculture to heavy industry and, in the more recent years, even to a consideration for consumer goods. Throughout the process, the Russian people maintained their allegiance to the Russian state and accepted the Communist ideology, not without some variation and reluctance in parts of Russia. Indeed, the Communist leaders at the Twenty-Fifth Party Congress held in 1976 could proclaim with some justification that the Soviet state had overcome major obstacles to develop into a superpower and that the Russian people had never had it so good. But over the past ten years, narrow cracks and even gaping holes have appeared in the seemingly monolithic Communist ideology and in the commitment of Russian society to communism.

THE RUSSIAN CIVIL WAR AND ITS AFTERMATH

Even with the signing of the Brest-Litovsk Treaty ending the Russian involvement in World War I, the new Communist government was faced with internal war. The Czech Legion, a group of about 30,000 Czechoslovakian prisoners and deserters from the Austrian army, armed by the provisional government, received permission to join the Western Allies. Because the Czech Legion was on the Eastern front, they undertook a journey using the Trans-Siberian Railroad from Vladivostok. The new Bolshevik leaders, concerned about 30,000 armed men traveling across Russia, ordered local militia commanders to disarm the Czech Legion. Their efforts failed, however, because at each stop the Czech Legion was too strong to be handled by the local commanders. Moreover, local anti-Bolshevik groups took advantage of the inability of the new regime to control the Czech Legion and formed resistance groups. This misadventure, coupled with the fact that the Socialist Revolutionaries within the Congress of the Soviets refused to accept the Brest-Litovsk Treaty and that the Western powers desired to find an alternative to the Bolshevik regime, precipitated the Russian Civil War. Moreover, anti-Bolshevik forces, taking advantage of these conditions, plotted actions against the existing regimes in the hopes of overthrowing the Bolsheviks and establishing their own regime.

In response, the Bolshevik regime nationalized the entire economy, mobilized workers, and moved militarily against the anti-Bolshevik forces, the White forces. Receiving assistance from the Western powers, the Whites were able to succeed initially in pushing the Reds back on all fronts. To protect the revolution, the Bolshevik leaders instigated a Red Terror, which was matched by White terror. Suspected Whites were arrested and summarily executed. In the course of events, many innocent victims became part of the Red Terror. The Whites were no less discriminating, pillaging, murdering, and looting while their armies appeared to be gaining a foothold in the territory controlled by the Bolshevik regime.

By the end of 1918, the Bolshevik leaders, recognizing the internal danger, organized a Red Army. Returning to the stern discipline of traditional armies staffed by experienced tsarist officers, the Red Army soon began overpowering the Whites. By 1920, with the war over in Europe and the attention of the West turned elsewhere, the White forces began disintegrating. The Russian peasants withdrew any support previously given the White forces. The Bolshevik government, with firm control of its own army, was finally able to defeat the various anti-Bolshevik elements.

In 1920, when it appeared that the internal wars would finally be over, the Polish War began. Poland, demanding borders with Russia that were more in the interests of Poland, invaded the Ukraine. The new Red Army, however, was not the incompetent force that the Polish government expected. Soon, the Polish armies were driven back into their own homeland, and only the intervention of the Western governments restored order and established an acceptable boundary. Thus, after almost a decade of war and internal struggle, the Bolshevik regime turned to tasks closer to home: consolidating the revolution and establishing order.

WAR COMMUNISM

War Communism, brought about by the necessities of civil war, was an attempt to organize the peasants, militarize labor, control what could be planted, distribute free food and clothing, and even abolish money. The ruling Bolsheviks felt that such a policy was required to control Red areas and to carry on the struggle against the Whites. Thus, the peasant was not only squeezed by the ravages of civil war, but he was also organized and controlled by the Bolshevik government to continue the struggle. Even when the Civil War was winding down and the Bolsheviks were convinced of victory, War Communism did not end.

Citing the ravages of the war—its disastrous effect upon agricultural production, labor, and what little industry there was—Trotsky convinced Bolshevik leaders that War Communism methods should be applied to Russian reconstruction. Labor was conscripted and assigned various tasks throughout the country. Citizens were registered and required to show papers indicating place of registration and nature and place of employment. Those who attempted to beat the system were treated as deserters, assigned to labor squads, and placed on reduced rations. Peasants were organized into armies to "attack" the fields. Many peasants preferred, however, to work in their own villages and resisted, as much as they could, attempts to mobilize them for work elsewhere.

War Communism was unable to solve the problems of Russian agriculture and industry. Indeed, the Russian people suffered from large-scale famines in 1921, a direct result of the Civil War and inability to restore agricultural production. Resentment grew and ultimately led to the Kronstadt naval base mutiny, in reality an expression of peasant discontent. Peasant hatred of collectivization and increased expectations and demands on the government left Lenin with no alternatives. He moved away from War Communism and introduced, instead, the New Economic Policy, a temporary accommodation to the capitalistic approach.

THE NEW ECONOMIC POLICY

In most simple terms, the New Economic Policy (NEP), introduced in 1921 at the Tenth Communist Party Congress, allowed peasants to use surplus production as they saw fit. At the same time, small plants reverted to private ownership while larger factories and major areas of commerce, such as banking, remained in government hands. The issue of the NEP goes much further than this, however: it was basically a matter of power and control. As one scholar notes,

. . . the maintenance of Soviet power had become the main preoccupation of the Bolsheviks, and Lenin certainly felt that the regime was in danger unless a period of consolidation and construction took place. He knew better than others to what extent this implied a retreat, and he always referred to NEP as such.[23]

For all practical purposes, the NEP established the guidelines for the first long period of Communist rule.

By 1929, the NEP had reached the end of its usefulness, at least in the eyes of the post-Lenin Bolshevik leadership. Significant pressures were generated to return to the orthodox interpretations of Marxism. Nevertheless, over a seven-year period, the NEP had succeeded in easing the discontent of the peasants and had provided the Bolshevik leadership with a breathing spell during which to consolidate their power.

With no landlord and no communes, the Russian peasantry enjoyed a relative freedom not to be known again under communism. With a return to individual peasant farming, existence of a free market, and the relaxation of government controls, agriculture recovered rather quickly. On the other hand, the overall economy was slow to recover. Industry was below pre–World War I levels, but inflation was rampant, and insufficient grain was available to feed the Russian people.

Nevertheless, the individualism introduced into the Russian system was creating autonomy in various sectors of society. This autonomy constituted a dilemma for Bolshevik leaders. It threatened not only to erode the fundamental concepts of Marxist ideology, but also to undermine the existing political order, that is, the Bolshevik leaders themselves.

Stalin and the Second Revolution

With the death of Lenin in 1924, the Russian Communist party became engulfed in an internal power struggle. The primary protagonists were Trotsky and Stalin. While Trotsky insisted upon a new direction for the economy, Stalin maintained that the NEP should continue (albeit temporarily). While Trotsky demanded inner-party democracy, that is, flexibility within the party for a wide-ranging discussion of issues, Stalin demanded unquestioning obedience to the party line. The conflict extended to foreign policy as well: Trotsky wanted to prosecute world revolution vigorously; Stalin insisted on "socialism in one country."

At the Fifteenth Communist Party Congress in 1927, Trotsky and other opposition leaders were expelled. Stalin became the acknowledged leader of the Communist party. With the rise of Stalin there began a second revolution in communist Russia, an attempt to socialize the economy completely and to correct the non-Marxist developments of the NEP. Summarizing the impact of the NEP and the purpose of the Stalinist policy, one scholar writes,

If we separate the areas of politics and economy from the rest of society we find considerable autonomy in each area and widely ranging norms within them. The area of politics became increasingly concerned with internal discipline and control; the economy was only partially controlled, though viewed with growing misgivings by the political leaders. Finally, the rest of society was left free from direct political control, thus producing an explosion of experiment and creative energy. After 1929, this period of experimental self-expression in society was over for good. Such experiments as would now take place were controlled from above, and limited to the fields of industry, technology and organization. The remainder of social life was committed to adapt itself to these priorities.[24]

The second revolution had a pronounced long-range impact on the Soviet Union. Not only did it produce the modern Soviet state, but it created the characteristics of modern Soviet society and linked these directly to the modern idea of Russian communism. By the end of the Stalinist period, the Soviet Union had changed its character: it had been transformed from a peasant-oriented society to a modern, industrialized, totalitarian state. More important for our purposes, the Communist party had become an important part of Russian society. Indeed, the very nature of the totalitarian system demanded that autonomous groups be destroyed and that all social groups be closely linked to the party. Stalin's rule and his control of the party structure provided the instruments by which Soviet society became penetrated by the party and the party eventually became entrenched in all sectors of society.

The end of the NEP coincided with the implementation of the first Five-Year Plan (the centralized planning approach is a fundamental characteristic of the Soviet economy). The objective of the first Five-Year Plan was to expand industrial output, increase electric power, and mechanize and collectivize the nation's farms. This was the beginning of the Soviet period of industrialization and also set the stage for the eventual total socialization of agriculture, which—it might be added—meant the destruction of the *kulaks* (peasant farmers) as a class.

By the beginning of World War II, ten years after the first plan, virtually all peasants were on collective farms. Peasants and farmers had resisted the socialization of agriculture. Nevertheless, under Stalin's leadership, the government forced collectivization. The initial results were starvation for many, destruction of farm animals and crops, and a significant decrease in agricultural output. Eventually, forced collectivization did produce a highly organized agricultural sector, but it failed to make the Soviet state agriculturally self-sufficient. Indeed, one of the major problems facing the Soviet Union today is agricultural productivity. Over the past years, the Soviets have frequently had to import grain from the West to overcome agricultural deficiencies.

Within two years over half of all Soviet agriculture production had been turned from private farming to co-operative and state farming. But seen from below by those involved it was primarily a heartbreaking story of futile peasant resistance, of large-scale slaughter of animals and, in many cases, desperate starvation.[25]

Pressure to industrialize and to increase agricultural output continued throughout Stalin's rule. The period involved consolidation of party and personal power. It included a series of purges that eliminated most of the old-time Bolsheviks and made Stalin an autocratic leader whose despotism exceeded even that of the tsars.

ELIMINATION OF OPPOSITION: THE PURGES

From 1934 through 1939, Stalin eliminated most of his opposition, both from the Right and from the Left. Seemingly motivated by the mysterious assassination of his close friend and subordinate, Sergei Kirov, Stalin demanded punishment for the "enemies of the people." No one was spared. Trials were staged. Prominent Bolsheviks were con-demned and shot. Stalin's secret police sought out former tsarist officials and summarily exe-cuted them. Thousands upon thousands of people, ranging from army officers and labor leaders, to artists and ordinary citizens, were arrested as suspects.

By 1939, the intellectuals and Bolsheviks who had initially opposed Stalin had disap-peared. The party had come under the iron rule of Stalin, and Russian society had come under the rule of the party. Stalin had become the party and the party, the state. The party determined state policy and had entrenched itself in all segments of Russian society. Indus-trialization and collectivization forced from the top had created new groups and new social relationships, and had established new power centers in the Russian political system.

During the Stalinist period, the individual was completely subordinate to the state, which, in turn, was controlled by the party. The Russian people were mobilized as never before in Russian history. Political organiza-tions surrounded the day-to-day existence of the Soviet citizen. The entire society was geared to follow the dictates of Marxist-Leninism as interpreted by Stalin. Dissent and opposition disappeared; strict guidelines for social and political behavior were estab-lished. And as Solzhenitsyn points out, the Stalinist period refined to a high degree the rule by fear and terror.[26] Labor camps and secret police became recognized instruments of Stalin's rule.

The death of Stalin left Russian leadership in disarray, as had the deaths of rulers throughout Russian history. Much of Russian society, the party, and the party leadership greeted Stalin's death with a sigh of relief. The heavy hand of one man's rule was lifted. For a two-year period following Stalin's death, there was significant political maneuvering within the highest circles of the party to estab-lish a legitimate heir. First Malenkov and then Bulganin sought to replace Stalin.

Meanwhile, Khrushchev was strengthening his control over the party.

Khrushchev and the Great Thaw

Khrushchev, a product of the Stalinist pe-riod, supported first one faction against Malenkov, and then another against Bulga-nin. Using the support of Stalinist conserva-tives, he was able to obstruct Malenkov's at-tempts at new directions in domestic and foreign policy. While Malenkov and sub-sequently Bulganin were deeply involved in administering the state, Khrushchev became first secretary of the party and strengthened his position in the Politburo, now called the Presidium (the highest policy organization in the party).

The leadership struggle was finally resolved when Khrushchev, using his position as first secretary of the party, placed most of his own men in key ministerial positions and in the Presidium. The final consolidation came dur-ing the Twentieth Party Congress, called by Khrushchev. It was during this congress that Khrushchev gave his famous speech denounc-ing Stalin and the cult of personality. The congress was virtually a one-man show put on by Khrushchev. There was no doubt in any-one's mind who controlled the party: Khrushchev had come through as the domi-nant personality and acknowledged leader.

During the following year, another attempt was made by an anti-Khrushchev group to oust him; but by a series of cunning political moves, the question of his ouster was placed in the hands of the Central Committee of the party, in which Khrushchev enjoyed wide support. By 1957, Khrushchev had support in the Central Committee of the party, in the Presidium, and from key ministerial posts.

The denunciation of Stalin and the cult of personality opened a relatively liberal era in Communist history. Although the economy re-emphasized capital goods and the need for industrial and military strength, promises were made to consumers of better things to come. Art, literature, and education soon reflected liberalization on one hand and forced compliance with certain socialist goals on the other. Moreover, it was during the Khrushchev period that Russia rather dramatically entered the Space Age with the launching of Sputnik I.

Khrushchev's major impact—mostly negative—was in the areas of domestic economic policy and foreign affairs. Eastern Europe's reaction to de-Stalinization led to the disintegration of the Communist monolith. Indeed, it was during the post-Stalin era that communism in the form of nationalism emerged to challenge Moscow's central control of Communist parties throughout the world. China, under Mao, developed her own version of Marxist-Leninism. There was violent reaction against Soviet rule in East Germany and Hungary. Polish and Rumanian Communist leaders became increasingly independent. In 1962, the attempt by the Soviet Union to place missiles in Cuba was frustrated by the United States. For many within the Kremlin, the latter was a humiliating defeat for Russia and one for which they blamed Khrushchev.

In world affairs the Soviet Union appeared to be losing its grip on satellites and other Communist parties. Moreover, Khrushchev's new Seven-Year Plan, with its high expectations and acknowledgment of consumer needs, ended in failure. While the Soviet people as a whole still had little to say about the government and state of affairs in general, it was nevertheless clear that significant changes in Soviet life were under way. As Wren notes,

By 1959 the physical condition of life and the atmosphere in the Soviet Union differed so markedly from life in Stalin's time that it seemed impossible that the old life could ever return. The remarkable and very considerable relaxation of tensions inside Russia, the reduction of controls upon Soviet citizens, and the apparent sincere efforts to improve cultural relations with the capitalist world were aspects of the "Great Thaw."[27]

The restlessness within the Soviet Union and the apparent failures of Khrushchev's economic and foreign policy led to his forced resignation in 1964. The Presidium of the Communist party demanded Khrushchev's ouster. Khrushchev, however, demanded to be heard by the Central Committee. But the committee supported the Presidium, and another change in leadership occurred. Leonid Brezhnev became the first secretary of the party, and Aleksei Kosygin was selected as the chairman of the Council of Ministers, both posts previously held simultaneously by Khrushchev. This was indeed a watershed in Soviet Communist history. Brezhnev and Kosygin are career bureaucrats and the first men to rule Russia since 1917 who had no direct involvement in the October Revolution, "the first men to rule Russia since 1917 for whom the October Revolution was an historic event rather than a personal memory."[28]

The New Leaders and the Modern State

With the ouster of Khrushchev came an attempt to turn back the clock. The new leaders felt that Khrushchev had moved too far too fast. Brezhnev, representing the party cadre, and Kosygin, the economic bureaucracy, were concerned that Khrushchev's "liberalization" policies would erode the power of the cadre and destroy the economic structures of the Soviet Union. Nevertheless, the forces set in motion by the Communist thaw during the

Khrushchev era have had a profound effect in subsequent years, despite attempts by Soviet leaders to put an end to them. Rebelliousness continues among the intelligentsia, and there is increasing reaction against secret arrests and trials of nonconformist intellectuals. According to some, the labor camps of the Stalinist era are still in operation. And it was in 1968 under Brezhnev's leadership that the Soviet Union crushed the Czechoslovakian uprising against Communist control.

The Brezhnev period initially brought with it a pragmatic approach to leadership and the institutionalization of dual leadership—in name, if not in reality. The president of the Soviet Union, the premier, and the first secretary theoretically share rule. But as the Twenty-Fifth Party Congress in 1975 showed, the real leadership rests in the hands of Brezhnev, the first secretary of the party.

In June 1977, Leonid Brezhnev, first secretary of the Communist party, was also appointed president of the Soviet Union, replacing Nikolai Podgorny. Thus, for the first time in the history of the Soviet Union, the first secretary of the party is also the top official of the state. It is too early to tell what the long-range result of this arrangement will be; however, it is clear that as president, Brezhnev can now negotiate as an equal with heads of state from other countries. Equally important, Brezhnev now occupies an important official state position from which to consolidate party control over state agencies.

The Russia of Brezhnev is a far cry from Stalinist Russia or Tsarist Russia. The Soviet Union under Brezhnev has consolidated its position as a major world power. Internally, the Soviet Union has continued its industrial growth and is now attempting to respond to consumer demands. Economic growth has created new groups within the Soviet Union: the managerial and technical groups (the Communists do not consider these classes) and the skilled administrators, as contrasted

to the ideologues and the party leadership. Moreover, there is significant evidence to suggest that Communist ideology as preached by Marx and Lenin, and revised by Stalin, is not motivating the masses to work for a socialist utopia. Indeed, some scholars argue that the young people in the Soviet Union are not willing to give up social pleasures and individual desires for collective welfare. Indifference toward the party is not only a phenomenon of the youth, but has extended to many sectors of Russian society. Dissidence, albeit still limited to small groups, has become a common characteristic of the Soviet system in the 1970s.

Meanwhile, the leaders of the Soviet state are faced with an economic system that cannot feed itself: agriculture is still a major problem. Moreover, there are constant struggles over continuing industrialization and the need for greater response to consumer demands. Problems of unification and centralization have become more pronounced as nationalistic resistance on the part of various ethnic groups within the Soviet Union has increased, perhaps as a result of the liberalization started by Khrushchev.

In a major sense, Brezhnev has inherited a Soviet Union that is just now reaching a point where economic and social change are influencing the political power base and the role of political actors. Communist ideology and the rules of the Communist political game have lost their revolutionary appeal; indeed, the Soviet Union is aging. With this phenomenon, new and perhaps more challenging problems have emerged. While the central control of the party remains unchanged and the oligarchic base of the system continues, there has been a lessening of controls on the average Soviet citizen. The terror of the Stalinist secret police has become history, and a social imperative has emerged which provides some basis for individual resistance to oligarchic controls.

The ferment leading to manifestations of greater independence and defiance of authority in recent years is still continuing and is likely to continue, despite efforts at repression. . . . But one has to have lived in the Soviet Union in Stalin's day to appreciate that, despite the efforts of the present leadership to turn the clock back, today's atmosphere still does not compare with the total police terror and the fear pervading the atmosphere at that time. One has to realize, too, that the Russians have been conditioned for centuries to accept controls that to us would be intolerable. I used to discuss at length with a Russian intellectual friend the differences between our societies. The point I could never get him to accept was the fact that we are not required to carry an internal passport, in which is recorded the holder's authorized place of residence and in which is registered every move, with a police stamp to confirm it.[29]

Throughout Communist rule, the role of the individual has been clearly subordinated to the needs of socialist ideology and collective welfare. This has led to the legitimacy of an oligarchy as the basis of Communist rule. Acting on the ideological premises of Marx and Lenin, and in reality providing a continuance of tsarist absolutist rule, the Communist party of the Soviet Union has clearly placed the individual in a tertiary position vis-à-vis the state and the party. While in the Brezhnev era the average Soviet citizen is relatively free to pursue his own life, he can do so only if he does not resist authority and if he accepts economic priorities and bureaucratic control as a way of life. Indeed, the average Soviet citizen has little real input to the Soviet system. More important, there are no legal alternatives or private organizations and institutions that can provide him with a vehicle for such input. It is the party that runs the state and serves as the sole political determinant of Soviet society.

Thus, even in the Brezhnev period, as in Tsarist Russia, economic and social control, as well as political control and planning, come from the top. Outside party channels, there is little that the Soviet citizen can do to change things. Indeed, the Soviet citizen has become socialized into accepting this state of affairs. The institutions of the Soviet Union have evolved and become institutionalized on the basic premise of Marxist-Leninism ideology in a society that has long accepted the subordination of the individual and the absolutism of the state.

The historical conflict between absolutism and anarchy is still present in modern Russia.

For the notion of the totalitarian state, perhaps useful for political scientists as a bird's eye view of Soviet society, misses the human quotient. It conjures up the picture of robots living a regimented existence. Most of the time, it is true, the vast majority of Russians go through the motions of publicly observing the rules. But privately, they are often exerting enormous efforts and practicing uncommon ingenuity to bend or slip through those rules for their personal ends.

Resignation is the characteristic Soviet reaction to the privileges of the high and the mighty. In Russian history, it has long been that way, Russians say, and this is fatalistically accepted. . . . "People don't want to change that part of the system, they want to beat it. . . . They don't say the system is wrong. They want exceptions made for them personally."[30]

The Soviet Constitutional Order

After fifteen years of work and some behind-the-scenes controversy, a new Soviet Constitution—the fourth—was published in 1977. It will be discussed by various groups across the Soviet Union before it is approved by the Supreme Soviet, probably with some minor changes. The new constitution maintains the essential features of the 1936 constitution, which it is supposed to supersede. For example, while more freedoms and rights are granted the Soviet citizen (for example, the inviolability of correspondence and telephone conversations, and the right to have a house, income, and savings), these are expressly qualified by the provision that "exercise by citizens of rights and freedoms must not injure the interests of society and the state, and the rights of other citizens."

It is still too early to assess whether the new constitution will have any significant effect on the operation of the Soviet political system.[31] Thus, it is perhaps more useful to look at several aspects of the 1936 constitution because it has been in effect for forty years, even though it has been amended frequently.

Given the nature of the Soviet political system and the totality of control exercised by the Communist party, one can reasonably ask why the student should be concerned with Russian constitutionalism. There are a number of important considerations. The constitution serves as a vehicle for expression of the Marxist-Leninist ideology; it provides a unifying factor for nationalities within the Soviet state; it establishes the basis for a stable regime; and it legalizes the social order. Although the main concern in this chapter is Communist ideology, we will touch briefly on these other considerations since there is a close relationship among all of them.

SOCIALISM AND FEDERALISM

The first part of the Soviet Constitution focuses on the social structure and proclaims that the Soviet Union is a socialist state in which power rests with the proletariat. This section states that the means of production is under socialist ownership, that is, both national and state ownership. Property not included in these categories is owned cooperatively by the people. Allowance is made for each family to have private use of a small plot. Although each person has a right to personal property (savings, home, household articles), the constitution requires that each ablebodied citizen work for the common good.

One of the basic principles outlined in the Soviet Constitution is federalism. There are fifteen union republics reflecting the divergencies of ethnic and regional forces. Tsarist Russia was faced with the problem of nationalities as is present-day Russia. Non-Russian nationalities, such as the Armenians, Georgians, Azerbaijanis, Lithuanians, Estonians, and Ukrainians, have been incorporated in the Soviet state, a number by the use of military force. The constitution outlines the rights of such nationalities and their relationship to the Soviet state.

The more important question is: How is Marxist-Leninist ideology reflected in this attitude toward nationalism? Marx viewed nationalism as a negative force, opposed to the concepts of socialism and the proletariat. Given the problems faced by the new Communist leaders in 1917, however, Lenin correctly viewed nationalism as an important force in the struggle against capitalism and, equally important, in the problems associated with governing the Soviet Union. Thus on the one hand, nationalism is recognized as a negative force in the long run; on the other hand, it is recognized by Communist leaders as being an important force to harness and manipulate in the short run.

The Soviet Constitution embodies some of the features of federalism, but these are counterbalanced by the central control exercised by the Communist party. Under the Soviet Constitution, the fifteen republics have a right to secede from the Soviet Union. They have the right to enter into direct diplomatic relations with other countries and to conclude treaties with them. The republics are even authorized to maintain their own military force. Republics can establish their own constitution, display their own flags, and use their own language.

The state structure also reflects the ambiguous nature of federalism. The Supreme Soviet is composed of the Council (Soviet) of the Union and the Council (Soviet) of the Nationalities. The Council of the Union is elected according to population while the Council of Nationalities is composed of twenty-five representatives from each Union republic, eleven representatives from each autonomous republic, five representatives from each autonomous region, and one representative from each national district (see Figure 5-1).

The members of the Supreme Soviet are elected every four years. One member in the Soviet of the Union represents 300,000 persons. The Supreme Soviet is supposed to meet twice a year, but actually meets less frequently. Its meetings usually last about seven days. Given the number of its deputies and the brevity of its meetings, little substantive work or serious deliberation can take place. It is interesting to note that, during the entire existence of the Supreme Soviet, not one dissenting vote has ever been registered, nor has there ever been disagreement between the Council of Nationalities and the Council of the Union.

The Presidium of the Supreme Soviet is elected by both chambers in joint sessions. It consists of a chairman, fifteen deputy chairmen (one from each union republic), sixteen other members, and a secretary. The deputy chairmen are usually the fifteen presidents of the Presidia of the Supreme Soviets at the union republic level. The Council of Ministers performs the functions normally associated with a cabinet in Western democracies. The chairman of the Council of Ministers parallels the role of the prime minister. The constitution identifies the Council of Ministers as the "supreme executive and directing organ of state power."

A similar organizational structure exists at the union republic level. Nevertheless, it is at the all-union level that central direction is given to economic planning and administrative coordination. Most important, it is at the all-union level that absolute control is exercised over the revenue and expenditures of the union republics. Moreover, there is no provision in the constitution for any union republic to challenge the authority of the organs at the all-union level. Indeed, the constitution states that it is the Soviet state that safeguards the sovereign rights of the union republics. In the final analysis, it is the all-union level that determines the meaning of phrases such as "All-Union significance" and ultimately decides the relationships between the all-union level and the union republics.

According to the constitution, the Supreme Soviet exercises exclusively the legislative power. In this sense, this institution serves to transform the will of the party into state law. In the performance of this function, representatives of the masses participate in the governing process. In reality, the party makes policy, and the institution representing the masses transforms policy into administrative rules and regulations. Marxist-Leninist ideology is thus reflected in the vanguard role played by the party in leading the masses toward a socialist state. In essence, the Supreme Soviet acts as a rubber stamp body at which the policy of the party is announced to an exclusive audience representing the masses. Nevertheless, it does serve as an institution to legitimize party policy and provides a sense of political participation by party members. The same procedure and impact is seen at the union level. There is, therefore, the perception that the union organs rule their own nationalities and play an important part in ruling the Soviet Union.

In reality, the party's centralized control and unitary organization, from the grass roots level to Moscow, enable it not only to negate the federalist reality, but to dominate the state structure as well. As one proceeds from

Figure 5-1: The Supreme Soviet and Federalism

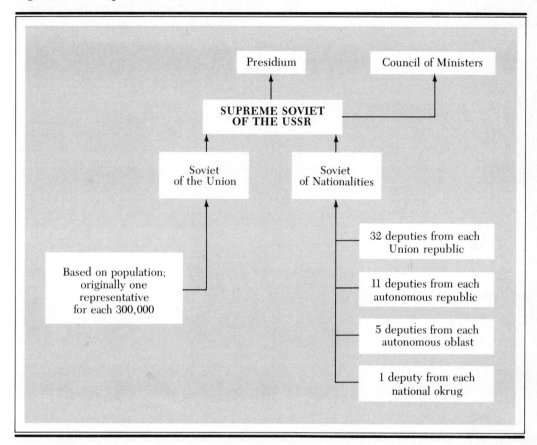

lower state organs to higher, the number of Communist party members in each organ increases accordingly. Thus at the all-union level, the Supreme Soviet represents the privileged elite of the Communist party and duplicates social membership of the organs of the party.

CIVIL RIGHTS AND FREEDOMS

The Soviet Constitution also guarantees civil rights and freedoms. For example, all citizens of the Soviet state are guaranteed freedom of speech, freedom of the press, freedom of as-

sociation, and freedom of demonstration. But these guarantees are contingent upon the exercise of such freedoms to strengthen the socialist order in the interests of the proletariat. Obviously, no criticism of the Communist party strengthens the socialist order!

The Constitution also proclaims the right of citizens to unite in voluntary associations and identifies the Communist party of the Soviet Union as being the vanguard of the proletariat and at the core of all organizations in the Soviet state, including voluntary associations.

Given the guarantees of civil rights and freedoms, the individual is in a position similar to that of the union republics vis-à-vis the all-union level. There is no procedure by which the individual can challenge the state or seek redress from violations of his individual rights and freedoms, except through the party.

The Soviet Constitution does provide for an administrative system through which complaints can be registered. This is a system of procuracy. In the Soviet Union, the procurators hold a special place. Soviet law makes the procurator responsible for ensuring that criminal trials proceed according to law. A procurator is involved in all phases of criminal trials. At any period during the investigation phase, the procurator may reverse the decision of state organs bringing the individual to trial, may transfer the case to other jurisdictions, or may release the accused and publish the necessary directives. Indeed, no individual can be brought to trial without the approval of the procurator. When the accused is brought to trial, the procurator acts as the prosecution. Thus he must not only act as a guardian of individual rights and assure that the trial is conducted according to law, but he must also prosecute the individual as representative of the state. The procurator also ensures that civil cases conform to the rules of law. Regardless of the legalistic purposes behind the procuracy system, however, its main purpose is to ensure that high-level party and state policy is carried out and without the arbitrary exercise of power by lower rank officials. Also, part of the procurator's responsibility is to fight graft and corruption in the economic system. The procurator has no power over the highest state and party officials.

Given these powers and responsibilities, the procuracy system and the general procurator of the Soviet System stand subordinate only to the national police (KGB). As a matter of fact, the procurators stand above judges and advocates in their power, responsibility, and training. The general procurator of the Soviet

Union is appointed by the Supreme Soviet for a seven-year term. He, in turn, appoints subordinate-level procurators for lesser terms. Local officers of the procurator's office perform their functions independent of any local authority. They are subordinate solely to the procurator general.

Another instrument for redress of citizen grievances is the party. Because the party is tied in directly to all state organs at all levels, and because the real power of the state stems from the party, a citizen is likely to find that his complaints are effective only if heeding them will strengthen the socialist state and is in accord with Marxist-Leninist ideology and party policy.

The detailed organization of state structures and administration spelled out in the Soviet Constitution is also a reflection of the Marxist-Leninist ideology. The last stage of socialism occurs when the organs of the state wither away. To achieve this last stage, however, there must be a socialistic structure led by the Communist party to ensure progression to "communism." Thus, even the organization of the state fulfills a specific role in the ideological progression of socialistic development. Moreover, according to Marxist theory, once the final stage is achieved, there will be no need to be concerned with bourgeois civil rights and freedoms: all persons will be equal in the communist state without relying on structures of the state or on legalistic principles or civil rights and freedoms.

The Soviet Constitution embodies the basic principles of federalism, includes guarantees of civil rights and freedoms, establishes specific powers and responsibilities of organs of the state, identifies the relationship between the all-union level organs and the Union Republic, and spells out the socialist purpose of the document. However, all of these power relationships, duties, and guarantees are very much circumscribed by the role of the Communist party and the need to strengthen the socialist order. In the final analysis, it is the party that provides the ideological guidelines and policy that "operationalizes" the principles of the constitution. Equally important, there is no channel by which any organ or individual may challenge the authority and decision of the party. Thus participation in the political system is required—indeed, demanded—by the constitution. But final decisions generally rest with the highest organs of the state and ultimately with the Presidium of the Communist party.

In retrospect, one can see that the constitution is generally a façade for the continuing control of the state by the Communist party. It describes a political world that has little relationship to reality. Nevertheless, it does serve a purpose and may provide a legal basis for the development of opposition to the absolutism of the party and to arbitrary official behavior. It has been the basis of appeals by some dissident intellectuals. Indeed, the demand for rights under the Soviet Constitution may be an increasingly important basis for opposition in the Soviet Union.

Summary

Historically, the Russian state has been under autocratic rule. Establishment of the tsar as both a secular and a religious ruler brought with it absolutism that remained until the eve of the Communist Revolution. While on one hand, pressures remained for centralized authority, on the other, impulses for anarchy persisted. The tsarist state provided no major channel for institutional change from below and gave the masses little opportunity for political involvement, except through extralegal means.

This condition was exacerbated by the political unrest in the 19th century. World War I proved to be the catalyst. In the fading years of the war, after humiliating and disastrous defeats on the battlefield and the breakdown of morale at home, the 1917 Revolution ended the tsarist system and inaugurated a new ideology.

The first decade of Communist rule in the Soviet Union was turbulent. But the new regime survived and institutionalized Marxist-Leninist ideology, an ideology based on specific precepts regarding politics, economics, and society. Regardless of contradictions of the ideology and the contradictions between Soviet society and the ruling circles, Communist ideology remains the basis for both national integration and state policy. Marxism-Leninism focuses primarily on collective justice and collective welfare, subordinating the individual to the state. The individual, according to this ideology, comes into his own only after the final stage of social revolution—communism—is reached. In the meantime, the Communist party, the vanguard of the people, rules in the name of the proletariat in order to achieve this final stage.

While the party is the key instrumentality for ruling, the state structure does play an important role. Through the constitutional order, the state provides the institutional manifestation of Marxist-Leninist ideology. Moreover, the state structure provides the institutional framework within which national integration is reinforced, while providing a "legal" basis for the entire Soviet structure. In the state structure also, the individual is clearly subordinate to the collectivity. There are no channels through which the individual may protect his "rights." On the other hand, the constitution does provide some basis for assessing the legality of the state structure. By appealing to the constitution, some dissidents have been able to focus attention on illegal state actions. In any event, the ideology, the party, and the state structure form a relatively coherent system through which the Soviet state is ruled.

The long history of autocratic rule, temporarily broken in 1917, is apparent in the present-day rule of the Communist party. An elite (oligarchy) controlling the instruments of power, based on a self-selection process through the Communist party, continues the traditions established by the tsars.

NOTES

1. *Khrushchev Remembers*, with an introduction and commentary by Edward Crankshaw (New York: Bantam Books, 1970), p. 1.
2. Hedrick Smith, *The Russians* (New York: Quadrangle, 1976), p. 8.
3. Louis Fischer, *Fifty Years of Soviet Communism* (New York: Popular Library, 1968), p. 10.
4. Melvin C. Wren, *The Course of Russian History*, 3rd ed. (New York: Macmillan, 1968), p. 245.
5. Ibid., p. 184.
6. The leaders of the Soviet Union, although preoccupied with ideological relevance, basically adhere to the general premises found in Marxist-Leninist ideology. Obviously, each leader reinterprets the ideology to reflect the exigencies of the age. Nevertheless, Marxist-Leninist ideology has remained substantially the same throughout the past sixty-year period.
7. Roy C. Macridis and Robert E. Ward, *Modern Political Systems: Europe* (Englewood Cliffs, N.J.: Prentice-Hall, 1963), p. 442.
8. Ibid., p. 442.
9. Stefan T. Possony, *Karl Marx, The Communist Manifesto* (Chicago: Henry Regnery, 1954), p. 37.
10. Arthur P. Mendel, *Essential Works of Marxism* (New York: Bantam Books, 1961), p. 77.
11. Possony, op. cit., pp. 39–40.
12. Karl Marx, *Capital* (New York: Modern Library, 1906), pp. 396 and 397.
13. Possony, op. cit., p. 82.
14. Ibid., p. 13.
15. Mendel, op. cit., p. 229.
16. Ibid., p. 231.
17. Ibid., pp. 171 and 224.
18. Macridis and Ward, op. cit., p. 447.
19. Mendel, op. cit., p. 270.
20. *Khrushchev Remembers*, op. cit., p. 616.
21. The "Russian Social Democratic Party, Bolsheviks" changed its name to "Russian Communist Party, Bolsheviks" at the Seventh Convention of the Bolsheviks, 1918.
22. Mendel, op. cit., p. 293.
23. J. P. Nettl, *The Soviet Achievement* (New York: Harcourt, Brace and World, 1967), pp. 79–80.
24. Ibid., p. 114.
25. Ibid., p. 118.
26. Aleksandr I. Solzhenitsyn, *The Gulag Archipelago* (New York: Harper & Row, 1973), pp. 144–178.
27. Wren, op. cit., p. 707.
28. *Newsweek*, October 23, 1967, p. 49.
29. Foy D. Kohler, *Understanding the Russians: A Citizen's Primer* (New York: Harper & Row, 1970), p. 148. 148.
30. Smith, op. cit., pp. 9 and 52.
31. For the first time, the new constitution provides for a first vice-president of the Presidium of the Supreme Soviet. Thus the president of the Presidium could be relieved of many of his administrative and ceremonial duties.

CHAPTER 6

SOVIET POLITICAL ACTORS: POWER AND LEGITIMACY

With its imposing Byzantine spires and protecting wall, the Kremlin looks as if it is the focal point of the Soviet political system. In fact, however, the focal point is a plain green-and-cream building at No. 4 Staraya Ploschad (Old Square). This is the headquarters of the Central Committee of the Communist party of the Soviet Union. Operating like a giant corporation, the party apparatus (*apparatchiki*) runs the Soviet Union. This is perhaps the first and foremost characteristic of the Soviet Union: it is a single-party state with all legitimacy in the hands of the rulers of the Communist party.

The Soviet Union has passed through a number of stages in the course of its transition from a primarily agricultural society to a relatively industrialized nation. As the society and economy have changed, so has the character of the political system. In recent years, a number of political actors have acquired influence in the system. This is not to suggest that the Communist party of the Soviet Union (CPSU) has become less powerful. Rather, the inputs to the party system have expanded and the ideological interpretations upon which the party bases its power have shifted. Moreover, the increasing industrial development within the Soviet Union, the first glimmerings of consumer pressure, and the increasing professionalization and specialization of the state and party structures have helped develop professional groups, technical cadres, and ethnic loyalties, all of which do provide inputs to the political system.

Political Actors and Power

Most students of the Soviet political system assign the primary role in the actual ruling of the Soviet state to the Communist party of the Soviet Union. Indeed, one can reasonably argue that, whether one assesses the state structure, the nature of the society, the ideology, or the important political power bases, one must start with the party. It is the CPSU that interprets the Communist ideology, applies it to the state, and ensures that all conform. Moreover, the party selects the top leaders and controls the selection of lower officials.

Thus the real power holders in the Soviet political system are party officials and, more specifically, those in the top party positions. Categorizing political actors as institutions, decision makers, groups, political influentials, and individuals would seem, therefore, to be a rather frustrating exercise, because classification would ultimately begin and end with the Communist party. Nevertheless, as we have suggested, Soviet society is now more complex than it was in Lenin's time. Moreover, the traditional concept of a totalitarian system based on a thoroughly monolithic order controlled by a rigid one-party system appears to be inaccurate. It is more correct to speak of a totalitarian order that is imperfect. The party is powerful but certainly not omnipotent. Dahl's label of "polyarchical" system, oligarchical in character, is an appropriate designation for the Soviet system.[1] Simply stated, this means that the Soviet system is totalitarian, but totalitarian does not necessarily mean a *rigid conformity* to the dictates of a small elite at the top. Rather, the Soviet system is one in which an oligarchy rules, recruits its own leaders, and establishes the basis of legitimacy, while a number of political actors interact with one another and the system to achieve places of prominence and power within the structure.

Many westerners have accepted George Orwell's image of totalitarian power, the bleak, remorseless, all-powerful state of 1984. In Orwell's vision the state and party allow no compromises. They control not only behavior but even thoughts. Orwell invented "Thought Police" to enforce the official orthodoxy. His Big Brother sees everything; no infraction goes unpunished.

The Soviet Union has not turned out that way. There is more bumbling, confusion, improvisation and luck involved in running the USSR than the traditional totalitarian image would allow. The country's rulers do not insist on limitless power in all things.[2]

Institutions

The formal institutions of the Soviet system are established by the Soviet Constitution as we discussed in the previous chapter. The constitution provides the basis of power for these institutions. It must be noted, however, that there is a significant overlap between state and party structures, which dilutes the legalistic grants of power to the state. Nevertheless, the Soviet Constitution is the basis for the administrative organization of the state. It also establishes the power and function of the governmental organs and spells out the role of the individual citizens with respect to "electing" the members of the state organs.

The Soviet Constitution of 1936 states that "All power in the U.S.S.R. belongs to the working people of the city and country as represented by the Soviets of Working People's Deputies" (Article 3). The constitution goes on to state that the "highest organ of state power in the U.S.S.R. is the Supreme Soviet of the U.S.S.R." (Article 30). The legislative power is to be exercised exclusively by the Supreme Soviet of the U.S.S.R., which consists of two chambers, one representing population and the other, geographical divisions or nationalities. (These features have not been appreciably changed by the new constitution.)

Herein lies another basic feature of the Soviet system. While the state organizations are theoretically the supreme legislative and executive organs of the Soviet system, it is the party that actually makes policy and controls the advancement of officials in both party and state structures. The people theoretically elect their highest officials; in essence, the Politburo of the CPSU makes all policy decisions and is "elected" by the Central Committee through the Party Congress. While the citizens of the Soviet Union are theoretically involved in both party and state processes, in reality they merely give symbolic confirmation of decisions already made by the Politburo. Moreover, the party structure and its overlapping membership through the state structures subordinate the state to the party. Thus, before we can speak of various political actors within the Soviet system, we must examine the relationship between party and state structures and the fusion of institutions within the state structure.

The essence of the party dominance of the Soviet state is contained in Article 126 of the 1936 Soviet Constitution (and explicitly reinforced in the new constitution).

. . . citizens of the USSR are guaranteed the right to unite in mass organizations—trade unions, cooperative associations, youth organizations, sports and defense organizations, cultural, technical and scientific societies; and *the most active and politically conscious citizens in the ranks of the working class, working peasants, and working intelligentsia voluntarily unite in the Communist Party of the Soviet Union, which is the vanguard of the working people* in their struggle to build communist society, and is the leading core of all organizations of the working people, both governmental and nongovernmental.[3]

What makes this provision of the Soviet Constitution so important in terms of the Communist party is that the "Supreme organ of the Communist party of the Soviet Union is the Party Congress." And, as we shall see later, the Party Congress responds to the dictates of the Central Committee and the Politburo.

The federal nature of the Soviet system was discussed in Chapter 5. In general, the major governmental units are those at the all-union level and the republics. Within some of the various republics there are autonomous republics and autonomous regions. The Soviet political system can generally be divided into four levels: the local soviets, province soviets, the Republic Supreme Soviet, and the U.S.S.R. Supreme Soviet. Each of these struc-

tures has its party equivalent, as shown in Figure 6-1.

THE SUPREME SOVIET

The Supreme Soviet is the major institution within the state structure that is afforded certain powers under the Soviet Constitution. The system operates on the principle of fusion of power, rather than on those principles apparent in the American political system (for example, the separation of powers and the system of checks and balances). Nevertheless, the Council of Ministers, the chairman of the Council of Ministers, and the president of the Presidium of the Supreme Soviet do have certain powers that are roughly equivalent to those of executives in Western parliamentary systems (see Figure 6-2).

Thus each unit within the state structure is accountable not only to the next highest level of administration but also to the appropriate party unit. This concept of dual accountability is a major unifying element throughout the system. Also, while the official political structure is theoretically federal, the party structure is unitary. Finally, it is difficult to ascertain the various powers of government, to identify the specific powers given the republic organs. Although certain powers are granted in the constitution on economic matters, for example, the economic centralization of the Soviet state makes it difficult to speak realistically of separate economic powers to the republics. Similarly, the overlap of membership, the dual accountability, and the basis of legitimacy impart a centralizing momentum to the Soviet system that is only partly offset by internal conflicts and the influences of various groups in society.

Not only are the soviets infiltrated by the party organizations, but also many of their operations are controlled, through the principle of dual subordination, by agencies' ap-

Figure 6-1: Soviet State and Party Structures

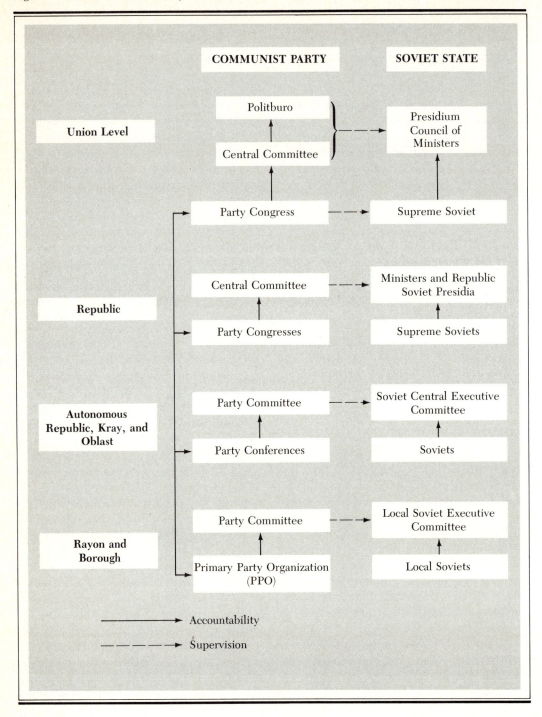

Figure 6-2: The Supreme Soviet

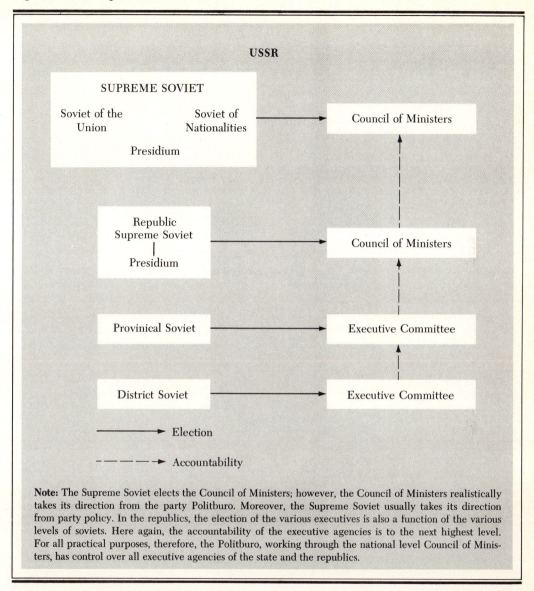

USSR

SUPREME SOVIET

Soviet of the Union   Soviet of Nationalities

Presidium

Council of Ministers

Republic Supreme Soviet

Presidium

Council of Ministers

Provinical Soviet

Executive Committee

District Soviet

Executive Committee

⟶ Election

------→ Accountability

Note: The Supreme Soviet elects the Council of Ministers; however, the Council of Ministers realistically takes its direction from the party Politburo. Moreover, the Supreme Soviet usually takes its direction from party policy. In the republics, the election of the various executives is also a function of the various levels of soviets. Here again, the accountability of the executive agencies is to the next highest level. For all practical purposes, therefore, the Politburo, working through the national level Council of Ministers, has control over all executive agencies of the state and the republics.

propriate ministries. According to this principle, the administrative subdivisions of local soviets are subordinated both to the executive committees of the local soviet to which they are accountable, and to the sections of ap-

propriate ministries—education, health, culture, finance, and so on—located in the territory in which the given soviet has jurisdiction.

Meeting semiannually, the Supreme Soviet has the function of legislative deliberation;

however, the main purpose of this relatively large body is to rubber-stamp the decisions of the top party leadership. In essence, the decisions are ratified after a set of speeches. There is no debate. Legislation, which has been previously introduced by government spokesmen, is given unanimous acceptance. Moreover, the fact that the Supreme Soviet usually meets for only about a week during each session means there is little time for serious debate. Despite these limitations, the Supreme Soviet does play a useful nonlegislative role in the Soviet system.

Except for limited commission activity, there is no institutional arrangement to facilitate legislative oversight, such as the question period in the British House of Commons or the committee investigation of the American Congress. One may well ask therefore, what the real purpose of the Supreme Soviet is . . . it impresses some segments of world opinion with the "democratic content" of the Soviet system.[4]

A meeting of the Supreme Soviet is also a learning process for the delegates. Because many represent the outlying provinces, the semiannual assemblage allows top leaders of state and party to socialize delegates into the party line while impressing them with their skill and power. In turn, the delegates are expected to transmit their impressions to the citizens they represent. Moreover, the leaders have an opportunity through indirect methods to sound out the delegates regarding the attitudes and opinions of various groups in Soviet society. In this sense, the Supreme Soviet does act as a link between the top leaders and the masses. Although the Supreme Soviet is at the apex of the entire state structure, by no means does it have the political leverage or power to be a significant political actor. Its role in the Soviet system is that of transmitter of policy and party guidelines. In addition, it is a valuable structure for socialization and implicit control.

We should also note that the Supreme Soviet does have a commission substructure similar to the committee system in the United States Congress. The way in which these commissions operate is not completely clear, but they appear to engage in limited deliberation regarding state policy. These deliberations normally follow rather rigid guidelines and are monitored by party stalwarts. Recently there has also been some public airing of proposed legislation. A particular policy may be announced in the newspapers in the form of a letter from an official. Soundings are then made of public reaction through newspaper letters. Thus the government-controlled newspapers provide a limited forum for discussion of some issues.

Both chambers of the Supreme Soviet have equal powers. The Soviet of the Union, originally based on one deputy for each 300,000 of the population, is now limited to 767 deputies. The Soviet of the Nationalities is based on fixed representation from the various geographic units. Each union republic has 32 deputies; each autonomous republic, 11; each autonomous province (oblast), 5; and each national area (okrug), 1. In most instances, the chambers meet jointly. Close to 75 percent of the deputies of the two chambers are party members.[5]

Each chamber has a chairman and four vice-chairmen, while the Presidium consists of the president, 15 vice-presidents, 20 members, and a secretary. Theoretically the Soviet Supreme Court and the procurator-general of the U.S.S.R. are part of the Supreme Soviet.

THE COUNCIL OF MINISTERS

As an institution, the Council of Ministers roughly corresponds to the cabinet in the Western parliamentary sense; but here again, the actual policy is determined by the party. Members of the Council of Ministers occupy cabinet-type posts in charge of various state functions. Thus the U.S.S.R. Council of Ministers includes such departments as the All-Union Agriculture Committee, State Committee for Science and Technology, and the State Planning Committee. In addition, there are a number of state committees, industrial ministries, and nonindustrial ministries. The union republic ministries and the republic council of ministers are directly controlled by the U.S.S.R. Council of Ministers.

The chairman of the Council of Ministers in 1977 was A. N. Kosygin, who came to power with Leonid I. Brezhnev after the removal of former General Secretary Nikita Khrushchev. Kosygin is also a member of the Politburo, another example of the interlocking of party and state. Although the top executive was split between Brezhnev (general secretary) and Kosygin in 1977, it is generally acknowledged that Brezhnev is the more powerful of the two men. Nevertheless, in the state structure, the chairman of the Council of Ministers exercises power similar to that exercised by the prime minister in a parliamentary system. Of course, the chairman of the Council of Ministers has little to do with parliamentary politics or majority rule by political parties. Rather, the position is a reflection of the stature of the individual in the top hierarchy of the Communist party. And indeed, the chairman of the Council of Ministers carries out his functions as determined by the top leadership of the Communist party.

The state structure is interlocked with the party structure through the Council of Ministers. A number of important members of the Council of Ministers are also members of the Politburo and hold posts in the Secretariat. For example, in 1973, two first deputies of the chairman of the Council of Ministers were also members of the Politburo. In addition, the minister of defense and the minister of foreign affairs were both members of the Politburo. Thus, not only has the party established its leadership over all state structures by virtue of its organizational structure, ideological le-

gitimacy, and professional skills, but it also has created institutional interlocking by duality of membership in key positions. The same relationships exist between the state and party at all levels (see Figure 6-1). This reinforces the point, made earlier, that the Soviet Union may well be a federal structure, but the commanding control of the party throughout the state structure makes the Soviet Union a "unitary" state, if not in name, certainly in fact.

Nevertheless, the Council of Ministers, and particularly the chairman, take part in national decision making. Although the priorities of the party come first, there is always the likelihood that members of the state structure will attempt to develop national priorities not wedded to rigid ideological guidelines. Indeed, they may try to develop their own political power bases within the state structures as occurred in the struggles after the death of Lenin and Stalin.

Decision Makers

Since the fall of Khrushchev and the emergence of Brezhnev as a leader in his own right, there has been much speculation regarding the "direction" of the Soviet Union. This speculation revolves around whether the Soviet Union is becoming more democratic or will see again the imposition of strong one-man rule. The initial leadership group of Brezhnev and Kosygin in 1964 led some to believe that the Soviet Union had seen the end of the "cult of personality." Indeed, officially, there is no leader in any of the organs of the party or the state. The party is led by the collective leadership of the Politburo, while the state is supervised through the collective leadership of the Presidium and the Council of Ministers. Yet, as is generally true, a strong personality opts for the leadership role, and the collective leadership shifts to approve or

Leonid Brezhnev (UPI photo)

Andrei Gromyko (UPI photo)

Aleksei Kosygin (UPI photo)

Vasily Kuznetsov (UPI photo)

Yuri Andropov (UPI photo)

A quartet of Soviet leaders pose in the Kremlin during a reception for foreign diplomats in 1977. (*Left to right*) President Leonid Brezhnev, Foreign Minister Andrei Gromyko, Vice President Vasily Kuznetsov, and Mikhail Georgadze, Secretary of the Presidium of the Supreme Soviet. (UPI photo)

The Great Kremlin Hall in Moscow. Opening of the Extraordinary 7th Session (9th Convocation) of the Supreme Soviet of the U.S.S.R. (Courtesy, Russian Embassy)

oppose individual acquisition of power. In this sense, the general secretary must be particularly sensitive to the alliances and attitudes of members of the Politburo and the Central Committee. One can reasonably argue that the system motivates key individuals to seek more power if only as a matter of self-protection. (One reflection of this was the election of Brezhnev as president of the Soviet Union in 1977—this in addition to his post as general secretary of the CPSU. Thus, for the first time in history, one man holds both posts.) Without a systematized process by which power is transferred, changes of leadership in the Soviet Union generally have resulted in massive power plays and a degree of chaos. This has been so not only because there is no institutionalized method for orderly transfer of power, but also because many of the positions within the apparat are dependent upon the nature of the leadership of the Politburo, not unlike the patronage systems within Western party structures.

Pictures of President Brezhnev began appearing in the summer of 1978 showing him in poor health. Following several stays in the hospital, these pictures rekindled speculation in Western circles regarding a possible successor to the Soviet leader. Since there has not emerged a clear line of succession, there was much debate as to what the leadership succession procedure might be if Brezhnev should be forced to retire from office because of health, or if he died while in office.

Since the Stalinist era, many within the party-state bureaucracy have come to fear anything that hints of one-man rule. Indeed, it is acknowledged that one-man rule places members of the bureaucracy in a vulnerable position—except, of course, those who happen to be allies and supporters of the leader. Thus the Khrushchev period, with its initial de-emphasis of Stalin, ushered in a brief period of hope that the party and bureaucracy would regain a pre-eminent position and be

free of purges and suspicions of loyalty. And so it was. But the pendulum continued to swing beyond the midpoint to where the party was being eroded by "democratization": meetings were packed by nonparty persons, and specialists and technicians outside the party played an increasingly more important role.

Table 6-1 shows the three major positions in the party/state structure, and the men who occupied them, including the present leader Leonid I. Brezhnev. As can be seen the chairman, Council of Ministers and general secretary of the Communist party were held at the same time by both Stalin and Khrushchev. At the present time, Brezhnev is both the general secretary of the Communist party and president of the Soviet Union (chairman, Presidium of the Supreme Soviet).

In reaction to "Khrushchevism," the Brezhnev and Kosygin leadership reverted to orthodoxy and conservatism in ideology and style. Indeed, the image of Stalin was rehabilitated and a sense of Stalin's positive impact on the Soviet Union restored.

The Brezhnev-Kosygin duumvirate was thought to be a solution in which the party and state leadership would counterbalance each other, while denying either Kosygin or Brezhnev a control monopoly. However, since 1965 and particularly since the invasion of Czechoslovakia in 1968, Brezhnev has increasingly taken on the role of "the leader" of the Soviet Union.

Earlier, Brezhnev had taken a lead in economic affairs, which was thought to be a preserve of Kosygin's. Moreover, since 1969, there has appeared what some say is a Brezhnev cult. The increased importance of Brezhnev as contrasted to Kosygin was also reflected in his appearances and speeches before the party congresses in the 1970s. Brezhnev clearly overshadowed Kosygin in this respect.

The stress on collective leadership in the post-Stalinist era has thus been eroded by the

Table 6–1: Succession to Leading Posts (July 1973)

Position	Name	Start of Service		End of Service	
Chairman, Council of Ministers[a]	Nikolai Lenin	Nov.	1917	Jan.	1924
	Alexei I. Rykov	Feb.	1924	Dec.	1930
	Vyacheslav M. Molotov	Dec.	1930	May	1941
	Joseph Stalin	May	1941	March	1953
	Georgi M. Malenkov	March	1953	Feb.	1955
	Nikolai A. Bulganin	Feb.	1955	March	1958
	Nikita S. Khrushchev	March	1958	Oct.	1964
	Alexei N. Kosygin	Oct.	1964	present	
Chairman, Presidium of the Supreme Soviet[b]	Yakov M. Sverdlov	Nov.	1917	March	1919
	Mikhail M. Kalinin	March	1919	March	1946
	Nikolai M. Shvernik	March	1946	March	1953
	Kliment Ye. Voroshilov	March	1953	May	1960
	Leonid I. Brezhnev	May	1960	July	1964
	Anastas I. Mikoyan	July	1964	Dec.	1965
	Nikolai V. Podgorny	Dec.	1965	present	
General Secretary of the Communist Party[c]	Joseph Stalin	March	1922	March	1953
	Nikita S. Khrushchev	Sept.	1953	Oct.	1964
	Leonid I. Brezhnev	Oct.	1964	present	

[a]Lenin, technically, was chairman of the R.S.F.S.R. council of people's commissars, his successors until 1946, chairmen of the U.S.S.R. council of people's commissars, and thereafter, chairmen of the U.S.S.R. council of ministers.
[b]Until 1924, these were chairmen of the All-Russian Central Executive Committee; thereafter, until 1936, chairmen of the U.S.S.R. Central Executive Committee; and, after 1936, chairmen of the Presidium of the Supreme Soviet.
[c]Khrushchev in 1953 adopted the title of first secretary. At the Twenty-third Party Congress in 1966, the designation of general secretary was restored. In 1977, Brezhnev was also elected president of the Soviet Union.

Source: Robert J. Osborn. *The Evolution of Soviet Politics* (Homewood, Ill.: Dorsey Press, 1974), p. 559.

emergence of Brezhnev as "the leader." Given the experience of the Stalinist period, however, there appear to be limits to the ability of one man to again reach the power heights of Stalin. It must also be remembered that the ability of the leader to exercise power rests, to a degree, on those who make up the system and whose major concern is their own security and the continuance of their power positions. Thus "the leader" represents those who make the system work.

The relationship of the leader and his entourage—so to speak—to the mass of people in the Soviet Union is well expressed by one observer who writes, "The men and women who make the Soviet system work lead different lives than do the ordinary Russians. . . . In many ways they are different people. In Russian they are called the *nachalstvo*, an untranslatable word, often used ironically, whose literal meaning is 'the authorities,' but whose true sense is more 'the big cheeses.' They live in a world apart."[6]

In brief, the decision makers in the Soviet Union are generally those associated with the Politburo, the Secretariat, the Central Committee, and to some extent, the Council of Ministers. The fact is that, in a number of instances, one individual may well hold a position in all of these groups and institutions. For all practical purposes then, decision makers, other than those who are commonly associated with lower level bureaucracies, are concentrated in the top echelons of the party.

Groups: The CPSU

It is clear that the Communist party of the Soviet Union is *the* political actor. Borne out of revolution and preceding the modern Soviet state, the party is the basis of legitimacy for all other institutions, groups, and individual activity. Based on the precepts of the Marxist-Leninist ideology, the party has control over policy decisions and their implementation.

As one scholar writes, "The Party has grown to be an intricate mechanism for coordinating the affairs of a centralized socialist economy and a centrally guided social order."[7] Indeed, the party has developed into a mechanism performing many functions normally associated with governmental agencies in other political systems. The "various levels of Party organization correspond to levels of government, and the territory covered by each Party organization coincides with a governmental jurisdiction."[8]

The party has developed a wide-ranging and professional structure through which control of the state is maintained and other political actors are "supervised." Thus, while the party membership may reach only about 15 million out of a population of over 250 million, the control mechanisms and organization perpetuate an elitist structure that reaches down to the grass roots level in all sections of the Soviet state.

Stalin had said that "in the Party there are about 3,000 or 4,000 leading officials whom I would call the Party generals. There are about 30,000 to 40,000 middle rank officials. These are our Party officers. Then there are about 100,000 to 150,000 members of the junior Party command staff. These are, so to speak, our noncommissioned officers."[9]

THE POLITBURO

The major party organization is the Politburo. Theoretically, the Politburo is elected by the Central Committee which in turn is elected by the Party Congress. Operating on the concept of "democratic centralism" and through a vast *apparatchiki*, the members of the Politburo, for all practical purposes, dictate the policy and determine the composition and direction of the Central Committee and the Party Congress. Figure 6-3 indicates the composition and relationship of the various organs of the CPSU.

Although the analogy must be stretched somewhat, the Politburo parallels the cabinet system in British parliamentary procedure. Little is known about the deliberation or procedures that take place in the Politburo. Its composition, however, indicates that the most powerful men in the party are members. The membership includes the general secretary of the party, the head of government (chairman of the Council of Ministers), and the chief of state (chairman of the Presidium of the U.S.S.R. Supreme Soviet). It may also include a number of Central Committee secretaries and several first deputy premiers. At times it includes the first secretary of the Ukrainian Communist party and the chairman of the Party Control Committee.

As noted earlier, the Politburo passes its decisions on to the Central Committee, whose work reflects the policy of the Politburo. Moreover, the Politburo issues directives to a number of government agencies. Thus the Politburo not only controls the party, but also links itself to the control and direction of government as well. The number of Politburo members varies from 10 to 25, depending on the power relationships at the top and the particular problems faced by the Soviet state. In 1976, the Politburo had a membership of 16.

The functions and power of the Politburo and the central structure of the CPSU are shown in Figure 6-3.

Serving as Brezhnev's board of directors, is the 16-member party Politburo. The Politburo, the

Figure 6-3: The Central Structure of the CPSU

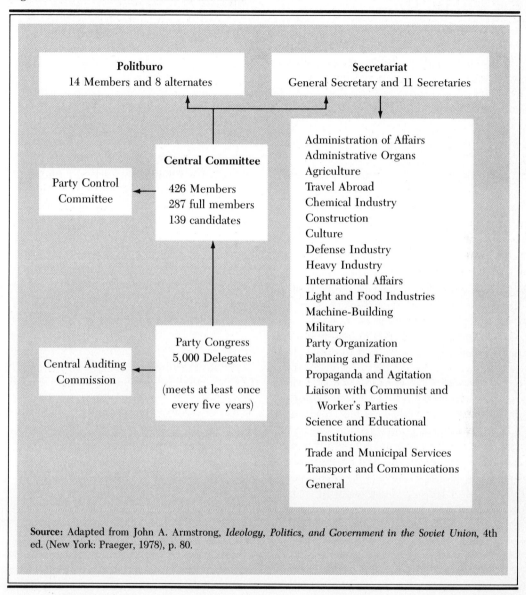

Politburo
14 Members and 8 alternates

Secretariat
General Secretary and 11 Secretaries

Administration of Affairs
Administrative Organs
Agriculture
Travel Abroad
Chemical Industry
Construction
Culture
Defense Industry
Heavy Industry
International Affairs
Light and Food Industries
Machine-Building
Military
Party Organization
Planning and Finance
Propaganda and Agitation
Liaison with Communist and
    Worker's Parties
Science and Educational
    Institutions
Trade and Municipal Services
Transport and Communications
General

Central Committee

426 Members
287 full members
139 candidates

Party Control
Committee

Party Congress
5,000 Delegates

(meets at least once
every five years)

Central Auditing
Commission

Source: Adapted from John A. Armstrong, *Ideology, Politics, and Government in the Soviet Union,* 4th ed. (New York: Praeger, 1978), p. 80.

country's principal policy-making body (although formally subordinate to the 396-member Central Committee), usually meets every Thursday. . . . The directives of the Politburo are passed along by the ten-man Secretariat, the party's nervous system. . . . The policies are handed down through party channels until they reach the basic party organization in every institution, plant or farm with three members or more.[10]

Decisions with the Politburo usually reflect the nature of the leadership; that is, a strong personality such as Stalin's is likely to subdue conflicting views and gather support for a unified leadership. On the other hand, the party has openly declared its adherence to "collective leadership." Thus, tendencies are always present to reflect a collective view, a procedure that allows some realistic discussion of policy alternatives.

THE CENTRAL COMMITTEE

Founded in 1898 with the First Party Congress, the Central Committee serves as the primary legislative and administrative organ of the party between Party Congresses. As such it is more directly involved with the power relationships within the Politburo than with the Party Congress. Moreover, the Central Committee has established a professional skill and organizational structure giving it an important controlling role over the various state agencies and the implementation of policy. Finally, it is supposed to direct

  . . . the activities of the Party, the local Party bodies, selects and appoints leading functionaries, directs the work of central government bodies and public organizations of working people through the Party groups in them, sets up various Party organs, institutions, and enterprises and directs their activities, appoints the editors of the central newspapers and journals operating under its control, and distributes the funds of the Party budget and controls its execution.[11]

The Central Committee is designated as the central controlling body of the CPSU. However, as noted previously, the Politburo, in effect, is the organ that determines party policy. Indeed, it is the relationships among the various Politburo members that determine, for all practical purposes, the direction and tenor of the Soviet political system.

  With a membership of 400, the Central Committee has become too large to serve as an effective executive for the Party Congress. Nevertheless, the Central Committee does reflect the various power groups within the party and does play an important role when disagreements emerge within the Politburo. For example, during the struggle between Khrushchev and Malenkov over the leadership of the party, secret sessions took place in the Central Committee supporting Khrushchev's claim to leadership. Lacking a unified focus in the Politburo because of the leadership struggle, the Central Committee became the focal point for the power struggle.

  As is true of the Politburo, membership in the Central Committee is a collection of party leaders to include many of the secretaries at the republic, province (oblast), and territory (kray) levels. Moreover, attention is given to ensure that various geographic areas, subnational interests, and formal state institutions are represented. As a political actor, the Central Committee does, on rare occasions, act on its own. But in the main, it is a conveyor of policy promulgated by the Politburo and is a reflection of Politburo power relationships. Moreover, the Central Committee has few formal functions to perform, other than those the Politburo directs it to perform.

THE PARTY CONGRESS

The Party Congress, although the formal supreme body of the CPSU, is primarily a ratifying body similar to the role played by the Supreme Soviet in the state structure. Meeting every five years (generally speaking) for a ten- to twelve-day period, the Party Congress forms the framework and forum for the ratification of party policy (a formality) and the channeling of party ideology. It is not a decision-making body but a forum used by the top party leaders to reinforce ideological purity and party loyalty.

  Because it has almost 5,000 members and

meets for so short a time, the Party Congress is not a decision-making body. Members are generally elected at province and local party level conferences. Representation is included from the military. Indeed, election to the Party Congress is a reward for party members below the central level.

The agenda of each Party Congress is carefully controlled. A number of representatives from foreign Communist parties and from the party rank and file are allowed to present speeches. Their speeches must be clearly within the guidelines established by the party leadership.

The Party Congress plays a negligible role as a political actor. Rather, it reinforces the political role played by the Politburo and, at times, the Central Committee. Moreover, the Party Congress is an appendage of the top party leadership and provides a forum for socialization and reinforcement of power in the party. It is a preserver of party power rather than a political actor in its own right.

Nevertheless, the Party Congress is not unimportant. It serves useful purposes in socialization and in forming a link between the rank and file and the top leadership of the party. Thus, although the Party Congress is essentially a gathering of the "faithful," it plays a useful role in party control.

According to one scholar,

The considerable investment of man-hours of important officials (for the congress and conference delegations embrace nearly all major Party and state officials in the U.S.S.R.) is justified by the experience these officials get in discussing problems with their peers and superiors, for higher officials obtain some idea of "grass-roots" feeling by talking with provincial officials. . . . The major assemblies, especially the All-Union Congress, provide a superb forum for setting forth and publicizing the Party line of the moment. Nearly 5,000 Congress delegates, meeting for only ten or twelve days, could not (even in the absence of manipula-

tion) debate and reach decisions on complex issues. But they provide an impressive backdrop for the speeches of the major leaders of the Soviet regime and an appearance of "monolithic" support for the regime's policies.[12]

PRIMARY PARTY ORGANIZATIONS

Primary party organizations are the basic unit of the party. They number approximately 350,000. Each of the primary party organizations has a secretary (although, generally, not full time). The primary party organizations are linked directly to the central organization through a pyramidal system; through district, province, republic, to the Central Committee. In addition, the secretaries beginning with the primary party organization are linked with secretaries on each higher level to the General Secretary of the CPSU.

Primary party organizations (PPOs) are found in virtually all Soviet enterprises and institutions. Normally, three party members in similar institutions or places of employment form a PPO. Every member of the CPSU must belong to a PPO. The PPO serves as the real working unit of the party, engaging in propaganda supporting party decisions, supervising party members, and recruiting new members.

According to the "Rules of the Communist Party of the Soviet Union,"

The Primary Party Organizations are the basis of the Party. Primary Party Organizations are formed at the places of work of Party members—in factories, state farms, and other enterprises, collective farms, units of the Soviet Army, offices, educational establishments, etc., wherever there are not less than three Party members. Primary Party Organizations may also be organized on the residential principle in villages and at housing administrations.[13]

INTERMEDIATE PARTY STRUCTURE

The Republic, territorial, provincial, area, city, and district Party Organizations and their committees take guidance in their activities from the Program and the Rules of the CPSU, conduct all work for the implementation of Party policy and organize the fulfillment of the directives of the CC CPSU within the republics, territories, regions, areas, cities, and districts concerned.[14]

The union republic more nearly parallels the central level than other subordinate agencies. A Party Congress, Central Committee, and Secretariat are the main organs at this level. Their responsibilities and functions are quite similar to those functions performed by similar agencies at the central level. All republics within the union, except the Russian Republic, have such structures. The Russian Republic is controlled by the organs at the central level.

Other intermediate structures of the CPSU are found at the district (*rayon*) and province (*oblast* and *kray*) levels. In general, these party structures parallel those at the central or all-union level. Organized on a territorial basis, a district party conference and province party conference usually meet every two or three years. These party conferences are convened by the district or province committees. The committees also elect the various bureaus and the committee secretaries—again theoretically paralleling the concept at the central level.

THE PARTY SECRETARIAT AND *APPARATCHIKI*

The Secretariat functions as the party's administrative structure and is one of the most important organs within the party. The Secretariat is headed by the general secretary of the CPSU. Theoretically, the Secretariat is elected by the Central Committee. Serving as the executive arm, the Secretariat directs the administrative structure and system of secretaries through the PPO. Additionally, it is organized in a number of departments paralleling the state structure.

Part of the importance of the Secretariat derives from its large representation in the Politburo itself. One-fourth of the full members and a majority of the alternates are also Secretaries. With the exception of Brezhnev, each Secretary exercises supervision over a specific sphere of operations.[15]

The importance of the Secretariat is its control over all levels of secretaries from the first secretaries at the republic level to the secretaries or bureaus of the primary party organizations. Implementation of party policy and supervision of party activity is the responsibility of the Secretariat. In addition, members of the Secretariat head various party sections whose power appears substantial, although the specific delineations of power are not clear. For example, a secretary heads the section on Party Organization, which is responsible for supervising ancillary party groups, such as the *Komsomol* (Communist Youth League) and trade unions. Another secretary heads the Administrative Organs Section, which is charged with the responsibility of supervising the functions of courts and prosecuting agencies. According to one scholar,

There is hardly any sector of Soviet life for which some branch of the Secretariat cannot claim responsibility. The Secretariat prepares reports for the Politburo, as well as background papers on current problems, policy proposals, and recommendations. It oversees the entire Party Machine and is responsible for the execution of Party policy decisions. It allocates the Party's manpower and controls its resources. It mobilizes the rank-and-file membership and enables the Party to act with a high degree of unity.[16]

The secretariat of the Central Committee "supervises" the apparatus of the Central Committee. In other words, the Central Committee staffs the central party machinery, and the Secretariat leads the party machinery. What is true of the Secretariat at the central level is generally true of secretaries at all party levels. Thus one can see that the post of General Secretary has emerged as the most powerful in the Soviet Union.

The *apparatchiki* (the party apparatus) are those full-time professional party men who are the party bureaucracy. Numbering about 225,000 in the 1950s (estimates now range from 100,000 to 250,000), the *apparatchiki* link the various party organizations with the party committees. While there is disagreement among scholars as to who are the members of the *apparatchiki*, it is clear that this category includes the party cadres.

Viewing the bureaucracies in the Soviet Union, one can identify various functions and purposes. Thus, according to the role played by the party, the *apparatchiki* is the most important on the power scale, followed by the Soviet administrative bureaucracy, the economic bureaucracy, and the social and cultural bureaucracy. According to one observer,

Each category of party member has a distinctive political role; collectively, the party's members indoctrinate and supervise the citizenry as a whole. In the highest ranks of the party command structure are full-time paid professional functionaries, often called cadres in Soviet publications, who include secretaries, deputy secretaries, department and section chiefs, and instructors of party committees. They are divided into four levels—in descending order—central, regional, local, and primary. They link the party committees with the network of subordinate party organizations and economic and cultural agencies, which they supervise. . . . These cadres, or professional rulers, are often referred to as apparatchikis.[17]

Success in party ranks leads to great advantages within society, including social prestige and professional recognition. Thus, selection to the party and subsequent promotion through various levels of the party hierarchy are significant matters for party members —indeed, for most professional men and women. Party control over such matters is based on two relatively simple procedures: *Recommendatsiya"* (recommendation) and *nomenklatura* (nomenclature). While *recommendatsiya* identifies the person to be promoted, the *nomenklatura* provides the key job categories and descriptions.

The Party's ultimate sanction for assuring both the loyalty and efficiency of state officials was the power of *nomenklatura*, perhaps best translated as "patronage," which is now a permanent feature of the Soviet system. All major appointments within any given jurisdiction must be approved by the top Party official in that jurisdiction, no matter whether the positions to be filled belong to the Party itself, the government, or nongovernmental organizations, including for example, the leading trade union posts and collective farm chairmanships. The *nomenklatura* list applies even to posts which are formally elective, for example, the chairman and executive committee of a city Soviet.[18]

It is no wonder that advancement in the party hierarchy reinforces orthodoxy and institutional loyalty.

The very nature of the Soviet system demands some type of control agency or watchdog over both party and state structures. Since the beginning of the Communist system there have been such agencies. Khrushchev established the Committee of Party-State Control (CPSC). Operated by various party secretaries, its function was to monitor all activities to ensure discipline and proper functioning of agencies. The CPSC had access to records and financial data to ensure that records and reports were not falsified. The committee also had power of reprimand, fine, and dismissal. Subsequent to Khrushchev's downfall, the CPSC was replaced by the People's Control Committee, which is primarily concerned with the state structure and appears to have less power than its predecessor.

The Party Control Committee under the Central Committee performs the same function as the People's Control Committee, but is primarily concerned with party structure. Clearly this labyrinth of party-state channels with its supervisory and control organs has developed into a vast and complicated bureaucratic structure with overlapping functions and distinct hierarchical patterns.

Other Groups

There is some disagreement among scholars regarding the degree of group activity in the Soviet Union outside the party. While some argue that meaningful group activity outside the party is virtually nonexistent, others argue that it is unrealistic to presume that a totalitarian system does not have some degree of group activity. Generally, there is always some internal conflict regardless of the type of political system. It is not the existence of conflict that is the important question, rather the degree and kinds of conflict. As should be evident, most political conflict and group activity in the Soviet Union takes place within party circles. There are, for example, conflicts between party ideologues and the "new" scientific and managerial personnel. Moreover, to a degree there is bureaucratic competition among the various organs of the party and state. Yet attention to only this aspect presumes that conflicts and "politics" occur only at the highest levels. Below this level there are sources of interest group activity and party-state conflicts, as well as intra-party struggles. Although these are certainly not articulated in clear or systematic terms, the

student should be aware of the existence of interest groups outside the party and interests that may temporarily cross party boundaries. To conclude, however, that such groups are political actors in their own right is to presume a degree of autonomy and power that does not exist outside party circles. As one observer notes,

The application of the group concept to political behavior in the U.S.S.R., it should be stressed, does not necessarily involve an interpretation of Soviet politics solely in terms of interest groups and group conflict. . . . The group approach however, sensitizes the observer to a realm of political activity that has gone almost unnoticed and thus facilitates our understanding of Soviet and other Communist systems in the course of their development.[19]

Since the death of Stalin (1954), the Soviet system has become less rigid and has developed a limited area of political activity. This activity can be categorized as institutional, noninstitutional, voluntary, nonvoluntary, and spontaneous, as was done earlier with regard to American political activity.

There can be no doubt that Communist society, in spite of its monolithic appearance and the claims of homogeneity made by its supporters, is in fact as complex and stratified as any other, and is divided into social classes and into other categories distinguished by factors such as nationality and religion. Each group has its own values and interests and each its sharp internal differences, and all are inescapably involved in conflict with other groups.[20]

In the Soviet system as contrasted to the American political system, the CPSU crosses the boundaries of all categories. Indeed, institutional groups such as the bureaucracy, voluntary groups such as labor unions and the Writers' Union, and nonvoluntary groups such as ethnic nationalities (for example,

Armenians and Ukrainians) owe their inception to the party. They cannot realistically exist in organized form outside party control. Ethnic nationalities, of course, exist regardless of the party. Indeed, some of the most important problems for the CPSU stem from attempts to integrate nationalities into the system and from increasing ethnic nationalism. Our discussion of groups in the Soviet Union must take into account the fact that all organized groups are legitimate only insofar as the party allows. Other activity is clandestine or latent, that is, not publicly articulated to such a degree that it creates regime response.

Major groups within the institutionalized category include the Security Police (KGB) and the military. The KGB has one of the most influential roles, aside from the party, in setting policy. Given the nature of the Soviet system, the problem of security is an inevitable consequence. There is always concern by top party leaders regarding control of the security forces, their function in perpetuating party discipline, and their ideological orientation. The history of the KGB has been replete with terrorism and torture, and purge after purge. Throughout the history of the modern Russian state, the leader of the KGB has been viewed with fear and suspicion by party leaders. Hence, steps have been taken to limit independence of action on the part of the police. The military has played an important role in this matter, checking the extent of police power and limiting the KGB as an independent political actor. Equally important, party officials have kept the officials of the secret police from gaining too much influence in the Central Committee and other higher party organs. The head of the Security Police is limited to membership in the Central Committee. Nevertheless, as with many vast intelligence agencies, the KGB has thousands of members (about 500,000 at last estimate), its own communications system, and a vast amount of power.

In recent years, the powers of the KGB have been somewhat circumscribed, not only by the military but also by pressures from an emerging Soviet public opinion, as well as from state agencies and party organs. The police have remained staunch supporters of the status quo and of orthodoxy in party matters. The police hierarchy has always considered itself strictly subordinate to top party officials.

The military, as in other political systems, considers itself apart from society as a whole. Primarily a conservative institution, the military supports the status quo. In the main, the military has been loyal to the party and supportive of its policies. Indeed, the party has exercised control over society with complete support from the military. Rather than seeking to become involved in the political system, the military has attempted to remain apart from the inner circles of the party. Military men who are involved in party matters are generally co-opted for this purpose. Yet when the party has taken a course contrary to the interests of the military, the military leadership has acted as a political interest group, more to defend its interests than to seek change or innovation. Its influence becomes considerable when Soviet society perceives an external threat.

The party leadership has historically been concerned about the political orientation of the military. This concern is reflected in the system of controls the party has established, including attempts to recruit all officers into the CPSU. Promotions are also influenced by party affiliation. Moreover, political officers assigned to units attempt to ensure political reliability by indoctrination and oversight of behavior. The Soviet officers corps is supported by the party as one of the privileged classes. Thus there is little incentive for the military to make major changes in the party-state-military relationship. Conflict does arise as the Soviet military becomes increasingly professional. Professional military views invariably come into conflict with party views on defense needs and military strategy. Indeed, within the Soviet state there is some concern about military "hawks" who are more interested in military defense budgets than in Soviet society, a view that finds some parallel in the American system.

There is no question that the Security Police and the military are the most influential groups in Soviet society. Yet even here one must be careful in ascribing to them autonomous roles as political actors. While they are essential instruments of party control, their legitimacy and status evolve from the party and their adherence to Party control and policy.

Two other groups should be mentioned, although their total impact on the policy process is not clear. The militia is the regular police force and is directed by the Ministry of Internal Affairs. Aside from its normal police functions, the militia is responsible for administering the internal passport system. Each Soviet citizen who has reached the age of sixteen must have an internal passport. This passport is used for a variety of matters, such as employment or travel within the Soviet Union. In addition, the militia is responsible for other functions, such as control of all reproduction equipment, communications equipment, photographic equipment, guns, and explosives.

The People's Guards is an auxiliary police organized to assist the militia. Since 1958, when it was first organized, the People's Guards has grown to include over seven million of the population. Units are organized by various party, *Komsomol*, or trade union organizations at places of work and residence, and at universities. Composed of unpaid volunteers, these units assist the militia in performing traffic control duties and maintaining law and order. Minimally trained, these units have caused some bitterness among the populace because of their involvement in deten-

tion and control. Moreover, the militia has, at times, come into conflict with the People's Guards because of numerous overlapping duties.

There are a number of groups ancillary to the party that remain under strict party control. The All-Union Central Council of Trade Unions (AUCCTU), for example, is led by a high party official. Similarly, the *Komsomol* (All-Union Lenin-Communist League of Youth) and its junior affiliate, the Pioneers, are also controlled by party functionaries.

Lawyers, industrial managers, economists, and writers are groups within society that may have some impact on the party and on the structure of the state. Only the writers have an association. While a number of the other members of this intelligentsia do not have formal professional associations, a few belong to academic institutions and to the Academy of Sciences. In any event, "political groups in the Soviet Union are seldom organized, and if organized, are dominated by functionaries who are usually not elected and not responsive to the wishes of their constituents."[21]

There is evidence to suggest, however, that leaders of the party and state are influenced by group action. Equally important, leaders recognize the existence of groups and their potential power base. Leaders use and manipulate groups to reinforce their own power or to support various views in controversies within party organs.

In addition, a number of informal channels exist by which groups such as the military can exercise some of the attributes of a political actor. For example, a number of professionals are used by party and state officials as consultants on various committees and commissions. This provides an opportunity for professional men to give an input into the system and, in the aggregate, have some impact and influence as political actors.

In many societies the mass media operate almost without government controls. This is clearly not true in the Soviet Union. Indeed, party leaders from Lenin to the present have recognized the importance of the written and spoken word. The party has consistently exercised strict controls over the mass media. In the Soviet Union today, the mass media are an arm of the state—more correct, an arm of the party. Controlled by the Ministry of Communications, the mass media must conform to the guidelines established by the party. Little leeway is allowed in criticism of the party or the Marxist-Leninist ideology. *Pravda*, for example, is the official organ of the party. It is known throughout the world and is the party mouthpiece. It expresses views on ideology and acts as an official interpreter of Communist views of the world. In the Soviet Union, the mass media do not have political actor status and are not a source of independent news. Pure and simple, the mass media are an extension of party socialization functions and an arm of the Communist leaders. In light of the Watergate exposé and the significant increase in investigative reporting in the United States, one can see a distinctly different role played by the mass media in the two countries. Nonetheless, the mass media, more specifically, the Russian press is used to test sentiment on policies and also serve as a link between the masses and the leadership.

. . . contrary to what many people think in the West, the Soviet press does offer a safety valve for minor grass roots dissatisfaction—letters to the editor. I was surprised to discover that it is a big business. *Pravda* gets close to 40,000 letters a month and has 45 people in its letters department . . . the regime finds letters useful. They give ordinary Soviets a chance to vent their frustrations at the notoriously inefficient bureaucracy, to sound off about poor consumer goods, and to let off steam generally. In the process, they give the Party an excellent means for monitoring the behavior of officialdom as well as the morals and attitudes of the general citizenry. In effect, letters trigger the press in its watchdog role.[22]

One of the most troubling issues for the party is the activities and interests of religious and nationality groups (nonvoluntary groups). Religion has been viewed by Communist ideology as anti-Communist and as "opiate of the masses." Although the Soviet Constitution provides for "freedom of religion," it also provides for antireligious propaganda. The antireligious groups supported by the party are clearly paramount. Nevertheless, the Russian Orthodox Church continues to exist, and some scholars even argue that there is a resurgence of religious activity in the Soviet Union. The party has allowed religious activities to continue not only as a symbolic gesture but also as a vehicle for use in worldwide matters such as religious congresses. Moreover, periodically the church can be used as a basis for mobilizing religious groups for support of the Soviet state, as it was during World War II.

There have been instances of active dissent by religious groups. For example, a militant anti-Soviet Slavophile group called the All-Russian Social Christian Alliance of Liberation of the People published a *Manifesto of Russian Patriots* which rejected Marxism out of hand and favored an orthodox Christian state.

Nationalities

Nationalities present a much greater problem to the Soviet leaders. Ethnic groups have always been a thorn in the side of the party.

Party leaders across the country are constantly on the attack against local nationalist sentiments in places like Lithuania, Georgia, Armenia, the Ukraine, Uzbekistan, because such feelings have broad latent popular support and contain the most serious threat of decentralization and disloyalty faced by the Russian-dominated Soviet state.[23]

While denouncing nationalities as contrary to the internationalism of communism, party leaders have had to recognize the realities that exist within the Soviet state. The nationalities in the Soviet system (See Table 6-2) have sentiments toward their own groups that have frustrated party and state attempts to integrate them into a rigid state structure.

The history of ethnic nationalism within the state has been characterized by an anti-Russian and anti-Moscow orientation. For example, the Ukrainians and Armenians not only have struggled to gain some measure of political freedom, but also have groups in other countries, such as the United States, who support their fight for political freedom. Periodically, reports do filter out of the Soviet Union of active resistance by non-Russian nationalities. In any event, there is a high potential for ethnic nationalities to develop into political actors in their own right. Even today, nationality policy must take into account non-Russian language and culture. Yet this observation must be interpreted cautiously. There are a number of counterbalancing forces to the ethnic renaissance some see in the Soviet Union.

The Soviet policy of cultural unification and Russification has been continuous and persists. To develop a high level of social mobility and achieve success in the highest circles of party and state, one must accept the Russian language and culture. In addition, economic policies that subordinate the republics to the center have done much to reduce the autonomy and, hence, the national identity of many groups. Finally, the party and state have instigated significant public pressures to integrate all nationalities into the Soviet system, a situation similar to that existing prior to World War I.

Political Influentials

Political influentials outside the party are a rarity in the Soviet Union. In recent years,

intellectuals such as Solzhenitsyn have made some impact as individuals by virtue of their repute as members of the intelligentsia. Again, for anyone to become a political actor by virtue of wealth, status, and prestige outside the party presumes autonomy, which is alien to the Soviet state.

There is little need to go into detail concerning book-length publications of dissidents such as Solzhenitsyn. There are a number of such writers, including Boris Pasternak, author of *Doctor Zhivago*, and Vladimir Dudintsev, author of *Not by Bread Alone*. The West has learned of the repression within the Soviet Union through such publications and also has witnessed the banishment or punishment of a number of intellectuals as a result. The fact remains, however, that the larger intellectual community strongly supports the policy of the state and the party—at least publicly. Nevertheless, there are a few individuals in the Soviet system who, by virtue of their stature in society, have been the focal point of some outspoken denunciations of the repression in the Soviet system. While these key individuals are allowed a degree of dissent, many who are not of national repute are quickly and violently suppressed.[24] The suppression of major intellectuals would attract the attention of the Western press and cause embarrassment to the Soviet state. In this respect then, such individuals do acquire some of the attributes of political actors.

A group of intelligentsia published a clandestine journal, *Chronicle of Current Events*. This publication included contributions from a variety of professions, but primarily from scientists. The general thrust of this publication was to recommend institutional changes and a freer intellectual climate. But again, the problems associated with publishing anything outside party channels provide little hope that such clandestine journals can have an impact on the Russian people. The same is true regarding the development of political influen-

Table 6–2: Nationalities and Soviet Republics (Estimates from the 1970 Census)

Nationality and Republic	Total Nationality Population in SSR, in millions
Ukrainian SSR	35.3
Uzbek SSR	7.7
Belorussian SSR	9.1
Kazakh SSR	5.3
Azerbaijan SSR	4.4
Armenian SSR	3.6
Georgian SSR	3.3
Moldavian SSR	2.7
Lithuanian SSR	2.7
Tajik SSR	1.7
Turkmen SSR	1.6
Kirgiz SSR	1.5
Latvian SSR	1.5
Estonian SSR	1.1
Total	113
Russian—RSFSR	110

Source: Adapted from Edward Allworth, ed., *Soviet Nationality Problems* (New York: Columbia University Press, 1971), p. 282.

tials. Regardless of the stature of some of the dissidents in Western circles, it is unlikely that they will have an important impact on the Russian people.

The organization of formal groups in the Soviet Union does serve an important party purpose. In addition to providing a channel for socialization into the Communist ideology and party procedures, groups serve as vehicles for mobilizing various persons in society and symbolically reinforce the concept that the people have input to the system. Equally important, formally organized groups, under the control and supervision of the party, provide a means of population control. Over the past years, as we have already noted, a degree of dissent has surfaced among intellectuals in the form of books and tracts about repression in the Soviet Union. Although there are a group of liberals within the Writers' Union, ". . . they do not ignore the fact that they function within a political and ideological framework which insists that there is only one truth—the absolute truth of communism."[25]

Individuals

In the Soviet system, the individual has an anomalous role. Having very little impact on politics and selection of leaders, the individual Soviet citizen remains virtually a subject of the state, accepting orders from above and carrying them out as best he can to avoid official reaction. Politics become *"they* the rulers" and *"we* the people." In essence, there is little meaningful input to the political system by individuals.

Apathetic acceptance of the system should not be construed as indicative of lack of support. Most people still are loyal to the system. It has given the Soviet people more than could be imagined under the tsars or during the early Stalinist period. The attitude and role of the individual are best summed up by Smith, who writes:

You also find an unbridgeable chasm between the leaders and the led; between "Them" at the top and "us" at the bottom . . . leaders do not seek exposure politicking among the people. Almost nothing is disclosed about their private lives or families. . . . For the common man, politics and power of the leaders are like the natural elements. No ordinary mortal . . . dreams of doing anything about them. They are simply a given fact, irresistible and immutable. State policy is like the weather. It descends from on high and the ordinary Russian trims his sails with stoic fatalism. He makes the best of whatever comes along, enjoying calm political seasons and trying to find shelter in rough ones. Not too surprisingly, most Russians are apolitical.[26]

One of the most visible roles played by the individual Soviet citizen is that of voter. Although the results of elections are known before election day, the voter does take part in a nationwide event which is primarily a mark of support for the existing government rather than a real contest between candidates. There is a complex and elaborate electoral system which may involve as many as two million candidates for the various soviets from the village to the Supreme Soviet of the U.S.S.R.

In reality, there is no election contest. Candidates are usually selected by groups such as the *Komsomol*, trade unions, and cultural societies. Only one candidate is selected to run for each post. Although voting is supposed to be conducted in secret, the voter is placed in a position where if he exercises his right to take a ballot into a booth, it is viewed as being an unpatriotic act. Because there is only one candidate running for each office, the voter normally picks up his ballot and simply deposits it in the ballot box without marking it, an indication of a positive vote for the candidate. Moreover, the Soviet Union can claim that at least 99 percent of its voters turn out (contrasted to a 50 to 60 percent turnout in U.S. national elections). This turnout is carefully monitored by party representatives. As each voter appears at the voting place, he is checked off a list. Thus as the day wears on,

any slowness in voting is corrected by party action groups who "induce" voters to come to the polls.

In the main, therefore, voting in the Soviet Union is a highly ritualistic affair associated with regime support. Given the possibility of severe party reaction against those who do not participate, the voter is highly motivated to participate. On the other hand, for many voting provides a visible means of participating in the political process and does fill a need for associating the party and state with the individual citizen. Moreover, the selection of the candidate and the need for him to discuss matters with local groups reinforces the linkage between the people and the party-state structures.

Discussion of issues, presentation of alternative policies, individual involvement in candidate support, and meaningful involvement in political campaigns are matters alien to the Soviet political process. Moreover, the citizen still remains relatively isolated from the realities of politics in the Soviet Union and quite limited in his ability to affect policy, either individually or collectively.

Summary

It is clear that in the Soviet Union, the Communist party is the foremost political actor. The top leaders of the party are the guardians of the Marxist-Leninist ideology. The party cadres attempt to ensure that the interpretations given to this ideology by the top leaders are implemented throughout the Soviet system. All other political actors, be they institutions or individuals, are completely subdued and subordinated to the party. Nevertheless, there are a number of political dynamics associated with regions, nationalities, religions, and intellectual groups which challenge the party interpretation of ideology. These groups and regional diversities increasingly place pressures on the party for flexibile interpretations which take account of a variety of interests. Similarly, intellectual dissent within the Soviet Union has shown that even the dogmatic ideological orientation of the party leaders is subject to criticism. It may also reflect the problems faced within the Soviet authoritarian system. Industrialization and education may be creating different values and attitudes toward the traditional Marxist-Leninist ideology and, indeed, a different set of political actors. Nonetheless, there is nothing to suggest that the present political system, resting on Marxist-Leninist ideology and controlled by the Communist party, will dramatically change in the foreseeable future.

NOTES

1. Robert Dahl, *Preface to Democratic Theory* (Chicago: University of Chicago Press, 1956).
2. Robert G. Kaiser, *Russia, the People and the Power* (New York: Atheneum, 1976), p. 104.
3. Robert J. Osborn, *The Evolution of Soviet Politics* (Homewood, Ill., Dorsey Press, 1974), p. 538.
4. John Armstrong, *Ideology, Politics, and Government in the Soviet Union*, 3rd ed. (New York: Praeger, 1974), pp. 162–163.
5. Ibid.
6. Kaiser, op. cit., p. 175.
7. Osborn, op. cit., p. 207.
8. Ibid.
9. As quoted in John Dornberg, *Brezhnev, The Masks of Power* (New York: Basic Books, 1974), p. 89.
10. *Great Decisions, 1975* (New York: Foreign Policy Association, 1975), p. 14.
11. Osborn, op. cit., p. 549.
12. Armstrong, op. cit., p. 75.
13. Osborn, op. cit., p. 553.
14. Ibid., p. 550.
15. Armstrong, op. cit., p. 91.
16. John S. Reshetar, Jr., *The Soviet Policy, Government and Politics in the U.S.S.R.* (New York: Dodd, Mead, 1971), p. 146.
17. Frederick C. Barghoorn, *Politics, USSR* (Boston: Little, Brown, 1972), p. 54.
18. Osborn, op. cit., p. 283.
19. H. Gordon Skilling, "Groups in Soviet Politics," in H. Gordon Skilling and Franklyn Griffiths, eds., *Interest Groups in Soviet Politics* (Princeton, N.J.: Princeton University Press, 1971), p. 23.
20. Ibid., p. 13.
21. Ibid., p. 382.
22. Hedrick Smith, *The Russians* (New York: Quadrangle, 1976), pp. 370–372.
23. Ibid., p. 429.
24. According to the *Chicago Tribune*, June 12, 1977, section 2, p. 1, "The Gulag Archipelago exposed by Alexander Solzhenitsyn has been partially dismantled. But taking its place in the Soviet Union is a system of 'special' psychiatric hospitals in which perfectly sane persons are confined to be 'cured' of their nonconformist views."
25. Ernest J. Simmons, "The Writers," in Skilling and Griffiths, op. cit., p. 260.
26. Smith, op. cit., p. 255.

CHAPTER 7

SOVIET POWER AND POLICY

Since the end of the Stalinist era, policy making in the Soviet Union has increasingly reflected differences of opinion among the top leaders of the party and state. In addition, the process and substance of policy is now being influenced by functional groups and local and middle level bureaucrats. Moreover, ideology does not translate easily into specific policy alternatives, particularly if both reformers and supporters of the status quo use the same ideology to justify their positions. Nevertheless, Communist ideology remains the primary guideline for the direction of policy and determines the kinds of policy changes that may be introduced. More important, Communist ideology and the party are, in the long run, the final authority regarding the legitimacy of policy. Thus, the policy process is determined by the dictates of the top leadership of the party and the general ideological perceptions of the period.

As discussed in the previous chapters, the party is the focal point for policy initiatives, while the state structure is primarily the channel for implementation. However, it should not be presumed that each of these institutions is immune to influence from the other or from external groups. Not only are

there overlapping memberships between the party and the state, but there are innumerable informal channels which cut across institutional lines. Moreover, while a number of members of the state bureaucracy enjoy a degree of autonomy as technicians and managers unencumbered by ideological directions, it is generally true that there is a "fusion" between party and state, a fusion—it might be added —that was envisioned by Lenin. Nonetheless, the increasing complexity of Soviet society and the Soviet Union's development as an industrialized state has created an environment that is increasingly susceptible to a broader-based policy input process.

The dominant Soviet political culture is "closed" and elitist, characterized by intense competition for power and a considerable range of policy perspectives among the highly placed participants who dominate it. However, the participants despite their often sharp mutual antagonisms, have common ideological outlooks and political training and experience. . . . Still, behind the facade of unanimity, there is the movement, ferment, and dynamism of real politics, replete with the lobbying, connivance, and bargaining characteristic of politics everywhere.[1]

Certain basic features of the Soviet system need to be re-emphasized before we study the policy process. First and foremost, the individual Soviet citizen has very little impact on the policy process. The nature of the Soviet legal system and the legislative process are such that individual impact is negligible. Similarly, groups outside the official structure of the party and state do not have a serious political existence as potential groups, as was noted in earlier chapters. All meaningful policy making takes place within the boundaries of official organs or those groups that have an official stamp of approval. Thus the policy process is rigid and inflexible, and is oriented toward satisfying the demands of the state. Yet, as will be made clear in the following paragraphs, a more open process has developed, and channels have been established to provide feedback into the system from the grass roots level.

In examining the Soviet political system, one can reasonably conclude that policy initiatives and implementation are primarily the responsibility of official organs and that there is a minimum of input from external sources. This is true not only in terms of associations and interest groups, but also with respect to the role of the mass media. In the main, domestic and foreign policies emanate from an oligarchy whose control of the political system limits participation in the policy process by the masses and by associations representing the masses.

The nature of the Soviet economy fosters this oligarchical control. It is a *command economy,* one in which economic goals are determined primarily by administrative directives and economic decision makers rather than by consumer action. Thus a command economy and a controlled political process have evolved from ideological precepts and decision makers whose responsibility and accountability are not to the people but to an elite—an elite, it should be noted, who per-petuate their own power, recruit their own leaders, and ultimately determine the proper interpretation of the communist ideology. It is with this in mind that we now turn to an examination of the policy phases within the Soviet system.

Emergence Phase

Policy in the Soviet system, as in all other systems, attempts to respond to obvious social and economic problems. In the Soviet system, much of this is done through intra-party debate and conflict, as well as through conflicts between state and party organs. Nevertheless, there is some response to policy that may emerge from passive resistance on the part of those directly affected by policy and from the indirect influence and impact of the intelligentsia and functional groups.

Local party officials in outlying provinces, for example, may bring policy problems to the attention of the party apparatus by publishing a letter in *Pravda* or *Izvestiya* regarding existing policies or the need for a new policy. Similarly, letters to the editors give official insights into the attitudes of the people. Yet, there is no systematic way for policy to emerge from the actions of individuals or groups outside the official structure. As one author suggests, there is no verbalization of policy needs.[2]

In the main, policy emerges through the highest party and state channels. Yet, this emergence can be stimulated by latent groups that have a potential of developing into interest groups with some political impact. As one scholar has concluded,

Today, the Soviet political system is again oligarchic, but its socioeconomic setting is now quite different. Soviet society is far more developed and stable, far less malleable and atomized. In the past, the key groups that had to be considered as potential political participants were relatively few. To-day, in addition to the vastly more entrenched institutional interests, such as the police, the military, and the state bureaucracy, the youth could become a source of ferment, the consumers could become more restless, the collective farmers more recalcitrant, the scientists more outspoken, the non-Russian nationalities more demanding. Prolonged competition among the oligarchs would certainly accelerate the assertiveness of such groups.[3]

Moreover, policy of the Soviet society in the late 1970s is increasingly being influenced by pressures of functional as well as institutional groups. In addition, there has evolved an environment in which policy emerges through diverse, innocuous, and unsystematized impulses. These are generally implicit; that is, there is not really a "demand" for a particular policy, nor the development of association or groups to "lobby" for a particular policy. Rather what emerges is "attention" groups in which individuals and local officials describe their experiences in letters to the editor or in discussions with higher level party officials, thereby getting attention and stimulating others to do likewise.

All this, it should be emphasized, is attempted in the name of Marxist-Leninist ideology, and there are numerous examples. One of the most obvious was the education reforms attempted in 1958 by former First Secretary Nikita Khrushchev. Concerned about the quality of higher education and the need for skilled labor, Khrushchev, in seeking to consolidate his power within the party (among other things), attempted to instigate educational reforms, stressing the need to "uplift" the working man and bring prestige to manual labor. Consequently, he developed a policy incorporating manual labor and higher education with a selection process to higher education which would provide greater opportunities to children of the working class. Thus, vocational education was to become a

key element in progressing to higher education.

During the course of the next few years, this policy was met by passive resistance of teachers in the regular academic curriculum, of plant managers, and of the intelligentsia in general. For example, a number of articles and letters to the editors were published explaining the impact of these policies—generally negative with the obvious hope of change or establishment of new policies. A sampling of such publications show the following:

Kh. Tammiste, "Why Desks are Unoccupied in the Evening Schools," *Pravda*, January 28, 1969.

B. Viktorov, "A Teen-Ager Quits School," *Pravda*, February 2, 1967.

Comments about inadequately trained and poorly motivated young workers, Pavel B. Katsuba in *Izvestiya*, April 16, 1968.

As a result of the comments of these attention groups and the persistent opposition to Khrushchev's leadership within the Politburo and the Central Committee, educational reforms were defeated. Of course, some of the reaction to these reforms was partly a result of the overall disenchantment with Khrushchev's performance during the early 1960s.

A key figure in emergence of policy is the first secretary of the local party organizations through province level. The role of the first secretary is to coordinate the activities of local agencies and enterprises, be they industrial plants or schools. Thus, the secretary is likely to be knowledgeable about the need for differing or new policies. These matters are inserted into the Secretariat channels and eventually reach the top members of the Secretariat. Moreover, the party apparently has many specialists involved in various aspects of Soviet domestic life. Their understanding and involvement in certain segments of society is bound to be reflected in the various party organs and ultimately in the highest organs of the party. Similarly the state structure reflects these matters and concerns.

It should be clear, however, that in a number of key policy matters, emergence takes place from within the highest circles of the party. In such estimates, the policy is dictated from within party circles or very limited areas external to the party in which discussion and debate may take place. Thus, the dictates of the party leadership, regardless of the impetus from lower levels, are paramount.

Identification

In the Soviet system, there is a close relationship between the emergence and identification phases of the policy process. Because most of the important policy proposals emerge from within the party hierarchy, the same groups and structures also propose the specifics of policy and develop the necessary tactics to ensure its approval. Clearly, many policy proposals move from emergence to identification and to approval rather quickly, given the nature of the Soviet system. Nevertheless, various groups within the hierarchy, although agreeing on the need for specific policy, may develop differing proposals to deal with the particular issues. Moreover, proposals submitted by certain groups within the party structure may generate a reaction from other groups within the party hierarchy.

The identification phase in the Soviet policy process thus becomes extremely important. While the process differs in scope and methods compared to the American process, the the purpose is identical: to ensure sufficient support for a particular policy. In this sense, the identification phase subsumes the approval phase to a major extent. The formal approval is almost pro forma, while the infor-

mal channels for approval—those within the party circles—are the determining factor regarding types of policies. Thus, while tactics and groups are coalescing to support a particular policy, the fact that a proposal evolves and is submitted more or less means that there is sufficient support to have it approved: it represents the policy of the highest circles of the party and thus must be accepted. Yet as one scholar notes,

The freedom of Soviet policy-makers is impinged on by several forces, which broadly speaking, fall into two categories. The first can be classified as the *alienated and unincorporated sectors* of Soviet Society—'latent oppositions'—which react negatively to specific Party policies but are not necessarily opposed to the entire value structure. . . . [Secondly], the emergence of 'loyal oppositions' [whose] challenge to the monopolistic decision-making power of Party leaders, a power that ranges from determining the price of a liter of milk to declaring war, is an important consequence of the rapid industrialization of the U.S.S.R. . . . Bargaining between Party leaders, experts, and representatives of interest groups tends to be carried on mainly behind the scenes, rather than in the open market of competing interests and ideas.[4]

Politics of the policy process were apparent in the industrial organization plan Khrushchev proposed in 1957, shortly after coming to power. This policy was intended to change the role of the party in the economic sphere while reinforcing the role of state structures and technical managers. Between the time Khrushchev proposed the policy in the Politburo and its formal approval by the Supreme Soviet several months later, much debate had taken place, both in the upper echelons of the party (Politburo and Central Committee) and in the newspapers. Although opposed by the majority of those in the Politburo, Khrushchev was able to prevail by developing significant support outside party circles. Managers, state ministries, and Khrushchev's allies within the party mobilized sufficient support to overcome the objections of Khrushchev's enemies within the Politburo. Of course, the fact that Khrushchev was first secretary of the Communist party helped significantly in mobilizing support and negating the opposition within the Politburo. This was also a test of strength for Khrushchev because he was struggling to establish himself as the power in the Politburo.

During a period of transition of leaders, such as the years immediately following the fall of Khrushchev, the struggles over power and policy are particularly serious. Once a member of the ruling elite establishes his supremacy, however, these struggles subside and members of the Politburo tend to follow the leader.

In all instances, to be correct and to appeal to the highest leadership of the party, policy must be based on some accepted ideological interpretation. Because the central party leadership is also the interpreter of the ideology, it becomes clear that policy is identified and approved by the Politburo. Thus, because policy initiative and approval generally stem from the same source—the party leadership —the emergence, identification, and approval phases of policy are closely intertwined in the Soviet system.

The point needs to be emphasized, however, that policy identification and, to some extent, approval does require support of a number of groups in the Soviet Union, but certainly not to the extent normally associated with policy in the United States. Policy proposals normally follow the kinds of discussions and debate associated with the British Cabinet. The biggest difference, of course, is that the British Cabinet must defend its policy to the large legislative body (the House of Commons) which has the authority to defeat the proposal. In the Soviet Union, support of the Politburo is virtually the only necessary procedure in the entire process. If there is disagreement within the Politburo, then additional groups are brought into the process to support one group or another. But the focal point remains the Politburo.

These observations regarding policy identification are best exemplified by problems within the Soviet economy. " 'Whose voice is louder?' was how Khrushchev once described the informal bickering that he said was often the determining factor in the making of economic choices in the Soviet Union. This struggle is always most important, and fiercest, in the ruling Presidium [Politburo] of the CPSU Central Committee."[5]

A brief study of the Soviet economic policy process is instructive in this regard. While not intending to provide a detailed analysis of the Soviet economic system, the following discussion will make more clear the relationship among leaders, party, the top party leadership, and external sources of policy input in the Soviet Union.

The Soviet economy has always been a major headache to Communist party leaders. A command economy presupposes central direction. The State Planning Commission determines the items to be produced by the economy; estimates the amounts of various semifinished products, raw materials, and equipment needed to produce these items; and coordinates transportation schedules and materials input to ensure a smooth production output. Industrial ministries are responsible for the proper functioning of the various industries, while the Ministry of Agriculture is responsible for supervising and directing collective farms and state farms to ensure they meet their quotas. Each plant has a quota it must fill, each agricultural unit has a quota, and all of the major transportation facilities must be geared to support these quotas, that is, to ensure distribution from, as well as input to, the major industries.

Manufacturing enterprises, all subordinated to central ministries, were not only told how many pieces or how many tons of a given product they were to make, but also how many component parts, how many workers, how much in wages, how much in capital investment they were to put into producing it. Enterprise managers and plant directors literally received instructions on the number of nuts and bolt they could use to assemble a steam shovel, how many buttons should be sewn on a shirt, how many nails to hammer in a packing crate.[6]

Soviet planners judge the effectiveness of the particular industry on the volume of physical output. In many instances, quality suffers as plant managers attempt to maintain and surpass quotas, and as a result there are constant complaints among Soviet consumers about shoddy products. Certain products are in short supply. When they are available, their prices are beyond the average consumer. For example, Soviet planners may determine that only about 250,000 automobiles can be built in any given year. To correlate demand with supply, the price of such automobiles can be adjusted to ensure that no more than 250,000 Russians can afford the product. Thus, the industrial manager finds himself under a variety of controls emanating from the central structure and dictating detailed economic procedures, regulations, and incentives.

Agriculture is the more serious problem in the Soviet Union. The Soviet economy has never been self-sufficient in agriculture. Regardless of the inducements, the Soviet agricultural worker's productivity remains low compared to that of his counterpart in the United States. Thus the Soviet Union is forced to import food products. In an effort to find solutions, Soviet planners have tried many devices, including giving capitalistic incentives and allowing private plots. In the main, these have stimulated Soviet farmers to develop their private plots while neglecting cooperatives and state-owned farms.

From the beginning of the modern Soviet state, there have been problems with agricultural development. Following Marxist-Leninist ideology regarding ownership of lands by the state, Stalin implemented a policy of collectivization. The more efficient and wealthier farmers *(kulaks)* as a class were liquidated. Estimates are that about five million peasants (wives, children, and close relatives) were uprooted from their farms, and at least half were killed or died. The *kulaks* fought the secret police and militia almost to a standstill. But following a lull of almost two years, Stalin reinstituted the policy in 1931, which culminated in complete decollectivization.

Khrushchev attempted to increase productivity and efficiency of agriculture by instituting the "virgin lands" policy, a policy intended to develop the vast farmlands of Siberia. The failure of this and related policies was a major cause of his downfall. His successor, Leonid Brezhnev, tried to correct Soviet agricultural policy. In a speech before the Central Committee, he announced a new agricultural plan which was to provide a better deal for the Soviet peasantry and establish a series of welfare measures. Nevertheless, after a period of five years, Brezhnev's agricultural plan succeeded no better than that of his predecessor. According to many, the disincentives built into the command economy invariably frustrate attempts to make the system more effective.

Early in 1965, the matter of economic reform was a major issue in the Soviet Union. With the end of the Khrushchev era of reforms, it was particularly important for the economy to develop in accordance with acceptable ideological guidelines. What was particularly important for the new leaders was to correct the perceived faults of "Libermanism."[7]

In 1962, Yevsei Liberman, a university professor, had advanced the idea that the communist economic system needed reform in an article in *Pravda*. This reform, he had suggested, should rest on such concepts as profitability, forces of supply and demand, incentives for labor and management, and cost accounting. Libermanism was an economic reform concept supported by Khrushchev, but considered heretical by orthodox economic managers and planners. Clearly, Libermanism was contrary to the basic economic precepts of Marxism. Equally important, the implementation of Liberman's proposals would have a serious impact on party-state relationships. For example, if economic managers were allowed autonomy in determining output, it would reduce the party control over economic enterprises as well as the economic bureaucracy.

Following the ouster of Khrushchev in 1964, Kosygin attempted to further Liberman-type economic reforms while continuing some important features of centralization. Concerned about incentives to increase production, Kosygin felt that enterprises should be allowed more flexibility in making economic decisions. On the other hand, the planners should concern themselves primarily with planning. The inference was that party cadres should be concerned primarily with overall planning and administration, while the economists and managers should be allowed to deal with the practicalities of economic problems on a day-to-day basis. The role of the party was not questioned in these debates; rather, attempts were made to distinguish between managerial and ideological guidelines.

Thus the matter of economic reforms became a struggle between Kosygin (state bureaucracy) and Brezhnev (party bureaucracy). The appointment of Brezhnev's friends and allies to key posts in the Central Committee soon gave Brezhnev the power base from which to subordinate Kosygin and the state

bureaucracy and to develop a degree of autonomy from the party. By the middle of 1966, Brezhnev was securely in the seat of power. As if to confirm publicly Brezhnev's consolidation of power, the party's Presidium was renamed the Politburo and the first secretary's title was changed to General Secretary. Both titles had been used during the Stalinist period. Since 1966, Kosygin and the state bureaucracy have been clearly subordinate to Brezhnev and the party.

In his speech of September 1965 before the Central Committee, Brezhnev presented his reform, which not only allowed a greater freedom for enterprises in managing their economic affairs, but it also abolished territorial party controls over economic enterprises. Brezhnev had to reassure regional party cadres, however, that this in no way reduced the role of the party; rather, that the party would enhance its central control over new ministries.

Nevertheless, within a few years the new economic reforms floundered, not necessarily because of the substance of the plan, but due partly to the entrenched conservative party cadres. Extremely suspicious of any diminution of their power, particularly in the economic field, the party cadres at the middle and lower levels, although not publicly disapproving of the policy, did not forcefully implement it, thereby vetoing it in effect. Moreover, complete approval of this policy was withheld not only by many lower party officials, but also by officials at the highest levels because of the fear that such reforms would erode the party position and, invariably, their own position.

In terms of policy emergence and identification then, the central planners have the primary role in the Soviet economy. When industries fail and agriculture is unable to increase food production sufficiently, policy is generated from the central party leadership to try to rectify the situation. Because the economy does not reflect market forces or the demands of the consumer, decisions regarding economic production and policy in general are made at the highest levels of the leadership. Moreover, the centralized basis of economic planning requires a vast bureaucracy controlled at the center. Not only does this circumvent the federal principle of the Soviet state, but from the policy point of view, it reinforces the party's pre-eminent position in all phases of policy and sustains party bureaucratic protection against meaningful reforms. As one expert concludes, "The Party bureaucracy seems unable and most unwilling to adjust its rule of Soviet society toward decentralization of economic decision-making and continues to subordinate other needs to the retention of total power."[8] Indeed, the same can be said of decentralization of political decisions in the Soviet system.

Approval Phase

Again the Politburo is the key to the approval of policies. As noted earlier, the approval and identification phases are closely related, and in many instances there is only a short time between the advancement of policies and their approval. Generally speaking, the Supreme Soviet legitimizes policy. This, however, is a pro forma matter.

The Central Committee of the party plays a key role in certain cases of policy approval whether it be for specific policies or for approval of leadership positions. This was readily apparent in the removal of Nikita Khrushchev as first secretary of the Communist party in October 1964. The problems of Khrushchev's leadership have already been discussed. In the main, the failure of Khrushchev's domestic policies, particularly agriculture, combined with his attempt at some liberalizing of the policy process were the reasons for his ouster.

While Khrushchev was away on vacation at his Black Sea resort, the anti-Khrushchev group implemented its strategy to depose the First Secretary. Brezhnev was aware of the general plan. The plotters, key members in the Presidium (Politburo), mobilized their support in the Central Committee to assure ratification of the decision already made by the Presidium. Khrushchev was ushered in to the meeting and was immediately met by charges from Suslov regarding failures of Khrushchev's policies. Most of the members of the Central Committee had already been approached by the anti-Khrushchev group and were assured of their support. Contrary to what took place in an abortive 1957 attempt to depose Khrushchev, the Central Committee ratified the decision of the Presidium, and Khrushchev was disposed. Leonid Brezhnev was "elected" first secretary. In this instance, the Central Committee served as the legitimizing agency for a policy deposing Khrushchev. In 1957 when anti-Khrushchev elements tried to depose the First Secretary, Khrushchev used the Central Committee as the power base to defeat his opponents. These events provide a clear example of the telescoping of policy identification and approval into almost one action.

While there is no clearly delineated approval function within the state structure, the state ministries most concerned with a particular policy must be involved in the approval phase if the policy is to be implemented successfully. The professional skills and bureaucratic expertise within the state structure, as well as experts from outside the party-state structure, are involved in the approval process to the extent that a particular policy does or does not have strong approval or support from the central organs of the party. Thus, as the degree of authority exercised by the general secretary decreases with respect to approval of policy, the resort to external groups in approval increases. For example, in assessing the role of groups of lobbies and the relationship to the power of Nikita Khrushchev, one scholar concludes that "lobbies had always existed, even under Stalin, and . . . they became active whenever Khrushchev's authority dwindled."[9]

Typically, a particular policy is presented within the Politburo, generally by the general secretary or another key member. The policy is debated, discussed, and approved—usually unanimously. Of couse, it is difficult to ascertain with any degree of certainty the proceedings within the Politburo. It is assumed that a policy that develops a high degree of coherency throughout the party structure has indeed been given the strong approval of the Politburo. Once the Politburo gives its support, the policy is passed on to the Council of Ministers, which in turn issues ordinances or regulations implementing the policy, implicitly providing approval. It must be remembered, or course, that the chairman of the Council of Ministers is, in a sense, the "prime minister" of the Soviet Union. More important, he is likely to be a key member of the Politburo. For example, the office of the chairman of the Council of Ministers has been held by Lenin, Stalin, and Khrushchev, as well as by a number of other important officials of the Politburo.

In sum, in a system such as that in the Soviet Union in which one party is paramount, the policy phases become virtually subsumed into one process. Because the top party leadership is at the center of the policy process, with few if any other political actors exercising a meaningful role in the process, emergence, identification, and approval can become intertwined to such a degree that it is difficult to identify where one ends and the other begins. Nevertheless, one can identify, even in this environment, clusters of actions within the party-state structure which give rise to policy phases and provide some visibility to the process by which policy

emerges, is identified, and approved. The unsystematic and nonarticulated process by which policy process is affected outside official party circles makes the process obscure and, at best, spasmodic even if influential at times. Thus, the student must ultimately return to the obvious: the party leadership, in the form of the first secretary, members of the Politburo, and at times members of the Central Committee, is the key to the Soviet policy process.

Implementation

As is true of virtually every political system, the bureaucracy in the Soviet Union is concerned about its power and maintaining its secure role in the system. As we have noted with respect to economic reforms, there is a large conservative element within the Soviet bureaucracy that is solidly entrenched and bases its power on existing relationships and orthodoxy of ideological perspectives. While there are liberal elements within the party and state structure, it is clear to the party *apparatchiki* that dramatic changes in policy or procedures are, in the long range, a challenge to the party and to the position of the party bureaucracy. Generally, the same holds true with the state bureaucracy. Nevertheless, there are constant tensions and conflicts not only within the various bureaucracies, but between the state and party bureaucracy. These develop not only from ideological disagreements, but also from the differences between administrative and managerial apparatus within the state and the ideological bureaucracy within the party.

Mainly, the state structure (administrative-managerial bureaucracy) is responsible for implementing policies. The major instruments are the All-Union Council of Ministers and the union-republic and republic ministries. The all-union ministries are similar to cabinet departments both in Great Britain and in the United States. In this structure, members of the Council of Ministers supervise the activities of a variety of state committees and ministries, such as the State Planning Committee (GOSPLAN). Each of the deputy chairmen is in charge of one of the major functional committees. In addition, as we saw in Chapter 6, the Council of Ministers supervises the operations of state committees and the industrial and nonindustrial ministries.

While the all-union ministries are responsible for all activities within their particular field, without any reference to the republic governments, the union-republic ministries function through their counterparts at the republic level. Thus the Union-Republic Ministry of Education would deal primarily through the minister of education in the republics (for example, Ministry of Education, Republic of Armenia). In assessing the various functions of the ministries, one can see that those ministries of prime importance to the Soviet Union as a whole, and those ministries that cut across republic boundaries, are at the all-union level (for example, Defense, Electronics, Shipbuilding, Railways). Other ministries, such as Public Health and Procurement, can be operated through republic channels.

Republic ministries are primarily concerned with matters within the specific republic and are solely responsible to the republic ministries. In any event, the hierarchical pyramid is clear: the Council of Ministers of the Soviet Union has overall responsibility for the operations of the councils of ministers from the republic level through the all-union level.

The implementation of policy is obviously affected by the nature of these pyramidal relationships, as well as by the involvement of the party apparatus in the administration of the state. Moreover, control committees in both party and state structures and at all levels provide control and direction for the implementation of policies. Perhaps more important, the Secretariat structure and the party apparatus provide a similarity of outlook and training that gives a great degree of coherency to policy implementation in the Soviet Union, something not always found in Western systems.

In the words of one scholar, "The Soviet regime operates one of the world's largest and most complex bureaucratic structures. It functions by means of ministries and related agencies, as well as government corporations and state-owned economic enterprises"[10] Given the nature of the Soviet regime and the innocuous role played by the individual citizen, the citizen's suspicion of the bureaucracy and its reputed inefficiency have created a visible "we-they" syndrome. Although this syndrome may exist in other modern systems, it is particularly exacerbated in the Soviet state for reasons discussed earlier. Moreover, the distrust of the bureaucracy appears to be a heritage from the tsarist period. The vastness of the Communist bureaucracy has simply compounded the problem. The fact that the people play a negligible role in the election of leaders militates against the democratic concept of bureaucratic responsibility to both the people and the elected official.

Yet another basic characteristic of the bureaucracy-people relationship in the Soviet Union is the fact that people can do little against the bureaucratic structure. Robed in the aura of Communist ideology, bureaucrats rule by virtual fiat. Indeed, the only recourse left to citizens with grievances is the Communist party, a massive bureaucracy in itself. It is difficult for any individual to be long out of the sight or impact of the bureaucracy. Every aspect of the citizen's daily life comes under scrutiny and influence of either the state or party bureaucracy. Indeed, some scholars argue that this pervasiveness of the bureaucracy and officialdom that permeate the life of the citizen has created a significant apathy and a longing to be left alone, characteristics that do not necessarily fit into the Marxist-Leninist scheme of things.

Feedback

As is true of emergence, the feedback phase of the policy process evolves primarily from the party-state bureaucratic structure. Nevertheless, feedback from groups external to the bureaucratic structure has become more important. For example, policies dealing with nationalities must take into account the reaction of non-Russian ethnic groups. Similarly, policies dealing with religious activities must eventually face the reaction of religious groups. The point is that the post-Stalinist era in the Soviet Union has created an environment in which there is a propensity for groups to act in the character of "interest groups" associated with an open society. While involvement in the identification and approval of policy by groups external to the official bureaucracy is still quite limited, the reaction of such groups, particularly in terms of grass roots attitudes, is important to the Soviet hierarchy.

The individual citizen, of course, has little recourse for resolving his grievances. Similarly, groups can accomplish little by "democratic" means, that is, by overt lobbying, demonstrations, letter writing campaigns, voting participation, group coalitions, and so on. However, indirect and implicit means can be used, as has already been discussed in the emergence policy phase.

One of the most significant examples of feedback in the Soviet policy process has to do with the top leadership, rather than with citizens and groups. The fall of Khrushchev marked the first time in the history of the Communist regime that a "leader" was deposed by his lieutenants, by a majority of the

Politburo. Khrushchev came to power as a result of the divided leadership following the death of Stalin in 1953. The struggle was between Khrushchev (representing the party), Beria (the secret police), and Malenkov (the government apparatus). First Khrushchev and Malenkov joined forces to eliminate Beria. Then the struggle ensued between Malenkov and Khrushchev. While Malenkov advanced the concept that the economy should stress consumer goods, Khrushchev favored heavy industry or, as some scholars point out, the "steel eaters" of the military-industrial complex.

Both men were maneuvering to consolidate their power in the Politburo and Central Committee. While Malenkov moved to make the state machinery superior to the party, Khrushchev attempted to place the party in a dominant position vis-à-vis the state. Their efforts were reflected in the attempts to develop a particular economic policy.

In a 1957 December meeting of the Central Committee, one of Malenkov's allies was placed in command of the Soviet economy, thus downgrading the role of the party. In February of the following year, Khrushchev announced at another meeting of the Central Committee an economic plan based on making the top party organs dominant in the economic structure. He reorganized economic management basing it on regional economic councils which would be responsible for the economy on a regional basis. These councils would be headed by party officials.

As a result of these decisions and the increasing problems associated with the virgin lands scheme in Siberia (which showed signs of disaster), as well as a number of domestic schemes, the opposition to Khrushchev increased in the Politburo to a point where he could not command a majority of the membership. Subsequently, the Politburo tried to remove Khrushchev, but he argued successfully that, since the General Committee had "elected" him, it should be the Central Committee that deposed him. The matter was thrown into the Central Committee.

In June 1958, at a plenum of the Central Committee, a spectacle took place which is rare in the Soviet Union. Indeed, it has never been repeated. There was a serious debate on the Khrushchev matter. Members of the Central Committee actually took the floor to speak on this issue. Khrushchev was victorious, and those who had tried to oust him were themselves voted out of the Central Committee, including Malenkov.

The situation in 1964 was the reverse. While Khrushchev was out of Moscow, his opponents organized their support not only in the Politburo but in the Central Committee. In the years following 1958, Khrushchev's policies had consistently gone against the orthodoxy of the party and had increasingly eroded the role of the party. Indeed, Khrushchev's attempt at some "democratization" of the party and state structure led to fears on the part of the official bureaucracy that their power was being permanently eroded. Moreover, the failure of the virgin lands scheme, the acrimonious nature of the Sino-Soviet split, and problems in both domestic and foreign policy gave many top officials the impression the "Khrushchevism" was self-defeating and almost as dangerous as Stalinism. The famous secret speech in 1956 by Khrushchev denouncing the cult of personality and Stalinism ironically set the stage for a reaction against a Khrushchev cult and ultimately led to his own downfall.

With a majority of the Politburo against him and the members of the Central Committee supporting the anti-Khrushchev move, Khrushchev was removed as first secretary and chairman of the Council of Ministers. For the first time in the history of the Soviet State, the "leader" was removed from office by a relatively "democratic" process of developing a majority against him and deposing him through institutional processes.

In this instance policy feedback on leadership was relatively clear, even if after the fact. It is not so clear in a number of other instances where feedback develops from lower organs of the party or state, or through reaction of various groups within the Soviet Union.

Foreign Policy

Although there is a linkage between foreign and domestic policies of most states, this is particularly true in the Soviet Union. The Marxist-Leninist ideology stressing proletariat class struggles was conceived as a worldwide phenomenon; therefore, what happens within the Soviet society is ideologically important for foreign policy considerations. Moreover, the Soviet leadership still conceives the Soviet Union as the leader of the Marxist revolution, hence the close ideological relationship between domestic developments and international environment.

The foreign policy process thus involves a significantly smaller circle of officials and party bureaucrats than normally associated with domestic policy (which in itself is the result of an oligarchical structure). Moreover, information about foreign policy matters and international environment is generally limited to a small group of officials. With the control of the mass media and the need to ensure a direct linkage between foreign and domestic policy, the party exerts herculean efforts to manipulate information about foreign policy.

The official agency for foreign affairs is the U.S.S.R. Ministry of Foreign Affairs. The ministry is directly under the Council of Ministers and its chairman (premier). As with other state organs, the ministry is a policy-implementing body rather than a policy-making body. All important foreign policy decisions emanate from the Politburo of the party. Generally such decisions are based on recommendations made through the Central Committee department responsible for foreign affairs.

While in the past foreign policy has been preoccupied with ideological considerations, the post-Khrushchev leadership seems to be increasingly influenced by pressures to view foreign policy systematically and pragmatically. This approach is generally reflected in the work done by two institutions of the U.S.S.R. Academy of Sciences: the Institute of World Economics and International Relations, and the USA Institute. Nevertheless, the supremacy of the party in foreign affairs is clear. Not only is policy made at the highest levels of the party, but in every embassy there is a party representative who reports directly to the Central Committee in Moscow. In addition, the Central Committee apparatus must approve all persons selected to fill key diplomatic posts. The subordination of the Foreign Ministry and foreign affairs to party structure is further seen in those persons occupying the post of foreign minister. These are usually career diplomats and technicians, not party functionaries or Politburo members. Given the paramountcy of the party in directing the affairs of the Soviet Union, the status of those being selected to the post of foreign minister is clearly subordinated to the most important party positions. Finally, there is a special relationship between the foreign ministry and the party. Penetrated at virtually every level by party controls and party officials, the ministry has very little independent action of its own. As noted earlier, the importance of ideological relevance in foreign policy and its linkage to domestic politics makes foreign policy one of the most important concerns of the party leadership.

One of the major foreign policy goals of the Soviet system is to retain the Soviet primacy in the Communist world. Thus there is a major preoccupation with ideological relevance and ideological purity. To ensure this worldwide credibility, domestic development must be closely linked to foreign policy, since the Marxist-Leninist premise assumes the Soviet model as the proper one. Moreover, the premise upon which foreign policy is based presumes that the socialist world is constantly struggling against the capitalist world. Therefore, a series of political, economic, and social measures must be implemented to ensure the primacy of the communist system. Again, much of this stems from the presumed superiority of the Soviet system not only over the capitalistic system but over other communist systems as well. Finally, national revolutions are encouraged to gain the dominance of the proletariat and, equally important, to provide credibility to the premises of the Marxist-Leninist ideology.

It should not be presumed, however, that the Soviet ideology is necessarily rigid in terms of foreign affairs. As a matter of fact, the tactics of Marxist-Leninist ideology provide a significant flexibility, even to the point of temporarily aligning the Soviet state with capitalistic countries, as was done in World War II. But in the long run, the strategic considerations prevail. Ideology is integrated into the institutional processes and perspectives of the party-state bureaucracy to achieve the goals of Marxist-Leninist ideology. Obviously, there is a vast amount of disagreement on the means, but the ends are certainly accepted as a cohesive tool for the behavior of party and state bureaucrats.

Accomplishments and Prospects

Prognosticating about Soviet politics is hazardous, perhaps more so than with other systems. The context within which Soviet decisions are made and political leaders emerge makes discerning trends and future directions highly speculative. Nevertheless, there are some indicators and trends that are useful for comparison with other systems and serve as a framework for understanding the Soviet system.

At the outset, however, we should note that scholars disagree regarding the future directions of the Soviet system. Generally speaking, there are four major positions. First, there are those scholars who argue that the Soviet regime will collapse. Given the party structure, the serious problems that will become insoluble, the highly conservative nature of the institutions, and the increasing irrelevance of the ideology, a prerevolutionary situation will be created. The inability of the regime to respond to such a situation will lead to its collapse and replacement by a yet unknown system, according to this view.

Another perspective presumes that there will be evolutionary development in which the problems developing from within and without the Soviet system will necessitate internal change. The new challenges will force a transformation of the party-state structure and the institutional orientation. As part of the evolutionary development thesis, some suggest that modernization of the Soviet state will cause fundamental changes in the system. Modernization is thought to lead to democracy and egalitarianism. Thus, as the Soviet state modernizes, it will foster the evolution of democratically oriented institutions and create a society that is egalitarian. Through this evolutionary process, the authoritarian base of the Soviet system will be eroded.

A variant of this modernization thesis is the so-called convergence thesis. This argues that the Soviet and American systems are becoming alike. Sharing common values, the Soviet and American systems are evolving similar economies and social systems. Using similar technology and committed to an industrial system, the Soviet system will, according to

this approach, develop a socialist type of market economy. While the Soviet system moves away from a command economy, it is thought that the American system will develop a sector of state-owned enterprises and a large welfare system and will give more attention to economic planning. Thus the Soviet and American systems, according to this view, are converging as a result of economic forces.

Similarly, there are those scholars who presume an increasing bureaucratization of the Soviet system and a parallel development in the United States. This bureaucratization perspective presumes that managerial elite and technicians (technocrats), by virtue of the demands of a highly industrialized society, will become the key power holders—political actors—in both societies. As a result, there will be a similar ideological orientation and professional perspectives. Thus, while the role of the party bureaucracy will decline in the Soviet Union, the role of elected officials will decline in the United States.

A final view is that the Soviet system will continue generally as it is now, at least for the foreseeable future. This continuation will be characterized by an increasing amount of dictatorial control or the development of one-man rule with entrenched institutions supporting the status quo. While there will be a certain responsiveness to social, economic, and political demands, the power holders—political actors—will remain essentially the same.

There are, of course, a number of variations of each of these perspectives. For example, there are scholars who would argue that there are variations of the present totalitarian model, ranging from an imperfect totalitarian system, to an authoritarian system to a bureaucratic model. Clearly then, Soviet futurism is a subject in its own right. The student should appreciate the variety of views and the difficulties inherent in identifying cause-and-effect relationships in politics.

POLITICAL-SOCIAL CHANGE AND
MARXIST-LENINIST IDEOLOGY

Although one need not agree with any of these propositions, it should be recognized that changes are taking place within the Soviet system, as with any system. These changes are likely to influence the political system and the types of political actors, as well as the basis of political power.

Soviet society is becoming increasingly industrialized and consumer oriented. This is not to suggest that there are not many "backward" areas in the Soviet rural areas and outlying villages. Nevertheless, the pace of industrialization and the increasing professionalization within Soviet society is creating a system that cannot rest on mundane definitions of the Leninist proletariat state. Indeed, there are those that argue that industrialization is gradually leading to an affluence normally associated with the bourgeoisie. This will undoubtedly cause friction between the consumer pulls of the economy and the drive for continuing industrialization, as well as the concern over increasing the efficiency of agriculture.

The Soviet system is far from becoming a consumer society, however. With its command economy and the unresponsiveness to market forces, economic decisions will undoubtedly continue to be made in response to bureaucratic decisions. But the push of the command economy against the pull of consumerism will surely create strains and tensions within the economy and social structure.

There also appears to be an increasing autonomy—as much as there can be within an authoritarian system—of special groups, such as military, police, state bureaucracy, youth, intelligentsia, and trade unions. In essence, such groups are developing an increasing institutional cohesion, probably as a result of the change in the economic system and of the type of leadership in the party-state structure. Concomitant with this phenomenon is a widening scope of elite participation. That is, professionals outside the party-state bureaucracy are exerting increasing influence over the policy process. This should not be presumed to mean a pluralistic system, but rather one in which there is increased political participation within a rather narrowly defined sphere. The latency of existing interest groups will decrease with emphasis being given to visible involvement in the political process. Given the strength of ethnic identities within the Soviet system, interest group activity representing subnationalities will create increasing pressure on the Soviet system.

The ideological relevance of Marxist-Leninism is also suspect, at least in terms of its economic premises. Moreover, the Soviet insistence upon its primacy, already under serious attack by other Communist parties, is likely to become less and less relevant in the Communist world. Indeed, the rise of China and Maoism has seriously challenged Soviet primacy and will continue to do so, while states in Eastern Europe—Romania, Poland, as well as Yugoslavia—further their own nationalistic brand of communism. Paralleling these trends is the emergence of a strong nationalistic sentiment, not only in the Soviet Union, but around the periphery of the Soviet state. Combined with the decay of ideological relevance, nationalism is likely to become a key factor in the sustenance of the Soviet state.

Soviet society, therefore, will not necessarily develop in terms of the Marxist-Leninist historical determinism. Rather, challenges of modernization and social mobility are likely to create economic and social classes and to make more definite the gradations in status and privilege that exist, to a degree, in the Soviet system already. The institutionalization of these relationships and the need for a revision of existing ideological premises will have some impact on the power structure in the system. Because our concern is to develop some understanding of political actors and their power base, we shall view the general patterns of political actors within the context of social and economic changes. These general directions can be categorized into three main areas: participation and competition, nature of political leadership, and role of the party.

PARTICIPATION AND COMPETITION

There appear to be increasing pressures within the Soviet system for expansion of political participation. While the system is far from allowing realistic involvement of individuals in selecting leaders and in influencing policy choices, the number of groups involved and the scope of political involvement seems to be widening. Thus, as the Soviet system becomes increasingly industrialized, the need for professional and managerial skills increases, giving some credence to the view that the professional and managerial elite will become power wielders. Moreover, the general demands for professionalization will undoubtedly create additional tensions between party and state structures. Institutional groups, such as the military and police, will increasingly demand institutional loyalty while developing institutional cohesion. Thus, it is likely that there will be increased competition not only between the party and state structures, but also between the various bureaucracies, economic, military, and police.

There do not appear to be serious signs of increasing involvement in politics by the individual Soviet citizen. Indeed, one of the underlying trends of politics has been the apparent apathy of the individual. The years of authoritarian leadership and "closed" politics have created an environment in which "being left alone" is the best alternative. This has been reinforced by the continuous barrage of ideological exhortations based upon Marxist-Leninism-Stalinism which has become increasingly irrelevant to important sec-

tors of the Soviet system. While lip service is given to the ideology, many Soviet citizens, in urban areas particularly, go about their own tasks, seeking ways to "beat the system." Thus a gap has been created between the party-state political actors and the mass of people, at least in terms of realistic political participation.

On the other hand, there is some evidence to indicate that primary party organizations—grass roots level organs—are becoming important in the policy process. Whether this is a result of the relatively open system since the Stalinist period or a result of the changing nature of the Soviet economic and social system is difficult to ascertain.

Dissent within the Soviet Union has been rather consistent over the past ten years. There is no reason to believe that it will decrease. Indeed, *samizdat* (underground publications) proliferate during times of crises, such as the Polish and Hungarian revolutions in 1956, in which the Soviet Union played such a heavy hand. More important for our purposes, dissent in the form of underground publications and visible demonstrations is no longer rare in the Soviet system. Students at the University of Moscow and the University of Leningrad were expelled or disciplined for their resistance to Soviet action in Hungary and Poland in 1956. Given the circulation and popularity of *samizdat*, it is reasonable to argue that there is an undercurrent of dissent within the major universities; however, this dissent has not become widespread. It is limited to a narrow circle of intelligentsia and should not be viewed as an indication of major dissatisfaction with the Soviet regime.

LEADERSHIP

Barring the return to a Stalinist type of leadership, it is more than likely that the leadership will reflect internal competition among various groups. The removal of Khrushchev by his subordinates, although a unique event in Russian history, does suggest that the general secretary of the Communist party needs to continually reassess his support not only in the Politburo, but also in the Central Committee. Leadership succession is neither clearly delineated nor institutionalized. Key leaders are thus motivated to seek power to assure their supremacy. In turn, the politics involved in the acquisition of power are likely to be reflected in the Politburo and the party apparatus in general. Rather than a monolithic totalitarian structure, therefore, one is likely to find a latent pluralism in the policy-making and administrative process.

As we saw in the assessment of the policy-making process in the Soviet system, the more that the general secretary's authority is challenged, the more likely that groups and professionals external to the party structure will be involved in decision making. It is conceivable, therefore, that the concern of the leadership to ensure its power base will create a dilemma in which key officials will have to seek allies outside the party structure and even beyond the state bureaucracy.

It has already been noted that there is likely to be increased group activity, particularly by those groups outside the party-state structure. Cultural groups, as well as ethnic and religious groups, may find an environment more conducive to articulation of their interests, especially if the leadership moves from a closed elite power structure to a "consensus" type of structure. This is not to suggest that a consensus type of process paralleling what one finds in the United States or other Western democracies will necessarily evolve, but Soviet leaders may seek allies, whether in or out of the party structure, avoiding the kind of "purge" mentality of the Stalinist era. In other words, a realistic political bargaining environment may be developing.

As some scholars have pointed out, these developments seem to be motivating the growth of a counterelite in the Soviet system, that is, an elite associated not with the party-state bureaucracy, but with the intelligentsia and academia which provide inputs to the policy process—not necessarily for the purpose of attaining more power within the party-state bureaucracy. Moreover, it is conceivable that such a counterelite can provide realistic alternatives to policy initiated from within the bureaucratic structure.

THE ROLE OF THE PARTY

These developments raise major questions for party leadership. On one hand, the increased industrialization and the nature of leadership has opened the Soviet system to a degree unknown in previous years. On the other hand, changes in the social and economic structures require some fundamental changes in the nature of the policy process and the role of the party. Thus major problems confront the Communist party of the Soviet Union. Any major changes in its power position suggest a diminishing of that power to a more pragmatic and rationalized system, assuming that professional and managerial elite are exerting pressures for change. Moreover, the apparent apathy of the Soviet citizens has not necessarily decreased the pressure from a latent consumerism. In addition, there appears to be some "grass roots" pressure from primary party organizations that may substitute (however inadequately) for "public opinion" in democracies.

In such circumstances, the party leadership is faced with a dilemma. For the party to respond effectively to these kinds of internal pressures requires some changes within the party, both ideological and substantive. The withering away of the relevance of Marxist-Leninist-Stalinist ideology will require some acceptance of a rational, pragmatic approach to the solution of problems. Yet the party's basis for power rests on the continued dominance of the ideological perspective for the Soviet state. A shift to other bases of power within the Soviet system is likely to diminish the role of the party.

Assuming that the party will not return to the harsh totalitarian rule of the Stalinist era, the party must then develop a more open policy process, while clarifying and institutionalizing its leadership transfer procedures. As we have learned, it is not clear in the Soviet system how policy emerges and what kind of impact various groups have on the policy process—if any. Moreover, the deliberations within the Politburo and the leader selection process remain a mystery. The Russian people are usually presented with a fait accompli and have little impact on the selection of leaders. Searching the Soviet Constitution and the Operating Rules of the Communist party, one cannot find any clear definition of the relationships between the party and the state or among the various organs of the party. Thus, much is left to the top party leadership and the *apparatchiki*, a situation that may become less tolerable given the competition between bureaucracies and the party-state tensions and conflict.

It is clear that the dominant political actor in all of the policy phases is the Communist party of the Soviet Union. The Politburo in conjunction with the Central Committee is at the center of the policy process. While there is some input from groups outside the party structure, this is minimal and only at the discretion of the party. The dominance of the party is reinforced by the interlocking membership of the party and state structure, particularly at the highest levels. Indeed, the clearest example is the recent election of party General Secretary Leonid Brezhnev to the presidency of the Soviet Union. The Soviet chief of state also holds the key post in the party, combining these posts for the first time in modern Soviet history.

There is, to be sure, a distinct state structure with nonparty input. But yet the fact remains that the state structure is a policy-implementing system rather than a policy-making system. Even in these circumstances, the party's primary and intermediate structures play a key role in the proper implementation of policy. While the federal structure seems to provide a relative autonomy in certain areas of policy, the unitary party system, in reality, negates this structure.

The rise of nationality groups and the glimmerings of dissent in conjunction with some input from the grass roots level do influence the party leaders in identifying some policy areas. In addition, experts and intelligentsia, working through various state and party committees, also manage to provide an alternative view to party ideologues. These inputs, however, are meaningful only if they are adopted by one or the other party organs and made a matter of party debate. In the final analysis, the politics within the Politburo of the party and the power of the "leader" determine policy for the Soviet Union.

Summary

In the final analysis, barring a cataclysmic event or confrontation with China or the United States, it appears that the Soviet system will continue in much the same fashion—with some revisions. While the internal contradictions of the system will require some important changes in the policy process and in politics generally, it is unlikely that the party will lose its dominant position. The Soviet system has institutionalized the role of the party at all levels of government and at all levels of political participation. These entrenched interests, buttressed by the demands of the command economy, make the party the primary actor. Although the state bureaucracy has gained prominence in its own right, many of the key officials maintain their position in the state by virtue of their party status. While the fusion that Lenin spoke of between party and state is far from being accomplished, there is an intertwining that does obscure the distinctions between the two.

The command economy is likely to become more efficient as a result of computerized technology. Coordination will become less difficult. The computerization of the system will also provide a more efficient communications and control technique making economic enterprises more responsive to commands from above.

For these reasons, the evolutionary theory is probably relevant in this analysis, although with qualifications. Thus, it is difficult to accept the thesis that evolutionary development ipso facto will lead to a democratic type of system. Modernization, social mobility, and a skilled populace do not necessarily lead to democratic enlightenment. Indeed, they may lead to orthodoxy and to a demand for conformity. Moreover, to presume that evolution ultimately leads to higher and better things is to neglect the study of humanity. War and the interstate conflicts have increased in their ferocity as humanity has evolved. On the other hand, there is some evidence to suggest that evolutionary development of the Soviet system may lead to a more open system characterized by a broader scope of political participation, the development of a counter-elite with alternative policies, and the increased influence of groups external to the party-state structure (including ethnic and religious groups). While this may not necessarily lead to a democratic system in relation to the development of communism in the Soviet state, it does indicate, to a degree, enlightenment and a lessening of ideological rigidities. Where the system will go from here is difficult to foresee.

It is also instructive to note that the concept of individual rights and liberties and the responsibility of the individual in the political system remains a subdued—or submerged—issue. The stress on the collectivity remains

the focus of Soviet politics and the policy process. While there are glimmerings of "individuality," the weight of the party-state bureaucracy and the fundamental premises upon which state policy rests evolve from the concern with the collectivity. The rights of the individual against the collectivity are at a primitive level of development. Given the nature of the Soviet regime and the perceived trends, it is unlikely that the Soviet system will place individual rights at the forefront of the policy process.

Finally, even with indications of change, it seems that the legitimacy of the Soviet system in the eyes of most Soviet citizens has increased since 1953, the end of the Stalinist era. Although the old guard—those in top leadership positions—will be replaced by death or retirement in the late 1970s and 1980s by a new breed of leaders, this does not necessarily pretend vast changes. Most Soviet people have grown up with a Communist system: they know no other. Moreover, in comparative perspective, the Soviet people have a higher standard of living than they have ever known before. In addition, the status of the Soviet Union in world affairs is also at a high level. Regardless of internal discontent and pressures, it is unlikely that these will cause fundamental changes in the Soviet system, at least in the foreseeable future.

NOTES

1. Frederick C. Barghoorn, *Politics, USSR*, 2nd ed. (Boston: Little, Brown, 1972), p. 239.
2. Barghoorn, op. cit., p. 239.
3. Zbigniew Brzezinski, "The Soviet Political System: Transformation or Degeneration," in Zbigniew Brzezinski, ed., *Dilemmas of Change in Soviet Politics* (New York: Columbia University Press, 1969), p. 20.
4. Albert Boiter, "The Origins, Structure and Growth of Soviet Pressure Groups," in U.S. Army Institute for Advanced Russian and East European Studies, 4th

Annual Soviet Affairs Symposium, *The Role and Influence of Soviet Pressure Groups on CPSU Policy* (Garmisch, Germany: June 8–10, 1970), p. 8. Hereafter referred to as Symposium.

5. Sidney I. Ploss, "Soviet Politics Since the Fall of Khrushchev," Foreign Policy Research Institute, Monograph Series No. 4, January 15, 1965, p. 23.

6. John Dornberg, *Brezhnev, the Masks of Power* (New York: Basic Books, 1974), p. 192.

7. The discussion of Libermanism is based on Dornberg, op. cit., pp. 192–193.

8. Donald E. Graves, "The Party and the Government," in Symposium, p. 24.

9. Michel Tatu, *Power in the Kremlin, From Khrushchev to Kosygin* (New York: Viking Press, 1969), p. 436.

10. John S. Reshetar, Jr., *The Soviet Polity, Government and Politics in the USSR* (New York: Dodd, Mead, 1971), p. 226.

CHAPTER 8

THE UNITED STATES AND THE SOVIET UNION: CONCLUSIONS

Although the concluding chapter of this book will review in a comparative framework the four political systems examined in this book, it is necessary to pause here for a brief review and comparison of the American and Soviet systems. The reasons for grouping the American and Soviet systems and the Chinese and Japanese systems were discussed in the preface. Suffice it to say here that the American and Soviet systems reflect a European heritage and are Western in perspective and in general political style. In this light, it may be useful to identify the major similarities and differences between them before we go on to examine the non-Western political systems of China and Japan.

There are many similarities as well as differences between the American and Soviet systems. It is not enough to say simply that one is democratic and the other, communist. Indeed, it is not enough to say that one is nonauthoritarian and the other is authoritarian. Simplistic and absolute delineations between political systems require serious qualification. Nevertheless, the American and Soviet political systems can be compared in

general conceptual terms as a basis for understanding these systems and for serious comparative research.

Returning to the purpose of our comparative approach, we can make general statements regarding the performance of the American and Soviet systems using the conceptual framework in this book: ideology, political actors, power and policy—all from a systems perspective. In addition to the major concern about performance, it may also be useful to ask: Are they becoming like us, or are we becoming like them? A number of Americans as well as Russians have speculated about this particular matter. Obviously, if Americans address the question, we are likely to find one set of questions. If Russians address the question, they are likely to find a different set of questions. In any event, we can draw some conclusions on this matter after we review the two systems in comparative perspective.

Ideology

One of the most important differences between the two systems is ideology. The

Marxist-Leninist-Stalinist ideology of the Soviet Union remains a basis for control by a small elite, perpetuating an oligarchy that is increasingly concerned about its power position and the relevance of the ideology to a changing, modern industrial system. While the ideology is rationalized on the basis of power to the proletariat, it is the party—an oligarchical structure—that exercises power in the name of the proletariat. The ideology provides the rationale for control of government and society by the party. Moreover, the party is the only official organ that has the right to interpret ideology. Thus, a party whose membership represents less than 10 percent of the total population of the Soviet Union has a virtual monopoly of power, determining the direction of the political system and the relationships between the state and the individual.

Moreover, Soviet ideology emphasizes the good of the collectivity. In the name of the state or the proletariat, power is legitimized. There is no concept of responsibility or accountability of officials to the individual. Indeed, the concept of individual rights and liberties is, at best, a minor consideration in the Soviet state.

Preoccupation with ideological relevance is an important characteristic of the Soviet leadership. Thus, there are frequent pronouncements regarding ideology, its application to the current state of domestic and external society, and its legitimizing function. Political actors, policy process, and the application of power are significantly affected because all of these must abide by the ideological principles pronounced by the party. There is little leeway for varying interpretations. Thus, it is the party that establishes the tactical and strategic guidelines for politics within the Soviet system.

In the United States, while there is no particular ideological code or fount of ideological legitimacy, there is a commitment to democratic rules of the game. Such an ideology does not provide the tactical nor even the strategic guidelines and goals for any political system. Rather, it provides a procedure or technique through which goals can be set for the political system. Individual rights and the need to maximize individual opportunity to achieve personal goals are fundamental concerns of the democratic ideology. Moreover, to ensure this maximization of individuality, the power of government is limited and officials are made responsible and accountable to the electorate.[1] In this limitation of governmental power, many groups and institutions outside government have developed power, something relatively unknown in the Soviet Union.

The American democratic ideology inherently perpetuates a heterogeneous society. This heterogeneity and the limitations on government with counterbalancing power outside government are reflected in the political system as a whole. Power is decentralized and diffused within and among various levels of government. Moreover, the nature of the ideology works against the development on an oligarchical structure.

In sum, the Marxist-Leninist-Stalinist ideology stresses the achievement of a particular goal under the direction of an elite who, acting in the name of the proletariat, exercise all power. This group is above the state and the individual. Power stems from the party. The American ideology, lacking distinctive goals or a particular map, stresses limited government, individual rights, opportunity, and political responsibility.

LEGITIMACY

Legitimacy in both political systems rests on perceptions regarding ideology. In the Soviet Union, therefore, political actors must consistently refer to the current interpretations of Marxist-Leninist ideology and justify their actions as being for the good of the collectivity and the socialist state. Moreover, in many instances, legitimacy requires the perpetuation of the Marxist-Leninist ideology on a worldwide scale. What also limits the range of legitimacy is the fact that the party is the interpreter of the ideology. Normally, the leader, such as Brezhnev, interprets the major tenets of the ideology, which are in turn applied by the party bureaucracy.

In the American system, the rules of the game within the general context of democratic ideology eschew a particular path or necessarily a particular interpretation of behavior. Moreover, politics and political power are not restricted to official institutions. Indeed, the ideological propensity to further the pluralistic environment provides a number of ways to acquire power, be they through official or private institutions. The wide range of activities legitimized within the democratic system encourages the development of a wide range of political actors from government institutions to private corporations and community groups. Legitimacy for their action rests on the accepted premise that political activity is legitimate so long as individual rights are respected and violence is avoided.

Obviously ideology and legitimacy do not operate within the political system as clearly as they may appear here. Counter Marxist-Leninist activity under the guise of communist ideology has operated in the Soviet Union (for example, the Liberman concept of economics). Similarly, the whole issue of equal rights and civil rights in the United States precipitated protest demonstrations aimed at violent confrontation, an activity bordering on illegality. Nevertheless, the paramount concern of systems is reflected in the basic tenets of the ideology. It is by reference to these matters that political actors gain legitimacy. In the Soviet Union there is a narrow basis for legitimacy. In the United States, there is a wide-ranging basis for

legitimacy. And in both states the types of political actors reflect these ideological considerations.

The nature of the ideology and the historical heritage are directly linked to the rules of the political game and the types and power of political actors. The dominance of one party in the Soviet Union based on an ideology of power and oligarchical rule considerably limits the role of political actors outside the party. Indeed, the very nature of the Soviet system is a hierarchical, autocratic, bureaucratic corporation which allows little autonomy for groups outside the structure. Not only is the political structure pyramidal, so is the economic structure. The focus on central planning and allocation of resources from a central institution considerably erodes the concept of Soviet federalism. Yet, central planning and a command economy have enabled the Soviet Union to achieve dramatic economic goals and develop into the second industrial nation in the world—within a period of about 50 years.

Political Actors

Political actors have historically been within the party-state bureaucracy in the Soviet system. The economic bureaucracy has also played an important role. Nevertheless, the scope of political activity has always been directed by the party apparatus. Yet, in the post-Stalinist period there are signs that functional groups or interest groups have a larger role to play in the system. Associational and nonassociational groups, such as the intelligentsia and ethnic and religious groups, have developed a potential for affecting the political system. Indeed, there are scholars who see the development of an "interest group" type system with the increasing industrial growth of the Soviet Union and its complex social and economic structure. However, for the immediate future, institutional groups play the major role as political actors, with the party being the dominant one. Thus, intra-party politics and party-state politics remain the major focus of political activity, while other groups are primarily unorganized and latent, operating to a limited degree on the fringes of politics.

In the United States, the broad basis of the ideology and the historical heritage provide a wide field for a number of political actors both in and out of government. Political parties, although important to the political process, are only one type of political actor. Contrary to the situation in the Soviet Union, there has always existed more than one party vying for national power. At the state levels, there have been a number of parties involved in the political arena. While institutional groups play an important role, associational groups and, more recently, nonassociational groups have major roles to play as political actors. Indeed, ethnic associations and professional associations, such as the American Medical Association, are major political actors. The interest group–government linkage has been a consistent characteristic of the American system. Labor unions, for example, have a close tie with the Department of Labor. Similar situations exist at the state and local levels. Thus, there is a diffusion and decentralization of power among many political actors, providing counterbalances to government power. Moreover, the existence of a free press provides and allows the population as a whole to have access to information which, in itself, provides a check to political actors in general. Finally, the role played by the individual, both as a consumer and as a "political being," has the final and most decided impact. The market economy is geared to consumer pressures, while political actors must ultimately receive their sanction from the individual voter, either directly or indirectly.

Although these are significant differences, one should be aware of a number of similarities in political actors. Professional groups, technicians, and managers play a major role in both systems. Given the nature of industrial society, both the Soviet Union and the United States have developed a complex managerial and technical elite. In both systems, this elite seems to have similar outlooks and professional status. Both systems require and have a large bureaucracy, and bureaucracies seem to have similar outlooks and seek similar power positions. In addition, social status and prestige in terms of bureaucracies, professions, technicians, and managers vis-à-vis society develop and perpetuate similar life-styles in both systems.

The fact remains, nevertheless, in the environment of the United States, with its multiplicity of levels of governmental power and its variety of political actors both in and out of the government, there are important counterbalancing forces to the development of any single overpowering political actor. In the Soviet system, even with the existence of political actors similar to those in the United States, the dominance of a single party, the overriding concern for the relevance of the ideology, and the oligarchical structure of the power system mitigate the impact of associational and nonassociational groups. Yet the singular difference in political actors is the role played by individuals. Although in the United States, the individual has minimal impact as a political actor, there are channels outside government which give voice to individual interests. For example, public opinion, elections, and consumer pressures are all crucial elements in the operation of the system. Yet, such things are, at best, rudimentary in the Soviet Union: they do not play an important role in the political process.

Perhaps the role of the individual in the political system of both states is one of the best indicators of the nature of the political system and the kinds of political actors that exist. In the Soviet system, the individual role is clearly subordinated to the bureaucratic party-state structure. Neither in the economy nor in the political system does the individual have an important impact. Decisions as to what is manufactured, where, and how much are made with little reference to the desires of the consumer in the Soviet Union. Although the Soviet Union has accomplished much toward reaching its economic goals, it is noncompetitive, and the productivity of individual workers and farmers does not compare to the productivity of their counterparts in the United States. For example, one American farmer does the work of ten Soviet farmhands, while the productivity of the industrial worker in the Soviet Union is about one-half that of a worker in the United States. Moreover, the poor quality of Soviet goods has become almost legendary. In the economic system, therefore, the individual is but a "cog," responding to a command economy in his roles as worker and consumer.

In the Soviet political system, the individual has little impact on who rules and what policies are made. Indeed, the separation between the rulers and the ruled remains so wide that it has given rise to an attitude most characterize as the we-they syndrome. Part of this is the fatalistic and apathetic attitude of the individual that nothing can be done about the system anyway. This should not, however, obscure the fact that the system enjoys a high degree of legitimacy in the eyes of the individual Soviet citizen and, indeed, that the individual is probably better off now than he has ever been. Nevertheless, political participation is primarily symbolic. Elections do not realistically offer alternatives. Rather, they provide support for the regime and a psychological feeling of having taken part in government. Furthermore, intelligent political activity presumes access to information and the opportunity to organize for political purposes. Both of these conditions do not exist in the Soviet Union. The mass media are

controlled by the party-state leadership and do not perform the important role of informing and providing alternative points of view. Nor do the mass media necessarily provide information regarding internal or external events.

The primary channel for political activity is the party. Because the party is not a mass organization—it represents less than 10 percent of the population—it is difficult for individuals to use these channels. Moreover, most of the party rank and file are viewed as workers, taking orders from above rather than being involved in realistic policy processes and leadership selections, although there appears some movement in this regard in the post-Stalinist era. Nonetheless, organizations, such as trade unions, youth groups, and professions, are under the umbrella of the party. Key party officials are leaders of such organizations and act under party orders.

Equally important, the whole concept of rights and freedoms of individuals and protection under the law is subordinated to the requirements of the state. The ambiguity of the law, the dominance of the party-state bureaucracy, and the need for ideological relevance give the official institutions a major role in determining the role of the individual vis-à-vis the state in the context of the legal system. Throughout the history of the Communist party, constitutionalism has been merely rhetoric and inconsequental to the legal rights of the individual. Since the middle 1950s, however, the surfacing of dissidence among the intelligentsia and the erosion of the relevance of Marxist-Leninist ideology has allowed more flexibility to those outside the party structure. The Soviet Constitution has emerged as a basis for legitimacy. Thus, dissidents claim to act in the name of the Russian Constitution and in defense of the rights of individuals. It is difficult to say how far such constitutionalism will be carried. In the final analysis, the individual remains a subject rather than a citizen; that is, he is allowed to take part in the political process as determined from above and has little voice in affecting policy decisions or who should rule.

In the American system, almost the opposite is true of the individual's role. To be sure, the individual in the American system can do little as an individual. Nevertheless, participation in elections and in the opportunity to organize for political purposes are crucial elements in the individual's relationship to the state. Moreover, his access to a free press and demands for responsibility and accountability of decision makers to the public provide the individual with important levers in affecting the political system. In the economy, the consumer orientation and market forces give the individual an important voice in what is produced, how many, and to what quality standards. Indeed, consumer demands and complaints have led to the organization of various consumer bureaus at all levels of government and to consumer input to corporate decisions. The capitalistic system also has provided the opportunity for individuals to be stockholders and share in the system. This should not obscure the fact that corporate structures completely dominate the individual role in the economy, leading to government regulation and control and to a mixed rather than a free economy. Nevertheless, individual consumer demands play an important role in the production of goods and the making of economic decisions.

Because both states base their governmental structure on the concept of federalism, the ways federalism operates in each system should be compared. The Soviet Union has a constitution that grants broad powers to the constituent states. For example, states can theoretically engage in foreign relations on their own, develop their own armies, and act almost autonomously in many matters. As a matter of fact, Belorussia and Ukraine have their own diplomatic representatives at the United Nations. Yet the fact remains that the Soviet Union is essentially a unitary state. No other conclusion can be reached after examining the party dominance, the party-state relationship, the central economic planning and control, and the ideological environment.

The Communist party of the Soviet Union is a unitary, oligarchical structure that reaches down to the local levels. The Secretariat and the control organs provide the bureaucratic structure to ensure a unified perspective and operation. Moreover, it is the party that determines the ultimate relationship between the states and the center. Given the party-state relationship and the overlapping of membership between the party and state bureaucracy, one can see that the states have little autonomy. This central control is reinforced by the vast bureaucracy that provides a singular unity to the planning, coordination, and operation of the economic system.

Ideologically and psychologically, the states have little basis for developing a realistic federal relationship with the center. Given the nature of power and the role of the party, little power evolves to institutions outside the party. Also, consistent "Russification" militates against developing power and structures outside a purely Russian orientation. Thus, if one expects to go far within the Russian political system, the learning of Russian and the acceptance of Russian culture and values are a necessity, regardless of the non-Russian nationalistic tendencies. Finally, the traditional relationship between the states and the center has been one of subordination. Thus, the experience over the past two generations has been to institutionalize a completely subordinate role for the states in which they act as agents for the center.

In the United States, federalism also does not necessarily operate as intended—but for different reasons. While the states retain much power in a number of fields, including education, police, and welfare, their power has been eroded because of their inability to deal with problems that are interstate in nature. During the early years of the United States, the states did exercise significant power vis-à-vis the national government. However, the growth of the United States as an industrial society and her development into a world power has, as a matter of necessity, subordinated the states in many areas.

Yet the fact remains that significant power is held by local and state authorities. Indeed, there are many areas in which the federal government is effectively subordinated, for example, elementary and secondary education and law and order.

Historically, there have been and still remain limits on the extent of federal power vis-à-vis the state governments in the United States. While the scope of state power has been narrowed, the traditional relationships and political and legal interpretations provide an area of autonomy for state governments. Indeed, it is correct to say that citizens in the United States are realistically citizens of two political systems, the national one and that of their own particular state. And each system has autonomous powers.

Equally important, in the United States, political party activity is most important on the state and local levels. There is no dominant party that controls the entire party process from local to national level. There is no single group that can realistically control one party throughout the national system. Moreover, party power is diffused at the various levels, from local to national, which in turn is further diffused and decentralized by the system of presidential-congressional government. The Congress is essentially a grouping of state representatives whose constituency and power rests with the state.

Even the growth of corporate structures and vast economic operations crossing many state lines has not precluded a significant amount of power diffusion and decentraliza-tion. In more cases than not, the growth of economic enterprises has been accomplished through cooperation with state and local authorities rather than through conspiratorial attempts by corporate structures to acquire power.

As we can see, there is a built-in tension between national and state power in the American system. On one hand, the growth of national government and the large-scale expansion of business enterprises has diminished the power of states. On the other hand, there is a firm constitutional basis for state autonomy which remains at the root of state initiatives and local power. The very nature of the power system in the United States encourages the development of local community groups. Moreover, the system also stimulates the proliferation of ethnic associations, professional groups, and a vast array of voluntary associations.

Similarities between the United States and the Soviet Union with respect to federalism are clearly overshadowed by basic differences. In the final analysis these differences are a result of differences in the ideological orientations and rules of the game in the two systems. Within the Soviet system, the party is the fount of all ideological interpretations and power; in the United States, power resides in the people, flows upward, and is limited at every level. The limits of power are imposed not only by constitutional directive, but also by tradition, custom, legal interpretations, and public expectations. Equally important, the concept of separation of powers provides decentralization of power at various levels of government. At the national level, there are autonomous grants of power to the executive, legislative, and judicial systems. While in both the Soviet and American systems the bureaucracies act semiautonomously, the fact remains that in the American system, bureaucracies share power and are responsible and accountable to elected representatives. No such parallel exists in the Soviet Union, where all power flows out of the Politburo of the Communist party.

Power and Policy

The politics of both the policy process and decision-making procedures differ considerably between the Soviet Union and the United States. Yet, the purpose and, to a lesser degree, the substance of policy are generally similar. That is, both states attempt to respond to the power of political actors and to the expectations of the people. Keeping in mind also that both states are industrial and aim at developing and maintaining a strong industrial capacity and productivity, policies to affect these ends may appear similar in the long run. Yet differences are substantial. Policies in the Soviet Union, for example, are viewed in terms of impact on the collectivity with attention to ideological guidelines. In the United States, the concern varies widely, but is focused primarily on the quid pro quo involved in satisfying the interests of labor, management, bureaucracy, institutional groups, professional groups, and the public. Thus policy process, substance, and impact, although similar in certain respects betweeen the two states, differ in many more important areas, a reflection of the differing ideologies, bases of legitimacy, nature of political actors, and general style within the political system.

The Politburo is the focal point of the policy process in the Soviet Union. Accomplished by means of secret deliberations, the policy process becomes primarily a matter of intra-party politics with little external input. Moreover, this secretiveness makes it difficult for other groups within the party and state bureaucracy to rally legal opposition. Thus, policy is announced from the top to be implemented by the state bureaucracy, which is watched over by the party apparatus. In this respect, it is useful to note that press conferences, public relations, and the entire range of mass media concern so apparent in the United States are completely absent in the Soviet system. The mass media, controlled by the party-state leadership, announce policy and give it support rather than suggesting and discussing alternatives.

The fundamental bases of the Soviet political system—command economy and controlled politics—are thus reflected in the policy process. Policy is made at the top, with primary reference to a closed group, supported by a hierarchical organization perpetuating an oligarchic structure. Yet the policy is affected by ideological considerations and the demands of a growing industrial state, an increasingly affluent society, and a vast backward agricultural sector. The input to the policy process is limited to the party-state bureaucratic structure with the primary input from within the party leadership. It is generally when the party leadership disagrees that external individuals and groups are co-opted into the policy process. While the process is primarily a directed process, there is some need to develop consensus among party-state leaders and the party apparatus if the policy is to be implemented as envisioned by the top leaders.

In the United States, the policy process, in the main, is a wide-ranging political phenomenon involving, at times, many groups —institutional, associational, nonassociational, and spontaneous—and at other times, a small number of bureaucrats. The policy process is not limited to a small group of elite shielded from the inquiries and power of other political actors.

While it is generally accepted that the president is the center of the policy process in the United States, other power centers and political actors can resist presidential power. The mass media, for example, play an important role in publicizing policies and alternative pol-

icy choices. Moreover, presidential control
over the actions of Congress is limited to say
the least. Given the power of Congress not
only over allocation of money, but in its role
as an investigating body, the president is
never free from countervailing forces. On the
other hand, once the president receives a
mandate—vast popular and/or overwhelming
congressional support—he is virtually free to
do whatever he desires. This is something
many Soviet leaders in the post-Stalinist era
undoubtedly seek to achieve in their own
right.

The policy process in the American system
is more accurately described as a conglomerate of subprocesses. That is, a number of political actors form various power clusters trying
to affect the policy process. This may involve a
political battle between groups both in and
out of government, between competing political parties, and within parties. While political actors within the government undoubtedly try to limit the involvement in the policy
process by other political actors, the fact remains that the existence of many power centers, the relative openness of the system, and
the role of mass media make it extremely difficult to remain secretive about the policy
process. Indeed, it is more than likely that
political actors involved in the process seek
the cooperation of other political actors to ex-
pedite policy through the labyrinth of the
bureaucracy and competing interests in order
to reach the presidential-congressional level
as quickly as possible. Thus, two of the most
important distinctions between the Soviet
and American systems are the degree of
openness and the number of political actors
involved. Finally, in the United States, the
policy process is based on consensus building,
while in the Soviet Union, ideological relevance, the status of the leader, and cohesiveness of the party elite are controlling
considerations.

The policy processes of the Soviet Union

and the United States are compared in Figure
8-1.

The Soviet Union is hierarchical, with policy decisions being made within a closely defined and narrow sphere of activity. Decisions
are made at the top, usually within the top
echelons of the party, and transmitted to the
various bureaucracies. In the United States,
however, the policy-making process normally
includes wide-ranging interactions and power
relationships between the president, Congress, and the bureaucracy. Equally important, the process is susceptible to the power of
a variety of interest groups, public opinion,
and the mass media. Rather than a pyramid in
shape, the process generally resembles a rec-
tangle, with major political actors involved in
the process.

In both the Soviet Union and the United
States, domestic policy is primarily concerned
with developing an industrial society. Thus,
there is much concern with education, population skills, proper housing, welfare, and
standard of living. While the concern of the
Soviet leadership is not necessarily focused
on consumers or the person as an individual,
policies that do not provide some material
benefits provoke consumer and individual resistance, although within the system and
rigidly prescribed limits. There is, in this instance, a similarity between the demands of
the Soviet consumer, urban skilled labor, and
professions and similar groups in the United
States. Policies reflect these similarities.

Yet, it should be remembered that the
Soviet focus is on the collectivity and "class"
structure, even though the Soviets do not
admit to having classes. The American system
still takes cognizance of individual rights and
freedoms. Indeed, many of the domestic
policies of the past two decades (for example,
welfare reforms, equal opportunity, civil
rights legislation) were an attempt to respond
to the individuality of the American citizen.

There is an overwhelming concern with the

Figure 8-1: Forces in the Policy Process

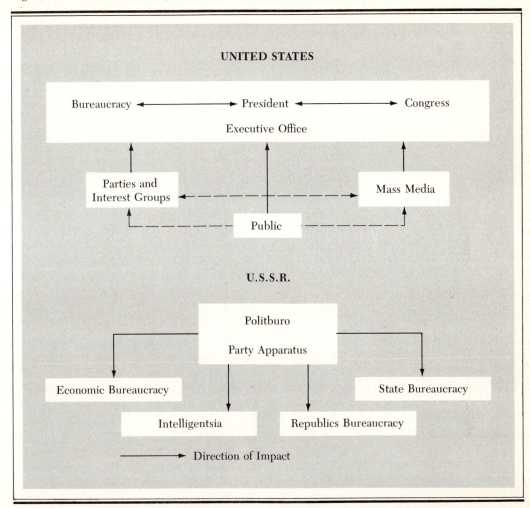

substance of economic policy by the Communist party of the Soviet Union. The reasons are obvious. Economic power, according to Marxist-Leninist ideology, is an important ingredient of political power and ideological relevance. The command economy dictates central planning and implementation. In the mixed economy of the United States, there is government control of some enterprises, and government regulation of others, but a large range of private enterprises are relatively free of control and the individual has an opportunity to become involved in private businesses or a partnerships, or to own stock. Thus, in the United States, there are a number of economic bureaucracies, sometimes competing, other times cooperating, but all operating within the general context of a market economy attuned to the concept of supply and demand.

In noting a main characteristic of the Soviet economic system and, indirectly, the substance and impact of economic policy, one observer states, "It would be difficult, probably impossible to separate decentralization of economic power from decentralization of political power; in Soviet society the two are intertwined. Economic power is a vital lever which helps the Party maintain its 'leading role'!"[2]

Soviet policy is based on a number of basic themes. First and foremost is the concern for ideological relevance according to the Marxist-Leninist concept of political systems and social structure. Thus, policy must always evolve within the framework of the prevailing interpretations of Marxism-Leninism. However, the communist ideology intertwines with the thread of Russian nationalism which stems from the concept of Mother Russia and is part of tsarist heritage. Historically, the Russian peasant has been bound to the soil, nurturing a deep love of the land. This led to a politico-religious symbolism of the state reflected in the close historical relationship between the ruler, the Russian church, and the religious convictions of the peasantry. These politico-psychological factors are also intermixed with policy premises that must account for the demands of industrial society and agricultural efficiency. Moreover, the increasing development of society stimulates changes within the socioeconomic structure developing an increasingly affluent society and intensifying consumer pressures. Thus policy must respond to rather obvious concerns such as housing, welfare, education, hospitalization and pollution. Finally, the Soviet Union is a heterogeneous society consisting of a vast number of non-Russian nationalities, as well as mixtures of Western and Eastern subsystems. Policy must therefore account for the heterogeneity of society, yet the ideology demands a homogeneous political system.

In the final analysis, it is much too simplified to characterize Soviet policy as Marxist-Leninist in context and industrial in substance. Indeed, one must also go beyond the concepts of command economy and controlled political system. There is much in Soviet policy that has evolved from historical considerations and much that is based on Russian nationalism. It is not a simple matter to extract specific policy ingredients from the total policy process.

Policy in the United States is rooted in the almost contradictory concepts of equality and individualism within the context of a general democratic theory. In the main, democratic theory is based on power to and from the people, leading to a number of factors such as official responsibility and accountability. But the commitment to equality and individualism is more difficult to reconcile than the Soviet ideology of equality and the collectivity. In the American system, the concept of equality can ultimately lead to conformity, while individualism can lead to a wide range of human stations in life. Thus policy is generally an attempt to reconcile these conflicting concepts. Yet, in the main, policy has not fallen to radical egalitarianism or aristocratic conservatism. This is another way of saying that policies tend not to support one extreme or the other. Policy is considerably affected by bargaining between groups, as well as within groups, reflecting a wide range of political actors with varying degrees of power.

Like the Soviet Union, the United States policy context is also affected by the demands of a highly industrialized society, increasing affluence, a consumer-oriented economic system, and a society that is increasingly based on goods and services. Policy concerns in the United States are similar to those in the Soviet Union (that is, housing, welfare, education, hospitalization, pollution); but obviously the ideological context, the rules of the game, and the means and ends of policy are unique to the particular system. The Soviet system is based on an oligarchical structure whose major concern is maintenance of power, with a political monopoly by one party. The United States system is fundamentally pluralistic, with realistic political competitive politics and power shifting periodically from one set of political actors to another. Finally, the role of the individual in each system is fundamentally different. The Soviet system is based on the complete subordination of the individual to the party and state. In the American system, the individual remains the focal point of politics and is protected by an impressive array of rights, liberties, and democratic concepts of official responsibility and accountability to the people. This is perhaps the underlying distinction between the two systems and is at the very root of the contrasting political philosophies.

Foreign Policy

The foreign policy process and goals of the two countries reflect the differences in ideology and governmental processes. While in the United States foreign policy is still vulnerable to the pressures of a number of interest groups and a multiplicity of views from within the bureaucracy and from elected officials, in the Soviet Union, foreign policy reflects a monolithic process and perspective. In both countries, however, foreign policy is less susceptible to the pressures of domestic forces. In the United States, the president and his national security staff have a great degree of freedom to identify and implement foreign policy goals. The role of the president as the chief foreign policy maker has not only been reinforced by tradition but has been legalized by the courts. In the Soviet Union, there is no question that only the highest circles of

the party are realistically involved in foreign policy.

The involvement of the United States in World War II was the most significant historical factor in propelling the United States into continual involvement in world affairs. The breakdown of the European world order and the rise of the Soviet Union as a world power were the major factors determining United States foreign policy for over two decades. Indeed, until the early 1970s, United States foreign policy was marked by a cold war syndrome, the legacy of World War II and the nuclear era. Since that time the United States has attempted to help re-establish some type of democratic world order, particularly in Europe. As a result, the United States has become involved in a series of multilateral, bilateral, and international agreements and treaties with the idea of creating order and preserving democracy.

Over the past generation, the emergence of Communist China, the breakdown of the colonial structure, and the development of nuclear technology have created even more difficult problems for United States policy. Historically the European powers have been the colonial powers, perpetuating a world order emanating from Europe. Thus, while a realignment and emergence of new powers was taking place with the breakdown of the colonial structure, the United States was embroiled in its ideological struggle with the Soviet Union. This struggle broadened in scope to include most areas in the world. Compounded by the ever-present danger of nuclear war, these problems have created a series of crises over the past twenty years and have involved the United States in Korea, Lebanon, the Dominican Republic, Cuba, and Vietnam. Moreover, the United States has expanded its economic and military aid extensively and now has numerous links with many noncommunist and some communist countries.

In the most recent period, the policy of détente with both China and the Soviet Union and the preoccupation with international economics and oil have overshadowed the cold war mentality of the 1950s. The space age and the continuing sophistication of nuclear weaponry have broadened the dimensions of international politics. Yet, the United States remains one of the key elements in the world democratic order, both ideologically and economically.

The Soviet Union's reaction in the aftermath of World War II was similar to that of the United States. Convinced of the basically antagonistic nature of capitalism and democracy as practiced in the United States, the Soviet Union embarked on protecting its boundaries in Europe by establishing a system of satellite countries throughout Eastern Europe. At the same time, the Soviet Union attempted to establish some buffer areas in Asia. Major conflicts with the United States in the immediate post-World War II period, however, were in Europe.

Matching the United States nuclear arsenal, the Soviet Union also engaged in economic and military aid to a variety of countries in various regions of the world. With the emergence of Khrushchev, the Soviet Union shifted from a basically antagonistic and threatening relationship with the West to a "peaceful" competitive posture, promoting the idea that the communist system would engulf the West. Diplomatic initiatives were taken throughout the world as the ideological and economic competition with the United States increased.

While there are a number of important post–World War II events that have shaped the foreign policy of the Soviet Union, four appear paramount: the emergence of China as the major Asian communist power, the militancy of the Arab world toward Israel and the entire Middle East situation, nuclear technology and the space age, and the breakdown of the colonial order. While these events were unfolding, the monolithic communist system eroded with the death of Stalin. Thus, while the Soviet Union has gained strength in terms of its own economic and political system, a multicommunist state system has emerged bringing with it a lessened enthusiasm for the Soviets as *the* world leader of communism. The current communist system includes a variety of ideological interpretations and states that refuse to accept dominance by the Soviet Union. The major antagonists in this drama are the Soviet Union and China. Indeed, these two major states are engaged in an ideological (and, at times, military) struggle that overshadows the struggle between the United States and the Soviet Union.

While both countries have attempted to avoid military confrontation, they have pursued policies that best advance their own ideologies. Moreover, the pursuit of foreign policy goals has reflected internal styles, political attitudes, ideological perspectives, and varying goals. Yet both countries now face a world with multicenters of political power, highly nationalistic sentiments, and distrust of "big" power politics. Ideological sentiments are not enough to maintain a cohesive external system in such a world environment.

Both major powers are thus faced with a different world in which other important powers are emerging whose ideology may be distinctly different. Moreover, attempts by both the United States and the Soviet Union to develop a system of friendly states while engaging in intense competition with each other have been marked by ambiguity. There are occasions where cooperation between the United States and the Soviet Union has proven mutually advantageous (for example, in the Middle East). Such cooperation has even taken place between China and the United States (for example, over the Angola issue in 1976).

In sum, the cold war posture of both the United States and the Soviet Union has been replaced by a more accommodating perspective—détente—and a recognition that nuclear war would be mutually destructive. Both countries have also become involved in economic activities, cultural exchanges, and political initiatives with one another, a far cry from the chill of the 1950s. Nevertheless, beneath all of the "friendly" thrusts, the fact remains that the Soviet Union and the United States have arrayed massive destructive nuclear forces against each other. They remain the strongest military and economic powers in the world and are conscious of the needs of their own security and the imperative to follow policies supportive of their own ideological posture. While their policies may coincide from time to time, there is nothing to suggest that the underlying ideological conflict has eased.

CONVERGENCE OR DIVERGENCE?

There is always much speculation from both Soviet and American scholars regarding the question: Are they becoming like us, or are we becoming like them? Answers or discussions of this question inherently involve a comparative perspective and focus on change within political systems. A number of scholars are fond of quoting a comparison between American and Soviet societies first expounded by Mikhail Agurski, who was a Communist Jew purged by Stalin.[3] And it is this view that is the focal point of our brief assessment of covergence or divergence between American and Soviet systems.

According to this theory, American society is depicted as follows:

On the other hand, Soviet society is as follows:

In American society, there is a vast freedom of movement between the walls, that is, within limits of democratic tolerance. The system is also quite stable. On the other hand, in the Soviet system, little if any movement is allowed, and the relative heights of the sides of the structure indicate an inherent instability: a sharp shock could jolt the ball out of place. Many would argue, however, that the Soviet system is quite stable and is viewed as legitimate in the eyes of most Russians. Indeed, if one were to revise the drawing, it is more than likely that the following could be reasonably accepted as a representation of the Soviet system:

There are limits, of course, to how far the Soviet system can widen the area of tolerance. Even with the revised model, it can be seen that there is a great difference between the tolerance of a democratic society, such as that found in the United States, and the Soviet communist system. If indeed the Soviet system were to go beyond certain narrow limits of tolerance, it is likely that the basic ideology and power structure would undergo major change. In this respect, many scholars argue that the Soviet system will probably evolve into a more adaptive system rather than degenerate or collapse.[4]

Summary

In light of the prevailing systems and ideologies in the United States and the Soviet Union, we can only conclude that there is a fundamental contrast between the two systems. While there are a number of similarities primarily associated with the characteristics and imperatives of industrial society, these are not overwhelming in terms of the role of the individual, ideology, and purpose of government. Thus, the convergence theory regarding the future of the two countries is not persuasive in our view. Without fundamental changes in the institutions and value systems in one country or the other, it seems clear that, for the foreseeable future, the United States and the Soviet Union will continue to represent clearly contradictory and distinctive political systems.

In his famous assessment of 19th-century America, de Tocqueville observed,

The American fights against natural obstacles; the Russian is at grips with men. The former combats the wilderness and barbarism; the latter civilization with all its arms. America's conquests are made with the plowshare, Russia's with the sword.

To attain their aims, the former relies on personal interest and gives free scope to the unguided strength and common sense of individuals.

The latter in a sense concentrates the whole power of society in one man.

One has freedom as the principal means of action; the other has servitude.

Their point of departure is different and their paths diverse; nevertheless, each seems called by some secret design of Providence one day to hold in its hands the destinies of half the world.[5]

NOTES

1. Irving Kristol, "The American Revolution as a Successful Revolution," in *The American Revolution: Three Views* (New York: American Brands, 1975), p. 43.

2. Robert G. Kaiser, *Russia, The People and the Power* (New York: Atheneum, 1976), p. 355.
3. See, for example, ibid., p. 173.
4. Zbigniew Brzezinski, "Concluding Reflections," in Zbigniew Brzezinski, ed., *Dilemmas of Change in Soviet Politics* (New York: Columbia University Press, 1969), p. 157.
5. Mayer, J. P., *Alexis de Tocqueville, Democracy in America,* translated by George Lawrence (New York: Doubleday, 1969), p. 413.

Further Readings

UNITED STATES

Abraham, Henry J. *The Judiciary: The Supreme Court in the Government Process.* 4th ed. Boston: Allyn and Bacon, 1977.

America's Continuing Revolution. Introduction by Stephen J. Tansor. New York: Anchor Books, 1976.

Barber, James David. *The Presidential Character: Predicting Performance in the White House.* Englewood Cliffs, N.J.: Prentice-Hall, 1972.

Bernstein, Carl, and Bob Woodward. *All the President's Men.* New York: Simon and Schuster, 1974.

Bone, Hugh A. *American Politics and the Party System.* New York: McGraw-Hill, 1971.

Boorstein, Daniel J. *The Americans: The Democratic Experience.* New York: Vintage, 1973.

Brzezinski, Zbigniew, and Samuel P. Huntington. *Political Power: USA/USSR.* New York: Viking Press, 1969.

Califano, Joseph A., Jr. *A Presidential Nation.* New York: Norton, 1975.

Congressional Quarterly, Inc. *Origins and Development of Congress.* Washington, D.C., 1976.

———. *Powers of Congress.* Washington, D.C., 1976.

Dahl, Robert A. *Democracy in the United States: Promise and Performance.* 3rd ed. Chicago: Rand McNally, 1976.

Greenwald, Carol S. *Group Power, Lobbying and Public Policy.* New York: Praeger, 1977.

Manheim, Jarol B. *Deja Vu: American Political Problems in Historical Perspective.* New York: St. Martin's Press, 1976.

Nie, Norman, Sidney Verba, and John R. Petrocik. *The Changing American Voter*. Cambridge, Mass.: Harvard University Press, 1976.

Ornstein, Norman J., ed. *Congress in Change: Evolution and Reform*. New York: Praeger, 1975.

Patterson, Thomas E. and Robert D. McClure. *The Unseeing Eye: The Myth of Television Power in National Elections*. New York: G. P. Putnam's Sons, 1976.

Peltason, J. W. *Corwin's and Peltason's Understanding the Constitution*. 6th ed. Hinsdale, Ill.: Dryden Press, 1973.

Richardson, Elliot. *The Creative Balance: Government, Politics, and the Individual in America's Third Century*. New York: Holt, Rinehart and Winston, 1976.

Ripley, Randall B. and Grace A. Franklin, eds. *National Government and Policy in the United States*. Itasca, Ill.: Peacock, 1977.

Rourke, Francis E. *Bureaucratic Power in National Politics*. 2nd ed. Boston: Little, Brown, 1972.

———. *Bureaucracy, Politics, and Public Policy*. 2nd ed. Boston: Little, Brown, 1976.

Schlesinger, Jr., Arthur. *The Imperial Presidency*. Boston: Houghton Mifflin, 1973.

Skidmore, Max J. *American Political Thought*. New York: St. Martin's Press, 1978.

Vogler, David J. *The Politics of Congress*. Boston: Allyn and Bacon, 1974.

Wattenberg, Ben J. *The Real America*. Rev. ed. New York: Capricorn Books, 1974.

Zeigler, Harmon L., and Margaret A. Hunt. *Interest Groups in American Society*. Englewood Cliffs, N.J.: Prentice-Hall, 1972.

SOVIET UNION

Allworth, Edward, ed. *Soviet Nationality Problems*. New York: Columbia University Press, 1971.

Armstrong, John A. *Ideology, Politics, and Government in the Soviet Union*. 4th ed. New York: Praeger, 1978.

Aspaturian, Vernon V., ed. *Process and Power in Soviet Foreign Policy*. Boston: Little, Brown, 1971.

Barghoorn, Frederick C. *Politics USSR*. 2nd ed. Boston: Little, Brown, 1972.

Brown, Archie and Michael Kaser, eds. *The Soviet Union Since the Fall of Khrushchev*. New York: Free Press, 1976.

Brzezinski, Zbigniew, and Samuel Huntington. *Political Power: USA/USSR*. New York: Viking Press, 1969.

Dornberg, John. *Brezhnev: The Masks of Power*. New York: Basic Books, 1974.

Gehlen, Michael P. *The Communist Party of the Soviet Union*. Bloomington: Indiana University Press, 1969.

Hollander, Paul. *Soviet and American Society: A Comparison*. New York: Oxford University Press, 1973.

Kaiser, Robert G. *Russia: The People and the Power*. New York: Atheneum, 1976.

Khrushchev, Nikita. *Khrushchev Remembers*. Translated and edited by Strobe Talbott. Boston: Little, Brown, 1970.

Lane, David. *Politics and Society in the USSR*. New York: Random House, 1971.

McLellan, David, ed. *Karl Marx; Selected Writings*. New York: Oxford University Press, 1977.

Morton, Henry W. and Rudolf L. Tokes, eds. *Soviet Politics and Society in the 1970s*. New York: Free Press, 1974.

Osborn, Robert J. *The Evolution of Soviet Politics*. Homewood, Ill.: Dorsey Press, 1974.

Reshetar, John S., Jr. *Government and Politics in the U.S.S.R.* New York: Dodd, Mead, 1971.

Rigby, T. H. *Communist Party Membership in the U.S.S.R.; 1917–1967*. Princeton: Princeton University Press, 1968.

Salisbury, Harrison. *Black Night, White Snow; Russia's Revolution 1905–1917*. New York: Doubleday, 1978.

Sharlet, Robert. *The New Soviet Constitution of 1977; Analysis and Text*. New York: King's Court, 1978.

Skilling, H. Gordon and Franklyn Griffiths, eds. *Interest Groups in Soviet Politics*. Princeton, N.J.: Princeton University Press, 1971.

Smith, Hedrick. *The Russians*. New York: Quadrangle, 1976.

Wren, Melvin C. *The Course of Russian History*. 3rd ed. New York: Macmillan, 1968.

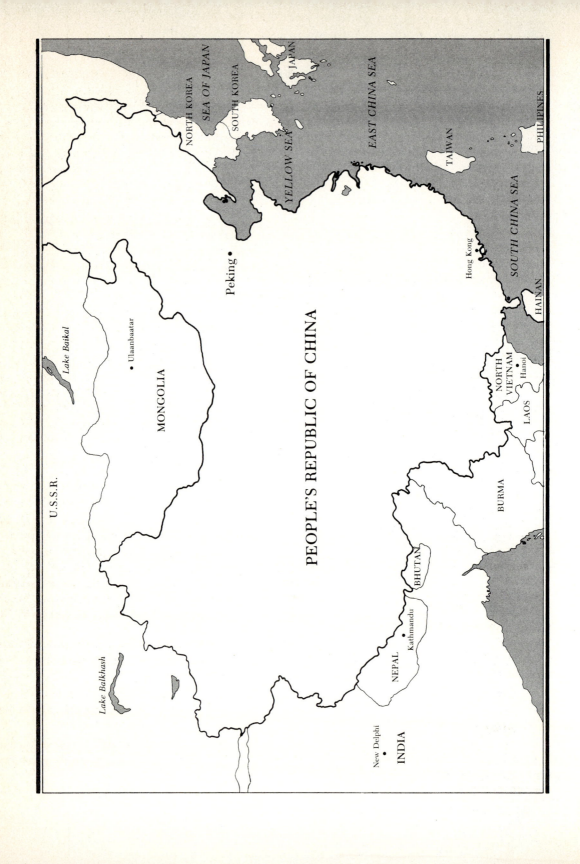

PEOPLE'S REPUBLIC OF CHINA

U.S.S.R.

Lake Baikal

Lake Balkhash

MONGOLIA

Ulaanbaatar

Peking

NORTH KOREA

SEA OF JAPAN

SOUTH KOREA

JAPAN

YELLOW SEA

EAST CHINA SEA

TAIWAN

PHILIPPINES

Hong Kong

SOUTH CHINA SEA

HAINAN

NORTH VIETNAM

Hanoi

LAOS

BURMA

BHUTAN

NEPAL

Kathmandu

New Delphi

INDIA

PART 4 *The Chinese Political System*

CHAPTER 9

CHINA: TRADITION AND MAOISM

From the point of view of the Chinese Communist party, "Ideology alone differentiates Communists from all others in the political marketplace, and ideological principles as interpreted by the Chinese provide the point of departure for their decisions and judgments."[1] The Chinese believe that Maoism, their own particular brand of communist ideology, has reached a higher level of dialectical evolution than the ideology of any other socialist (Communist-led) state, and therefore is superior to all more or less similar ideologies.

The concept of ideology provides a convenient framework in which to consider Maoism and tradition. In a somewhat narrow sense, tradition here means the intellectual ideas that historically powered Chinese society from the Han dynasty (206 B.C.–A.D. 220) until the 20th century. This set of ideas was derived from the selective adaptation of the views of many thinkers into what became known as the Han Synthesis. It has been attributed, perhaps romantically, to the greatest of them all, Confucius. Hence, we shall use "Confucianism" as synonymous with "tradition." Many prefer to regard Confucianism as a system of ethics which guided the organization of Chinese society for over two thousand years, so it is not usual to speak of Confucianism as ideology. Nevertheless, it is appropriate to treat Confucianism as an ideology in the meaning discussed in the introduction to this book.

Tradition: Confucianism

If we were to characterize in one word the Chinese way of life for the last two thousand years, the word would be "Confucian."[2]

The Confucian perception of the world developed in the few centuries preceding the birth of Christ. Crystallized in the Han Synthesis, it was institutionalized in the Chinese state and society over the ensuing centuries. Geographically isolated from other major centers of civilization, China was intellectually isolated from systems of thought and religious currents in other parts of the ancient world. Therefore, Chinese society and its patterns of thought and behavior developed independently with essentially no Western influence.

Confucius (551–479 B.C.) was a contemporary of the early Greek philosophers and of the historical Buddha, both of whom created lasting and influential schools of thought. But probably more than any other individual in history, Confucius has most deeply influenced the thought of more people over a longer period of time.

During the intellectual ferment of the waning years of Chinese feudalism, Confucianism emerged as the dominant of several schools of thought. It sought to find the causes of the collapse of the old political order. In so doing, it reconsidered the broadest possible questions about man—his relationship with other men and the relationship of men to their government—and about "heaven." "Heaven" was not conceived in the Christian sense, but as a comprehensive integrating concept closely related to what we call "legitimacy."

HUMANISM AND THE INDIVIDUAL

The early leaders of the various Confucian schools of thought, although differing one with another in certain premises or assumptions, stressed humanism and development of the individual within the group. This development was in accord with certain desired character attributes. In the common view of things, appropriate self-cultivation of the individual led to harmonious family relations which, in turn, led to harmony and good government at the village and all higher levels of government. Leadership was based on ethics and moral example. If the leader were virtuous, the followers would emulate his virtue. Moral power, not laws, would govern Chinese society.

THE LEGALISTS: ANTI-CONFUCIANISM

This general review of man and government did not go unchallenged in China during the 4th and 3rd centuries B.C. Although Con-

fucianism eventually won out as the dominant and orthodox philosophy, it met its strongest challenge from the Legalist school. The ideology of this school is best summarized in the classic collection of writings titled *Han Fei Tzu*, after its putative compiler, Han Fei (280–233 B.C.). Some major ideas of the Legalists are summarized here not only because that school was the ideological basis of the Ch'in dynasty (221–206 B.C.), but also because the authoritarian, ruler-centered Legalists illustrate an early and continuing alternative to the humanistic Confucian school.

While Confucianists reacted to the warfare and political chaos of their time by developing ideas of morality and ethics, the Legalists reacted by insisting upon the need to preserve and strengthen the state. In one sense, warfare of that time was civil war because it pitted Chinese state against Chinese state; on the other hand, it was interstate warfare in a modern sense when the objective was to defeat, subjugate, and absorb the enemy into one's own domain, albeit in a common continental and cultural setting. The *Han Fei Tzu* was a handbook for the ruler written in a time of political chaos. It gave guidance for the conduct of interstate relations when force ruled, and outlined techniques for domestic control. Perhaps it was, after all, better suited than Confucianism to an understanding of the ruthless pursuit of self-interest carried on by feudal lords of that day.

The Virtue of Law The Legalists had neither use nor respect for ancient customs and "professed to have no use for morality whatsoever."[3] *Han Fei Tzu* scorned the humanism of Confucius and other scholars, inveighing against their worship of ancient sages and their impracticality and contradictions, and referring to their teachings as "stupid or deceitful." The Legalist ruler does not lead by moral example nor does he expect people to do good of themselves. His technique is do whatever is necessary to prevent people from doing evil, so he "does not busy himself with morals but with laws," laws severe in their sanctions and applied equally to all.

The Legalist ruler considers ignorant those who say good government will come when the ruler is able to "win the hearts of the people." The intelligence of the people, wrote Han Fei, is "not to be relied on any more than the mind of a baby." The worth of the individual could be found only in his value to the state or to the ruling class.

The Preservation of the State   Now the Legalists were interested in domestic stability and preservation of the state. An orderly state could be maintained by supporting men of integrity and character and by eliminating the "five vermin" of the state. These vermin included scholars who cast doubts on the "law of the age," the "itinerant speakers" who used foreign influence and deceptive arguments for selfish purposes, the "free-lance fighters" who would challenge the state, "courtiers" who corrupted officials and sought to avoid military service, and tradesmen and craftsmen who dealt in inferior goods and took advantage of the peasantry. In other words, those who opposed the state or detracted from its welfare or threatened its stability had to be silenced. Ideological conformity was a major tenet of state policy.

Power as the Goal   The dominant goal of the Legalist system was enhancement of its own power. Major policies to support this goal were quite similar to those adopted by much more recent and "modern" totalitarian societies. For instance, the four methods to maintain domestic order included encouraging the peasant to till the land to provide a strong economic base for the agrarian society, levying taxes in cash and in grain to provide against famine and to support the army, and

using severe penalties to ensure compliance with the law. Finally, the Legalist sovereign must insist on a strong army based on universal military service. Those engaged in pursuits not essential to the state were to be eliminated along with the dysfunctional "five vermin."

The ideas of the Legalists as systematized by Han Fei were adopted in practice by the feudal state of Ch'in, which emerged as the unifying dynasty in 221 B.C. This dynasty lasted a scant fourteen years, but its impact on China was both revolutionary and enduring. It was revolutionary because it completed the destruction of feudalism which had begun centuries earlier. The feudal land tenure system gave way to the buying and selling of land, serfs became free peasants who could sell their labor, and traditional ceremonies and obligations fell into disuse. Newly acquired territories were not redistributed as fiefs, but incorporated into the state as lesser administrative subdivisions subject to centralized control. These and other fundamental changes under the Ch'in (which is the source of our name for China) transformed China into a centralized unitary state. Under the subsequent Han dynasty, this state was administered by a bureaucracy selected on merit. The impact of the Ch'in was enduring in the institutional sense, because the centralized unitary bureaucratic state, despite many ups and downs, was the model for Chinese political organization into the 20th century.

The End of Legalism   In a quite different way, the memory of the Ch'in dynasty has endured in the Chinese consciousness. The Legalist system ultimately failed to satisfy the needs of the people and could not, by even the harshest methods, stamp out opposition. Attempts to control the people by "enacting laws and harsh penalties" failed, and Legalist policies were "discredited for centuries to come." The Ch'in dynasty came to symbolize "evil and oppression in Chinese history" and to serve as an example of the fate of rulers who substitute "force and tyranny" for humanity and justice.[4]

With the overthrow of the Ch'in dynasty, the new rulers turned to Confucianism as the ideological basis for the state. Over the succeeding few centuries, the Han dynasty erected a political and ideological edifice which endured as the official orthodox philosophy of government until the establishment of the People's Republic in 1949. Although the Confucian ideology was frequently violated in practice, it remained the ideal of Chinese society.

Both Confucianism and its antithesis, the Legalist school, evolved in the intellectual quest for solutions to the problems manifest in the political chaos attendant on the decline and fall of the previous dynasties, problems of war, hunger, injustice, and man's relation to his government. Let us now examine some of the ideas of Confucian ideology and outline the means by which social order could be brought out of chaos.

THE SUPERIOR MAN

Like Plato, Confucius would have sages be kings, and government administrators be "superior men" *(chün-tzu)*. The concept of the superior man is central to the Confucian ideal. This ideal is rooted in government by man, not by laws; and not government by any man, but by men schooled in the Confucian Classics. The ideal of the superior man was applied to the intellectual elite (literati) and their associates, the landlords, bureaucrats, and military men who governed China. The three lower classes (peasants, artisans, and merchants) were to be led by moral example and by the virtue of the fulling class. So even in the earliest times, Chinese society was roughly divided into the two classes, the rulers and the ruled.

The superior man could be developed through education. Education consisted essentially of mastery of the texts of the several works which constituted the so-called Confucian Classics, the main corpus of Chinese learning. The ancient Chinese approach to learning was not analytic or scientific, nor was it inquiring in the Western sense. It was essentially pragmatic, intuitive, synthetic, ethical in tone, socially group-minded, and historical, if anecdotal, in content.

Models to guide the conduct of the individual or to explain man's relationship to other men and government could be found in the study of the ancient sages. Confucius wrote in *The Analects* that he simply transmitted what was taught to him, adding nothing of his own. His purpose, then, was not so much to impart knowledge; rather, it was more to inculcate moral principles, form character, and transmit intact the great tradition of the past. Mencius, who lived about a century after Confucius and stands second only to Confucius among the ancient greats, amplified this view, saying, "Follow the rule of the Former Kings, and it is impossible that you should go wrong."[5] To the Confucianist, the past was perfect.

HARMONIOUS SOCIETY

The goal of traditional Confucian teaching was a frictionless, harmonious society led by men of virtue. Confucius himself finessed the question of man's ultimate nature, that is, whether man is inherently good or evil. Perhaps for this reason, some of his followers divided on this point which, at least to Westerners, is essential. While some held man's nature to be inherently good, others advanced the opposite point of view. Interestingly enough, these opposing points of view led to the same conclusion; namely, that man could be improved by right learning, was educable and hence perfectible. What Confucius did emphasize was a basic egalitarianism: all mankind may not be equal by inheritance, but all men possess a basic moral equality. Until his time, the "superior man" was a man of good birth, whose ancestors ranked above the common herd. No man of mean origins could aspire to that rank. Confucius insisted that the superior man was entitled to that appellation solely on the basis of his virtue and that no man was so entitled solely on the basis of birth. Theoretically, then, careers (as scholar-officials) were open to men of talent, but the advantages lay with sons of scholars and the wealthy. Nevertheless, upward mobility based on merit was another ideal of Confucian ideology, and peasant sons entered government often enough to maintain the vitality of this ideal.

Humanity, too, is central to Confucian ideology and to the development of the superior man. Humanity consists, in one formulation, of five virtues. The man who is courteous is never humiliated, he who is magnanimous wins the multitude, he who is of good faith wins the trust of the people, the diligent man attains his objective, and he who is kind can get service from the people. Without these characteristics, "a man cannot long endure adversity, nor can he for long enjoy prosperity."

The superior man could be created, it was believed, by inculcation of these attributes, and only he who possessed them was fit to rule. What other type of man could have the vision to see beyond personal profit to the broader interests of mankind?

Most early Confucianist writings seem to lack coherent structure and tend to be composed of parable-like anecdotes from history and of aphorisms suggesting the crystallized folk wisdom of earlier centuries. But the classic, *The Great Learning*, outlines the process by which a harmonious and peaceful world can be achieved:

The ancients who wished clearly to exemplify virtue throughout the world would first set up good government in their states. Wishing to govern well their states, they would first regulate their families. Wishing to regulate their families, they would first cultivate their persons. Wishing to cultivate their persons, they would first rectify their minds. Wishing to rectify their minds, they would first seek sincerity in their thoughts. Wishing for sincerity in their thoughts, they would first extend their knowledge. The extension of knowledge lay in the investigation of things. For only when things are investigated is knowledge extended; only when knowledge is extended are thoughts sincere; only when thoughts are sincere are minds rectified; only when minds are rectified are our persons cultivated; only when our persons are cultivated are our families regulated; only when families are regulated are states well-governed; and only when states are well-governed is there peace in the world.[6]

The development and flowering of the individual must arise from education. "By nature, men are pretty much alike," said Confucius, "it is learning and practice that set them apart. Virtue and ability cannot be left to chance, so tradition held there ought to be some education for all (ability does not depend on birth) and profound education for the few capable of absorbing and applying it. The state is a cooperative enterprise, and it cannot be effective and harmonious unless understood and supported by its citizens.

THE FAMILY AND THE INDIVIDUAL

In the Confucian scheme of things, the family was the basic unit of social organization. For the individual, "virtue is to love men," and this love began with the family. Its foundation lies in filial piety, the love, reverence, and respect of the child for the parent. Unfilial conduct was the most serious of crimes, and in the *Book of History*, the Duke of Chou declared the unfilial and unbrotherly worse than thieves and murderers. Confucius seems to have regarded filial piety as a social duty as well as a family duty, but he gave priority to the family.

As a microcosm of the political order, the family stressed that each member had his own place and his own role. Like each citizen of the state, if each family member knew his duty and fulfilled his obligations, the social order would be secure. The basic family relationships, which probably had their origins in the family as the basic economic unit of China's ancient agrarian pre-Confucian past, are expanded and universalized in *The Mean:*

There are five relationships which concern all men and three virtues by which they are fulfilled. The relationships of ruler and subject, father and son, husband and wife, older and younger brother, and of intercourse between friends—these five are the relationships which pertain to all men, knowledge, humanity and courage—these are the three virtues which apply to all men, and that by which they are practiced is one . . . [7]

Clearly three of the five Confucian relationships are purely familial, but all five become familial if one conceives of the state as an extended family embracing all of society. The ruler is the father and the subjects, his sons; friends become brothers to all men; all men become friends.

Two important observations are derived from this discussion. Chinese society rested on the subordination of the individual to a complex, hierarchical, patrilineal, male-dominated family system ideologically supported by, and in practice strongly supporting, the Confucian tradition. The second observation is that this system inculcated in all Chinese a profound feeling for the past and deep sense of cultural continuity in a system that did not encourage change or the seeking

of alternative models of social or political organization.

These entirely too brief sketches of the goals of self-cultivation and social integration of Chinese society lead us to the subject of how the traditional Chinese related to nature and to government.

Man and Government

The integrating concept is the triad of heaven, earth, and man: "Heaven has its seasons; earth has its resources; man has his government."

The operation of heaven is timeless and unchanging. The revolutions of the stars, the alternation of the seasons, all things in nature occur in harmony with their cycle of growth and decay. The causes of this are not knowable, but the results are visible. Man, therefore, must use the resources of earth in harmony with the cycles of heaven.

Man is responsible for proper harmony between heaven's seasons and earth's resources; ultimately man's government embodied in the person of the ruler bore this responsibility. The ruler's role is symbolized in the written Chinese character for king *(wang)*, which consists of the three parallel horizontal lines, representing heaven, earth, and man, and a vertical line which joins the three principles. The king is the intermediary between heaven's seasons and earth's resources and regulates for man the harmonious functioning of all things.

THE MANDATE OF HEAVEN

The emperor's legitimacy—his right to rule—depended on his virtue, on his righteousness. When righteousness prevails in the world, wrote Mo Tzu (470–391? B.C.), there is order. When righteousness does not prevail, there is chaos. Now the son of heaven (emperor) is entrusted with this standard, but he takes it from heaven and causes it to be applied throughout the social and political hierarchy. The function of the ruler, then, was to harmonize man's activities with the unchanging cycles of nature. Failure to do so would bring calamity—flood, drought, famine—sure evidence that the ruler lacked the virtue to rule, and hence was unfit to bear the "mandate of heaven." The evidence of unfitness became more clear when natural calamities coincided with, or were basic causes of, deficiencies in the administrative system, such as inability to collect taxes; failure to maintain such public works as transportation, irrigation, or flood control facilities; or the incapacity to maintain public order throughout the empire or to repulse barbarians on the border.

The mandate of heaven justified and required government by moral prestige, and the emperor was the exemplar of that morality. Although his authority was theoretically absolute, it necessarily was carried by a central government bureaucracy which staffed the ministries in the capital and provided administrative leadership in the provinces and districts, leaving considerable autonomy at the village level. These administrators were the cream of the literati in China, a meritocratic corps d'élite whose entry to government service was attainment of the highest calling in traditional China. Selection for entry was based on mastery of the Confucian orthodoxy. These scholars made the empire their own and, while reverencing the emperor, simultaneously served as a check on potential excesses inherent in an "absolute" imperial system. The requirement for the emperor to act in accordance with the mandate of heaven provided the ideological basis for restraint of the emperor. The emperor remained the focus of the entire hierarchy of society and the harmonizer of man and nature. But he was not indispensable. When dynasties crumbled,

the mandate of heaven provided the ideological rationale for the overthrow of his dynasty and provided simultaneously legitimization of his successor, who, by definition, had demonstrated the virtue necessary to rule.

But this doctrine was not a sanction for revolution in the sense that revolution entails fundamental changes in the political, social, and economic organization of a society. It was, rather, justification for a revolt against a ruler who did not "complete the way" in a Confucian sense. Its objective was not change in an innovative way, but change to ensure harmony with the traditional way of doing things. In other words, it was "restorationist," not "revolutionary."

Of course what has been treated here as the Confucian view of things was not, at any given time, an accurate perception of reality. Throughout its long history, China experienced good government along with the bad; it suffered despots, albeit unwillingly; famine, hunger, and warfare were not done away with; the material well-being and security of the people were not always provided for. Nevertheless, the Confucian tradition was never seriously threatened as the orthodox state philosophy, and it remained the Chinese ideal for more than 2,000 years. Confucianism developed over centuries, undergoing changes wrought by new interpretations, competition with opposing or variant schools of thought, and always subject to changing times and man's perception of these changes. It did present a generalized, yet coherent, view of how things *ought* to be, and provided a prescription of how to change the world from what it was to what it should be. Confucianism further satisfies our earlier definition of ideology by supplying the values through which the normative goals could be achieved. The "Confucian ideology" has been the "most successful of all systems of conservatism," writes America's pre-eminent Sinologist, John King Fairbank. He adds, "Nowhere else have the sanctions of government power been based for so many centuries upon a single consistent pattern of ideas attributed to one ancient sage."[8]

The Dynastic Cycle

Before turning to a discussion of the transition from Confucianism to Maoism, let us see how Chinese historians have conceived of change during China's long history. The dynastic cycle is the major interpretive theme in the successive rise and fall of various hereditary ruling families who exercised political control over all of China, or over its most important areas. In briefest outline, the cycle of a given dynasty was seen to follow through in this way: a strong capable man (at times from the peasantry) seized power by military force and brought to the people internal peace and prosperity; in time the ruling family lost its vigor; administrative efficiency decreased because the ruler showed favoritism to those who were incapable, and corruption and effeteness came to characterize the government. On the economic side, the early ease of tax collection and efficient allocation of resources for civil works and defense was replaced by difficulties arising from withdrawal of land (the chief source of government revenues in the agrarian society) from the tax base. Land was withdrawn to be placed at the private disposal of members of the imperial family or their favorites; and as central government efficiency lessened, those who could escape from the exactions of the capital did so. Progressively, the increasing needs of the capital had to be satisfied from the decreasing tax base, and the peasants were forced to pay the price for imperial luxury and maladministration. Peasant revolts were a frequent result.

A lack of attention to defense requirements invited probes and aggression by non-Chinese groups on the borders of China. Failure to spend adequate funds to maintain civil works for irrigation and flood control invited agricultural disasters in north China where rainfall is always marginal and flood is often devastating. When the old regime had been weakened sufficiently by a concatenation of inept leadership, dwindling tax resources, ineffective military forces, peasant revolt, and natural disasters, some new leader emerged to initiate once more a dynastic cycle.

CONFUCIAN PERCEPTIONS

Two observations can be made about the dynastic cycle interpretation of China's history. In all instances of the alternation of dynasties, the new dynasty found its model and values in the past as perceived through the lens of Confucian ideology. In this sense, it was conservative, pessimistic, and did not look to the development of new forms of government, new values, or new group attitudes when time-tested values were successful and available. The cyclic view can be contrasted with the liberal and optimistic Western view of man's development as a kind of linear progression, with regressive periods to be sure, but generally the trend was onward and upward to a better life. Modern Chinese acceptance of Marxist-Leninist views has required a reversal of the traditional cyclical view of history.

YIN AND YANG

The second observation is that the recurring rise and fall of dynasties can be explained in the Chinese terms of *Yin* and *Yang*, the two opposites (passive and active, negative and positive, female and male, moon and sun, decay and growth) which describe the ebb and flow of all natural phenomena in their cycles, but which also are the two components of the Great Unity. Hence, Chinese traditionally perceived the world and man's affairs in terms of this "unity of opposites. The cycle of dynasties was unity-disunity-unity. Maoist doctrine insists on unity-struggle-unity. These ideas are not far different from thesis-antithesis-synthesis and Marx's application of these ideational terms to the real world as dialectical materialism.

The Transition from Tradition to Maoism

The transition from Confucian ideology as the orthodox state philosophy to its replacement by Maoism (Mao Tse-tung Thought) extends over a complex period in China's history. This period, roughly from the 1830s to the establishment of the People's Republic of China in 1949, was, in the Chinese view, "a century of humiliation." It is also the story of how Chinese leadership reacted to external pressures from an expansionist and imperialist Europe, Japan, and the United States, and to internal pressures traditionally seen as part of the decline of a dynasty. The Chinese responded in a variety of ways. First they doggedly maintained the traditional Chinese attitude that Confucianism was superior to all other philosophies and resisted all Western encroachments. Later they sought, with minor successes, to integrate Eastern ethics with Western technology. In 1911 the dynasty succumbed to a variety of pressures, and a representative parliamentary government emerged temporarily. In the 1930s and 1940s, the Chinese Communist party developed a coherent ideology with concrete programs and established itself as an alternate government controlling a significant portion of China's people and territory. By 1949 Chinese Communist armed forces had driven the republican government from power and established the People's Republic of China.

THE MANCHU DYNASTY

By 1800 China had been ruled for more than 150 years by the alien Manchu conquerors. Despite the outward splendor and stability of the dynasty, the dynastic cycle was well into the period of decay. Population had increased markedly in relation to available resources. The government was losing its ability to rule effectively. Confident of its cultural superiority, China rejected Western overtures to expand trade beyond the traditional trade center at Canton and refused diplomatic relations with European countries, which claimed they wished to deal with China on an "equal" footing, but which, in actuality, sought all kinds of privilege.

In the face of superior Western military technology, China was forced to capitulate and was opened to a veritable flood of alien influences. Diplomatic relations were established with several countries which set up the Treaty Port system, provided for most-favored-nation treatment, extraterritoriality, and other measures that disrupted China's pattern of economic and cultural self-sufficiency.

These actions eroded the literati's belief in Confucian superiority which underlay and justified this autarky. China was forced against its will outwardly to discard traditional ideas of the world and to deal with Western concepts of an international order theoretically composed of equal coordinate states. But it was all too clear to the Chinese that this system placed China in inferior status. The unequal treaties were their proof.

The T'ai P'ing Rebellion   These Western encroachments coincided with the devastating T'ai P'ing Rebellion (1850–1864) which had its origin in increasing peasant discontent (there was a significant rebellion somewhere in China during each of the ten years preceding), the humiliation of the Opium War with

England (1841–42), the absence of any abstract loyalty of the Chinese rebels to the state and its Manchu rulers, Peking's lack of timely information about developments in south China's coastal areas, and the congruence of these circumstances with the emergence of a charismatic leader using a distorted version of Christianity to support his call for establishment of a Heavenly Kingdom of Peace on earth. After fourteen years, the movement collapsed from administrative ineptitude, the senseless destructiveness of its troops, the corruption of its leadership, and its inability to win over the Confucian literati. Peking re-established order, but the rebellion had cost 20 to 40 million lives.

The near success of the T'ai P'ing Rebellion showed the ineptness of the regime in dealing with a combination of events characteristic of the dynastic decline and the intrusion of an alien ideology. A new and vigorous conservative leadership asserted itself in Peking in the early 1860s and sought to "restore" the traditional order. It succeeded in defeating the rebels and revitalizing moral leadership and tried to administer the state on Confucian principles. For the next generation, Chinese leaders devoted their efforts to the "self-strengthening" movement. They believed that a combination of Chinese ethics and tradition and Western technology could somehow strengthen and "modernize" China, fend off the Western imperialists, and assure China of its proper place in the world. The idea was basically unworkable: the literati were too successful in their conservatism and impeded "modernizing" change. The traditional disdain for business and contempt for the profit motive prevented significant industrial development. Western technology, machines, and gunboats "had their own philosophy."

The Collapse of the Dynasty   In 1894–95 the Sino-Japanese War was fought for control of Korea. Contrary to the expectations of West-

erners, who still stood in awe of China's civilization, Japan won easily, and China soon came to be regarded as the "sick man of Asia." Russia, England, France, Germany, Japan, and others rushed in to carve up the Chinese melon by reserving their own spheres of influence. In 1898, younger Chinese leaders attempted the wide-ranging "100 Days Reform," but it too failed to relieve China's distress. With the support of the Manchu court controlled by the Empress Dowager Tz'u Hsi, the Boxer Rebellion of 1900 threatened the lives and property of foreigners, but it was quelled by an 8,000-man combined expeditionary force of foreigners who occupied Peking. Thereafter, disintegration of the Confucian state accelerated.

THE REPUBLIC OF CHINA

The Manchu dynasty collapsed in 1911 and was replaced by a group of nationalistic revolutionaries led by Dr. Sun Yat-sen. They established the Republic of China, meant to be a Western-style parliamentary republic. It soon foundered, partly because the Chinese were unprepared to use such a system, but mainly because the new government could not control the provincial military leaders. Centralized control was really never established, and in a few years a decentralized pattern of control of China by regional military commanders emerged and was aptly named the Warlord Era (1916–1928).

Despite taking part in World War I as one of the Allies, China refused to sign the Versailles Treaty because Japan was given Germany's former sphere of influence in Shantung. This blatant disregard of China's sovereignty, as well as the accumulated humiliation and shame of the unequal treaties, sparked the riots of May 4, 1919. This nationalistic denunciation of foreigners later grew into the May Fourth Movement, which stands out as a watershed date in Chinese history because of the impact it had on the social, literary, and economic aspects of Chinese life.

The Kuomintang and the Communists   Unable to assert control in Peking, a minority of the parliamentarians established a rival regime in Canton in 1921 with Sun Yat-sen as president. Sun's Nationalist party (Kuomintang) sought and received advice from the young Soviet regime. The Soviet communists provided money, some arms, and the organizing talents of Comintern agents, who left their imprint on the Kuomintang, clearly modeled on the Communist party of the Soviet Union. A faithful military advisor to Sun, Chiang Kai-shek, was chosen to develop the Kuomintang armed forces, and when Sun died in 1925 without having gained control of China, Chiang assumed leadership of the Nationalist party.

Chiang moved quickly to unify China by military force. He drove the Communists into hiding, and by 1928 formally ended the warlord regime in Peking. In fact, however, Chiang was never able to consolidate his power throughout China. He was unable to destroy the core of the Chinese Communist party. Some provincial governors retained considerable autonomy. China still suffered unequal treaties, and Japan was always a threat to China's territorial integrity. Nevertheless, the KMT achieved some remarkable results. China was unified for the first time in two decades. The armed forces were improved. The Kuomintang introduced many modern techniques into the economic infrastructure and drafted a constitution designed to establish a democratic government when conditions were right for it.

The failure of Sun's Nationalist party to achieve its goals of a unified democratic republic, totally sovereign and internationally respected, can be ascribed to several internal and external factors. Internally, the remnants of the Chinese Communist party regrouped in south China in the late 1920s and there established the Kiangsi Soviet, a self-sufficient base area defended by Communist troops. The Kuomintang undertook five "annihilation campaigns," and yet failed to defeat their enemy. The Communists withdrew to Yenan (1934–35) on the famous 6,000-mile Long March, there to establish another base area from which to make their claim to lead China. Externally Japan continued its policy of the 1890s: to prevent the emergence of a strong China. The Japanese army stationed in Manchuria, without the knowledge of the Japanese Foreign Ministry or even its own military superiors in Tokyo, created an incident in 1931 and swiftly carried out well-developed plans to seize Manchuria by force. China was powerless to retaliate, and the League of Nations was impotent. So Manchuria was detached from China in 1933, and the "independent" Empire of Manchukuo was established under the actual control of the Japanese army. In this time of troubles, the Kuomintang reacted in the traditional way by appealing to Confucian morality to revitalize Chinese society.

Japanese Invasion   Japan initiated all-out aggression against China in 1937, and the Kuomintang was forced to withdraw to the interior to fight for its life. During the Sino-Japanese War (1937–1949), Sun's Nationalist party was nominally allied with the Chinese Communist party in a united front against Japan, but it was the Kuomintang that bore the main burden of combat and suffered the major losses of territory, people, resources, and industry. The Nationalist-Communist united front was not regarded by either side as anything more than a temporary accommodation so long as the survival of both was threatened by Japan. Chiang's view of the dual threat to his government is clear from his remark that Japan was a cancer of the skin, but the Communists were a "cancer of the soul."

The Allied victory over Japan in 1945 was

not a victory for the Kuomintang. In short order, the Chinese Communist and Nationalist forces became entangled in a massive civil war from which the Communists emerged in 1949 as the sole de facto government on mainland China. The Nationalist leadership was defeated by the effective organization and superior military capabilities of the Chinese Communist forces, and also because of their own strategic military errors, their inability to deal with the wartime and postwar inflation, governmental corruption, repressive measures that turned the people against them, and because they offered no hope for better things. The Nationalist government and remaining armed forces escaped to Taiwan to re-establish the Republic of China. For many years it was generally recognized internationally as the *de jure* government of China, but its international status has decreased markedly since its expulsion from the United Nations in 1972. Most nations of the world now recognize the People's Republic of China as the legitimate government of China.

Maoism

The "Revolution of 1911," the overthrow of the Manchu dynasty and the establishment of a parliamentary republic in 1912, was essentially a conservative phenomenon. Its ideology called for the trappings of Western governmental institutions combined with Sun's principles of people's nationalism, people's democracy, and people's livelihood. Ultimately, as their words and actions demonstrated, Sun and his heir, Chiang Kai-shek, both sought to preserve traditional Confucian ethics and the social system on which they rested. Yet others desired radical change for China, and the Russian Revolution of 1917 showed the way. A variety of leftist groups appeared in Shanghai and Peking, and

the leaders were professors and students, heirs to the tradition that the literati should lead. The Chinese Communist party was formally organized by twelve Chinese in Shanghai in July 1921.[9]

THE RISE OF THE COMMUNIST PARTY

This section recounts the history of the Chinese Communist party up to its seizure of power in 1949 by military victory over the Nationalist party, outlines the Chinese Communist ideology in its major tenets, and essays a comparison of tradition and Maoism. From the outset, the Chinese Communist party committed itself to the overthrow of the capitalist classes, "to enter upon the battlefield with the world workers who protect the proletariat motherland—Soviet Russia," to join the Comintern, to have a "serious, centralized disciplined organization," and to be communist in speech and action.[10] During the period of the First Revolutionary Civil War (1921–1927), the Chinese Communist party was a numerically small conspiratorial group, closely tied to Comintern. At the Third Party Congress (1923), the Chinese Communist party decided to enter the First United Front with the Kuomintang, which was then reorganized by the Comintern agent Michael Borodin. Kuomintang membership was open to any Chinese Communist party member who would swear allegiance to the Kuomintang, and Chou En-lai and Mao Tse-tung both had posts in the Kuomintang organization. During Chiang Kai-shek's military movement to the north in 1927 the Russian advisors and members of the Chinese Communist and Nationalist parties were expelled.

The First Revolution   The Chinese Communist military forces tried to seize control in the August uprising at Nanchang, but Chiang suppressed the rebellion ruthlessly. Thousands were killed and sizable Communist-led organizations, such as labor unions and the Communist Youth League, were disbanded. Defeated everywhere, the Communist forces infiltrated into the Chingkangshan area (May 1928) to form the Fourth Red Army. The Comintern-directed policy of cooperation with the Kuomintang aimed at seizure of power from within had failed. Thereafter the Chinese Communist party was no longer simply a conspiratorial group seeking to seize state power.

The Second Revolution   During the early part of Second Revolutionary Civil War Period (1927–1937), the Chinese Communist party initially placed itself outside the reach of Nationalist military power, established Chinese soviets in central-south China, worked to improve its own military forces, and experimented with carrying out an agrarian revolution. Leading party elements insisted, as did Soviet ideology, that the way to power was through control of the urban proletariat and armed uprisings in the cities, the so-called Li Li-san line, advocated by that leader of the Political Bureau of the Central Committee. On the other hand, Mao and other leaders of the Kiangsi Soviet pursued their own policy of self-strengthening and brought about, in 1930, the renunciation of the Li Li-san line and his removal from office. Once more the Moscow perception of conditions in China was deemed erroneous.

Although the Kuomintang effectively suppressed the urban activities of the Chinese Communist party, the Fourth Army avoided defeat in Kiangsi and escaped to Yenan. En route an important conference took place at Tsunyi in Kueichow province. Here Mao formally assumed leadership of the Chinese Communist party, his opponents were removed from leading positions, and the decision was made to combat the Japanese who had already incorporated Manchuria into

their empire and were threatening all of north China.

The War of Resistance   The War of Resistance against Japan began with Japan's open aggression against China in July 1937. By the summer of 1938, the Japanese had penetrated as deeply into China as at any time during the eight-year war. Wang Ching-wei, former leader of left-wing Kuomintang, was now Japan's puppet leader of occupied China. The Kuomintang had been driven into the Szechwan Basin in central China; the Chinese Communist party occupied areas of northwest China and had its headquarters in Yenan.

Communist policy for this period was clear. Defeat of Japanese imperialism, because it was a prerequisite to continuation of the revolution, took precedence over seizure of government power. Yet the Chinese Communist party would act independently and autonomously when necessary.[11] In his speech on the "Problems of War and Strategy,"[12] Mao said, "Every Communist must grasp the truth: 'Political power grows out of the barrel of a gun, but the Party must always control the gun.'" Mao's strategy was to accumulate power through guerrilla warfare to prepare for regular warfare, which alone could decide the anti-Japanese campaign. The goal of this strategy (New Democracy) was to destroy China's "colonial, semi-colonial and semi-feudal politics, economy and culture."[13]

This Second United Front (the Communist-Nationalist cooperation against Japan) never had the highest priority for either the Nationalist or the Communist party. It collapsed when the Kuomintang attacked the Communist Fourth Army in January 1941. Both sides attempted to keep up appearances of harmony, but the goal of each was clearly to eliminate the other. The Chinese Communist party continued its development as a "political-military organization that sought systematically to use the forces of social revolution.[14] A "rectification campaign" removed unreliable persons from the party apparatus, land was redistributed to the peasants, and capital was confiscated. Economic self-sufficiency was a necessary goal. The Chinese Communist party developed the organizationally skilled and highly motivated cadres who expanded the Communist area of control and did so with popular support. By 1945, Mao claimed 1,200,000 party members in areas populated by 90,000,000 people.

Japan's defeat in 1945 meant the end of a four-year war to Americans; but to the Chinese Nationalists and Communist it was the beginning of the final and decisive struggle for domination of China. The Chinese Communist party classifies the years 1945 to 1949 as the Third Revolutionary Civil War; in effect, this period was a continuation of the second phase of the struggle from 1927 to 1937, uncomplicated by the Japanese.

The two parties clashed first in the competition to take the surrender of Japanese forces, to acquire their weapons, and to establish their own political control in areas occupied by the Japanese. The Kuomintang secured the surrender of most of the Japanese forces, in part through the help of the United States, which air-lifted and sea-lifted Nationalist troops to pre-empt Communist occupation in many areas. But the Chinese Communist forces were closest to the vital northeastern area, and the Soviet Union, which entered the Pacific War on August 8, 1945, gave important help to them.

The Chinese Civil War At first both sides were reluctant to engage in all-out civil warfare because time was needed to prepare for it. Both sides appreciated the war-weariness of the Chinese people, and both knew the United States wished to prevent a civil war. President Truman sent George C. Marshall to China (December 1945–January 1947) to try to reconcile the opposing factions. General Marshall succeeded in gaining a truce. Chiang Kai-shek probably accepted the mediation efforts because United States assistance would be needed if he were to win. On the other hand, Mao Tse-tung resented the interference and accused Truman of hypocrisy. Mao engaged in negotiations on the political level but carried on combat in the field. He was confident that his well disciplined and motivated political-military organization would prevail. Eventually the Marshall Mission failed to prevent the outbreak of full-scale civil war, which was probably inevitable.

The Chinese Communist military forces (now called the People's Liberation Army) began a full-scale offensive in mid-1947, called on the people to overthrow the Nationalists and to establish a "democratic coalition government," and gained wide popular support for redistribution of land to the peasants. Mao pursued wisely the tactics of destroying Nationalist forces wherever they could be caught, arming peasants with captured weapons, and gradually demoralizing Nationalist troops isolated by their own city-holding tactics. In April 1949, the Nationalist capital at Nanking was lost, and the People's Liberation Army overran all of China by the end of the year.

The People's Republic of China The People's Republic of China was established on October 1, 1949. Some of its important theoretical underpinnings are found in Mao's article commemorating the twenty-eighth anniversary (June 30, 1949) of the founding of the Chinese Communist party.[15] Mao called for the transition from his New Democracy to a "people's democratic dictatorship" based mainly on the alliance of workers and peasants, under the leadership of the working class, but including, for the time being, the petty and national bourgeoisie. These groups make up the "people" who exercise "dictatorship" over the all reactionaries, that is, those who oppose the revolution of the "people." "Democracy" applied to the "people"; "dictatorship" applied to all others. Members of the reactionary classes would be "educated" and "remolded" under the leadership of the party; the uneducable would be "eliminated for good." In general orientation the party would "lean to one side," that is, look to the Soviet Union for guidance: "The Communist Party of the Soviet Union is our best teacher and we must learn from it." In Mao's words:

To sum up our experience and concentrate it into one point, it is: the people's democratic dictatorship under the leadership of the working class (through the Communist Party) and based upon the alliance of workers and peasants. This dictatorship must unite as one with the international revolutionary forces. This is our formula, our principal experience, our main programme.[16]

The year 1949 is roughly the mid-point between the founding of the Chinese Communist party (1921) and today. For the first half of its existence, the party ideology was that of a group seeking power through the overthrow of a counterrevolutionary government. For the second half of its existence, the Chinese Communist party has been a revolutionary government in control of the largest population in the world.

DEMOCRATIC CENTRALISM

From the mid-1930s until 1949, the Chinese Communist party was a movement, a besieged government, a military force, and the standard-bearer of revolution in China. Its ideology was deeply influenced by its military experience, especially in terms of organization and leadership. The "organizational principle of the Party is democratic centralism,"[17] a term familiar in its Soviet context, but which

in its Chinese context consists of two nouns "democracy" and "centralism."

Centralism is the creation of an organization with vertical chains of command which merge at the top. Information moves up the chain; commands move down the chain. In a military organization, each higher command commands the next lower level: all subordinates are expected to obey the orders of the commander. So is it with the Chinese Communist party. According to the 1973 Chinese Communist Party Constitution:

The whole Party must observe unified discipline: The individual is subordinate to the organization, the minority is subordinate to the majority, the lower level is subordinate to the higher level, and the entire Party is subordinate to the Central Committee.

Further, all organs of state power, such as the People's Liberation Army (which includes ground, air, and naval forces) and mass organizations "must all accept the leadership of the Party." Centralism extends to all people in China from the primary party organization at the lowest level—in a factory, a school, or a military unit—to the highest level, reaching its apex in the leadership of the party.

Centralism, perfected, is overrigid. It must be balanced with its opposite, "democracy," which must never be taken in its Western sense, but which theoretically provides flexibility in thought and action. While military operations require obedience to commands, efficient operations require that those commanded understand the objectives of an operation, that they provide information to assist in the overall mission, and that subordinates be permitted enough flexibility to encourage initiative and spontaneity at the lower levels. This is "democracy" in the Chinese sense. It is forced, but not decisive, participation in gathering information for decision making. This was especially important in guerrilla operations (such as those from 1937 in northwest China by the Chinese Communist party) where command and control were extremely difficult.

This inherently contradictory principle of military organization, democratic centralism, was developed in times of military strife and civil war. It has been carried on in the peacetime organization of the Chinese Communist party by its leaders of some four decades, men who developed as both military and political leaders. What "democracy" requires is "positivism and creativity, not only enthusiastic, absolute obedience for individuals, but also what might be called creative obedience. This is the capacity to make decisions of an independent nature but absolutely in accord with the intent of a party resolution."[18]

THEORY OF CONTRADICTIONS

The second major element of Chinese Communist ideology, the theory of contradictions, was explained in Mao's speech titled "On the Correct Handling of Contradictions among the People" (February 1957).[19] Mao distinguished two types of social contradictions, antagonistic and nonantagonistic. Antagonistic contradictions are classic Marxist contradictions, between hostile social classes and between hostile social systems, contradictions "between ourselves and the enemy." Nonantagonistic contradictions are "totally different in nature." They occur among the "people" themselves. An explanation of the terms "people" and "enemy" is needed to understand this difference.

In Maoism, "people" means all those social classes, strata, and groups which "favor, work for and support the cause of socialist construction"; that is, all who support the Chinese Communist party are "people." All who oppose it are "the enemy." The antagonistic contradiction between the proletariat and bourgeoisie is resolved by socialist revolution; that between colonies and imperialism, by national revolutionary war. Nonantagonistic contradictions among the "people" are solved by the "democratic method, the method of discussion, of criticism, of persuasion and education," never by coercion or repression. Essentially, antagonistic contradictions are irreconcilable and are resolved by violence; contradictions among the people are reconcilable, and nonviolent solutions are appropriate.

The title of Mao's speech insisted on the "correct" handling of contradictions. It is a question, in Mao's words, of who is "right" and who is "wrong." The correct solution is the "right" solution, that is, the party solution. The handling of contradictions is governed by the first major ideological element of democratic centralism. Centralism dictates obedience to the party solution, but the method of decision requires "democracy" in the sense discussion and criticism are necessary to reach the "correct" solution. Some "people" (those who retain bourgeois characteristics) are certain to give expression to their own ideologies, and these are to be countered by discussion, persuasion, and criticism. In fact, wrong ideas must always be criticized and "noxious weeds" fought wherever they crop up. The 1975 Constitution of the People's Republic of China adds, "These contradictions can be resolved only by depending on the theory of continued revolution under the dictatorship of the proletariat and on practice under its guidance."

THE MASS LINE

In turn, the method of handling contradictions correctly has given rise to the many slogans and mass mobilization campaigns[20] to educate the masses to the correct political point of view. Linked to these very numerous slogans is the third important element of Chinese Communist ideology, the concept of the "mass line." This concept recognizes that the party membership, which now constitutes only 3.5 percent of the Chinese population, cannot alone sustain its policy; rather, the party must depend on the masses for enthusiastic and broad support cultivated not only by broad mass participation but also by useful policy input in the form of discussion and criticism of specific policies directed to solution of practical problems. At the same time the mass line performs a control function on bureaucrats, party members, and intellectuals who may tend to place personal or institutional interests above those of the party. The mass line assures vigorous interaction between the officials and the masses, and provides the means constantly to reconcile theory and practice.

Maoism and Marxism-Leninism

These three major elements of Chinese Communist ideology—democratic centralism, the theory of contradictions, and the mass line—are not unique in communist ideology. Maoism is deeply indebted to Marx, Lenin, and the example of the Russian Revolution for its basic assumptions about dialectical materialism and historical development, the inevitable triumph of socialism, the role of imperialism, class struggle, and the dictatorship of the proletariat. But the Chinese did alter some basic Soviet concepts to fit Chinese conditions. For example, the Chinese Communist party argued that the peasants could be the vanguard of the revolution to rationalize away the fact that the minuscule Chinese urban proletariat could never be the revolutionary base. We have already learned that the Chinese Communist party repudiated Comintern advice in the 1920s and rejected the Soviet-endorsed Li

Li-san line. In five decades of leading China's great struggle (according to the general program of the Chinese Communist party, April 14, 1969), Mao Tse-tung has "integrated the universal truth of Marxism-Leninism with the concrete practice of revolution, inherited and defended Marxism-Leninism, and has brought it to a higher and completely new stage."

With this general discussion of the major elements of the "prescription" element of ideology, let us now turn briefly to the Chinese Communist perception of the world and its normative view of how things ought to be.

The world is viewed generally in classic Marxist terms and interpreted in terms of the theory of contradictions, as a continuing struggle between the "people" and the "enemy." The international situation, as seen at the adoption of the new constitution of the People's Republic of China in January 1975,[21] was characterized as "great disorder under heaven," itself a direction favorable to the "people" because it meant that "all the basic contradictions of the world are sharpening." Détente was seen as a more and more intense contention of the two superpowers (the United States and the Soviet Union) for world hegemony. Throughout the world the factors for revolution and war were increasing, and the "people" of all countries were told to "get prepared against another world war." This view of the world, at once both optimistic and paranoid, can be substantiated over the years as a constant in the world outlook. One certainly questions whether it is believed by Chinese. Perhaps it is not widely believed. Nevertheless, it is the party line and Chinese Communist leaders follow the line in conduct, or alter the line to justify conduct at variance with an earlier line.

The internal situation in China was viewed with similar optimism and a warning of struggles ahead. Having passed successfully through the Great Proletarian Cultural Revolution, adopted a new party constitution in 1969, and rid China of revisionist elements by August 1973, the party announced its new constitution for the People's Republic of China in 1975. The National People's Congress (which approved the constitution) demonstrated the great unity of the people and the "flourishing vigor of the socialist homeland." But the work of the socialist revolution is not yet complete, and the people were exhorted to study the works of Marx, Engels, Lenin, and Mao, and to "implement the principle of *grasping revolution, promoting production and other work and preparedness against war*" (Italics in original).

As with the general Marxist scheme of things, the normative state sought by the CCP is not described in detail. Essentially it is expressed in negative terms, such as the overthrow of imperialism headed by the United States, the overthrow of Soviet revisionism, and the overthrow of reactionaries in all countries. These are steps that will lead to the emancipation of all mankind by eliminating exploitation of man by man everywhere. In its positive aspects, it looks to the development of China as a "powerful modern socialist country."

Comparison of Tradition and Maoism

What you have learned so far has probably suggested some similarities as well as differences between Confucianism and Maoism. This section summarizes them.

In modern as well as in traditional China, the written word is highly respected and carries great weight. The Confucian Classics were the source of knowledge for the literati; the *Quotations from Chairman Mao Tse-tung* (Little Red Book) was the constant beacon for hundreds of millions of Chinese. While the classics were available to few, the press runs for the Little Red Book exceeded 500,000,000 copies.

There was but one orthodox school of traditional thought in Confucian China; in the People's Republic of China, no dissent is tolerated. Mao Tse-tung thought is the sole guide to acquisition of the correct political point of view, the absence of which, Mao has said, is like "having no soul."

In both periods of Chinese history, leadership has been exercised by an elite selected on the basis of merit which is determined by the individual's mastery of orthodoxy and its practical application.

Subordination of the individual to group goals has also characterized Chinese social structure under both systems, traditionally to family goals, currently to Communist party goals. In neither case has the concept of individual freedom, individual choice, or priority of personal goals held any importance. At the same time, both ideologies have encouraged the individual to be self-reliant, thrifty, diligent, and to "struggle hard." Communist ideology exhibits puritanical traits not found in Confucian society, but which it shares with most revolutionary movements.

A final point of similarity is that both ideologies laid claim to universality.

Differences in the two ideologies seem far more fundamental. Although some scholars have argued that Maoism is little more than another "neo-Confucianism," the evidence suggests otherwise.

Confucianism is clearly an independently developed Chinese system of thought, albeit altered from time to time by such non-Chinese accretions as Buddhism. Its development and flowering was a centuries-long process. Maoism is basically a Chinese adaptation of a comprehensive view of world history derived from Western civilization and imported within the last six decades, well within the adult years of some of China's current leadership. Essentially Maoism is an offshoot of Marxism-Leninism deriving its operative assumptions and interpretations from the Soviet experience. While Confucianism looked to the past for its ideals, Maoism looks to a romantic undefined future where no man will be exploited by another. If Confucianism was pessimistic in the Chinese tradition, Maoism is optimistic in the Western tradition.

While Confucianism idealized family loyalties and approved local patriotism, Maoism will have none of either. Family loyalty has been replaced with party loyalty which, insofar as it has succeeded, is utterly destructive of the traditional social fabric.

Although both traditional and Maoist societies can be characterized as unitary, centralized bureaucratic states, it is also true that the People's Republic of China has extended its influence far beyond the district level to the control of the daily activities of every Chinese to an extent undreamed of in Confucian China. Mass movements, pervasive indoctrination and criticism, and self-criticism discussion groups have been the methods.

Confucianism sought a stable harmonious society in tune with a harmonious universe, quiescent in nature and adjustable by compromise. Maoist insistence on the existence of contradictions (even among the "people") accentuates the stresses, struggle, and conflict in human relations and insists that they persist, even in a socialist society. The correct handling of contradictions is a requirement to elevate societal development. Where tension exists, the Communist party uses it; where it does not exist, the Communist party creates it.

A final point concerns legitimacy, or acceptance of the regime. In Confucian China, the emperor derived his legitimacy from his virtue and acted in accord with superior authority conceived as the mandate of heaven. If the Emperor lacked "virtue," his legitimacy was negated; his rule could be overthrown by the people. In the Maoist scheme, the Chinese Communist party alone has the right to rule. The party alone is correct, and no alternative exists for the people of China. Under Confucianism, the limits to rule were nearly explicit; under Maoism there are no explicit limits.

The Chinese Constitutional Order

The 1975 constitution was a far simpler document than that which it replaced (the 1956 constitution), having been reduced from 106 to 30 articles. The preamble noted that socialist society covers a long historical period, that class struggle, contradictions, and the struggle between the socialist road and the capitalist road will continue. Concerning international affairs, the constitution promised that China will "never be a superpower." With socialist countries, China will strengthen its unity; to oppressed peoples and nations, it will give support; toward nations with different social systems, it will seek relations based on the Five Principles: (1) mutual respect for sovereignty and territorial integrity, (2) mutual nonaggression, (3) noninterference in each other's internal affairs, (4) equality and mutual benefit, and (5) peaceful coexistence.

Unlike it was in the Stalin constitution of 1936, the role of the party in the organization and functioning of the Chinese state mechanism is quite clear. Marxism-Leninism-Maoism is the theoretical basis guiding the thinking of the nation; the working class exercises leadership over the state through its vanguard, the Communist party of China, "the core of leadership of the whole Chinese people." All power in the People's Republic of China belongs to the "people," and the National People's Congress is the "highest organ of state power"; yet the National People's Congress is explicitly "under the leadership of the Chinese Communist party."

Party control of the People's Liberation Army is equally emphatic. The People's Liberation Army and the people's militia are "led by the Communist Party of China," and commanded by the chairman of the Central Committee of the party. This provision stresses equally party control and the importance of the role of the People's Liberation Army. The dictatorship of the proletariat is the "magic weapon" with which the Chinese people vanquish enemies and protect themselves: the People's Liberation Army and the militia are the "pillar of the dictatorship of the proletariat." Military service is the "honorable obligation of citizens," and it is the "lofty duty of every citizen to defend the motherland and resist aggression."

In short, the 1975 Constitution is designed to institutionalize the leadership role of the party, which created the machinery of state to serve its revolutionary goals. The explicit concentration of power in the party is meant to assure the continuation of the revolution. The elimination of the position of chairman of the People's Republic of China is to assure submission of the state to the party and to eliminate the power base used by Liu Shao-ch'i to usurp party power. Similarly, designation of the chairman of the Central Committee to command the country's armed forces is intended to guarantee that no more Lin Piaos arise to try to seize power by a coup d'etat.

Chou En-lai reminded the congress that the Great Proletarian Cultural Revolution "personally initiated and led by our great leader Chairman Mao" was the most important event in Chinese life since the First Congress in 1954. The new constitution thus reaffirmed the party's dedication to continuing revolution.

Summary

Since pre-Christian days, Chinese society has been guided by some orthodox ideology, which articulated an agreed perception of the world; an idealized normative state of things, which was its goal, and general ideas about how society could be altered from the current state to the desired state.

Confucian tradition guided Chinese society until the 20th century. This ideology perceived the world as a corruption of the romanticized ideal Chinese society of the ancient sage kings, when the emperor ruled by his virtue and regulated in harmony the relations of man, earth, and heaven. The willed reality, or desired state of things, could be achieved by emulation of the ancients, cultivation of their virtue and character by mastery of the classics, the development of the "superior man" as both the exemplar and the administrator of the unitary Chinese state operated by a bureaucracy based on merit. The concept of mandate of heaven provided the rationale for the overthrow of a dynastic leader who lost virtue, and simultaneously legitimized the successor regime.

Since 1949, the Chinese Communist party has been a revolutionary government in control of the largest population in the world. Communist ideology views the world as a continuous struggle between socialists and all others, between the "people" and the "enemies of the people." It is described in terms derived from Marxism-Leninism, dialectical materialism and historical determinism. Its view of the world is both optimistic and paranoid. The normative state of things sought by the ideology is not described in detail, but it looks to a future where no man is exploited by another. The program to reach "willed reality" is more specific, yet subject to change as dictated by circumstance, internal and external. The means is the people's democratic dictatorship led by the Communist party and based on the alliance of workers and peasants. The theoretical principles governing the party are democratic centralism, the theory of contradictions, and the mass line.

Confucianism and Maoism share some characteristics: emphasis on a core of written works, intolerance of dissent, leadership by a very small elite, chosen for its mastery of the orthodoxy, and a claim to universality. The differences are more important. Maoism seeks to destroy the idealized family relations of Confucianism and the traditional social fabric. It extends its influence deeply to control the individual's daily life in ways undreamed of in traditional China. Where Confucianism sought harmony, Maoism posits unending struggle and conflict. Confucianism was rooted in the past. Maoism is rooted in the future.

The Chinese Constitution of 1975 institutionalizes the Maoist ideology and the role of the party. Not only is the party the state, but it also controls the People's Liberation Army. The theme of the constitution is the continuation of the revolution under the guidance of the Chinese Communist party.

NOTES

1. John Wilson Lewis, *Major Doctrines of Communist China* (New York: Norton, 1964), p. 78.
2. Wm. Theodore de Bary, ed., *Sources of Chinese Tradition* (New York: Columbia University Press, 1964), Vol. I, p. 115.
3. See Burton Watson, trans., *Han Fei Tzu* (New York: Columbia University Press, 1964), p. 7. For another translation of excerpts of *Han Fei Tzu*, see de Bary, op. cit., pp. 124–136, on which much of this portion is based.
4. de Bary, op. cit., p. 139.
5. Arthur Waley, trans., *The Analects of Confucius* (New York: Vintage, 1938), p. 17.
6. de Bary, op. cit., p. 115.
7. Ibid., p. 120.
8. John King Fairbank, *The United States and China*, 3rd ed. (Cambridge, Mass.: Harvard, 1972), p. 50.
9. For "A Chronology of the Communist Movement in China, 1918–50" (revised 1963), see Conrad Brandt, Benjamin Schwartz, and John K. Fairbank, *A Documentary History of Chinese Communist* (New York: Atheneum, 1967), pp. 29–47.
10. "First Program of the Communist Party of China, 1921" and "Decisions of the Second Conference of the Communist Party of China, 1922," quoted in Claude A. Buss, *The People's Republic of China* (Princeton, N.J.: Van Nostrand, 1962, pp. 93–101.
11. Mao Tse-tung, "The Question of Independence and Autonomy within the United Front" (November 5, 1938), in *Selected Works*, vol. 2 (New York: International Publishers, 1954, pp. 262–266.
12. Mao Tse-tung, "Problems of War and Strategy" (November 6, 1938), in ibid., pp. 267–281.
13. Mao Tse-tung, "On New Democracy" (January 1940), in ibid., vol. 3, pp. 106–156.
14. Franz Schurmann, *Ideology and Organization in Communist China* (Berkeley: University of California Press, 1966), p. xii.
15. Mao Tse-tung, "On the People's Democratic Dictatorship," in op. cit., vol. 4, pp. 411–424.
16. Ibid., p. 422.
17. "The Constitution of the Communist Party of China," in *Peking Review*, nos. 35, 36 (September 7, 1973).
18. See H. F. Schurmann, "Organizational Principles of the Chinese Communists," in *China Quarterly*, no. 2 (April–June 1960).
19. See John Wilson Lewis, op. cit., pp. 89–105.
20. See list compiled by Alison Huey in Lucian W. Pye, *China an Introduction* (Boston: Little, Brown, 1972), pp. 281–292.
21. "Press Communique of the First Session of the Fourth National People's Congress of the Peoples Republic of China, January 17, 1975," in *Peking Review*, no. 4 (January 24, 1975).

CHAPTER 10

CHINESE POLITICAL ACTORS: POWER AND LEGITIMACY

Chairman Mao has taught us: "The Chinese Communist Party is the core of leadership of the whole Chinese people. Without this core, the cause of socialism cannot be victorious."[1]

The People's Republic of China is an authoritarian system rationalized by an ideology that is concerned mainly with the state and society as a collectivity. The overwhelmingly dominant role of the party in all fields of activity, a role legitimized by the ideology, has resulted in the control and use of state power by a small and highly select group of party members. This group retains for itself the major decision-making posts in important Chinese institutions. For these reasons the full range of political actors discussed in Chapter 1 is far less characteristic of China than it is of Japan and the United States, and even the Soviet Union.

Political Actors and Power

The formal roles of the two major political structures, the Chinese Communist party and the People's Republic of China, have been expressed in their respective constitutions, but the actual operation of the political system has not always accorded with constitutionally expressed "ideals." It is true that "law" in the Western sense does not play a prominent role in Chinese society. Nevertheless, the party attaches great importance to such quasi-legal constitutions, and each of the four most recent National Party Congresses (1945, 1956, 1969, and 1973) have approved a new party constitution. State constitutions were promulgated in 1954 and 1975.

Each party Congress and party constitution since 1949 has legitimized and given formal status to a new, apparently stable and temporarily acceptable distribution of power among the three major political actors. Each new distribution of power reflected the result of struggles over certain broad policy issues, such as the proper role of the People's Liberation Army in relation to the other political actors, the red versus expert controversy, national defense policy, and the appropriate strategy for economic development. In Chapter 11 we consider in some detail the problems of economic development, the Great Leap

Forward (1958–1960), and the Great Proletarian Cultural Revolution (1965–1969). Suffice it to say here that the Cultural Revolution was a thorough-going mass movement intended to destroy those people in the party who had betrayed the revolution and taken the "capitalist road." Its intent was to restructure Chinese society, to create new attitudes and behaviors, and to make a new kind of man. This chapter explains the roles of the party, the state structure, and the People's Liberation Army in the establishment and consolidation of power after 1949. China's experiment (1969–1971) with Bonapartism (the elevation of Marshal Lin Piao to formal status as Mao's successor and the vital role of the People's Liberation Army in restoring public order to China after the Cultural Revolution) is treated in this chapter because it shows the intimate relationship of the three political actors.

Institutions

THE CHINESE COMMUNIST PARTY

In the People's Republic of China, it is unrealistic to make differentiations between the Chinese Communist party as a group and as an institution. The party is the state—in more emphatic form than in the Soviet Union. In China there have not developed even rudimentary groups outside the party structure. Moreover, China's status as a developing nation has not brought about the political-social-economic development and modernization to stimulate the growth of group structures which provide inputs to the political system. The Chinese political system is unitary, reflecting its historical structure and the present-day impetus for control and direction from the center. Political actors outside the official structure are peripheral to the system: they hardly exist at all in a realistic sense. The point is, the Chinese Communist

party, although it can be conceived as a group in standard studies of party systems, is more correctly an institution in the political system.

Throughout its history, the Chinese Communist party (CCP) has tenaciously guarded its role as the corps d'élite of China's society, as the "political party of the proletariat, the vanguard of the proletariat." A revolutionary party whose "ultimate aim" is the "realization of communism," the party has been the leading institution and the major political actor in China. The party is the source of ideological orthodoxy and guides the entire nation. The second major political actor is the state apparatus of the People's Republic of China (PRC), which carries out the day-to-day functions of government and assures the execution of party decisions. The People's Liberation Army (PLA) is the third major actor in Chinese politics. Theoretically a part of the state and always subordinate to the party, the PLA has nevertheless acted with some autonomy to influence significantly both policy and action.

THE ROLE OF THE PARTY

The mission of the Chinese Communist party expressed constitutionally is comprehensive in scope, integrating the "universal truths of Marxism-Leninism with the actual practice of China's revolutionary struggle." The General Programme of the 1956 constitution[2] stated that the party's fundamental task was to bring about the "industrialization of the country," and took due notice of the "illimitable possibilities for the gigantic development of the productive forces of society." This economic optimism was justified by the party's accomplishments in the eleven years that had passed since the Seventh Party Congress in 1945. By 1956 China was well into its first Five-Year Plan (1953–57), which emulated the Soviet model of large-scale, centrally planned development of basic industry. The goal of China's planned economy was to produce a "powerful modernized" industry, agriculture, and national defense to satisfy the people's material and cultural needs. This goal was soon actively sought in the Great Leap Forward.

The party constitution required all members to place party interests above their own personal interests, to be diligent, to work hard, to study, to practice criticism and self-criticism, and to conduct their activities in accord with the mass line and the organizational principle of democratic centralism (see Figure 10-1).

THE POLITBURO

The Politburo is the true locus of authority and power in the Chinese Communist party and hence in the People's Republic of China. The party constitution (Article 37) conferred on the Politburo the authority to exercise the powers and functions of the Central Committee when the latter is not in session. The chairman and vice-chairmen of the Central Committee are concurrently the chairman and vice-chairmen of the Politburo. Since the office of chairman of the Central Committee of the Chinese Communist party was created in 1945, its sole incumbent, until his death in September 1976, was Mao Tse-tung. Mao used the Politburo, of which he was also chairman, as the center of decision-making authority. It is possible that Mao personally decided who would be elected to the Politburo, although decisions on its membership are most likely the result of factional bargaining. The Politburo has been a small group, ranging in membership from eleven at the time of the establishment of the People's Republic of China in 1949 to a high of 26 in 1973. Membership includes both regular and alternate members, but there is no precise

information on roles of these two classes of membership.

The organization principle of centralism is carried to its extreme in the party by the establishment of a Standing Committee of the Politburo, the smallest and yet the most important group of decision makers. Both the full Politburo and the Standing Committee are empowered by the party constitution to exercise the powers and functions of the Central Committee when it is not in plenary session. The special position of the Standing Committee is emphasized by the fact that it is elected, not by the full Politburo, but by the Central Committee itself. The number of members of this very select group has varied from five to nine.

Analysis of Politburo membership suggests "a finely balanced factional system,"[3] which consisted of 21 regular and 4 alternate members, representing central bureaucrats, Shanghai and Nanking regional leaders, "leftist" elements identified with Mao's wife, Chiang Ching, and men with long-term politico-military experience. The Politburo had nine members: Mao Tse-tung; Chou En-lai, Central Committee vice-chairman and premier of the State Council; Kang Sheng, Central Committee vice-chairman and head of Security; Marshal Yeh Chien-ying, Central Committee vice-chairman and vice-chairman of Military Affairs Committee; Li Te-sheng, Central Committee vice-chairman and commander of Shenyang Military Region; Wang Hung-wen, Central Committee vice-chairman and secretary of the Shanghai CCP; Marshal Chu Teh, chairman of the National People's Congress; Tung Pi-wu, acting chairman of the People's Republic of China; and Chang Ch'ün-ch'iao, first secretary of the Shanghai CCP and chairman of the Shanghai Revolutionary Committee. The "old, middle-aged, young" formula was not reflected in the Standing Committee, whose youngest member was Wang Hung-wen (born 1937)

Figure 10-1: Organization of the Chinese Communist Party, Eighth National Party Congress, 1956

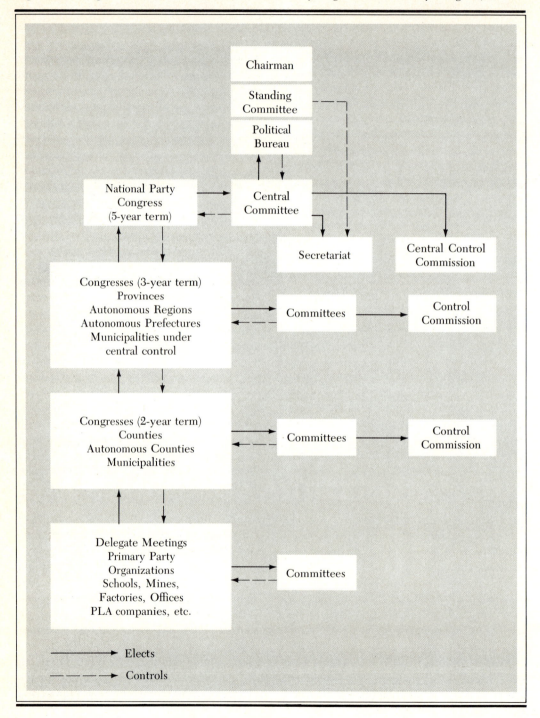

and second youngest member was Li Te-sheng (born 1914). The others were old, even by Chinese standards, and five members have since died: Tung Pi-wu (1886–1975), Kang Sheng (1898–1975), Chou En-Lai (1898–1976), Chu Teh (1886–1975), and Mao Tse-tung (1892–1976). Teng Hsiao-p'ing was added to the Politburo in January 1975. Exactly one year later, he was elected vice-chairman of the Central Committee and member of the Standing Committee of the Politburo, only to be dismissed from all posts both inside and outside the party on April 17, 1976, by decision of the Central Committee on the proposal of Chairman Mao.

THE CENTRAL COMMITTEE

An important role is played at the national level of the party by the Central Committee, which is elected by the National Party Congress. The Central Committee is responsible for carrying out decisions of the National Party Congress and, when the latter is not in session, for directing the entire work of the party. The Central Committee also is responsible for the overall operation of the state apparatus. The People's Liberation Army (actually a tri-service force consisting of ground, naval, and air forces) must carry out its mission in accord with instructions of the Central Committee. In its plenary session, the Central Committee elects the Political Bureau (Politburo) and the Politburo Standing Committee, which is the real decision-making organ of the party. It elects the party Secretariat, which supervises the functional departments and committes of the party, and it elects the officers of the Central Committee. The 1956 Central Committee, with an original membership of 97 regular and 73 alternate members, was constitutionally mandated to meet twice annually and did meet twelve times in plenary session from 1956 to 1969, less than half as many times as required. Some meetings lasted for but a single day, while others lasted up to three weeks. Meeting infrequently and for short periods, the Central Committee could not serve as a deliberative body on matters of substantial importance and complexity. The importance of the Central Committee lies less in its formal actions and more in the nature of its membership. Essentially the Central Committee is an assembly of leaders from all parts of China and all major functional organizations which provides a close link between the small Peking-based group of party decision makers and the varied functional and geographic interests of the party as a whole. The Central Committee forms a reservoir of talent from which are selected the members of the inner elite, the Politburo.

The Ninth Central Committee was enlarged to a total of 279 members (170 regular, 109 alternate) from 170 at the Eighth Party Congress. Mao was elected chairman of the Central Committee, and Marshal Lin was the only vice-chairman. The 64 percent increase in Central Committee membership permitted increased PLA participation without markedly reducing the numbers of other representatives, whose relative strength was nevertheless diluted. The election of one vice-chairman instead of five, as had been done in 1956, enchanced Lin's new status as successor to Mao. Of the 170 regular Central Committee members, 64 (38 percent) were military representatives, as were 41 (38 percent) of the 109 alternates.[4] Reportedly, at least 53 PLA officers with the rank of "general" were included in the Central Committee.[5] Of 25 Politburo members (only 9 were carryovers), 13 were identified as military. The Politburo Standing Committee consisted of five members: Mao, Lin, Chou En-lai, Ch'en Po-ta, and Kang Sheng, the latter two from the Cultural Revolution group. Three former members of the Politburo of the Eighth Central Committee were purged: Liu Shao-ch'i, Ch'en Yün, and Teng Hsiao-p'ing. A fourth, the aging (83) Marshal Chu Teh, was demoted to Politburo member.

THE PARTY CONGRESS

The enumerated powers of the National Party Congress (Article 32), theoretically the highest body of the party at the national level, were: (1) to hear and examine the reports of the Central Committee and other central organs; (2) to determine the party's line and policy; (3) to amend the constitution of the party; and (4) to elect the Central Committee. Execution of these broad powers was manifestly beyond the capability of a group of more than 1,000 who met only for two two-week periods (in 1956 and 1958) over a thirteen-year span. Nevertheless, the Congress does have important functions: (1) to focus national and international attention (as when convened in 1956, 1969, and 1973) on new programs and policies; (2) to give authority and legitimacy to party actions decided elsewhere, and (3) to clarify policy and persuade delegates to party positions. The delegates themselves "achieve not only distinction but also find the excitement that deepens their commitments to the party and reinforces their bond with the leaders."[6]

The National Party Congress is to be convened every five years. The Central Committee in plenary session carries out the duties of the Congress when it is not in session. In turn, the Politburo and its Standing Committee act for the Central Committee when it is not in session. The current Tenth Central Committee held one plenary meeting immediately after the August 1973 Party Congress and a second three-day session in January 1975 preparatory to the adoption of the revised Chinese Constitution. Duties of all bodies are constitutionally vague. Provisions exist for party congresses in the localities and at PLA regimental level, convened triennially, subject to approval by higher party echelons. These congresses all have parallel party committees with standing committees, secretaries, and deputy secretaries. There are similar provisions for primary organizations of the party (party branches, general party branches, and primary party committees) to be organized in factories, mines, communes, offices, schools, shops, neighborhoods, and PLA company-level units.

The Eighth National Party Congress (1956) consisted of more than 1,000 members elected by the membership of the next lower level party congresses. Delegates to the Congress were elected for a term of five years, and the Congress was to be convened annually at the call of the Central Committee. In practice these constitutional provisions (Article 31) were violated. The Eighth Congress was not convened each year; instead, it met only once for a two-week session in 1958.[7] The term of office expired in 1961, and no National Party Congress was convened until 1969.

The Ninth Party Congress officially terminated the Cultural Revolution. Mao Tse-tung Thought was declared superior to competing ideologies; obedience to Mao's dictates was decreed for all. China was ready to move forward "aiming higher and achieving greater, faster, better and more economic results."[8] But reconstruction of the party seems to have proceeded slowly, and the anticipated party unity was more apparent than real. Unlike the early 1950s, the PLA did not "return to the barracks" and hand over political power; rather, its leaders sought to maintain the hard-won influence gained by supporting Mao against the radicals.

Four years later the Tenth Party Congress was called into session, August 24–28, 1973. Unlike the well-publicized 25-day Ninth Congress, which celebrated the historical triumph of the Cultural Revolution, the Tenth Congress began with no fanfare and ended with a short press communiqué. It was limited in scope "to the minimum necessary for formally disposing of the Lin Piao affair and certifying the reconstituted leadership organs."[9]

The Lin Piao affair was dealt with officially

by Premier Chou En-lai's report.[10] Chou traced its origins to the political report of the previous Party Congress drafted by Lin and Ch'en Po-ta. Both were said to oppose "continuing the revolution under the dictatorship of the proletariat" while "contending that the main task was to develop production." These views were the "same revisionist trash that Liu Shao-ch'i" and Ch'en had "smuggled" into the Eighth Congress in 1956. Chou said Lin's draft was rejected by the Central Committee, and Lin "grudgingly" agreed to read Mao's revision. Later, however, Lin rebuffed Mao's efforts to "save him" and planned a counter-revolutionary coup d'etat which was aborted in August 1970. Finally, in September 1971, Lin "launched the coup in a wild attempt" to kill Mao, but the conspiracy collapsed and he fled "as a defector to the Soviet revisionists in betrayal of the Party and country." All in all, Chou averred, smashing this conspiracy of the "bourgeois careerist, conspirator, double-dealer, renegade and traitor Lin Piao" had good results. The entire party, People's Liberation Army, and hundreds of millions of people had discussed the affair and their indignation aroused all "to unite to win still greater victories."

More to the point was Chou's statement that Lin Piao wanted to have everything under his command and everything at his disposal, but ended up with command of nothing and nothing at his disposal. Clearly, Lin did not comprehend the irrefutable truth of Mao's teaching that "correctness or incorrectness of the ideological and political line decides everything." Chou played down the significance of Lin's Bonapartism by recalling that in the past half century the ever-victorious Chinese Communist party had gone through ten major struggles between the two lines (bourgeois and revolutionary) and that the smashing of Lin Piao's antiparty clique did not mean the end of the two-line struggle within the party. In fact, Chou said the two-line struggle will recur ten, twenty, or thirty times in the future, and Lin Piaos and Liu Shao-ch'is will appear again.

The 37-year-old political *arriviste* from among the Shanghai radicals, Wang Hung-wen, stressed the continuity of the Ninth and Tenth Party Congresses in his report to the Congress.[11] Quoting Mao frequently, Wang pointed the way for the future: "Great disorder across the land leads to great order. And so once again every seven or eight years" (Mao in 1966). Wang said the true Communist must "dare to go against the time [revisionism], fearing neither removal from his post, expulsion from the Party, imprisonment, divorce, nor the guillotine." The party must guarantee its survival and keep its color by following "a correct line and correct policies, but [we] must train and bring up millions of successors who will carry on the cause of proletariat revolution."

Most of the 1,249 delegates to the Tenth Party Congress were worker, peasant, and soldier party members. Over 20 percent were women. By secret ballot, the Congress elected a 319-member Central Committee (195 regular and 124 alternate members) which embodied "the combination of the old, the middle-aged, and the young."[12] The election of a large Central Committee (26 percent of the total Congress delegates) continued a trend which had increased its size from 70 in 1945, to 170 for the Eighth Congress, and to 274 for the Ninth Congress. The Central Committee elected its officers on August 30, 1973, naming Mao Tse-tung chairman and electing five vice-chairmen nearly two years after the death of the previous sole vice-chairman, Lin Piao.[13] The Tenth Central Committee reduced military representation (from 43 to 32 percent), kept party and government cadres about the same (28 percent), and increased representation of the "revolutionary masses" (from 29 to 40 percent). Especially interesting was the restoration to high party status of 52 officials who had been deprived of status during the Cultural Revolution.

In the final analysis the Chinese Party Congress performs functions similar to the Party Congress of the Communist party of the Soviet Union. It acts as a legitimizing body to the directions of the Politburo and the Central Committee. The Party Congress is not a policy-making body, nor does it act autonomously from the higher leadership of the party. It does serve a socializing function for party members and is a forum for publishing party policy. In addition, it serves as an educational channel, teaching party members the "right" party view.

OTHER PARTY ORGANS

Other important party organs at the national level (1956–66) were the Secretariat and the Central Control Commission (see Figure 10-1). The Secretariat (Article 37) was supposed "to attend to the daily work of the Central Committee under the direction of the Politburo and its Standing Committee," by supervising the execution of party policies and decisions throughout all levels of the party organization. The Central Control Commission, elected by the Central Committee, was supposed "to examine and deal with cases of violation of the Party Constitution, Party discipline, Communist ethics, and the state laws and decrees on the part of Party members; to decide on or cancel disciplinary measures against Party members; and to deal with appeals and complaints from Party members" (Article 53).

Subordinate level party organizations replicate the organization at national level. Delegates to the Party Congress at provincial level were elected for a three-year term, and the number of delegates and procedures for their election were determined by the provincial level committee. These committees,

like the Central Committee at national level, carried out party decisions when the provincial congress was not in session. They allocated party cadres, directed the work of "leading party members" in the local state organs and reported, not only to the local congress, but also to the Central Committee at national level. Party organization at county level was similar.

PRIMARY PARTY ORGANIZATIONS

The basic level of party organization consisted of the primary party organizations (PPOs) formed in factories, mines, schools, companies of the PLA, in towns, and in the late 1950s, in communes. A PPO required at least three regular party members. With 100 members or more, a PPO could hold a "delegate meeting" and elect a primary party committee to perform the functions of higher level committees and control commissions. A "general branch" committee could be set up by 50 or more party members with organization and functions like those of a "delegate meeting."

The locus of grass-roots basic political activity was the PPO (Article 50), which tied together the activities of the workers, peasants, intellectuals, and other patriotic people with the party. Specifically PPOs were charged: (1) to carry on propaganda and organizational work among the masses; (2) to pay constant heed to the sentiments and demands of the masses and report them to higher party organizations; (3) to recruit new party members, to collect membership dues, to examine and appraise party members, and to maintain party discipline among the membership; (4) to lead the masses to give full play to their activity and creative ability, to strengthen labor discipline, and to ensure the fulfillment of the production and work plans; (5) to promote criticism and self-criticism, to expose and eliminate shortcomings and mistakes in work, and to wage struggles against the violation of laws and discipline, against corruption and waste, and against bureaucracy; and (6) to educate the party members and the masses to sharpen their revolutionary vigilance and to be constantly on the alert to combat the disruptive activities of the class enemy.

THE CULTURAL REVOLUTION AND ITS AFTERMATH

During the Cultural Revolution, Mao assaulted the party structure with a nonparty organization, the Red Guards. To restructure and consolidate the party, Mao relied greatly on another nonparty organization, the People's Liberation Army. In the summer of 1968, Mao and Lin confronted two major problems: (1) how to restore the legitimacy of the party primacy, and (2) how to ensure real party control of the military. At the conference of an "enlarged" Eighth Central Committee, packed with additional military personnel, called to prepare for a new Ninth Party Congress, Liu Shao-ch'i (chairman of the People's Republic of China) was finally expelled from the Chinese Communist party by name (heretofore he had been identified only as "China's Khrushchev"). A massive campaign was launched to unite all of the country behind the actions of the Central Committee.[14] Party congresses were convened by military commands and revolutionary committees. A new draft of the party constitution was widely discussed, and 1,526 delegates were "chosen" to attend the Ninth Party Congress, which met in Peking, April 1–24, 1969. The new party-PLA power balance required formal constitutional approval.

The Party Congress approved the policies associated with the Cultural Revolution, legitimized the leadership changes, and confirmed Lin Piao's new status. It publicly affirmed that the theoretical basis guiding the

Chinese Communist party was now Mao Tsetung Thought, that is, "Marxism-Leninism of the era in which imperialism is heading for total collapse and socialism is advancing to worldwide victory."

In his address to the delegates,[15] Lin Piao damned those in Liu Shao-ch'i's gang who had taken the capitalist road, restated the absolute necessity of the Cultural Revolution, and lauded Mao's wisdom crystallized in the "Correct Handling of Contradictions." Although the Ninth Party Congress was convened at a time when a "great victory" had been won in the Cultural Revolution, Lin emphasized Mao's words: "The question of which will win out, socialism or capitalism, is still not really settled." Lin demanded unity under Mao's leadership: "Whoever opposes Chairman Mao, whoever opposes Mao Tse-tung Thought, at any time or under any circumstances, will be condemned and punished by the whole Party and the whole nation."

The new party constitution[16] was much shorter than the 1956 document it replaced (reduced from 60 to 12 articles). It gave greater prominence to the People's Liberation Army, but clearly stipulated that the PLA, like the organs of state, the Communist Youth League, and other revolutionary mass organizations, must "accept the leadership of the Party." The constitutional designation of Marshal Lin Piao as "Comrade Mao Tse-tung's close comrade-in-arms and successor" was unique in the constitutional history of socialist states and communist parties.

THE NEW PARTY CONSTITUTION

The constitution adopted by the Congress reaffirmed provisions of the 1969 constitution relative to the party's guiding ideology, basic program, and basic line of the program. The paragraph concerning Lin Piao was, of course, deleted.

Aside from Lin's excision from the 1973 party constitution, the changes were few, but relatively significant. No mention is made of a "Control Commission" nor of a party Secretariat, a body that was eliminated during the Cultural Revolution and not mentioned in the 1969 constitution. The long-time (1956–66) party secretary, Teng Hsiao-p'ing, was purged during the Cultural Revolution. Formal reconstitution of the party Secretariat might have been construed to be divisive by introducing one more potentially divisive power base in intra-party conflicts; however, provision is made for "a number of necessary organs" to handle the day-to-day work of the party, the government, and the PLA in "a centralized way." Perhaps surprisingly, the 1973 constitution omits the earlier claim that Mao has brought Marxism-Leninism to a "higher and completely new stage." This particular claim appeared in Lin Piao's introduction to the *Quotations from Chairman Mao Tse-tung* (Little Red Book). In late 1971, several weeks after Lin's aborted coup, the *Quotations* disappeared from book stalls. When it reappeared, Lin's introductory panegyric to Mao had been deleted. This may be due to a reinterpretation that Maoism is really suitable only to the Chinese condition, or it may be accounted for by a decision to play down the "cult of Mao."

The constitution requires all leading bodies of the party to be elected on the principle combining the old, the middle-aged, and the young, and stresses democratic centralism. On the democratic side, a party member with views at variance with party decisions or directives has the right to bypass the immediate leadership and report directly to higher levels, including the chairman of the Central Committee: "It is absolutely impermissible to suppress criticism and to retaliate." On the centralism side, Wang stated, "Of the seven sectors—industry, agriculture, commerce, culture and education, the Army, the government and the Party—it is the Party that

exercises overall leadership." The constitution requires all state organs, the PLA and the militia, labor unions, lower and lower-middle peasant associations, women's federations, the Communist Youth League, the Red Guards, the Little Red Guards, and other revolutionary mass organizations to accept the centralized leadership of the party. Society is guided to walk the narrow tightrope of democratic centralism in the unity of opposites.

Confirmation of the new power structure was the main business of the Tenth Party Congress. The aftermath of the Lin Piao affair included the removal of one-third of the Politburo and great personnel turbulence in the highest levels of party, government, and the PLA. The Cultural Revolution, getting rid of the stale and bringing in the fresh, resulted in huge increase in party members. This trend continued after 1969, and in four years, party membership had increased by one-third (7,000,000), to a total of 28,000,000, nearly three times that of 1956 (see Table 10-1). Party leadership had been formally reconstituted and legitimized by the action of the Tenth Party Congress, but the called-for unity remained elusive.

THE STATE STRUCTURE

The second major institutional political actor in China is the state structure of the government of the People's Republic of China. As a creation of the Chinese Communist party, its organization and principles of operation derive from and reflect party doctrine. Although the Chinese Communist party seized administrative and political control of all of mainland China in 1949, the establishment of a formal state structure was delayed until 1954. The structure described here was theoretically in effect through the Great Proletarian Cultural Revolution (1966–1969) and much of it applied until a revised state structure was

Table 10–1: Growth of Chinese Communist Party

Year	National Congress	Place	Number of Members
1921	First	Shanghai	57
1922	Second	Shanghai	123
1923	Third	Canton	432
1925	Fourth	Canton	950
1927	Fifth	Hankow	58,000
1928	Sixth	Moscow	40,000
1945	Seventh	Yenan	1,200,000
1956	Eighth	Peking	10,700,000
1969	Ninth	Peking	21,000,000
1973	Tenth	Peking	28,000,000

decreed by the new Chinese Constitution of 1975.

National People's Congress In theory, all power in the People's Republic of China belongs to the people. This power is exercised through the National People's Congress, the "highest organ of state authority" and the "only legislative authority in the country" (see Figure 10-2). Its 14 enumerated powers included the enactment of laws, election of the chairman and vice-chairman of the People's Republic, approval of the chairman's recommendations for premier and other members of the State Council, approval of the state budget, and "to decide" on questions of war and peace. Although elected for a four-year term, the National People's Congress has been elected only three times since 1954 (in 1959, 1964, and 1975). Like the National Party Congress, the National People's Congress has a large membership and meets infrequently. Similarly, its functions are delegated to its subsidiary "permanently acting body," the Standing Committee of 80 to 100 members. The National Defense Council and Supreme State Conference, both chaired by the chairman of the People's Republic of China, were advisory/consultative bodies with vague constitutional status. The Supreme People's Procurator is responsible for

ensuring observance of the law. The administration of justice is the duty of the Supreme People's Court.

The Fourth National People's Congress of the People's Republic of China was convened in Peking, January 13–17, 1975, to adopt a revised Constitution which had been in preparation for almost five years.[17] After "extensive democratic consultations and discussions," 2,885 deputies were elected from all parts of the country. Worker, peasant, and soldier deputies accounted for 72 percent of the total. Deputies were elected from 54 minority nationalities, and over 22 percent were women. The press communiqué of the Fourth National People's Congress called for unity in following Mao's line, support for and unity with the oppressed nations and peoples of the world, support for the "third world" in its struggle for independence and of the "second world" against the superpowers, and to follow Mao's principle to "dig tunnels deep, store grain everywhere, and never seek hegemony."

The Fifth National People's Congress met in Peking during the first week of March 1978. This was a particularly significant session because it was an important indicator of the relationship of Maoism to the new rulers of China. The five thousand delegates sitting under the huge portraits of Mao and Chairman Hua Kuo-

Figure 10-2: Organization of the People's Republic of China, 1970

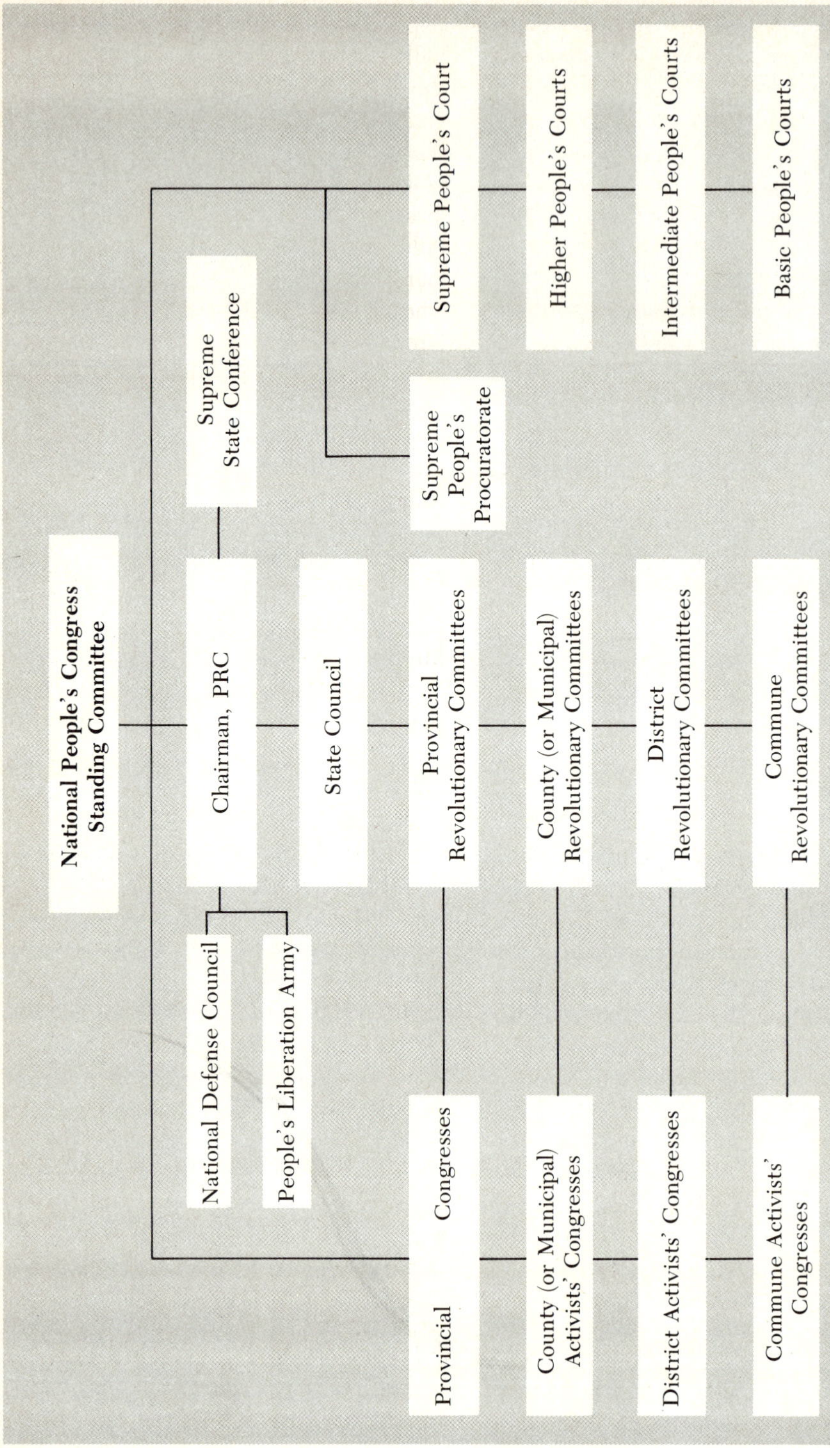

Source: Donald P. Whitaker et al., *Area Handbook for the People's Republic of China* (Washington, D.C.: U.S. Government Printing Office, 1972), p. 238.

feng approved the pragmatic approach of the new leaders. Breaking with the Maoist stress on social origin, it appeared that the new rulers were committed to the idea of political behavior rather than family origin. The Fifth National People's Congress also ushered to prominence Vice-Premier Teng Hsiao-ping, age 74, whose ideas on socialist democracy appeared to replace Mao's concept of perpetual revolution. Teng's pragmatic approach led him into conflict and political demise under Mao. But now it appeared that the vice-premier had become a political power and a major contributor to the direction of China under new leadership.

It will be some time yet before the impact of this "new" direction can be determined. In the meantime, social and economic changes within China are sure to stir peasant and worker demands.

The 2,885-member National People's Congress has a five-year term of office. Its functions are to amend the Constitution, make laws, approve the national economic plan, and to "appoint and remove the Premier of the State Council and members of the State Council *on the proposal of the Central Committee of the CCP*" (italics added). The permanent organ of the National People's Congress is the Standing Committee of 167 members. Its duties are to interpret laws, ratify and denounce treaties, receive foreign diplomatic envoys, and enact decrees. Accountable to the National People's Congress and the Standing Committee, the State Council is the "Central People's Government," and it consists of a premier, twelve vice-premiers, and heads of 29 ministries. Its duties encompass direction of state affairs, drafting and executing the national economic plan and state budget, and overall leadership and coordination of the work of the ministries and local organs of state nationwide.

The Chairman of the PRC   The chairman of the People's Republic of China was elected by the National People's Congress for a four-year

term. Constitutionally, his status lacked independence because his duties were essentially to act in pursuance of decisions made by the body electing him or by its Standing Committee. At the same time he commanded the People's Liberation Army and was empowered to convene the Supreme State Conference. The position was thus not without influence and status. Mao was elected chairman of the PRC in 1954 and served until 1959 when Liu Shao-ch'i was elected to replace him. Liu's election as chairman was interpreted to signify his elevation to rank as the number two man in the ruling oligarchy and his confirmation as Mao's eventual successor. Liu served until he was purged during the Cultural Revolution.

The State Council   The real locus of state power resided in the State Council, the "executive organ of highest state authority." Members of the State Council were appointed or removed by the chairman of the People's Republic of China in accord with decisions by the National People's Congress or its Standing Committee. The State Council is partly analogous to a cabinet in Western governments in that it consists of a premier, a number of vice-premiers, several ministries and commissions, and a secretariat. On the other hand it alone is responsible to submit bills to the National People's Congress, and to "coordinate and lead the work of local administrative organs of state throughout the country." The position of premier is a powerful post, and Chou En-lai was the only man to serve as premier from 1954 until his death in January 1976. The premier's power derived not only from his control of the wide-ranging apparatus of the state, but also from his high position as a member of the party Politburo.

Centralized leadership of the party over all organs of state at all levels of government is indirectly emphasized constitutionally by not providing for a "chairmanship of the state." The senior executive of the operating state apparatus is the premier of the State Council, but his appointment and tenure of office, as well as those of his subordinate ministers, are totally dependent on the wishes of the Central Committee of the party.

In China, the National People's Congress and the State Council with its various ministries play a role similar to the Supreme Soviet in the Russian system. These organs translate party policy into action; that is, the state structures become the administrative arm of the party. In this capacity the state structure's primary function is to implement policy, acting as the bureaucratic arm of the party. While there is no question that key state ministers and members of the bureaucracy are members of the party and "wear more than one hat," the fact remains that, in China, the state structure has developed into a highly technical and administrative institution. Indeed, the Chinese make a distinction between policy making and administrative policy. Policy making is solely the preserve of the Politburo, Central Committee, and organs of the party. Administrative policy making refers to those administrative decisions made to implement the general line (political decisions). Due to these distinctions and the focus of the state apparatus, there have not evolved distinct lines and functions of state machinery—in contrast to the Soviet system.

The State Council, because of the subordination to political decision making and its narrow focus on technical and administrative matters, cannot be equated to a cabinet system in the West or to the cabinet functions in Japan. Similarly, the various heads of ministries are administrators rather than major political figures in Chinese politics.

THE CENTRALIZED STATE

At the national level, certain broad comparisons to the Soviet Union suggest themselves. Both the People's Republic of China and the Soviet Union are highly centralized states dominated by a Communist party. Both nations embrace a variety of "minority groups," but the methods of dealing with them differ. While the Soviet Union is a federated state with subordinate national administrative units (Belorussia and the Ukraine) which are nominally accorded the right to conduct their own foreign relations and are members of the United Nations, the People's Republic of China is a unitary state, and no attributes of sovereignty are accorded any constituent unit. Soviet nationality groups are given special symbolic importance in a two-house chamber, but Chinese minorities are given only token representation in the National People's Congress. The major minority groups in the PRC are permitted "autonomy" in the five autonomous regions (ARS); the Inner Mongolian AR, Ninghsia Hui AR, Sinkiang Uighur AR, Kwangsi Chuang AR, and the Tibetan AR.

Below the national level, governmental organization follows the pattern at the center. In addition to the autonomous regions, the major administrative subdivisions are the twenty-one provinces and the three special municipalities of Peking, Shanghai, and Tientsin. At the second and lower levels, the local congresses were not important power centers, and the People's Councils were dominant in executing policies determined by higher level councils and the State Council. Theoretically lower levels of government were given enough latitude and initiative in testing and adjusting policy to local conditions to satisfy the requirement for flexibility in practice and the "democratic" part of democratic centralism. During the Cultural Revolution, People's Councils were replaced by "revolutionary Councils."

Local organs of state power are provided for in provinces and municipalities directly under central control, and the lower levels of prefecture, city, county, rural people's communes, and towns. People's congresses at all levels have "permanent organs" called revolutionary committees which are responsible to the appropriate congress and to the state organ at the next higher level, but the revolutionary committees may be elected or recalled only with approval of the higher state organ.

The Supreme People's Court and local courts at all levels exercise "judicial authority." The procuratorial functions are handled by the public security organs at all levels. The courts are not independent, but are accountable, at each level, to the people's congresses and revolutionary committees which appoint and remove presidents of the people's courts.

THE PEOPLE'S LIBERATION ARMY

The People's Liberation Army (PLA) is the third major institutional political actor in China. From its inception in the 1920s, the PLA has theoretically been subject to party control: "The Party commands the gun, and the gun must never be allowed to command the Party."

Preceding victory over the Chinese Nationalists in 1949, civil-military conflicts were minimal, partly because the leaders in these overlapping spheres of activity were virtually the same people. Then, from 1949 to 1952, PLA leaders generally controlled the country directly. When other civilian-dominated institutions were established, the PLA obediently "returned to the barracks," that is, the PLA handed over political power and resumed its primary military role. The PLA remained under firm civilian control for the next decade because ideology required it and because PLA leaders continued to hold important party and government posts and were involved in major decisions.

Throughout the 1950s, the PLA functions changed from counterinsurgency (to eliminate Nationalist pockets) to mass mobilization of peasants for reconstruction, and then to party-building. Demobilized PLA cadres became local administrators, and the PLA itself engaged in postwar reconstruction of the infrastructure and mobilized the masses for nonmilitary purposes.

The PLA brought military victory to the party in 1949, and during the Korean War (1950–1953) the PLA gained valuable experience in the successful conduct of large-scale conventional military operations against modern and well-trained United Nations Forces. With massive Soviet assistance, the PLA became a relatively modern and professional force. The transformation of military forces from a guerrilla force to a professional organization always brings forth professional interests which may conflict with those of the political leadership.

The professional interest of the PLA required highly trained, disciplined combat formations equipped with standardized weapons of modern design, mechanized formations, and a larger and technically proficient air force. The Korean War taught PLA leaders that much of Maoist ideology for a "people's war" applicable to the Chinese civil war did not apply to a foreign war against modern forces using close air support, massive firepower, and infantry-armor-artillery teams.[18] Military leaders wanted a PLA that could hold its own internationally and they wanted close ties with the Soviet Union to achieve it. They accepted Soviet military doctrine and, as professionals, kept abreast of international military developments. These views and aspirations put them in direct conflict with those who thought the primary use for the PLA lay in nonmilitary tasks. Despite the interlocking nature of political and military leadership in China, the PLA, or rather its proper role in Chinese society, became an issue that is not yet permanently resolved in a manner acceptable to the three main political actors.

The State and the PLA   Officially, the 1954 Chinese Constitution converted the PLA to an organ of the state structure, subor dinate to the Ministry of Defense, one of the many ministries subordinate to the State Council. The armed forces of the People's Republic of China "belong[ed] to the people," and their duty was "to safeguard the gains of the people's revolution and the achievements of national construction, and to defend the sovereignty, territorial integrity, and security of the country" (Article 20). Command of the PLA was vested in the chairman of the People's Republic, who also was named chairman of the Council of National Defense (Article 42). Mao Tse-tung, chairman of the party's Central Committee, was also chairman of the People's Republic of China (1954–1959). In this position he nominated the membership (for election by the National People's Congress) of the National Defense Council and he also nominated the premier of the State Council whose duty it was, inter alia, to supervise the Ministry of Defense.

During 1959, Mao relinquished (he later said he was forced to give up) his position as chairman of the People's Republic of China to Liu Shao-ch'i and thus, constitutionally, was no longer commander of the PLA. Nevertheless, the role of the party and its Military Committee (of which Mao *was* chairman) remained influential. This committee directed a reorganization of the PLA in late 1959 following the purge of Minister of Defense P'eng Te-huai, whose career was terminated after he opposed Mao's policies during the Lushan Plenum in the summer of that year.

Lin Piao, the new minister of defense, streamlined the PLA organization by reducing the seven general departments to three, making the General Political Department the authoritative command center and actual power throughout the PLA. This organization is shown at Figure 10-3.

The CCP and the PLA   Under Lin's leadership the PLA turned away from the purely professional interests pursued by his predecessor and turned to the task of assuring

party dominance of the People's Liberation Army. The principle of collective leadership at all command levels was restated to enhance the role and prerogatives of the unit political officers. Strong efforts were made to demonstrate the common interests and identity of the PLA members and the people by emphasizing agricultural and industrial production projects and nonmilitary construction and public works.[19]

Yet again in 1966 and 1967, during the Cultural Revolution, the PLA intervened actively in political affairs, expanding its role well beyond normal military missions and displacing party and government organizations to enforce direct military rule. Several factors contributed to PLA intervention: a severe conflict among the civilian leadership, a breakdown in social order resulting from Mao's means to resolve this conflict, and Mao's use of the PLA (with the acquiescence or willingness of its leadership) to coerce his domestic political opposition. By 1969 the PLA had not simply expanded its role, it had a new role. It was the savior of the society and had rescued China from radical revolutionary chaos by intervening massively on the side of conservative social and political forces. As Chang has pointed out,[20] the PLA did not seek political power through a premeditated coup. On the contrary, its power expanded as a direct result of Mao's pressure on it to restore order.

If the PLA significantly increased its power among the party organs at the center, it was even more successful in increasing and consolidating its strength in the regions. In the spring of 1969, the military occupied 21 of 29 posts as chairmen of provincial revolutionary committees and 90 of 250 vice-chairman posts. They also held 22 of 29 first secretary positions in Provincial Party Committees and 95 of a total of 158 other provincial secretary positions.[21]

Lin Piao's rapid ascent in the political hierarchy to become Mao's successor was ac-

Figure 10-3: Organization of the People's Liberation Army, 1959

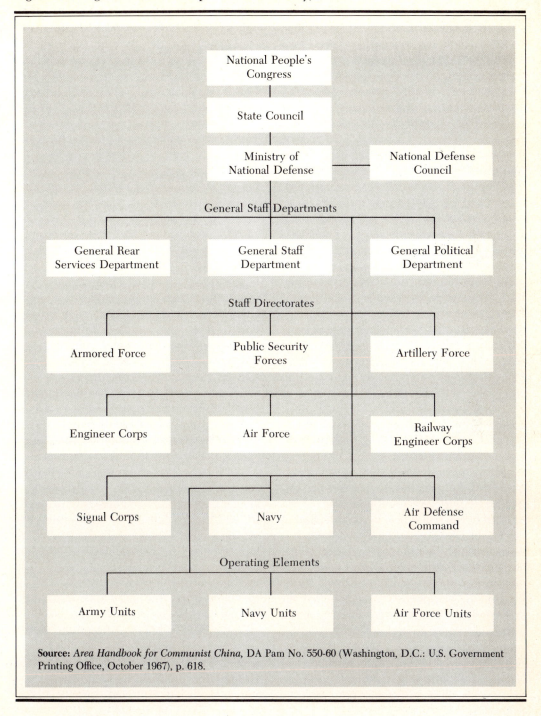

Source: *Area Handbook for Communist China*, DA Pam No. 550-60 (Washington, D.C.: U.S. Government Printing Office, October 1967), p. 618.

companied by expansion of the PLA's institutional power in many areas. This development was ideologically unpalatable to party civilian leadership and led inevitably to increased tension between the military and civilian leadership. At the Central Committee Plenum in Lushan in 1970, Marshal Lin Piao's top PLA supporters rose to deliver a "surprise attack," challenging Mao's earlier instructions that a new Chinese Constitution to replace the 1954 document should not provide for (and hence eliminate) the post of chairman of the People's Republic. Mao counterattacked, re-emphasizing that "the gun must not be allowed to command the Party," and launched a criticism campaign against Lin's supporters. In January 1971, Mao relieved the commander of the 38th Army, which had been stationed in the capital on Lin's orders since 1966, and moved that unit out of Peking.[22] Thereafter the PLA leaders contending for power apparently undertook serious planning for Mao's assassination in conjunction with an open seizure of power by selected units of the PLA. The plan for this military coup bore the memorably transparent code name "Project 571" (the numerals read in Chinese are a homonym for "armed uprising"). Reportedly the plan was leaked to Chou En-lai by Lin Tou-tou, daughter of Marshal Lin, just in time to avoid Mao's execution by the plotters. Along with his wife, Yeh Ch'ün, and his son, who was deputy director of operations of the Air Force, Lin fled China in the direction of the Soviet Union aboard a British-built Trident jet, which took them to their deaths in a burning crash in the Mongolian wastelands early in the morning of September 13, 1971. Lin's fellow conspirators were rounded up and arrested. Nearly three dozen generals posted in various central organs of the PLA soon lost their positions. By early 1973 almost fifty provincial-level party secretaries and about three-fourths of the military commanders or political commissars had been removed from office.[23]

In assessing the causes of the Lin Piao affair,

Mao's desire to eliminate the post of chairman of the People's Republic of China and Lin's opposition to it may be regarded as a clear focal point for resolution of interest conflicts, both personal and institutional. Mao had been chairman of the People's Republic of China from its establishment in 1954 until he relinquished the post in 1959 to Liu Shao-ch'i, Mao's previous "heir apparent." Liu held the post until purged during the Cultural Revolution. By 1971 the post had been vacant for several years and was clearly unnecessary to the functioning of government organs. Lin's status as "successor" to Mao had been proclaimed in the 1969 constitution, but his "successful succession," had the opportunity arisen, would have required the broadest possible base of support and the enhanced legitimacy of his claim which would derive from being chief of state. The realities of Chinese politics required Lin to seek the position for both personal and institutional interests and to try to consolidate his power in other areas. At the same time, these actions were necessarily counter to Mao's interests in maintaining his own power, contrary to Mao's interests in a unified party, and in opposition to the party's ideological imperative to monopolize power and authority. The Central Committee later made public some of the Project 571 documents which itemized policy differences between Lin and Mao: disaffection among the impoverished masses of peasants, the cadres who lost out in the Cultural Revolution, the young intellectuals sent to forced labor in the countryside, workers whose wages had been frozen, and cadres who had been forced into May Seventh Schools for thought reform. But policy differences alone do not satisfactorily explain the coup attempt.[24] Wary of Mao's penchant for "divide and conquer" tactics so skillfully demonstrated during the Cultural Revolution, the conspirators probably decided, after Mao's initiatives in late 1970 and early 1971, that they were next on the list.

With the death of Lin Piao in 1971 and the

reconstitution of the party in 1973, several actions were taken by Mao to drive home party victory over the PLA personnel who had supported Lin. Having diluted military influence at the center before and during the Tenth Party Congress, Mao moved to reduce it in the regions. He caused the reassignment of nearly all of the PLA commanders in the eleven military regions, men who had acquired political power during the Cultural Revolution and maintained it through Lin's fall from power. The purpose was to cut them loose from local power bases and to reemphasize the authority of the central organs.[25] The general effect was further to demilitarize Chinese politics as a continuation of the first major step in that direction, the removal from power of those associated with Lin's coup attempt.[26]

Using the past to criticize the present is a respected tradition in China, and a major campaign during 1974 was the "Criticize Confucius" campaign. Criticism of Confucius had earlier (1971) been a vehicle to castigate Liu Shao-ch'i, who allegedly "opposed the dictatorship of the proletariat" and had gone all out to propagate the "testaments" of Confucius. Confucius, himself a member of a decadent aristocratic family of the slave-owning class, so the interpretation reasoned, opposed economic reforms in order to preserve the economic base of slavery. Liu and his "gang" were accused of similarly using the ideas of all exploiting classes to corrupt the masses and to restore capitalism. Hence, both Confucius and Liu were counterrevolutionary and revisionist.[27]

Lin Piao was linked closely to Confucius throughout the 1974 campaign. He was depicted as having been a Confucianist at heart all along, who advocated "benevolence," "loyalty," and "filial piety" in order to rule others and to work for the "dupery, stultification of the workers and peasants in the interests of landowners and capitalists." Lin peddled the Golden Rule when he ought to have known that, in the class struggle, the rule is, "Do

unto others what you don't want others to do unto you." Mao had no use for the "asinine ethics" of Duke Hsiang.[28] The campaign stressed the need to prevent re-emergence of antiparty cliques whose activities were tied to the "Soviet revisionist renegade clique [which] has not given up its dream of subjugating China." The campaign was also related to the Tenth Party Congress' call to transform the "superstructure" in which criticism of Lin and Confucius was termed a "political and ideological struggle" by means of which Marxism prevails over revisionism. This was, indeed, a difficult task because reactionary Confucianism was "fairly deep-rooted," having been ceaselessly inculcated for some 2,000 years. The Criticize Confucius and Lin Piao Campaign was necessary to consolidate the dictatorship of the proletariat.[29]

Civil-Military Relations This 1975 formulation of PLA missions is substantially unchanged from that of two decades earlier, but civil-military command and control relationships have been clarified constitutionally. The 1975 Constitution formalized "civil-military" relationships which were confused by the 1966 purge of Liu Shao-ch'i, chairman of the PRC and titular commander of the PLA, and the 1971 flight and death of Lin Piao, sole vice-chairman of the Central Committee and minister of defense. For years there was no chief of state or commander-in-chief of the PLA, and there was no minister of defense from Lin's death in September 1971 until Yeh Chien-ying was named to succeed him in January 1975.

Authority over the PLA was restored to the party by the 1975 constitution. With the elimination of the post of chairman of the People's Republic of China, command of the armed forces was returned to the chairman of the Central Committee. As chairman of the Central Committee, Mao Tse-tung provided overall command to the PLA; as chairman of the Politburo of the Central Committee, he exerted policy control over the State Council, which supervises the Ministry of Defense; as chairman of the Party Military Commission, he exerted lateral policy control over the Ministry of Defense and, with that office, shares administrative control over the PLA chief of staff. If the 1954 constitution theoretically converted the PLA from a party organ to a state organ, the 1975 constitution reconverted it theoretically and actually from a state organ to a party organ. The fundamental mission of the armed forces (PLA and militia) is that of "a fighting force." Having the sole legitimate claim to a monopoly on the use of force, the PLA must be a substantial element in any analysis of power in the republic. For this reason, the military capabilities are considered here as they relate to the defense policy of China, and as a prelude to a summary of foreign policy in Chapter 11.

Organization and Capabilities PLA organization and capabilities were strongly influenced by two decades of experience in guerrilla and conventional mass infantry operations against the Chinese Nationalists and the Japanese within the territorial limits of China. In these years Mao's views became fixed on "people's war" and on tactics summarized as "when the enemy advances, we retreat; when the enemy halts, we harass; when the enemy seeks to avoid battle, we attack; when the enemy seeks to retreat, we pursue."

It has been claimed that the PLA is a people's army of a "new type, created and commanded by our great leader Chairman Mao and the Chinese Communist Party."[30] Constitutionally the PLA "is at all times a fighting force, and simultaneously a working force and a production force." The missions of the "armed forces" of China (which include the PLA and the people's militia) are (1) to defend the sovereignty, territorial integrity, and the security of the state; (2) to safeguard

the achievements of the socialist revolution and socialist reconstruction; and (3) to guard against subversion and aggression by imperialism, social-imperialism and their lackeys.

Soviet aid to China during the Korean War was followed by equipment modernization assistance estimated to be worth about two billion U.S. dollars by mid-1957. Soviet advisors were influential in modernizing the PLA until the late fifties.[31] Modernization meant that PLA officers became increasingly aware of the complexity of modern military operations, and this awareness cast doubt on the value of the pre-1949 experience. While profiting from the Soviet model, the PLA was also conscious that Chinese circumstances differed significantly from the Soviet situation in the context of party-military relations and overall defense needs.

Command and control organization, as well as the the force structure and the strategy adopted by China, have been greatly affected by the red versus expert issue, a conflict about which is more important, political control over the PLA or military combat efficiency. In China this issue has loomed larger than elsewhere because of the party's insistence that the essence of the PLA is its "revolutionary" character, and by the assertion that the acquisition of modern weapons is simply an external aspect of the PLA, unrelated to its basic nature. In short, men are more important than weapons: the decisive factor in war is men, and politics controls men. Therefore, the party uses "political commissars" and party committees within military units to ensure joint leadership.

Decision Makers

With regard to decision makers as political actors in China, only a few observations are necessary. From a methodological point of view, this category is least relevant in examining political actors. There are relatively few individuals in major posts in the party leadership who have exercised power for an exceptionally long period of time. Mao Tse-tung dominated both the red and expert points of views. Although the procedure is unpalatable to professional military officers, so long as Maoist doctrine prevails, the system is likely to retain its vitality. As Joffe summarized it, the "man-over-weapons" doctrine has been the major assumption justifying party supremacy over the PLA; the political control system provides its organizational basis.[32]

Moreover, similar to the Soviet Union, most of the decision makers are concentrated at the top of the party hierarchy. Unlike the Soviet Union, the Chinese political-economic system has not developed to a point where there has evolved some clearly distinguishing characteristics among the party leadership, the state structure, and the economic elite.

In the final analysis, one cannot speak of decision makers in the Chinese system without acknowledging the role of Mao and Maoism. Mao dominated the party (albeit not without challenge from time to time) from 1933 until his death in 1976. His genius for articulating party ideology and for giving force to programs is suggested by the eulogistic terms used to describe him: "Chairman Mao is the Red Sun in our Hearts. He is our Pole Star. The Great Helmsman." If Mao was the activist, the prime mover, and the originator and master of strategy achieved by alternating surprise, tension, and easement, as Edgar Snow has written, then Chou En-lai (1898–1976) was his perfect counterpart. Working together with Mao for four decades, Chou gained a wide reputation as a practical man, the perpetual compromiser, and the "indispensable man," handling deftly the planning and execution of policy which bored Mao. Tung Pi-wu, Marshal Chu Teh, and Marshal Yeh Chien-Ying all served the party in positions of great responsibility for forty years. Party leadership of the 1930s remained highly cohesive for several

decades, although the two major aspirants for Mao's mantle, Liu Shao-chi and Lin Piao, were eliminated during and after the Cultural Revolution. The decision makers owed their power to the institutional political actors which they tried to control: the party for Mao, the state structure for Chou, and the PLA for Lin.

Groups

Interest groups as political actors (except the party) have no autonomy in the Chinese political system. For all practical purposes, all groups are appendages of the party. This is particularly true of peasants and laborers. For example, in 1949 the party permitted the creation of an All-China Federation of Trade Unions. But when its objectives or policies came into conflict with those of the party, the party removed its leaders, and during the Cultural Revolution, dissolved the group. From time to time, work stoppages occur, but these are most likely the result of local dissatisfaction, not of organized labor activity, and are, of course, contrary to policy. Peasants are a vital force in Chinese life and have been organized more completely than ever in China's history. Nevertheless, the organizing activity is for party purposes and not for autonomously conceived social, economic, or political objectives. Farmers do make their needs and demands felt through passive resistance, sabotage, siphoning off of produce, or work slowdowns—and, of course, through the operation of the mass line. Youth have been mobilized in several organizations, for example, in the Red Guards. When party purposes were no longer being served, the Red Guards, for instance, were shut out of political activity by the PLA near the close of the Cultural Revolution. In general, interest and associational groups are not independent of party policy, are activated by party policy, and play an insignificant role in policy formulation.

Their major purpose has been to serve as a transmission belt for higher level directives.

Regionalism, however, is a persistent phenomenon in the Chinese political system. A continuation of the Warlord Era of the 1920s, regionalism is based on regional sentiments of the Chinese peasant against excessive demands from the center. This is reinforced by the tendency of many units of the PLA to be identified with a particular region as a result of their stationing and peasant background. Thus, regional government, regional identification, and association of units of the PLA with these regional structures provide a political base to resist policies from the center. This was particularly evident in the struggles over leadership in 1976 after Mao's death. Earlier this was seen in the response of regions to the Cultural Revolution.

In the Chinese system, some distinctions can also be seen between the ideologues and technicians and managers. The highly educated element of the Chinese state structure may have less commitment to the idealistic principles of Maoism than the party ideologues. Given the still rudimentary nature of the Chinese economic structure, however, the distinctions have as yet remained muted under the national effort to develop and mobilize national resources against perceived threats from the outside, particularly the Soviet Union. The point is that such groups and distinctions have not reached a stage of development to sufficiently articulate views in opposition to the party line, except as mobilized by party elite to support one or another leadership faction.

Political Influentials and Individuals

As we have discussed earlier in this chapter, the individual has no role in the Chinese political system. Rather it is the mass line—that is, the people as a mass, a socialized group—that is important to the Chinese system. Thus, the concept of individual is irrelevant to the total structure. Indeed, the individual is meaningful only in the context of an organized unit. Given the nature of Maoist ideology, the party and state structures, and the PLA, it is clear that individual rights and goals are emphatically subordinated to the party and the state.

What has been observed about the individual is generally true about political influentials. Indeed, any individual who becomes or tries to become influential outside party circles will soon find himself branded a bandit and, at the least, ostracized, isolated, and reduced to humble status. Political influentials evolve only as a result of their position in the highest organs of the party. Thus, it is generally true that political influentials as a separate group do not exist in China, at least in this stage of the development of the political system. The category of political influential or individual as a meaningful political actor is methodologically of little relevance in the Chinese political system. The lack of such categories, rather their inapplicability, suggests the centralizing features of the Chinese system and the character of the political process, political actors, and power.

Summary

The number and variety of political actors in China are limited compared to the United States or Japan. The Chinese Communist party, the state structure of China, and the People's Liberation Army are the major institutional political actors.

The party, the "core of the leadership of the whole Chinese people," is a revolutionary party whose ultimate aim is the realization of communism. It is the source of ideological orthodoxy and guides the entire nation. The 28,000,000 party members are a small elite, comprising no more than 3.5 percent of the population. The major party organs are the National Party Congress (1,249 members), the Central Committee (319 members), and the Politburo (and its Standing Committee), which is the real locus of decision making. Democratic centralism is the organization principle of the party. Constitutionally, the party leads industry, agriculture, commerce, culture and education, the PLA, the government, and the party, and all revolutionary mass organizations must accept this leadership. The party guides China, it formulates policy, mobilizes and controls society for party purposes, and supervises the state apparatus and the PLA in policy execution.

The Chinese state structure is a creation of the party. In theory all power belongs to the people and is exercised by the 2,885-member National People's Congress, which, like the Party Congress, meets infrequently and serves mainly as a legitimizing body. The real locus of state power is the State Council (the "executive organ of highest state authority") whose chairman (prime minister) can wield great power because he is also a powerful member of the Politburo and is the personal link between that body and the state apparatus. The 1975 Chinese Constitution further strengthened the prime minister by eliminating the position of chairman of the People's Republic of China. It formally reduced the powers of the state apparatus relative to the party by clearly stating the leadership role of the Chinese Communist party. Nevertheless, the role of the state apparatus in defining policy choices and implementing policy is vital.

The People's Liberation Army is theoretically subject to party control: "The Party commands the gun, and the gun must never be allowed to command the Party." It is both a military and a political force, "a fighting force, a working force, and a production force." With the primary mission to defend China, it has also served at times as a developmental and organizational model for all Chinese, as the savior of the party during the Cultural Revolution, and as the major threat to party dominance and the springboard for Lin's attempt to overthrow Mao. For the latter reason, the PLA was placed under the command of the party's chairman of Central Committee in the 1975 constitution.

The role of decision makers and groups in the Chinese political system are so incorporated into the party-state-PLA structure that it is unrealistic to speak of the former as political actors. This applies with even greater emphasis to political influentials and individuals as political actors. The essence of the political actors in the Chinese system lies in the triad of party-state-PLA, with the party clearly the dominant structure.

It is also important to note that the lack of serious political actors in the categories of groups and the subsuming of policy phases into one or another phase is an indicator of the type of political system that has evolved in China and the nature of the political process itself. Moreover, the minimal delineations in the policy process and the limited political actors are important bases for comparison. Such characteristics generally reflect a closed system and a centralized ideology.

NOTES

1. "The Party Exercises Overall Leadership," in *Peking Review*, no. 27 (July 5, 1974), p. 8.
2. The 1956 Chinese Communist party constitution is found in John Wilson Lewis, *Major Doctrines of Communist China* (New York: Norton, 1964), pp. 115–139.
3. Thomas W. Robinson, "China in 1973: Renewed Leftism Threatens the 'New Course,'" *Asian Survey*, vol. 14, no. 1 (January 1974), pp. 3–4.
4. Y. M. Kau and P. M. Perrolle, "The Politics of Lin Piao's Abortive Coup," *Asian Survey*, vol. 14, no. 6 (June 1974), p. 572.
5. Ralph L. Powell, "The Party, the Government, and the Gun," *Asian Survey*, vol. 10, no. 6 (June 1970), p. 460.

6. Franklin W. Houn, *A Short History of Chinese Communism* (Englewood Cliffs, N.J.: Prentice-Hall, 1967), p. 87.

7. See Parris H. Chang, *Power and Policy in China* (University Park and London: Pennsylvania State University Press, 1975), Appendix C, "Known Party Meetings (1949–66) and Their Possible Agendas," for a list of meetings of subordinate party organizations.

8. Constitution of the Chinese Communist Party, *Peking Review,* no. 18 (April 30, 1969), p. 36.

9. Richard Wich, "The Tenth Party Congress: The Power Structure and the Succession Question," *China Quarterly,* no. 58 (April/June 1974), p. 232.

10. Chou En-Lai, "Report to the Tenth National Congress of the Communist Party of China," *Peking Review,* nos. 35, 36 (September 7, 1973), pp. 17–25.

11. Wang Hung-wen, "Report on the Revision of the Party Constitution," ibid., pp. 29–33.

12. "Press Communique of the Tenth National Congress of the Communist Party of China, August 27, 1973," ibid., p. 6.

13. "Press Communique of the First Plenary Session of the Tenth Central Committee of the Communist Party of China," ibid, p. 10.

14. Powell, op. cit., p. 448.

15. For text, see *Peking Review,* no. 18 (April 30, 1969), pp. 16–35.

16. For text, see ibid., pp. 36–39.

17. See *Peking Review,* no. 4 (January 24, 1975) for the press communiqué, for Chou En-lai's "Report on the Work of the Government," for Chang Chün-chiao's "Report on the Revision of the Constitution," and for the text of the PRC Constitution.

18. William W. Whitson, *The Chinese High Command: A History of Communist Military Politics, 1927–71* (New York: Praeger, 1973), pp. 524–525.

19. *Area Handbook for Communist China,* DA Pam. 550-60 (Washington, D.C.: U.S. Government Printing Office, 1967), p. 619.

20. Parris H. Chang, "The Dynamics of Party-Military Relations in China," paper given at Conference on Civilian Control of the Military: Myth and Reality in Developing Countries, sponsored by SUNY, Buffalo, New York, October 18–19, 1974.

21. Kau and Perrolle, op. cit.

22. Ibid., pp. 560–561.

23. Ibid., pp. 561–562, 575.

24. Ibid., p. 565.

25. Wich, op. cit., p. 248.

26. John Bryan Starr, "China in 1974: 'Weeding Through the Old to Bring Forth the New,'" *Asian Survey,* vol. 15, no. 1 (January 1975), pp. 12–13.

27. "A Criticism of Confucius' Thinking on Education," *Peking Review,* no. 38 (September 17, 1971), pp. 6–9.

28. Yen Feng, "Confucius' Benevolence, Righteousness and Virtue and Lin Piao's Revisionist Line," *Peking Review,* no. 29 (July 19, 1974), pp. 6–9, 20. Footnote to the article reads "Duke Hsiang ruled the State of Sung in the Spring and Autumn Period during the 7th century B.C. In 638 B.C., that state fought the powerful state of Chu. The Sung forces were already deployed in battle positions when the Chu troops were crossing a river. One of the Sung officers suggested that, since the Chu troops were numerically stronger, this was the right moment to attack. But the Duke said: 'No, a gentleman should never attack anyone who is unprepared.' When the Chu troops had crossed the river but had not yet completed their battle alignment, the officer again proposed an immediate attack. Again the Duke said: 'No, a gentleman should never attack an army which has not yet completed its battle alignment.' The Duke gave the order for attack only after the Chu troops were fully prepared. As a result, the Sung troops suffered a disastrous defeat and the Duke himself was wounded."

29. Mass Criticism Group of Peking and Tsinghai Universities, "Struggle Between Opposing and Worshipping Confucius Over the Last 100 Years," *Peking Review,* no. 26 (June 28, 1974), pp. 6–11.

30. Excerpts from speech by Defense Minister Yeh Chien-ying on forty-fifth anniversary of the founding of the PLA, *Peking Review,* no. 31 (August 4, 1972).

31. Ellis Joffe, *Party and Army: Professionalism and Political Control in the Chinese Officer Corps, 1949–1964,* Harvard East Asia Monographs (Cambridge, Mass.: East Asian Research Center, Harvard University, 1965), pp. 40–41.

32. Ibid., p. 57.

CHAPTER 11

CHINESE POWER AND POLICY

In the Chinese system, as in the Soviet system, there are clear concentrations of power within the party. Yet there are major differences between the two systems. These are a result of several factors which include the nature of the Chinese revolution requiring a protracted guerrilla war; the role played by the armed forces in China during the years of struggle; the need for a large Chinese Communist bureaucracy to govern areas under its control during the struggle; and the personal impact of Mao and his philosophy. These led directly to the rise of three major political actors in modern China: the party, the state structure, and the People's Liberation Army. Moreover, the Maoist philosophy allowed little opportunity for the emergence of political actors separate from the institutional framework of party-state-PLA. This is not to suggest, however, that Maoism did not stimulate various interpretations and the development of factions. Indeed, a major characteristic of Chinese political life since the success of the Chinese Communists in 1949 has been continuing internal power struggles over the interpretation and application of Maoism. Moreover, Mao's views did not go unchallenged, and he was criticized at times for the wrong line or political mistakes. Nevertheless, Mao's pragmatic approach and his political astuteness allowed him to overcome these temporary setbacks. And, in the final analysis, Mao was the basis of moral authority.

The Policy Phases

In examining the power and policy phases of the Chinese system, therefore, one must be aware of the power interplay among the party-state-PLA political actors to the exclusion of virtually all other political actors of any importance. Indeed, the evolution of political actors, such as technical and managerial groups, has been deliberately obstructed by the Maoists for fear of the erosion of party influence. While technicians and managers do have important roles, these generally remain wedded to the Maoist philosophy and the official institutions of the party-state-PLA.

The primary focus of power and policy struggles takes place among the elite of the party and among party elite and those in the state structure and the PLA. Additionally, there are significant intra-elite struggles with various factions attempting to mobilize the masses for support. The masses, then, have no independent role to play in the policy phases except in "feedback," a reflection of the role of the masses during the dynastic period. Thus, while the number of political actors involved is generally limited to the three major institutions, there is much conflict and interplay among the elites within these institutions.

Moreover, in referring to the state structure, the focus is on the bureaucratic organization and the power exercised by the various ministries, rather than on policy approval as exercised in legislative process. As noted in earlier chapters, the 1975 Chinese Constitution is clear in its identification of the party as the leading organ. Moreover, the power that is given to the party in the constitution is designed to ensure the continuation of the revolution. In contrast to the provisions of the Soviet Constitution of 1936, the role and power of the Chinese party is made explicit: the party rules with all organs of the state designed to serve the party.

Mao's philosophical thrust was to develop a "new Man" and to effect a complete transformation of the Chinese political and social system. In such a system with its humanistic dimension, no one would derive personal gain or advantage without benefits to all. Mao's greatest fear was that the revolution, once started, would become subsumed in technical and managerial imperatives and that the Chinese Communist party would become "bourgeoisie" oriented, as he believed that the Soviet party had become. Indeed, the fundamental purpose of the Cultural Revolution was to revitalize the revolution and to prevent the Maoist philosophy from being taken over by bureaucratic and technical political actors.

One must not lose sight of the fact that the modern Chinese Communist state had been ruled by one man since its foundation. From 1949 to 1976, Mao Tse-tung was the guiding light and the basis for all moral authority.

Thus, the very basis of power and the purposes of policy had to develop a direct link with the Maoist concept of party and state. While Mao was sensitive to the masses and insisted that the masses become involved in the struggle, there is no question that the initiatives in policy were to come from the party. This has led to struggles between the party and the state structure as well as the PLA. One of the most serious struggles, for example, between the party and the PLA was about party control of the armed forces.

Emergence, Identification, Approval

Examining the policy phases of the Chinese system, therefore, reveals rather clearly that, in the areas of emergence, identification, and approval, the focus is primarily on the top leadership of the party. While this is generally true with the Soviet system, in China there is little external to the party to provide the kind of "interest group" activity that was identified with the Soviet system. Moreover, the Chinese system remains but one generation beyond its success and is still struggling for institutionalized patterns for the revolution, a major factor in the intra-elite struggles. Finally, the fact that China is a developing system suggests that interest group activity or the evolution of political actors outside the official institutions is severely limited both ideologically and by the character of developing societies in general.

Implementation and Feedback

Policy phases in the Chinese system are best examined by focusing on emergence, identification, and approval as one process, through the major elites within the institutions, while identifying implementation and feedback as actions not only within the bureaucratic structures, but also in terms of the response of the masses. On further examination of the Chinese system, one is struck by the inextricable intertwining of the various policy phases, particularly in terms of the elite-bureaucratic relationship. Given these fundamental characteristics of the Chinese system, it is more useful to focus on major periods of Chinese development over the past 25 years in a case study perspective to reveal the power and policy character of the system. Thus, rather than identify the various policy phases, as we have done for the United States and the Soviet Union, we shall examine the policy phases by focusing on case studies of particular events in China over the past 25 years.

One qualification needs to be made. Historically, the Chinese system has been susceptible to regionalism. Indeed, the Warlord Era in the 1920s is a clear reflection of this characteristic. In the modern Chinese system, the problems of regionalism persist. During the Cultural Revolution, for example, regional loyalties emerged to obstruct many activities of the Red Guard. Similarly, regional needs are more clearly perceived by the masses than some of the exhortations of the mass line. Moreover, PLA units, state bureaucrats, and party officials associated with a particular region do tend to develop regional concerns in opposition to the Peking perspective. Mao and his lieutenants were quite aware of these tendencies, hence the serious concern with party control over the PLA and the institutionalization of the revolution and control over party activities within the various regions. Nevertheless, the peasants of China are still primarily concerned about the immediate environment and regional concerns and loyalties have not disappeared. In this sense, regionalism can be considered a latent political actor. However, the fact that there is no articulated and accepted regional power focus

militates against autonomous political actors reflecting this view.

This chapter discusses the use of power in domestic politics, using as its vehicle the theme of internal economic development, and outlines the Great Proletarian Cultural Revolution. It treats the use of power in international politics by summarizing China's foreign policy objectives and means to achieve them. It concludes with an assessment of China's achievements and prospects.

Moreover, in this chapter we will again see how various phases or categories that are relatively clear in other political systems are hardly distinguishable in the Chinese political system. Because of the dominant role of the Communist party and the relatively long and dominant rule of Mao, most of the important policy decisions took place—and still do—at the highest organs of the party.

Economic Development in the 1950s

The politics of Communist China, like those of any other Communist state, are the politics of forced-pace economic growth. . . . The Maoist slogan "politics in command of the economy" is not an empty ideological statement, nor the expression of a determination to override objective economic laws. It is a concept which arises logically from the nature of Maoist economic activity.[1]

Economic theory is the heart of socialist doctrine. Economic development has been a major objective of the Chinese Communist party. At the same time, the party has sought the equally important objective of the political integration of society.

Tracing some of these developments since 1949 provides a means to clarify the main thrust of Chinese domestic politics, to outline some major policy changes, and to explain in ideological terms the interaction of theory and practice. This approach also serves to describe the allocation of resources and distribution of political power among various institutions and political factions. The emphasis on development strategies is not meant to downgrade other concepts for analysis of Chinese politics.[2]

ONE PROCESS: EMERGENCE, IDENTIFICATION, APPROVAL

With victory in 1949, the Chinese Communist party set about the reconstruction of the nation, apparently broken in morale, riddled by inflation, uncertain about its future, but hoping for a "new China." To restore productive capacity and the transportation system, and to establish political control over newly acquired urban areas and consolidate the rural areas, the party waged several campaigns to mobilize the Chinese masses in support of the new government. These campaigns were designed to involve them personally, directly, and deeply in carrying out socialist revolution.

The former ruling classes (Chinese Nationalist landlords) had to be eliminated and their power transferred to hundreds of millions of peasants. The peasants had to liberate themselves, and "liberation" meant the establishment of "people's courts" where decisions were made on how to carry out the provisions of the Agrarian Reform Law of 1950. Although China avoided the trauma associated with the Soviet elimination of the *kulaks* in the 1930s, one to two million landlords were executed by 1952. Few of them could have owned more than a dozen acres.[3] On balance, however, violence as a technique for control was less important than persuasion, indoctrination, and forced mass participation in "campaigns."

Throughout the Korean War (1950–1953), China was fully mobilized. Strenuous efforts were made to strengthen the Communist party hold on the Chinese people. The Three Antis campaign of 1951, fought against "corruption, waste, and bureaucratism," was a continuation of an earlier "rectification" campaign to tighten control over party cadres who did not meet rigid standards of conduct. The leadership role of this elite was vastly complicated after the seizure of power in 1949. Its capacities were severely tested by the enormous tasks of rationalizing government procedures and agrarian reform, of securing loyalty to the new regime, of bringing about economic recovery, and of conducting military campaigns in Korea and Tibet. Standards slipped. This attempt to improve leadership by demanding selfless devotion to party and eradication of bureaucratic ideas of self-importance was complemented by continuing efforts to uncover and destroy counter-revolutionary elements.

The "Five Antis" campaign of late 1951 served both political and economic ends. The five acts to be opposed were bribery, tax evasion, theft of state property, cheating on government contracts, and stealing state economic secrets. The primary targets were capitalist merchants and manufacturers. The campaign resulted in destruction of much of the urban middle class by nationalization of its assets and provided funds to help finance the war.

The period of economic reconstruction (1949–1952) closed with industrial production more than doubled at an annual growth rate of 34 percent, war-damaged productive capacity restored, and large increases in employment.[4]

THE FIRST FIVE-YEAR PLAN (1953–1957)

With morale raised by victory in the Korean War and relieved of the defense expenditures connected with it, China embarked on the First Five-Year Plan (1953–1957). Inspired by the Soviet model, this plan gave priority to development of basic industry through large-scale, centrally planned, integrated plants, and depended greatly on massive Soviet support (see Tables 11-1 and 11-2).

One Process China adopted the following major features of the Soviet model: (1) state ownership of important industrial, financial, and transportation facilities; (2) tight, centralized control over allocation of key commodities and over division of resources for investment, defense, and consumption; (3) a development strategy of forced-draft industrialization giving priority to investment and, within investment, to heavy industry; (4) growth targets in the framework of five-year plans; (5) a massive bureaucracy to oversee, in detail, execution of the plans; (6) organization of party units at every level to transmit details of the plans and to monitor their day-to-day execution; (7) further extension of party control over the economy through mass organizations, such as peasant associations, labor unions, women's associations, and professional bodies; (8) collectivization of agriculture; and (9) the use of foreign trade to get machinery and technology not available in China and for the ultimate objective of economic self-sufficiency. During the 1950s, more than 12,000 Soviet engineers and technicians worked in China and thousands of Chinese were trained in the Soviet Union. The core of China's industrial development was about 250 modern Soviet projects—steel mills, machinery plants, and electric generating stations—which had been completed by the time Soviet personnel were withdrawn in 1960.[5]

Professor Gray explains Mao's concept of economic development[6] as based on the assumption that local rural communities would have the means and could be given the incentives to modernize for themselves in the many-faceted and interacting processes of the

growth of production, institutional change, political consciousness, and cultural advance. This concept requires decentralized decision making in local units small enough to provide direct participation for those affected. It assumes that the local community can, by cooperation, increase production, generate savings for limited capital investment, and become self-sustaining. At some stage, assistance from the state sector is needed and national integration begins. A new "achievement ethic" develops, and "entrepreneurship" (in a collectivized context) becomes a habit. But the process is not self-sustaining if the political aspect of the economic process is left out. Individuals or groups may value self-enrichment over group interest. Leaders may violate the mass line by arbitrary or bureaucratic decision making, or by alliance with the right or left, those who resist change or those who see it prematurely. This, Gray adds, "is why politics must be in command."

Implementation Rural collectivization began in the early 1950s with the formation of mutual aid teams. This was the first stage in a four-stage process designed to overcome the results of the initial redistribution of land from landlords to individual peasant owners and to achieve a full-scale commune system. Mutual aid teams were voluntary associations of five to ten households who pooled their labor and privately owned resources during planting and harvesting seasons. This type of cooperation was ages old in China. What was new was external pressure to eliminate the voluntary aspect, local social pressure to assure conformity, and the demand for change from temporary to permanent organization for mutual aid at this lowest level. By 1954 the permanent teams numbered about ten million members comprising 58 percent of all peasant households.[7]

The basis for the second stage of collectivism was formed by elementary agricultural

Table 11–1: China's Development Phases, 1952–1974

Phase	Description
1953–1957, First Five-Year Plan: "Leaning to One Side"	Maximum rate of fixed capital formation. Priority for development of basic industry. Forced draft industrialization; large-scale, centrally planned, integrated plants, Soviet style. Acceptance of principle of developing local industry serving local needs and utilizing local resources, but more lip service than practice.
1958–1960, Great Leap Forward: "Walking on Two Legs"	First signs of rejection of Stalinist model of industrialization in favor of Maoist all-out mass mobilization and mass participation. Proliferation of small-scale, inefficient local enterprises with backyard technologies. Nurturing of local initiative and regional self-sufficiency.
1961–1965, Great Crisis and Readjustment	Economic crisis forces shift of priority to agriculture. Return to Liuist approach: centralized planning and administration by professionals at national and provincial levels; return to economic rationality (uneconomic Great Leap plants closed). Rural industrialization pushed vigorously.
1966–1969, Cultural Revolution	Reversion to Maoist principles, pitting masses against technical and managerial elites. Worship of nativism and renewed pitting of red against expert. Destruction of party bureaucracy; sporadic economic disruption.
1970–1974, Post-Cultural Revolution	Return to economic order; new wave of industrial expansion. Shift in planning and decision making to regional and provincial levels, and further development of decentralized industrial plants in outlying regions. Use of the more advanced industrial centers to spread industrial systems into hinterland.

Source: *China: A Reassessment of the Economy—A Compendium of Papers Submitted to the Joint Economic Committee, Congress of the United States* (Washington, D.C.: U.S. Government Printing Office, July 10, 1975), p. 684.

producers' cooperatives (APCs). The APC often consisted of one village of from 20 to 40 households. Land, tools, and animals remained under private ownership but the specific use of them was decided by annual plans designed by the APC management. Members of the APC were to be compensated in proportion of their capital input and their own labor.

During 1956, the government moved into the third stage of collectivization by consolidating the elementary APCs into advanced APCs which included about three-fourths of all peasants. Several small villages, a large village, or perhaps a county of 100 to 300 households made up one advanced APC. Peasants no longer held any private claim to their former land holdings or other capital; instead, they held a share of the collective equity. Compensation to peasants was based solely on the amount of work performed. The burden of the agricultural tax was shifted from the individual and became the collective obligation of the advanced APC. By October of 1957, 96 percent of peasant households were in APCs.

Feedback Peasant discontent resulted. The serious debate about how best to increase agricultural production, which had charac-

Table 11–2: Major Economic Indicators, 1949–1974

Year	GNP, billions of 1973 dollars	Per Capita GNP, 1973 dollars	Midyear Population, millions	Industrial Production[a]	Agricultural Production[a]	Steel Output, millions of metric tons	Grain Output millions of metric tons
1949	40	74	538	20	54	0.16	108
1952	67	117	570	48	83	1.35	154
1953	71	122	583	61	83	1.77	157
1957	94	147	641	100	100	5.35	185
1958	113	172	657	145	108	11.08	200
1959	107	160	672	177	83	13.35	165
1960	106	155	685	184	78	18.67	160
1961	82	118	695	108	77	8	160
1965	134	179	747	199	114	12.5	210
1966	145	190	763	231	116	15	215
1969	157	192	817	265	118	16	220
1970	179	214	837	313	129	17.8	240
1974 (prelim.)	223	243	920	432	141	23.8	255

[a]Index of 1957 = 100 is used for industrial and agricultural production.

Source: *China: A Reassessment*, op. cit., p. 23.

terized China's development politics from the beginning, increased in tempo and temper. Chang outlined the two contending approaches to socialist construction.[8] The "radical" approach stressed subjective factors, such as class consciousness and attitudinal changes which are susceptible to political mobilization. It favored early agricultural collectivization to use land and labor more efficiently and to ease state collection of surpluses and the accumulation of capital. The "conservative" approach emphasized material incentives to the cultivator and the provision of advanced technology, such as chemical fertilizer along with some agricultural machinery. The Soviet experience strongly influenced this approach, which argued mainly that collectivization ought to be postponed until domestic industry could support it.

For his part, Mao believed that rapid industrialization in China could come about only after a sustained large-scale effort to increase agricultural production and that collectivization was the proper method for both political and economic reasons. It would strengthen the party control over the people and provide for accumulation of capital. Others in the central leadership disagreed, so the collectivization program encountered difficulties. Some problems, such as the heavy weather damage to crops in the fall of 1956, were beyond political control, but others were seen as political failures. Peasants and leaders both blamed the too hasty collectivization process for the scarcity of some goods. Many farmers withdrew from the larger APCs. In some areas the government reduced the size of, or dissolved, the APCs. The leadership realized that China was not on the brink of achieving, as the 1954 party constitution had stated, "the illimitable possibilities for the gigantic development of the productive forces of society."

The lag in agricultural development was sharply criticized, despite the substantial gains in the industrial sector which resulted from Soviet aid. Following Mao's call in 1956 to "let one hundred schools of thought contend; let one hundred flowers bloom," the volume and intensity of criticism increased. Thereupon Mao issued in 1957 his essay titled "On the Correct Handling of Contradictions Among the People." This essay established the limit of permissible dissent. Nonantagonistic contradictions among the "people" (those who support and work for the cause of socialist construction) are both necessary and desirable in pursuit of the socialist transformation. But antagonistic contradictions between the "people" and those who resist the revolution and sabotage it are neither necessary nor desirable. The "enemies of the people" could not be tolerated. The Anti-Rightist campaign of mid-1957 expanded into the larger Rectification campaign, and the intellectuals once more became a target of the regime. These campaigns foreshadowed the re-emergence of the "radical" line of agricultural development known as the Great Leap Forward.

THE GREAT LEAP FORWARD (1958–1960)

One Process. The Third Central Committee Plenum of the Eighth National Party Congress met for the unusually long time of 20 days in September and October of 1957. It was decided that emphasis on heavy industry (Soviet credits were then nearly exhausted) must give way to "walking on two legs," the simultaneous balanced development of industry and agriculture. Debate over the speed and scope of development was ended temporarily. As Liu Shao-ch'i stated it in his "Report on the Work of the Central Committee, May 5, 1958,"

The current mighty leap forward in socialist construction is the product not only of the successful development of the anti-rightist struggle and the rectification campaign but also of the correct implementation of the Party's general line—to build socialism by exerting our utmost efforts, and press-

ing ahead consistently to achieve greater, faster, better and more economical results.[9]

The Great Leap was not a fully drawn explicit plan for development. It was an intensively political mass movement proclaimed and urged on in a rhetoric of unrestrained optimism: "twenty years in one day." Its methods were exhortation, experimentation, reliance on the mass line, decentralization, and enormous efforts to "advance on all fronts."

Mao apparently made the decision to take the Great Leap in the spring of 1958 and to make the commune its organizational basis. His concept publicized in July 1958 was:

Our direction is to combine, step by step, and in an orderly manner, workers (industry), peasants (agriculture), businessmen (exchange), students (culture and education), and soldiers (military) into a large commune, which is to constitute our nation's basic social unit. In this kind of commune, industry, agriculture and exchange are the people's material life; culture and education are the people's spiritual life which reflect their material life. The total arming of the people is to protect this material and spiritual life.[10]

This concept was approved by the Politburo and published in a resolution of the Central Committee on August 29, 1958.[11] The Central Committee resolution saw the emergence of the people's communes as an "irresistible" development rooted in the "all-round continuous leap forward in China's agricultural production" and the ever-rising political consciousness of the peasant.

Implementation To combat resistance among the cadres charged with carrying out the Great Leap, the *hsia fang* movement of 1957–58 resulted in the "transfer down" of literally hundreds of thousands of provincial cadres from higher to lower levels of authority. The "demotions" were meant to eliminate the "commandism" and "bureaucratism" of recalcitrant cadres in the APCs. Other cadres seemed too closely identified with the interests of some of the more prosperous peasants who had benefited from the material incentives of the previous few years. The apparently ineradicable contradiction between socialism and capitalism had sharpened, and both peasants and cadres had therefore to take part in the Socialist Education Movement. The party held many conferences for cadres in late 1957 to bring into the open the negative views of those tending to the "capitalist road" or dragging their heels. The technique of "free debate" and opposing negative views with party "positive views" is a prime example of the great value placed on ideology as a tool to remold the views and alter the behavior of those who doubt the correctness of the party line.

In conjunction with the expanded antirightist campaign in the winter of 1957–58, millions of peasants were mobilized for immense projects for irrigation and flood control in the "water conservancy campaign." Increased agricultural production demanded such huge public works programs, which were carried out generally without central assistance or investment, along with campaigns to improve the soil, to plow deeper, to destroy insects, and so on. Local planning initiative and reliance on local resources was the takeoff point for a wide variety of construction and low-level labor-intensive manufacturing efforts to use the rural labor surplus to provide the investment that could not be provided by the urban industrial sector. These various campaigns convinced the central leadership that the APC organization was too small and too limited in function to carry forward the policies for rapid increases in rural production. APCs took on broader functions which conflicted with those of the regular government, such as education, credit and bank-

ing, public works, and handicraft industries. The adherents of the "capitalist road" were now defeated economically, politically, and ideologically. In some areas, it claimed, the agricultural output had increased ten- or twenty-fold. Demands for rural industry, mechanization, and electrification required the transfer of manpower from agriculture and the erection of a structure for large-scale cooperation cutting across old administrative divisions.

The Central Committee resolution claimed that transformation of the countryside had become a "common mass demand" with the support of the "poor and middle-class" peasants, that is, those who were more numerous, less productive, and most likely to gain from consolidation. The transformation was indeed rapid (see Table 11-3). The 26,000 communes averaged 5,000 households and 10,000 acres, but ranged upward in size from 2,000 households.

Democratic centralism was proclaimed to be the organizational principle of the communes. Three levels of administration were established, the commune, the production brigade, and the production team. The latter two corresponded roughly to the earlier higher level APC and the lower level APC. The commune held responsibility for overall economic planning, for the militia, for political, cultural, and educational affairs, and for large-scale agricultural, commercial, industrial, and conservancy projects. The party had parallel organizations at the two higher levels. A party secretary and six committees (organization, propaganda, youth, women, military affairs, and political) were set up at commune level, and a corresponding party branch with branch committees was set up at brigade level. Fundamentally, China now had a *new* basis for organization of the entire countryside, and the commune supplanted governmental organs specified in the 1954 Chinese Constitution. But the "fundamental

Table 11–3: Development of Socialist Agricultural Units in the People's Republic of China

	1950	1952	1956	1957	1958	1961
Seasonal/ permanent mutual aid teams	3,124,000	8,026,000	0	0	0	0
Lower level APCs	18	3,634	682,000	72,022	0	0
Higher level APCs	1	10	312,000	680,081	0	0
Rural Communes	0	0	0	0	26,578	26,000
Percent of peasant households organized	10.7	40.0	96.3	97.0	99.1	Not available

Source: Frederick W. Cook, "The Commune System in the People's Republic of China, 1963-1974," in *China: A Reassessment*, p. 373.

question," according to the party, was to strengthen the party's leading role, realize the principle of "politics in command," and "merge the Party and Commune into one."

Centralization of power at commune level meant the regimentation of daily life to an unprecedented degree. Stakhanovite measures were demanded of all workers. "Backyard furnaces" were erected to increase iron production. Workers' spare time was eaten up by all types of minor improvement projects. Production brigades, unlike earlier APCs which worked the land in a given locality, were shifted from place to place for agricultural and other projects. The individual's economic activity, his place of residence (often a dormitory separated from his family), his working conditions, and his entire outlook were disciplined in new ways. Centralization of power in the new, larger communes meant concentration of authority in the hands of persons unaccustomed to that new and untried organization. Great disruptions in personnel and in the allocation of functional responsibilities were inevitable in the attempt to develop new planning, production, marketing, and distribution relationships.

Feedback   Clearly the Great Leap had vital faults. Generally it tried to do too much in too little time. Work incentives reached a new low in the communes, which reduced and often eliminated the traditional private plots. Incentives diminished further with experiments to pay labor according to need rather than by work units performed. In some instances, more efficient villages saw their surplus redistributed to less efficient neighbors. Decentralized accounting and statistical systems lacked standardization and were inadequate for economic planning. The psychological stress and strain on hundreds of millions of Chinese were exacerbated by the Great Leap which followed more than a decade of almost constant change in a period charged with individual uncertainty. Finally, bad weather and disastrous harvests brought an end to the Great Leap.

The magnitude of the disaster of the Great Leap is suggested by reference to Table 11-2.

The significant gains made through 1958 were the result of the nearly frantic all-out mobilization of the Chinese people and gave rise to unjustified and overly optimistic estimates of grain output. Despite the diversion of some agricultural labor into other production, the party estimated grain production would rise to 250 million metric tons in 1958 and to 270 million metric tons in 1959. Actually the 1959 output was near the level of 1953, but the population had increased by nearly 90,000,000 people in the interim. By 1960 the leadership knew quite well that the Great Leap Forward was no such thing. It failed to achieve its objectives to

abolish exploitation of man by man, and to build a classless society in which the difference between city and countryside, between mental and manual work will disappear and the idea of "from each according to his ability, to each according to his needs will become the order of the day."[12]

The leaders of the People's Liberation Army played a conspicuous role in the intra-governmental conflict about the excesses of the Great Leap Forward. This conflict reached its climax of the Eighth Central Committee during the summer of 1959 at Lushan, in Kiangsi Province. Marshal P'eng Teh-Huai, minister of defense, mounted a direct frontal attack against the Great Leap policies in "the most serious" intra-party opposition Mao had encountered since 1942.[13] In part, P'eng's attack had its origins in PLA professional reaction to party policies that, for example, forced the PLA to expend 59 million workdays on agricultural tasks in 1958. It was also related to P'eng's desire for military collaboration with the Soviet Union, which was frustrated by the party's decision to sever completely all the military arrangements between the two countries only two weeks before the Lushan Plenum. Whatever P'eng's dissatisfaction over defense policy, his attack

concentrated on Maoist economic policies and he was joined by others. P'eng criticized the Chinese Communist party for poor planning of the Great Leap, for leftist tendencies which led to the optimistic and erroneous view that China could leap into communism in one big step, for prematurely diverting peasant labor into such industrial projects as the backyard furnaces, and for substituting the principle "politics in command" for certain economic laws. Mao marshaled enough support to defeat P'eng and to remove him from office along with Huang K'o-cheng, chief of staff of the PLA. Marshal Lin Piao and General Lo Jui-ching became minister of defense and chief of staff, respectively. Both were purged later.

One Process: Policy Revision   Mao's victory over his critics at Lushan presented a dilemma. Actual conditions seemed to require retreat from the Great Leap policies. Yet it was also necessary to continue those very policies to demonstrate Mao's ideological correctness and to prevent public tarnishing of his image. What occurred was essentially a retreat, but the retreat in agriculture began even before the Lushan meeting. In early 1959 the communes started to shift ownership of most means of production down to the production brigade. Even the brigade was too large to manage and motivate farmers effectively, so in 1961, the production team of 20 to 30 households was made the basic agricultural unit with ownership and control of most of the means of production. This decentralization did not mean the commune system ceased to exist. On the contrary, the communes retained functions best centralized at that level, for instance, coordination of production, water control, and some health activities, while education (after 1968) was delegated to production brigades along the small-scale water conservation and other subsidiary projects. Private plots were returned to peasant control in 1962, and the incentive system was changed to make the pay suitable to the work done.[14]

These measures were part of the 1960 decision to abandon "walking on two legs" for an "agriculture-first" policy with agriculture as the "foundation" and industry as the "leading sector." Economic planning was recentralized, uneconomic Great Leap projects were closed out, and industry supporting agriculture got priority treatment. By 1962 the party had swung to the right and economic rationality was the order of the day.

In April 1959, as we have seen, Mao relinquished his post as chairman of the People's Republic to Liu Shao-ch'i. Presumably Liu enjoyed Mao's confidence as a hard-line advocate of the Great Leap, but seems to have reversed his field to direct the general retreat from Mao's Leap with the assistance of Ch'en Yün (vice-chairman of the Central Committee and Politburo), P'eng Chen (Politburo member and mayor of Peking from 1951 to 1966), Po I-po (chairman of the State Economic Commission from 1956 to 1966), and Teng Hsiao-p'ing (general secretary of the Chinese Communist party and member of the Politburo Standing Committee, from 1956 to 1966). All members of the group were purged during the Cultural Revolution as "capitalist roaders," "freaks," "demons" "counterrevolutionaries" who were guilty of "heinous crimes." So Mao's diminution of power was only temporary. He retained the support of China's "indispensable man," Chou En-lai, chairman of the People's Republic's Council of Ministers, and won the support of the PLA controlled by Marshal Lin Piao after P'eng's purge.

Lin Piao led the portion of top PLA leadership that opposed overdependence on Soviet military support and supported Mao. As minister of defense and second to Mao in the party Military Affairs Committee, Lin faced the formidable tasks of reasserting party control over the PLA, restoring its morale, and heightening its political consciousness. For the PLA this meant adoption and rigid practice of Lin's (and Mao's) principle of the "four firsts": human factor first, political work first, ideological work first, and living thought first. PLA men with "dogmatic" and "purely military viewpoints" had to undergo re-education which had begun in 1958 under Lin's predecessor in the so-called officers to the ranks campaign.[15] All officers were directed to spend one month yearly in the ranks as an ordinary soldier to make the officers red as well as expert. Reportedly, 150,000 officers and 160 generals took part by February 1959, with generals pulling sentry duty and others doing dismounted drill with privates.

Lin's primary contribution to refastening party control over the PLA was in organized political work. Company-level party committees were revived in 1960 and made the basic unit for control and political education in the PLA. Within several months, the PLA's General Political Department had investigated 20,000 company-level party branches, purged about 2,000 party members, recruited 229,000 new party members, and claimed that 100 percent of company-level units had branch committees. This was a truly massive party infiltration of the PLA.[16]

So successful was Lin that the PLA became the model for all other institutions in the society, a position exemplified in the Learn from the People's Liberation Army campaign begun in 1963. Mao called on the whole nation to imitate PLA methods of organization, operation, and ideological training. In a sense, it was a rebuke to the party, and Chang sees it as the gradual buildup of the PLA as a "counterinstitution" to the party. Mao ordered party and state organizations to establish networks of "political work departments" modeled on the PLA. In some instances, these departments were staffed by PLA cadres or by civilian cadres trained by the PLA.[17] Not only did Mao tighten his grip on the PLA; he tightened his grip on other institutions with PLA assistance. Mao now had in place the ultimate power base for the massive shake-up and restructuring of the party known as the Great Proletarian Cultural Revolution (1966-1969).

The Great Proletarian Cultural Revolution

The Great Proletarian Cultural Revolution was a mass movement in the tradition of party campaigns but qualitatively different in the enormity of disruption and turmoil it visited on the Chinese people. Designed to change the attitudes and behavior of the Chinese people, it clearly had links with the cultural reform activities of Chinese intellectuals of the May Fourth Movement, and even earlier.

ONE PROCESS

In the early 1960s, Mao became increasingly dissatisfied with the rational economic policies of Liu and others which brought recovery from the disasters of the Great Leap. Mao worried about the direction internal policies were taking. He seemed to fear that Liu's pragmatism would lead China along the road to revisionism and the restoration of capitalism. Clearly, this view of the origins of the Cultural Revolution maintains, the Chinese revolution had lost its momentum. The unexpected consequences and the failures of the Hundred Flowers campaign and the Great Leap Forward had resulted from a lack of spiritual strength on the part of the leadership and its inability to understand Chinese Communist ideology. Mao's policies were not in error; success would reward ideological purification and renewed spirit. According to this view, the Cultural Revolution was meant to revitalize the party and the people by providing a synthetic revolutionary experience.

Another view of its origins holds that the Cultural Revolution was primarily the outgrowth of a power struggle. Mao was being deprived of power, it argues, by the bureaucratic "experts" directing the country's economic recovery. He could not abide the debasement of the revolution and permit the country to be run by bureaucrats and technicians. Having withdrawn to "reign" rather than "rule" in the early 1960s, as Professor Pye puts it, Mao found himself blocked when he tried to resume full control of Chinese affairs in 1962.

In short, the two major reasons advanced for the Cultural Revolution are that it resulted from conflicts over ideology or over the internal distribution of power. Neither is definitive. Power and ideology are so closely linked it is hardly rewarding to try to separate the "causes" neatly.

Mobilization preparatory to the formal declaration of the Cultural Revolution began in September 1965 when Mao secured Politburo approval of his five-man committee appointed to intensify the ideological campaigns begun in the Socialist Education Movement (1962–1964) and the subsequent "everybody be a soldier" campaign which extolled the virtues of the PLA. This group consisted of high level party officials who specialized in propaganda and information activities. By mid-1966, Mao was ready to call the Central Committee into session to approve his decision to mount an all-out attack on his enemies.

Mao presided over the Eighth Central Committee of the Chinese Communist party, which met in Peking for the first twelve days of August 1966.[18] With characteristic optimism the Central Committee communiqué boasted of the successes achieved by the Chinese people in the preceding four years as a result of Mao's "brilliant policies": the consolidation of the communes, big increases in the output and variety of products, the mass movements to study and apply creatively Mao's works, and good harvests for four straight years. Throughout the land, it stated, "an invigorating revolutionary atmosphere prevails" and "a new all-round leap forward" was emerging.

The Central Committee decision concerning the Great Proletarian Cultural Revolution consisted of "sixteen points." A deeper and more extensive stage of revolution was declared, one that "touches people to their very souls." Thematically the sixteen points were a restatement of goals of earlier campaigns. The Socialist Education Movement was to continue seeking the "four clean-ups" to purify politics, ideology, organization, and the economy. The masses were charged to liberate themselves through resistance to the cropping up of the "four olds" (ideas, culture, customs, and habits) of the bourgeoisie. The leaders were told not to take any measures on behalf of the masses, but to trust them and to reply on their initiative: "Don't be afraid of disorder." Mao's emphasis on the correct handling of contradictions was repeated. Every revolutionary was exhorted to develop the "communist spirit of daring to think, daring to speak, and daring to act." The Cultural Revolution was "to achieve greater, faster, better and more economic results in all fields of work," language identical to that used in Liu's 1958 remarks on the Great Leap.

The main target of the Cultural Revolution was "those within the Party who are in authority and are taking the capitalist road." The antiparty, antisocialist rightists had to be "fully exposed, hit hard, pulled down and completely discredited and their influence eliminated." Mao's instrumentality to destroy his enemies was the youth of China, the Red Guard.

IMPLEMENTATION

Six days after the close of the Central Committee plenum, Mao greeted one million Red Guards at Tien An Men Square in Peking.

Millions of Chinese youth enlisted in the Red Guard and set about their task to eliminate anti-Maoist elements by intensified attacks on the "bourgeoisie," mass denunciation meetings, and the Great Poster campaign (the display of large character posters revealing the crimes of antiparty and "capitalist road" elements). Reportedly eleven million youths were brought to Peking on trains run by the People's Liberation Army to take part in mass rallies to energize them for further attacks on the establishment. Formal education came to a halt. By late fall 1966, the party central organs were generally inoperative. Red Guards were dispatched throughout the country to dismantle provincial and local party bodies and to replace them with revolutionary organs. The Red Guard slogan "seize power" was the keynote for the direct attack in January 1967 on the party hierarchy at all levels. But not all Chinese submitted meekly to the disruptive and destructive acts of the Red Guard. Workers in Shanghai and Hankou resisted. Even Red Guard faction fought Red Guard faction. By summer, China was engulfed in anarchy. The Red Guards were able to carry out their depredations because the PLA did not intervene. But in July 1967, Ch'en Tsai-tao, PLA commander of the Wuhan military region, suppressed the Red Guard activity. The ultra-leftists of the Cultural Revolution, led by Chiang Ching (Mrs. Mao), secured the dismissal of Ch'en and, apparently emboldened by the victory, sought to purge the PLA leadership. At this point the PLA leadership decided to defend itself. It succeeded in causing Mao to purge most of the extremists (except for his wife and Ch'en Po-ta) and began to take firm action to oppose the Red Guard. Mao took a more moderate line, and the PLA assumed control of most provincial revolutionary committees. In July 1968, after a last resurgence of disruptive activity, Mao authorized the PLA to destroy the Red Guards as an organized political force. Within a few months, the PLA secured control of Revolutionary Committees throughout China. PLA commanders disarmed and demobilized the Red Guards. Order was restored.

FEEDBACK

The Cultural Revolution, which began as a "children's crusade" to purify the party and drive out the capitalist roaders, terminated in a new balancing of domestic political forces. Indeed, the purge of the leadership was dramatic. Four of the five original members of the September 1965 group lost power. The chairman of the PRC and heir-apparent to Mao (Liu Shao-ch'i) was purged along with Teng Hsiao-p'ing, longtime general secretary of the Chinese Communist party. Only seven members of the Politburo and 54 of 180 Central Committee members survived the turmoil. The State Council had ceased to operate and only three of sixteen deputy premiers were left in office. The Foreign Ministry's work came nearly to a standstill, and all ambassadors except one (in Cairo) were recalled. China had withdrawn from the world for nearly three years to reassess and redefine her essence in ideological and political terms. The Ninth National Congress was called to affirm the victory of the Maoists, a victory made possible only by the active intervention of the PLA. By 1969 the PLA controlled China and its reward was the designation in the text of the party constitution of Marshal Lin Piao as Mao's "close comrade-in-arms and successor."

The Cultural Revolution brought forth a strange anomaly for a socialist state, a dictatorship of the proletariat led by the military. But it was not to endure. Mao and the party soon reasserted control by diluting the power of the PLA and then conferring legitimacy on party policy and actions at the 1973 Tenth Party Congress and the 1975 National People's Congress.

Foreign Relations

There are two broad approaches to the analysis of China's foreign relations. One approach tries to explain China's behavior in terms of its "aggressive" ideology, which is hostile to the West, supports wars of national liberation, and trumpets the inevitable triumph of socialism. The second views Chinese foreign policy as essentially defensive, more pragmatic than ideological, more nationalistic and less interested in worldwide socialist revolution. The objectives of China's foreign policy have been outlined in varying degrees of abstraction. At the relatively strident ideological level, the General Programme of the Chinese Communist party seeks the overthrow of "imperialism, modern revisionism and all reaction" and the "abolition of the system of exploitation of man by man, so that all mankind will be emancipated." It does so by upholding proletarian internationalism and fighting to oppose the "hegemonism of the two superpowers—the United States and the Soviet Union." In more concrete terms, former U.S. Secretary of State Dean Rusk outlined Chinese foreign policy objectives to the Senate Foreign Relations Committee (March 6, 1966) in this way: (1) to bring China on the world stage as a great power; (2) to seek "dominance within Asia and leadership of the world communist revolution, employing Maoist tactics"; (3) to seek "to restore traditional influence or dominance in South, Southeast, and East Asia." To Professor Oksenberg, foreign policy goals have remained much the same over the life of the People's Republic: the search for national security, and for a "dignified role" in international affairs, one in which China helps write some of the rules of interstate intercourse.[19]

In 1949, China was diplomatically isolated. Internal political consolidation and economic reconstruction required secure borders. The new government's ideological ally and sole source of diplomatic support was the Soviet

Union, which extended diplomatic recognition on October 3, 1949. The next February the People's Republic of China and the Soviet Union concluded a 30-year Treaty of Alliance and Friendship which contained mutual defense obligations against Japan or any power (the U.S.) allied with Japan. After the Soviet-backed North Korean armed forces invaded the Republic of Korea in June 1950 and were defeated by the United Nations Command in October 1950, hundreds of thousands of Chinese "volunteers" crossed the Yalu and fought the United Nations forces to a stalemate along the waist of Korea. In response to Chinese intervention, the United Nations declared in February 1951 that China was an "aggressor." Thus branded as an international renegade, China sought to strengthen its international diplomatic position through other means.

COOPERATION AND PEACEFUL COEXISTENCE

The major theme of Chinese foreign policy for the mid-fifties was expressed in the meeting of 28 African and Asian nations at the Bandung Conference in Indonesia in April 1955. China subscribed to Indian Premier Jawaharlal Nehru's five principles of "peaceful coexistence": mutual respect for each other's territorial integrity and sovereignty; mutual nonaggression; mutual noninterference in other's affairs; equality and mutual benefit; and peaceful coexistence. Two decades later these principles continue to be a vital element of Chinese declaratory policy. They were written into the constitution of 1975 and were made part of the Chou-Nixon communiqué of February 1973.

This posture of cooperation and coexistence can be attributed, in part, to the realization that American attitudes toward China continued to harden in regard to areas other than Korea and that states that felt threatened by China would certainly seek United States protection. The Mutual Defense Treaty between

the United States and Japan became effective in 1953. In 1954, United States Secretary of State John Foster Dulles masterminded the establishment of the eight-nation regional collective security arrangement known as the Southeast Asia Treaty Organization (SEATO). Three months later, in December 1954, the United States and the Republic of China signed a treaty which stated, "Each party recognizes that an armed attack in the West Pacific area directed against the territories of either of the parties would be dangerous to its own peace and safety and declares that it would act to meet the common danger in accordance with its constitutional processes." A serious crisis arose in August 1958 when the People's Republic of China increased its military forces in Fukien Province directly opposite Taiwan and began heavy artillery attacks on Nationalist-occupied Quemoy Island, only one mile off China's coast. Fearing that an invasion by the People's Republic of China was imminent, President Eisenhower told both China and the Soviet Union that the United States would protect the islands, and reaffirmed its pledge to support the Nationalists. To assuage Chinese fears that the United States might "unleash" Chiang to attack the mainland, the United States made it clear that she would not support such a move. Apparently denied Soviet military support, China relaxed its pressure on Quemoy; nevertheless, in 1976, PRC artillery units still continued to fire propaganda shells into Quemoy for up to two hours every other day. The Nationalists maintain about 60,000 troops on Quemoy,[20] and the Chinese Communists are as determined as ever to incorporate Taiwan into the People's Republic of China.

THE SINO-SOVIET DISPUTE

China's relations with the Soviet Union dominated the foreign policy of the People's Republic of China during its first two decades.

The so-called Sino-Soviet Bloc was widely regarded, particularly in the United States, as the major element of "monolithic international communism." This general impression of impregnable and permanent solidarity was illusory, for the two countries came to disagree on several basic issues.

The Sino-Soviet dispute probably began with Premier Nikita Khrushchev's denunciation of Stalin at the February 1956 meeting of the Communist party of the Soviet Union (CPSU). This act, which condemned the cult of the individual, was taken as a criticism of Mao. The Soviet Union later criticized the Great Leap, which the Chinese Communist party lauded as a major advance in the application of socialist theory, as proof of the Chinese party's right to claim ideological leadership of the peoples of the third world nations seeking independence, liberation, and revolution. Soviet technicians and aid to China were halted precipitately in 1960, at the precise time when China desperately needed help to counteract the disastrous effects of the Great Leap. The controversy was now out in the open, exacerbated by Soviet neutrality in the Sino-Indian clashes in 1959 and active support of India in 1962. Khrushchev was roundly condemned after the Cuban missile crisis of 1962 for being "adventurous" in emplacing Soviet missiles on Cuban territory in the first place, and for having caved in to American threats in the second place.

With increasing self-confidence, the Chinese Communist party (CCP) accelerated efforts to justify its role as leader of the world socialist movement. In a widely cited speech on September 3, 1965, Defense Minister and CCP Central Committee Vice-Chairman Lin Piao claimed the whole cause of world revolution hinged on the current struggles in Asia, Africa, and Latin America. He stated that Mao's theory is "of outstanding and *universal* practical importance" (italics added). He charged that the revisionists' (Soviet Communists') belief that the "oppressed will be liberated" when all follow their (the Soviet) lines of "peaceful coexistence, peaceful transition, and peaceful competition" simply showed the Soviet leaders in their "true color as the accomplices of imperialist (U.S.) gangsters."[21] Applying the general CCP idea of the struggle of "rural versus urban" to the world scene, Lin foresaw ultimate defeat of the urban states of North America and Western Europe by the rural areas of Asia, Africa, and Latin America. Some observers saw Lin's speech as a new blueprint for world revolution, but its main thrust was to undermine the CPSU's pretensions to world ideological leadership and to conceptualize in simple terms the fact that China had joined the "third world" as leader of the "rural" regions. This construct, by definition, eliminated the Soviet Union.

From 1966 to mid-1969, the People's Republic of China virtually isolated itself from foreign contacts, but two events highlighted Sino-Soviet antagonism. The first was the unexpected and highly efficient invasion of Czechoslovakia by Soviet troops in August 1968 to oust the government of Alexander Dubcek. This act was justified by the "Brezhnev Doctrine," the idea that socialist countries have the right to intervene by force when other socialist states give evidence of slipping away from Soviet control in some act that might "endanger the Socialist community as a whole." It was, to the CCP, an entirely gratuitous presumption of "limited sovereignty" for socialist states other than the Soviet Union. The second event was the outbreak of military engagements at several places along the 4,000-mile Sino-Soviet border in the first half of 1969 which caused both countries to increase their military forces in the area. In 1976, an estimated one million Soviet troops[22] were deployed opposite the Chinese forces. Together, the PRC and Soviet forces numerically exceed those deployed in the NATO-Warsaw Pact confrontation, which divides Europe from the Baltic to the Adriatic.

A NEW SINO-AMERICAN RELATIONSHIP

Until 1971, Sino-American relations were best described as mutually hostile. In the late sixties, while heavily engaged in a war against North Vietnam, a contiguous and "fraternal socialist state" of the PRC, the United States also took steps to decrease Chinese distrust. These included the withdrawal of the U.S. Seventh Fleet from the Formosa Straits and the 1969 announcement of the Nixon Doctrine: (1) the United States would keep all its treaty commitments, (2) the United States would provide a nuclear shield if a nuclear power threatened the freedom of a nation allied to the United States or whose survival was vital to United States or regional security, and (3) in case of nonnuclear aggression, the United States would furnish, as appropriate, military and economic assistance, but look to the threatened nation to assume primary responsibility for its defense and to provide the manpower for that defense.[23] In June 1971, President Nixon removed trade restrictions against China, and announced the next month that he would visit China in early 1972.

China was ready to respond to United States moves to reduce tensions in East Asia. China was concerned about United States–Soviet cooperation on the nonproliferation of nuclear weapons and Strategic Arms Limitation Talks (SALT) Agreement, and therefore sought some accommodation with the United States to lessen the possibility that the two superpowers might act jointly to oppose China's vital interests. China's full acceptance into the world of international organizations occurred on October 25, 1971, when the United Nations General Assembly adopted an Albanian resolution to seat the People's Republic of China and to expel the representatives of the Nationalist China.

The Shanghai Communiqué signed by President Nixon and Premier Chou En-lai on February 27, 1972,[24] is the keystone of current Sino-American relations. The United States objectives were to involve China in "a new structure of peace in Asia characterized by mutual restraint of the great powers" and "to arrive at a new appreciation of their relationship in which common elements were seen to predominate over the differences flowing from our varying societies, philosophies, and positions in the world."[25] Both parties subscribed to the five principles of cooperation and peaceful coexistence, and agreed to work toward normalization of relations, to expand trade, and to oppose any nation or group of nations seeking to establish "hegemony" in the Asia-Pacific region. The communiqué also outlined areas of disagreement. The People's Republic of China supports the struggles of oppressed peoples and nations for freedom and liberation: "countries want independence, nations want liberation, and the people want revolution." The United States supports individual freedom and social progress for all, free of outside pressure or intervention. While China states all United States forces must be withdrawn from Taiwan and holds that "Taiwan is a Province of China," the United States position is to "progressively reduce" its forces and installations in Taiwan as tension lessens. The United States acknowledged that "all Chinese on either side of the Taiwan Strait maintain there is but one China and that Taiwan is part of China."

For more than six years following the Shanghai Communiqué, tangible results of the "new" Sino-American relationship were few. Trade increased from zero to nearly a billion dollars in 1974, but slipped to half that amount in 1975. However, in December of 1978, President Carter surprised the world with his announcement of a formal exchange of diplomatic recognition between the United States and the People's Republic of China. At the same time, the United States continued full diplomatic relations with Taiwan.

Accomplishments and Prospects

No observer of China today doubts that the Chinese Communist party has made substantial progress in providing the Chinese people a material standard of living higher than they have known in the past, a standard that is relatively low, but equal. The actual size of China's population is unknown,[26] but some estimates put the population over 900 million for 1976. China seems close to self-sufficiency in food grains, but much greater productivity is needed to mobilize capital and to free labor for industrial development. The commune system, introduced in 1958, has developed greatly since 1963. Communes now number about 50,000 and function as the basic unit of local government. China has not been a major trading nation, but significant increases in trade have occurred since the Cultural Revolution. Total trade tripled from 1970 to 1974 from $4.3 billion to $13.7 billion. Although China will avoid dependence on foreign countries, foreign trade will likely expand. China's overall economic performance is far below that of its neighbors, such as the Republic of Korea, the Nationalist government in Taiwan, and Japan.

REVOLUTIONARY FLUX

The constantly changing distribution of political power within the Chinese Communist party and the People's Republic reflects a nation and people in revolutionary flux. The formal distribution of power was outlined earlier. Yet it is clear that formal structures are more a result of ideological structures and a specific distribution of power among leaders than a cause for its allocation in a particular way, more extraconstitutional than constitutional. Although a very few men have held the posts of real power for three decades, Professor Chang has demonstrated that the policy-making process is, indeed, "pluralistic."[27] Mao's views did not always prevail, a fact made clear by the operation of the dialectic in Chinese politics — the alternating pattern between conservative and radical policies which reflect the powerful advocacy of conflicting interests. His power was never absolute. Both supporters and opponents have had an important influence on policy.

LEADERSHIP CHANGES

Nevertheless, Mao's death in September 1976 was a profound loss to the Chinese Communist party, for he combined uniquely in his person the roles of ideologue, political balancer and arbiter, and innovator in the policy process,[28] not to mention his function as the source of moral authority. The leadership succession has been a thorny problem complicated by the deaths of Chou En-lai, Kang Sheng, Tung Pi-wu, and Chu Teh, all part of the inner leadership group for four decades. For a while it seemed that Teng Hsiao-p'ing would succeed to Mao's titles, if not to all of his power. By mid-1977, Teng had once more sunk into obscurity and Hua Kuo-feng had been elected to Mao's post as chairman of the Central Committee, replaced Teng as chairman of the PRC Council of Ministers, and presided over the editing and publication of volume five of Mao's *Selected Works*. Hua's accession to power was opposed by the "gang of four," consisting of former vice-premier Chang Ch'ün-ch'iao and three other Politburo members: Chiang Ching (Mao's widow), Wang Hung-wen, and Yao Wen-yuan. These "radicals" have generally been charged as being "counterrevolutionary" and both anti-Mao and anti-Chou. The severity of this power struggle is suggested by reports (May 1977) that 50 to 60 members of the Central Committee have been removed along with nearly half of the Politburo members. Hua seems to have got much of Mao's power, but no man can duplicate Mao's aura of morality, prestige, and transcendent legitimacy. The struggle for power is likely to continue, mostly hidden from the outside world, until legitimized more or less permanently at a subsequent Eleventh Party Congress.

Hua Kuo-feng (UPI photo)

Li Hsien-nien (UPI photo)

Yeh Chien-Ying (UPI photo)

Wang Tung-Hsing

Teng Hsiao-p'ing (UPI photo)

244

Premier Chou En-lai, accompanied by Chiang Ching, wife of Chairman Mao, and Yeh Chien-Ying, member of the Central Committee, during May Day celebration in Peking in 1973. (UPI photo)

Members of the armed forces march through Teinanmen Square in 1977, celebrating the closing of the 11th National Congress. Portraits are of the late Chairman Mao Tse-tung and his successor, Hua Kuo-feng. (UPI photo)

Chairman Mao's widow, Chiang Ching, and Chou En-lai extend greetings to the throne at a mammoth rally held in Peking's Teinanmen Square. (UPI photo)

Former Chairman of the Chinese Communist Party Mao Tse-tung is surrounded by "admiring young people" following a mass rally in Peking in 1966, celebrating the "Great Proletarian Cultural Revolution." (UPI photo)

Commune members in Chinhua County in China's Chekiang Province tending spring crops. (UPI photo; source, Hsinhua News Agency)

Within wall of Old Chinese capital a view of Morrison Street, one of the most modern thoroughfares within the Tartar City section of Peking. The streets are wide, and in normal times the merchants transact a flourishing business. (ACME and UPI photo)

THE CHINESE PEOPLE AND THE CCP

An important question transcends the death
of Mao: Has the Chinese Communist party
succeeded in its efforts to recast the Chinese
people, their thought and behavior, into a
new type of human being? The cyclical interpretation of history has given way to "progress," and 800 to 900 million people have been
subjected in all areas of human life to the
comprehensive and repetitious influence of
mass organizations and mass campaigns to
root out improper thoughts. The complete
tradition of China's golden past has been denounced again and again, with the people
being told to get rid of old thoughts, old customs, old habits, and old culture. The continuation of criticism campaigns leads to the
belief that the leadership is far from convinced
that its efforts to create a "new" communist
man have succeeded. But the attempts will
not cease. The bourgeoisie is still in the party,
in the government, in the PLA, and in the
various spheres of culture, waiting to seize
power and overturn the socialist revolution.
Mao's answer to this problem was continuous
revolution: "Will there be a need for revolution a hundred years from now? Will there still
be a need for a revolution a thousand years
from now? There is always need for revolution." With "faith in dialectic," Mao wrote,
"The supersession of the old by the new is a
general, eternal and inviolable law of the universe." . . . "Without struggle there is no
progress. Can 800 million people manage
without struggle?"[29]

The conduct of China's foreign policy in its
search for national security to permit internal
revolutionary development has depended
broadly on its relations with the Soviet Union
and the United States. Well into its third decade, China attempts to contain the Soviet
threat by normalizing relations with the
United States and consolidating a variety of
ties with Japan, and the third world. Although
the Chinese defense budget may be the

world's third largest, the People's Liberation
Army (with a stockpile of 200 to 300 nuclear
warheads) currently receives a lower budget
priority than during the late 1960s when war
with the Soviet Union seemed more likely.
The present PLA goal seems to be slow and
persistent weapons modernization while de-
terring a Soviet nuclear or conventional attack, contingencies which now seem de-
emphasized for the short run.[30]

China's general perception of the international situation and of Soviet and American
foreign policy was made clear in Chiao Kuan-
hua's speech to the U.N. General Assembly
in September 1975.[31] Recapitulating policy
views stated frequently in the past few years
by Chinese Communist leadership, Chiao repeated the litany that the "danger of war is
visibly growing." Détente is viewed as a
façade behind which contention for world
domination by the two superpowers is "bigger
and fiercer." The contradictions between the
two are irreconcilable and one must over-
power the other. Chiao's strident conclusion
was that the United States and the Soviet
Union are "bound to go to war some day. This
is independent of man's will," an attitude
aptly summed up in the Chinese proverb "sit
on a mountain and watch the tigers fight."

Ideological rhetoric aside, the People's Republic of China will continue to seek redistribution of international power in ways to
further its own interests. The triangular
Peking-Moscow-Washington relationship is
central to all policy moves. To date, Peking's
relations with Washington seem to serve
Chinese purposes, and the Soviet threat may
have lessened despite Peking's continuing characterization of Russia as the "most
dangerous source of war."[32] It is by no means
certain that the essential points of the apparent Sino-Soviet enmity are irreconcilable.
Nor is it unreasonable to question whether
the successors to current leadership of the
Chinese Communist party and the Communist party of the Soviet Union may not, in

fact, find bases for a renewal of their cooperation of the 1950s.

Summary

A major fact of Chinese political life since 1949 has been the continuing series of internal power struggles among the party elite concerning the proper interpretation and application of Maoist ideology to the solution of a variety of theoretical and concrete issues. Under Mao's leadership and in accord with ideology, policy initiatives come from the party. In fact, the society is so structured as to minimize the emergence of such political actors as technical and managerial groups, and policy formulation lies in the party-state-PLA complex, whose top leaders share power in the Politburo. The emergence, identification, and approval of policy is focused mainly in this party leadership and can best be regarded as a single act. Implementation and feedback occur within the bureaucracies of the three major institutional actors, but also in the response of the masses.

Placing "politics in command of the economy," the party embarked on agrarian reform in 1950 and its first Five-Year Plan (1953–1957) (for heavy industry development) in close imitation of the Soviet model. With the land almost totally collectivized by 1958, Mao shifted to the "walking on two legs" policy of balanced industrial and agricultural development in the Great Leap Forward. This movement did not produce the desired results, and opposition from influential elite in the state structure and the PLA forced a shift to a policy of retrenchment based on rational economic decision making by professional bureaucratic managers and technicians. Prominent PLA leaders were dismissed, but Mao was forced to bow out as chairman of the People's Republic of China.

The Cultural Revolution (1966–1969) meant a reversion to Maoist principles and the masses and the Red Guards were pitted against the technician-managerial elite. The party bureaucracy was nearly destroyed while the PLA remained essentially uncommitted until it intervened at the decisive moment to save the party, extracting in return the designation of Lin Piao as Mao's successor. After Lin's coup d'etat aborted in 1971, the party removed many PLA leaders from their party positions and returned once more to economic order. The new distribution of power was formalized by new party (1973) and state (1975) constitutions, but soon altered in the wake of the deaths of Mao, Chou, and other Politburo members. Hua Kuo-feng has taken Mao's place as chairman of the Central Committee and Chou's place as prime minister, but top-level turbulence will continue.

Internally, China seeks elusive political stability, but has achieved a relatively higher, but still low, material standard of living for its people. Externally, it has provided for its national security, despite Soviet hostility, and seeks a role in international affairs where it can help write the rules. It subscribes to the five principles of peaceful coexistence and has gained a permanent seat on the United Nations Security Council. The People's Republic of China will continue to seek redistribution of international power so as to further its own interests.

The Chinese political system remains an amalgam between the old and the new value systems. The ideology has yet to be institutionalized to a point where it is generally accepted not only as a basis for legitimizing the system, but also as a basis for the "peaceful" transfer of power between leaders. While the general principles of Maoism are used as the basis for the current leadership, the fact remains that various interpretations of Maoism have evolved. Moreover, Maoism has failed to develop the institutional and revolutionary commitment that were crucial concerns during the final years of Mao and particularly reflected in the Cultural Revolution.

Thus, while China appears to be developing a relatively effective administrative structure, and achieving some of the economic and social goals of its ideology, the political goals and guidelines established in the Maoist ideology remain unfulfilled.

NOTES

1. Jack Gray, "Politics in Command," in William A. Robson and Bernard Crick, eds, *China in Transition* (Beverly Hills, Calif.: Sage, 1975), p. 30.

2. See Michael Oksenberg, "Political Changes and their Causes in China," in ibid., pp. 99–118, for an outline of six approaches.

3. Lucian W. Pye, *China an Introduction* (Boston: Little, Brown, 1972), p. 186.

4. *China: A Reassessment of the Economy—A Compendium of Papers Submitted to the Joint Economic Committee, Congress of the United States* (Washington, D.C.: U.S. Government Printing Office, July 10, 1975), p. 150. Hereafter cited as *China: A Reassessment*.

5. Ibid., p. 47.

6. This summary is based on Gray, op. cit., pp. 35–37.

7. John G. Gurley, *Challengers to Capitalism Marx, Lenin and Mao* (Stanford, Calif.: Stanford Alumni Association, 1975), p. 124.

8. Parris H. Chang, *Power and Policy in China* (University Park and London: Pennsylvania State University Press, 1975), pp. 9–46.

9. Liu Shao-ch'i, "Report on the Work of the Central Committee, May 5, 1958," quoted in John Wilson Lewis, *Major Doctrines of Communist China* (New York: Norton, 1964), pp. 284–285.

10. Chang, op. cit., p. 83. Ch'en Po-ta quoting Mao in "Under the Banner of Chairman Mao," *Hung Ch'i* [Red Flag], July 16, 1958.

11. For full text, see John Wilson Lewis, *Major Doctrines of Communist China* (New York: Norton, 1964), pp. 288–293.

12. Gurley, op. cit., pp. 125–126, quoting *Peking Review,* 1959.

13. See Chang, op. cit., "The Showdown at Lushan," pp. 110–121.

14. Frederick W. Crook, "The Commune System in the People's Republic of China, 1963–1974," in *China: A Reassessment*, pp. 371–372.

15. See Ellis Joffe, *Party and Army: Professionalism and Political Control in the Chinese Officer Corps, 1949–1964,* Harvard East Asian Monographs (Cambridge, Mass.: East Asian Research Center, Harvard University, 1965), pp. 133–137.

16. Ibid., pp. 138–139.

17. Chang, op. cit., pp. 174–175.

18. See Special Issue, *China Pictorial*, no. 9, Peking (1966), for texts of the "Communique of Eleventh Plenary Session of the Eighth Central Committee of the Communist Party of China, August 12, 1966," and the "Decision of the Central Committee of the Chinese Communist Party concerning the Great Proletarian Cultural Revolution, August 8, 1966."

19. See Michael Oksenberg, "The Strategies of Peking," in *Foreign Affairs*, October 1970.

20. William Armbruster, "Quemoy's Long War," *Christian Science Monitor,* March 30, 1976.

21. Lin Piao, "Long Live the Victory of the People's War," Foreign Broadcast Information Service Daily Report Supplement Far East No. 171 (4s)–1965, September 3, 1965.

22. *The Military Balance 1975–1976* (London: International Institute for Strategic Studies, 1976), p. 9.

23. Richard Nixon, *U.S. Foreign Policy for the 1970's: A New Strategy for Peace*, a report to the Congress, February 18, 1970, pp. 55–56.

24. For text of Joint Communiqué, see *Peking Review,* no. 9 (March 3, 1972), pp. 4–5.

25. Department of State, "U.S. Policy toward the People's Republic of China," a news release on the prepared statement of Assistant Secretary of State for East Asian and Pacific Affairs Philip C. Habib, before the Subcommittee on Investigation of the House Committee on International Relations, December 17, 1975.

26. Leo A. Orleans, "China's Population: Can the Contradictions Be Resolved?" in *China: A Reassessment*, p. 71. Leo A. Orleans takes at face value the 1971 statement of Li Hsien-nien that PRC officials in the grain department use a figure of 800 million, officials outside the grain department use 750 million, the Ministry of Commerce "affirms the number is 830 million," and the planning department "insists the number is less than 750 million."

27. Chang, op. cit., pp. 176–196.

28. Ibid., pp. 188–189.

29. "The Great Cultural Revolution will Shine For Ever," *Peking Review*, no. 21 (May 21, 1976), pp. 9–10.

30. *Strategic Survey 1975* (London: International Institute for Strategic Studies, 1976), pp. 100–104.

31. Full text is in "Speech by Chiao Kuan-hua, Chairman of Chinese Delegation," *Peking Review,* no. 40 (October 3, 1975), pp. 10–17.. Chiao was chairman of the PRC delegation at the 30th Session of the United Nations General Assembly and minister of foreign affairs.

32. See "Soviet Social-Imperialism—Most Dangerous Source of War," *Peking Review,* no. 5 (January 30, 1976), pp. 9–13.

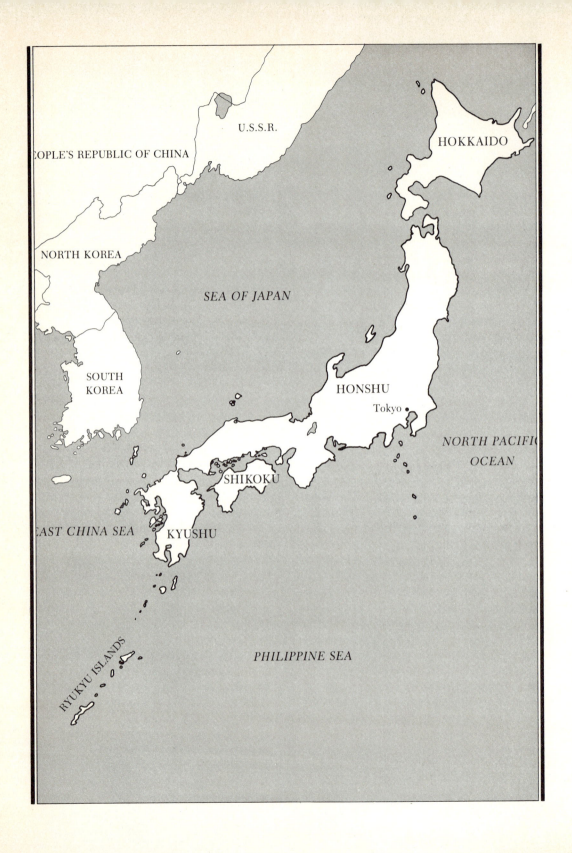

U.S.S.R.

PEOPLE'S REPUBLIC OF CHINA

HOKKAIDO

NORTH KOREA

SEA OF JAPAN

SOUTH
KOREA

HONSHU

Tokyo

NORTH PACIFIC

OCEAN

SHIKOKU

EAST CHINA SEA   KYUSHU

PHILIPPINE SEA

RYUKYU ISLANDS

PART 5 The Japanese Political System

CHAPTER 12

JAPANESE IDEOLOGY: TRADITION AND MODERNITY

Like China, Japan has a lengthy, distinctive, and strongly unified cultural tradition. In contrast to China, Japan was never a "giver of civilization," but was the recipient of massive importation of foreign religion and political thought and institutions. At the same time the indigenous religious base had shown remarkable tenacity. The importation of Buddhism in the 6th century, the introduction of Chinese (Confucianist) intellectual perceptions in the 7th and later centuries, the more recent and diverse infusions from the West in the 19th century, and the American influence in the mid-20th century did not replace what was there formerly. These influences have been consecutive accretions in a layering effect, so that Japan's ideology retains parts of all of them to varying degrees. While Japan has, for much of its history, perceived the world through essentially Confucianist eyes, Japan has also demonstrated unique skill in adopting some ideas and institutions, adapting others, and in the end, making them Japanese.

Today Japan is a democratic constitutional monarchy embodying British and American principles governing the relationship of its citizens to the state in which sovereignty lies with the elected representatives of the people. These principles are formalized in the Constitution of 1947 drafted by the Allied occupation authorities and imposed upon the people of Japan. During the early years after World War II, many foreign observers argued that Japan could never accept an alien ideology apparently so incompatible with traditional Japan. Until World War II, Japan was essentially a predominantly rural, hierarchical, authoritarian, oligarchic society presided over by a theoretically absolute and divine emperor. Nevertheless, three decades later, the Japanese seem to have embraced firmly these alien concepts and have made them the living fabric of their political and social life.

The transformation of the militaristic and internationally aggressive Japan of the 1930s into the democratic, peaceful, and internationally cooperative Japan of the post-occupation years was indeed remarkable, but some preconditions for the introduction and acceptance of a truly democratic system had not been entirely absent in Japan.

This chapter treats the development of Japan's ideology, emphasizing the impact of foreign influences, the historical gap between the locus of theoretical and the exercise of real power, and the centuries of nondemocratic tradition, all of which are vital to any assessment of the durability of Japan's new ideology under the 1947 Constitution.

Early Japan

No one knows when the Japanese became a coherent racial group, but certainly by the 3rd or 4th century A.D., the rulers of Yamato (a plain in central Honshu) more or less controlled other hereditary groups of families. By this time, the ideas of hereditary right and the role of the soldier as aristocrat were well-established. The religious faith of this preliterate Japan was called *Shinto* ("the way of the gods"). Shinto legend (a variation of the solar myth) provided an explanation of the origin of the Japanese people and legitimacy for the imperial family, now reckoned to be in its 124th generation of unbroken succession.

SHINTOISM AND BUDDHISM

Based on a rather vague conception of the universe composed of myriads of sentient parts, Shinto was a type of nature worship in which man, nature, and spirits live in intimacy. *Kami* ("gods") were perceived not only in the awe-inspiring, but also in the most common of natural features, a rock, a bubbling stream, or a pine tree, which even today one may espy adorned with strips of "holy" paper. Lacking speculative and philosophical elements, Shinto was "primitive." Yet its emphasis on love and gratitude toward nature, rather than fear, contributes still today to the sensibility and appreciation of nature so characteristic of the Japanese and so eloquently reflected in the art of flower arrangement, for example.

The religion and political organization of the Yamato rulers were challenged by the introduction of Buddhism and Chinese learning in the 6th century. Years of intrigue and strife resulted in the accession to power of a pro-Buddhist pro-Chinese group as the ruling oligarchy of Japan. Even this early in Japan's history, the emperor reigned rather than ruled. Prince Shōtoku (574–622), acting as regent during the reign of his aunt, set about reforming the government to enhance its power and prestige in the eyes of foreign and domestic rivals alike.[1] With A.D. 604 as the traditional date, Prince Shōtoku issued the Seventeen Article Constitution. At first glance the document seems to be little more than a series of moral injunctions found in Buddhist and Confucianist writings. In fact, it is of great importance because it is the first evidence of a considered body of government *ideals* in Japan and the expression of these ideals is clearly non-Japanese in origin.

CHINESE INFLUENCES

In addition to Buddhist injunctions to revere the Three Treasures (the Buddha, the scriptures, and the monastic orders), to cease from gluttony, and to avoid wrath, these "laws" of Prince Shōtoku included Confucian emphasis on harmony, decorum, rewards and punishments, and the fulfilling of one's duty. More important, the constitution enunciated the theory of a centralized state:

In a country there are not two lords; the people have not two masters. The sovereign is the master of the people of the whole country. The officials to whom he gives charge are all his vassals. How can they, as well as the government, presume to levy taxes on the people?[2]

One provision stressed the precedence of public interest over private interest. Another required that decisions on important matters be discussed with many. From the content of Shōtoku's constitution one can make some inferences about Japan at that time. It was decentralized and lacked a statement of government ideals. Clan leaders contended for power and tax levies at the expense of the imperial family. The people were not harmonious, and private and public morality left something to be desired. The constitution was supplemented by other acts in imitation of the Chinese system, including adoption of the Chinese calendar which implied acceptance of Chinese suzerainty and the introduction of a court rank system identical to that of contemporary China.

This first attempt to emulate the Chinese system did not revolutionize life in Japan. Early in 645, the new emperor, Kōtoku, summoned the nobles to court and proclaimed "the doctrine of absolute monarchy." To symbolize the changes he planned for Japan, he gave to his reign the name Taika ("great reform"). The following year he promulgated a four-paragraph edict, usually called the Taika Reform, which abolished private title to certain types of land, established a capital and provided for a local government, ordered population registers to be prepared to permit equitable distribution of land, and introduced a new tax system. As Sir George Sansom wrote, it was a "bold attempt" to apply to Japan the land tenure, taxation, and governmental systems in effect in contemporary T'ang China (618–906).[3] Further reform took place with the promulgation in 702 of the Taihō code, so named for the era, "Great Treasure." These administrative regulations organized Japan into sixty-six provinces and established a central government patterned closely after the Chinese ministries. Japan departed from the T'ang model in one major aspect. A Department of Worship (*Jingikan*), for which there was no Chinese counterpart, took precedence over the Council of State, which coordinated the ministries. Despite the acceptance of Confucian ethics, the Japanese did not accept the Chinese theory of the mandate of heaven. On the contrary, they maintained and strengthened their concept of a sacred and inviolable emperor whose claim to the throne is based on inheritance alone.[4]

In several ways Japan expanded its borrowing from China. A permanent capital (710–784) was established in Nara, and the street plan duplicated that of Ch'ang-an, the Chinese capital. The Chinese language became the language of government, religion, and literature. The earliest written histories of Japan were completed in the early 8th century. The development of Chinese sects of Buddhism was indeed remarkable, with the accretion of great power to the Nara sects. For a short period of time, it seemed Japan might become a Buddhist country. Emperor Shōmu declared (749) that he was a "servant" of the Three Treasures of Buddhism. Twenty years later Empress Shōtoku seemed ready to abdicate her throne to Dōkyō, a Buddhist leader.[5] These initiatives were repulsed and the imperial capital was moved from Nara thirty miles to the north to Kyoto, where it remained from 784 to 1868.

Near the end of the 9th century, Japan's contact with China ceased. Japan was left to modify and adapt further the massive Chinese influences. Over the next few centuries the Chinese influences in government, ethics, religion, art, and literature became Japanese. The power of the Buddhists was curtailed and converted to support of the central government, and their ideas were fused, to some degree, with Shinto. The Chinese civil service system did not become vital to the operation of Japan's government because its basic idea of a meritocracy had no appeal in a society where rank derived solely from birth. Japan did not develop a bureaucracy as China had done. In Kyoto, power was held by the Fujiwara family, which became so powerful at court that all emperors had to marry Fujiwara ladies. Real power was exercised by a Fujiwara regent for a minor emperor or by a Fujiwara civil dictator for adult emperors. Central government control of the provinces lessened for many of the same reasons that this phenomenon appeared in the dynastic cycle in China. The decrease in Kyoto's control was accompanied by the rise of tax-free manors in the provinces and the emergence of regional military leaders.

INTERMITTENT WARFARE AND THE SHOGUNATE

Four decades of intermittent warfare among powerful regional military leaders culminated in 1192 in the seizure of temporal power by Minamoto Yoritomo, upon whom the emperor bestowed the title of Barbarian-Subduing Generalissimo (Sei-i Taishōgun). The *Bakufu* ("tent" or military government) was established in Kamakura, just south of present-day Tokyo, far removed from the imperial family. The power of the Minamoto family lasted a scant three generations and was replaced by the Hōjō clan (1226–1333), which wielded real power as regents for child shoguns appointed from the court nobility in Kyoto. Thirteenth-century Japan is a marvelous example of indirection in government: a hereditary Hōjō regent held real power on behalf of a puppet shogun from the imperial family or the Fujiwara family, who was appointed by an emperor or abdicated emperor in whose person resided legitimacy and, theoretically, absolute power.

The Hōjō regency was remarkably effective and is perhaps best known for repelling two Mongol invasions in 1274 and 1281, aided substantially by typhoons which destroyed the invasion fleets and purportedly by the efficacy of powers to the Buddhist and Shinto deities. The typhoons which saved Japan from

enemy invasion (the only attempt in recorded Japanese history) were called Wind of the Gods *(kamikaze)*. Expenses incident to the defense of Japan and discontent of the military led to the overthrow of the Hōjō regency in 1333 and the short-lived attempt of Emperor Go-Daigo to assert direct imperial rule with the assistance of dissident feudal lords. A war of succession between competing claimants resulted in the formation of a new shogunate (1338–1573), this time in Muromachi, a district of Kyoto, under the Ashikaga family.

By the 15th century, centralized government had broken down. Civil war became endemic. For nearly two hundred years the people of Japan saw their land rent by intermittent and inconclusive internecine warfare among great feudal lords *(daimyō)* who were truly independent of imperial or shogunal rule. By a process similar to that in China just prior to the Ch'in dynasty, Tokugawa Iyeyasu emerged as the most powerful feudal lord and was named shogun in 1603.

THE TOKUGAWA PERIOD (1603–1868)

Japan's ideology, its perceptions of the world and its values, was rooted in ancient Japan and flowered during the two and one-half centuries of peace under Tokugawa rule. The ethic of the governing *samurai* (warrior-administrator) was generalized to include the entire population. This ethic was an amalgam of several elements. Shinto gave it a particular loyalty to the emperor. Military organization required initially loyalty to individual military leaders, but this loyalty later shifted to a class loyalty. The ideal of selfless devotion was provided by the Buddhist monk. Confucianism reinforced loyalty and filial piety. It emphasized learning, virtue, and class responsibility for correct governing of the other classes. The Japanese samurai class steadily expanded its horizons to include all social and political concerns. Tokugawa ideology stressed "system maintenance," and the samurai ethic laid the basis for the "goal attainment" orientation of recent Japan.[6]

The nonaggressive feudal military dictatorship of the Tokugawa was an extension into peacetime of the command control of wartime. The fundamental document, Rules for the Military Houses (*Buke Sho-hatto*), promulgated in 1615, laid down the rules for behavior of the military class and was never substantially changed. Its thirteen articles generally exacted absolute obedience from the military class and enjoined moral behavior and a frugal life-style. An earlier order (1613) governing the conduct of the Imperial court in Kyoto left no doubt that it was completely subject to Tokugawa, but provided for continuation of its ceremonial functions.[7]

Iyeyasu established his shogunate in the village of Edo (now Tokyo). The shogun was advised by a rotating group of elders who supervised lesser officials charged with a variety of tasks, including supervision of lesser rank lords, public works, shrines, finances, and government of the capital. Local government officials appointed by the shogun were limited to key Tokugawa estates and to the castle governors in Osaka, Kyoto, and Sumpu (the Tokugawa family castle). Most of Japan consisted of self-governing fiefs, and government in these areas tended to emulate that of Edo. A large bureaucracy operated to secure the strict and minute control of a rather ponderous feudal system, compassing the range from military training to peasant dress.

Inner and Outer Lords   The three-fourths of Japan's territory not ruled directly by Tokugawa was parceled out to about 270 *daimyo* who generally fell into two categories, the inner lords (*fudai*) and outer lords (*tozama*). Inner lords were those who actively and loyally supported Iyeyasu in his campaigns to seize power. They were placed in fiefs so located as to check potential anti-Tokugawa

movements. Some were athwart strategic lines of communication and others were located to be a constant threat to the rear of possible dissidents. Outer lords, on the other hand, had fought against Iyeyasu in 1600 or had considered themselves his equal and remained passive. Among the outer lords were the strongest and richest clans of Japan, some wealthier even than the main Tokugawa house. In particular, strong western clans such as Satsuma (in southern Kyushu) actually operated as autonomous states, free of control by Edo, and handling their own military defense, taxes, and in some instances, foreign trade.

Certain measures to weaken the outer lords were taken shortly after Iyeyasu's victory. The outer lords, and others, were forced to contribute heavily to the construction of the magnificent Edo castle. In 1635 the initiation of *sankin-kltai* strengthened shogunate controls. This system of "alternate attendance" at the shogun's court required daimyo and their families to spend part of each year in Edo, and when the daimyo returned to his fief, his family remained hostage to the shogun. Ever watchful for dissident daimyo, the Edo government had a well-organized and competent secret police system. To minimize the potential for anti-Tokugawa coalitions, bridges and roads were allowed to deteriorate, barriers were erected between fiefs, and a rigid passport system was established.

Social System   The social system of Tokugawa Japan, like its government, was an extension of the past. The imperial family and about 130 families of court nobility stood at the top of the hierarchy. Highly respected in protocol, they were financially poor, politically impotent, and useful mainly to sanction the Tokugawa military rule and perform ceremonial functions. The *samurai* (warrior) class, next highest in rank, consisted of about two million people, or 7 to 10 percent of the total population. Supreme within this rank was the shogun and his military court, followed in rank by samurai classed as lords, that is, those warriors with incomes in excess of 10,000 *koku*. Several lesser ranks of samurai existed, the lowest being the foot soldier (*gōshi*) who worked his land but responded to calls to arms. Samurai were not vassals who had plural lords. To the fundamental principles of personal faith and honor characteristic of European feudalism there was added, in Japan, absolute and unlimited devotion to the lord, fulfillment of which sometimes required self-immolation (*seppuku*). One-sided emphasis on the virtues of the vassal gave the relationship a peculiarly spiritual, self-sacrificing character. A samurai's entire life was theoretically devoted to acquiring the discipline necessary in the moment of ultimate emergency. This discipline was encouraged and forced from above by the minute direction of the details of a samurai's daily life, by training the body in martial arts, by training the mind and spirit through study of the Chinese classics, and by developing proficiency in the arts of the tea ceremony and versification. The samurai were a rough analog to the literati in traditional China as administrators and intellectual leaders, but also were the military defenders of the regime. This combination of roles was not seen in China, where the military class traditionally was viewed as inferior to the literati. The samurai qualities developed so highly in the Tokugawa period—loyalty, self-sacrifice, proficiency in the military arts—were translated into staunch loyalty to the emperor in the mid-19th century and proved an invaluable asset to modernization after the Meiji Restoration in 1868.

Peasants were the most numerous class and ranked next below the samurai, recognition that agriculture was the real basis of the society. Despite his social rank, the lot of the peasant was sometimes wretched, and *jacqueries* (peasant revolts) were not uncommon in the latter years of the Tokugawa period. As in China, the next lower ranks were the artisan and the merchant. Outside the four social classes were the *eta* and *hinin*, pariahs who performed functions such as cremation and butchery (which were sources of pollution to Buddhists), beggars and professional players, un-persons required to live apart from others, uncounted in the census.

This rigid hierarchical social system was a powerful force in the Tokugawa pursuit of its primary objective: to enhance its power as the temporal ruler of Japan and to maintain the status quo. The success in securing obedience of its vassals, ensuring domestic peace and rule by feudal "law," also provided the environment for the emergence of forces subversive to continued Tokugawa rule. Japan remained an agrarian state, but the growth of cities, the alternate attendance system, and the resulting increases in consumption led to the growth of a money economy. The lords living in Edo consigned their rice revenue to merchant-brokers. These and other purveyors to the ruling elite gained economic power, often to the distress of the samurai, but this power went unrecognized by enhanced social status. The peasant continued to be a "machine producing rice for the samurai to swallow" and did not share in the general rise in the standard of living.

Seclusion A policy of seclusion was the second major technique to preserve the status quo. In the last half of the 16th century Japan felt the influence of the expansion of Europe and was host to Christian missionaries who enjoyed successful ministries in western Japan and some influence at court. Early Spanish and Portuguese Christian interest was soon followed by British and Dutch commercial overtures. Official attitudes were ambivalent to these influences, but with consolidation of shogunate, the fear of external subversive influences took control. All foreigners were expelled from Japan except for the Dutch, who maintained a very small trading post in Nagasaki and served thereafter as Japan's window to the West. In 1638 a peasant revolt in Kyushu led by Christian samurai was ruthlessly suppressed. The revolt was not mainly religious in character, but the Tokugawa regarded it as such and open Christian worship ceased.

Generally successful in preventing the import of subversive religious and economic influence, the Tokugawa failed, in the long run, to avoid the spread of subversive doctrine from within Japan. The orthodoxy on which the shogunate rested was essentially Confucianist, moderate, conservative, and practical, with loyalty to the established system at its core. It was well-suited to keeping the status quo with everyone in his proper place justified by a systematized ethic. The samurai who operated the system, finding themselves with no more wars to fight, departed from concentration on the martial arts and the study of things Chinese and undertook critical study of the history of Japan, particularly of its two major political institutions, the shogunate and the emperor. Oddly enough, the major impetus for such studies came from the Mito branch of the Tokugawa family. This school of nationalist historiography contributed, in the 19th century, to the conviction among anti-Tokugawa elements that the shogunate was indeed a usurpation of imperial power and that the emperor ought to be restored to his proper place. The overall effect of nationalist studies was to reinforce and heighten loyalty to the emperor and resentment of the shogunate, to praise things Japanese while strengthening anti-Chinese and antiforeign sentiments.

Despite Tokugawa efforts to deny Japanese access to outside knowledge, the great semi-independent clans of the west—Satsuma, Choshu, Hizen, and Tosa—acquired much technical knowledge and political information from the Dutch. Taken together this information was called Dutch Learning (*Rangaku*)

and became the focal study of eager and inquisitive young samurai. Ardent young reformers emerged in western Japan presenting ideas for better administration, the strengthening of clan and national defenses, and even for overseas expansion. The growing conviction of the mutability of the shogunate was joined to relative discontent among the samurai, peasants, and merchants. Tokugawa conservatism was no longer a vital force. The precarious internal balance of power in Japan was upset by the arrival of American ships under Commodore Matthew Calbraith Perry in 1853, demanding the opening of Japan to international intercourse. Unable to cope with the external crisis and unable to control the western clans, the shogunate grew progressively weaker in the 1860s. The western clans, allies with the imperial court, defeated the shogun's forces in the field, secured his relinquishment of power in 1868, and "restored" the fifteen-year-old Mutsuhito as emperor to begin forty-four years of rule under the reign name of Meiji.

The Meiji Restoration   The Meiji Restoration occurred at the conjunction of two processes: the internal decline of feudalism and the arrival of Western military power in Japan. Sir George Sansom wrote, "Every force but conservatism was pressing from within at the closed doors: so that when a summons came from without they were flung wide open, and all those imprisoned energies were released."[8]

From Feudalism to Constitutionalism

Tokugawa ideology provided the sanctions and the basis for the changes following the Meiji Restoration. The imperial myth was strengthened and the emperor became the focus of the loyalties previously diffused to feudal lords. The familistic aspects of Confucianism were expanded to embrace the emperor (himself descended from divine emperors) as the father of all Japanese conceived as an extended family. Leadership of the country was taken by intelligent, forceful, aggressive samurai who exemplified loyalty and service to the throne, and were oriented to "goal attainment." The goals were to protect and preserve the Japanese polity in its uniqueness and to avoid the fate China suffered at the hands of the West. The means were liquidation of the Tokugawa political order and the borrowing and adaptation of Western institutions and technology.

THE DISSOLUTION OF THE SHOGUNATE AND REFORM

The immediate consequences of the restoration were the dissolution of the shogunate and its replacement by a new oligarchy composed chiefly of younger samurai from the clans of western Japan, men who virtually monopolized political power through the end of World War I. The oligarchy had the new emperor broadly outline their approach in the Charter Oath in 1868. The statement called for unifying all classes, discarding all customs, establishing deliberative assemblies, and seeking knowledge "throughout the world so as to strengthen the foundations of imperial rule."[9] The government was organized with the nomenclature used in prefeudal times, and the transfer of authority was dramatized by renaming Edo, Tokyo ("Eastern Capital"), and installing the imperial court in the former shogun's castle.

Over the next few years, the oligarchy carried out thorough-going reforms: abolition of the fiefs and establishment of prefectures governed by imperial appointees, dissolution of the class system, standardization of the monetary system, elimination of all taxing authority except Tokyo, establishment of compulsory elementary education, and formation of a conscript army. The oligarchy was determined to blend its knowledge of the West with Japanese culture to develop a national state capable of self-defense and worthy of equal treatment by the West.

The flurry of wide-ranging changes directed from above affected all segments of society, most important, the former members of the samurai class. Some members of the oligarchy were opposed to specific changes and to the rapidity of others, but the most serious split occurred over Takamori Saigo's proposal to punish Korea for alleged "slights" to the new government. A pillar of the restoration and first commander of the new national military force, Saigo resigned in 1873 to return to Kagoshima when the majority of the oligarchy decided internal development must have priority over a Korean punitive expedition. Dissatisfaction with several policies which lowered the status of the samurai class led to minor uprisings in Kyushu from 1873 to 1876, and in 1877 Saigo rose in revolt. This Satsuma Rebellion was limited geographically to the island of Kyushu, but its suppression required mobilization of all the central government's forces and seven months of heavy fighting, and cost more lives than the Sino-Japanese War of 1894–1895. Government victory ended organized military resistance to the new regime and assured that the oligarchy could carry through its policies capsulized as *fukoku-kyōhei*, a rich country with a strong military, preserving internal security and territorial integrity.

While dealing effectively with military opposition, the new government simultaneously faced political challenges to its authority at the very time the oligarchy itself was uncertain how best to accomplish its major task to restructure the government. The Charter Oath had promised "deliberative assemblies" and "public discussion" of issues. Works of major Western political philosophers—Mill, Locke, Rousseau, Montesquieu, and others—were translated into Japanese and provided potent stimuli as well as alternatives to rule by a small ex-samurai oligarchy and an imperial bureaucracy. At the national level by 1871, four successive organizations had been created which could lay some small claim to being "deliberative." The last of these even drew up plans for a bicameral body whose appointed members would later be replaced by elected members. Although some "progressive" bureaucrats favored such ideas, the oligarchy clearly did not intend to share its power with any deliberative assembly. Nevertheless, a Prefectural Governors Conference was held in 1875, and local assemblies, with advisory functions only, were set up in forty-eight prefectures between 1871 and 1879.[10]

DEVELOPMENT OF THE PARTY SYSTEM

The beginnings of political parties appeared, but there was no institutional context for their operations. Leadership for the parties came principally from the ex-samurai agrarian elite, and from a few frustrated ex-members of the oligarchy with minor additions from the commercial-industrial world. Their activities were restricted by government laws concerning newspapers and public gatherings. At the same time, the dissidents of the first decade of the Meiji period had "grasped both the *idea* of parties as potent weapons of peaceful opposition (in a period when military opposition was becoming increasingly difficult) and the *ideology* of liberalism as derived from Western experience."[11]

Organized political party activity really began with the Imperial Rescript of October 12, 1881, which announced that a parliament would be established in 1890. Within a week

the *Jiyuto* (Liberal party) was formed under the presidency of Taisuke Itagaki, a former oligarch from Tosa. Indebted to Rousseau's ideas, the Liberal party sought the extension of freedom under a constitutional government and advocated popular rights. As the most radical party, it found its support in rural areas. The *Kaishinto* (Progressive party) appeared the same month, formed by another former member of the inner circle, Shigenobu Okuma of Hizen. Led by several former bureaucrats, it was devoted to the interests of the wealthier classes and found most of its support in urban areas. A very large number of political parties soon appeared, but they generally were unimportant individually. To counteract the activities of these parties, the government established in March 1882, under Genichiro Fukuchi, the *Rikken Teiseito* (Constitutional Imperial party). This party drew its rather small membership from the rising bureaucracy and government workers throughout Japan, but it was not without influence because of the status of its members and its control of important segments of the press.[12]

Increased political party activity aided the spread of Western ideas of popular rights and representative government. An increasing number of public demonstrations and the scope and intensity of agitation caused grave concern to the oligarchy. The government reacted by abolishing the prefectural assemblies and by calling out troops at times. It also relied on enforcement of the Peace Preservation Law of 1887, which prohibited secret societies and assemblies and permitted the police to halt such activities "whenever they deem such a course necessary." The same day the Peace Preservation Law was enacted, Home Minister Aritomo Yamagata, acting in accord with his new authority, forcibly removed from the Tokyo area more than five hundred persons prominent in agitating against the government.[13] Some leaders of the parties were bought off by the oligarchy and foresook their parties and principles to accept positions in the government.

CONSTITUTIONAL DEVELOPMENT

Throughout this period, Hirobumi Ito's committee to draft a constitution labored on in secrecy. On February 11, 1889, the anniversary of the legendary founding of the imperial family, the emperor graciously bestowed the constitution on the people of Japan in a private ceremony attended only by high dignitaries and a few foreign diplomats.

The structure of the state formalized in the Meiji Constitution owed far more to Western form than to Western principles. Presented to the people as a token of imperial benevolence, it rested on the traditional Japanese theory of state *(kokutai)* and decreed for Japan an absolute constitutional monarchy. The emperor, "sacred and inviolable," was central to the whole system, reigning over the empire in a "line of emperors unbroken for ages eternal."

The Emperor In his person the emperor combined the "rights of sovereignty and exercises them according to the provisions of the constitution."[14] His extensive powers included (1) exercising legislative power with consent of the Diet, (2) convoking and proroguing the Diet, (3) dissolving the House of Representatives, (4) issuing imperial ordinances in the place of law when the Diet is not sitting, (5) exercising supreme command of the army and navy, (6) declaring war, making peace, concluding treaties, and (7) determining the organization of the different branches of administration and the appointment and dismissal of all civil and military officials. Theoretically the emperor was absolute; in reality, he "reigned," to use the precise wording of the constitution. His manifold powers were exercised only with the advice of his principal advisors.

The Genro There was no constitutional provision for the most important of these advisors, the extraconstitutional group called the *genro* which exercised decisive control of government policy until the 1920s (see Figure 12-1). It was originally composed of five men, appointed by the emperor for life: Hirobumi Ito (Choshu), in charge of drafting the constitution; Aritomo Yamagata (Choshu), home minister and builder of the armed forces; Kaoru Inoue (Choshu) and Masayoshi Matsukata (Satsuma), financial and taxation experts; and Iwao Oyama (Satsuma), outstanding field marshal. General Taro Katsura (Choshu) and Prince Kimmochi Saionji later were admitted to membership. For all except five months of the first twenty-three years of the constitutional period, members of this group served as premier.

The Privy Council The Privy Council, first formed in 1888, was a group of twenty-six men appointed for life who served as the highest constitutional body advising the emperor in appointments of the premier and other matters as required. As highest personal advisor to the emperor, the lord keeper of the privy seal was custodian of state seals, advised on the appointment of premiers, and very important, generally controlled access to the emperor.

The Cabinet Like the Privy Council, the Cabinet was a preconstitutional body established in 1885. No formal provision was made for it in the constitution, which simply stated, "The respective Ministers of State shall give their advice to the emperor and be responsible for it" (Article LV). The Cabinet was responsible to the emperor and was not accountable to the Diet for its policies or actions. Among the cabinet ministers, a special and unusual role was played by the army minister and the navy minister. This role was not explicitly stated in the constitution be-

The Crown Prince and Princess in their traditional court robes on the occasion of their wedding in September 1964. (Courtesy, Public Information Bureau, Ministry of Foreign Affairs, Japan; UPI photo)

Emperor and Empress Hirohito. The emperor remains a unifying symbol for the Japanese people, signifying hundreds of years of tradition. (Courtesy, Consulate General of Japan)

The Japanese Cabinet in 1978 with former Prime Minister Takeo Fukuda in the center, front row. (Courtesy, Consulate General of Japan)

Emperor Hirohito reads opening message at a special session of the Japanese Diet in 1964. (UPI photo)

The Diet is the highest law-making organ in Japan, consisting of the House of Councillors and the House of Representatives, elected by secret ballot. (Courtesy, Consulate General of Japan)

This seventeen-story Imperial Hotel occupies the same spot as the Old Imperial Hotel designed by Frank Lloyd Wright. Built at a cost of $60 million, the hotel has 900 guest rooms (1,400 including the East building) and parking for 700 cars. (UPI photo)

Construction of the Daibutsuden or Hall of the Great Buddha of Todaiji, Nara, began around A.D. 745. It is thought to be the largest and oldest wooden structure on earth. (UPI photo)

Skyscrapers in the Shinjuku district of Tokyo are shown in this aerial view. (UPI photo)

Figure 12-1: Organization of Japan's Government

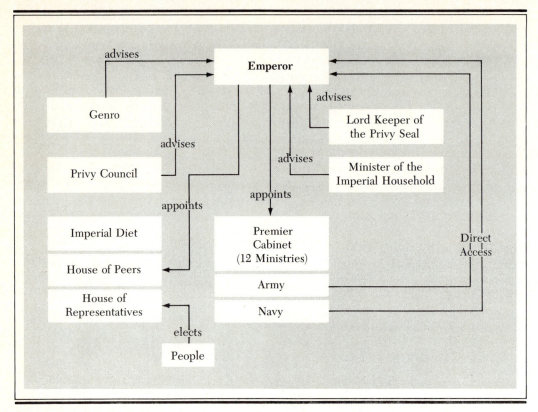

cause it had been developed prior to 1890, but the constitution did provide for the emperor's right of supreme command *(tosuiken,* Article XI). The right of supreme command belonged to the military staff and was not assigned to the government,[15] so it was possible within this framework for decisions of the military to be sanctioned as expressions of the "Emperor's direct will."[16] This preconstitutional principle was elaborated in 1900 by the legal requirement that the army and navy ministers had to be serving officers at three-star rank or higher and the service nominees had to be accepted by the premier. Thus, the army and navy, which controlled nominations of ministers for their service, could prevent the formation of a cabinet; in the opposite case, they could force the resignation of their minister.

The Diet   The bicameral Imperial Diet consisted of the House of Peers and the House of Representatives. A peerage had been established in 1884, and its members were given substantial constitutional power in 1890. The House of Peers had an original membership of 292, which later averaged about 400. Its six classes of membership included princes of the blood and the two highest ranks of the nobility who sat by hereditary right, lesser ranks who sat for seven years, and some imperial appointees who had seats for life. The House of Representatives (originally 300, later 466 members) was composed entirely of elected members. The franchise was limited to males and by property and tax qualifications to the extent that only about one percent of the population could vote. The lower house was in no sense representative of the general population. The two chambers were co-equal in powers to initiate legislation, pass laws, levy taxes, and approve the national budget. Conservative purposes were served because no bill rejected by either house could be reconsidered during that session. The Diet had but limited control of finances, and if the budget was not voted on, the government carried out the budget of the previous year.

Summary   All in all, the Meiji Constitution was not intended to establish a democracy and it did not. It did establish a structure of government whose component parts resembled those of Western governments, while maintaining distinctly Japanese devices, such as the *genro*, and enhancing the unique ideology of the divine descent of the emperor ruling in a line "unbroken for ages eternal." The oligarchy succeeded in reserving control of Japanese affairs to itself and did so by building on traditional values associated with cultural homogeneity and Confucianism.

Japanese society, then as now, was homogeneous, and there were no significant religious, ethnic, or racial groups outside the mainstream to contest traditional principles of social organization. The strong sense of family solidarity carried with it the idea of unity at family, village, and later, at national level, and reinforced concepts of a fixed hierarchy while rejecting Western ideas of individualism and self-importance. Inequality in family and national life was a recognized principle. The very brief Imperial Rescript on Education (1890) set forth the basic principles for nurturing the empire. The Confucian virtues of "loyalty and filial piety" unite the subjects of the empire who were enjoined to fulfill the Con-

fucian relationships. "Ye, Our subjects, be filial to your parents; affectionate to your brothers and sisters; as husbands and wives are harmonious; as friends true." Subjects were to advance the public good, always respect the constitution, and observe the laws, and "should emergency arise, offer yourself courageously to the state." The "way" set forth in this rescript was "infallible for all ages and true in all places."

This curious amalgam of constitutional and educational principles and theory, drawing heavily on Western institutions, Confucian ideas, and the revitalization of constitutionally expressed dogmas of an increasingly nationalistic Shinto myth, provided the oligarchy with the structure by which it pushed Japan to modernization, international equality, and status in world affairs.

Constitutionalism in Action, 1890–1945

The oligarchs filled all of the key government and military posts for the twenty-three years prior to promulgation of the constitution. They did not intend to share power with the "representatives of the people" in the lower house of the Diet, and they believed the carefully constructed constitution would assure their power to rule as advisors to the emperor. On the other hand, party leaders believed they could play a genuine role in policy formulation and mistakenly hoped even to control the legislature, as well as the executive, by having one of their members named premier. Given these opposing concepts of how the constitution should operate, conflict between the oligarchs and party members in the lower house was inescapable.[17]

Major developments in this conflict over the first four years of the constitutional period are recounted here in some detail because several precedents were established: (1) government interference in the electoral process, (2) selection of the premier by the *genro*, (3) arbitrary dissolution of the lower house, (4) alternation of the premiership between the Choshu and Satsuma factions, (5) the use of imperial prestige for political purposes, and (6) the Privy Council as interpreter of the constitution.[18]

OLIGARCH-PARTY CONFLICT

The tenor and intensity of the oligarch-party conflict was apparent during the initial election of the lower house on July 1, 1890. General Yamagata became the first premier under the constitution, and he directed prefectural governors, all of whom were appointed from Tokyo, to stand above and not be influenced by parties in their governance of the prefectures. Nevertheless, the one percent of the Japanese who held the franchise returned a lower house in which only 84 government candidates were elected, while the opposition Liberal (130 seats) and Progressive parties (4 seats) commanded the majority. The parties attacked, with little success, the government for its failure to secure treaty revision (to restore tariff autonomy and eliminate extraterritoriality), and with some success, the budget. Directly on assembling for its first session in November 1890, the lower house reduced the budget by 10 percent, mostly in the area of salaries for the bureaucrats who supported the oligarchs against the parties. To avoid damaging Japan's reputation in Western eyes, Yamagata did not dissolve the lower house. He prorogued it for a week, ruled that the budget could not be reduced by legislative action, bought off some opponents, and hired thugs to intimidate others. Yamagata carried the day. The independence of the executive from the legislative branch was increased. But criticism forced Yamagata's resignation in May 1891.

Yamagata's successor was chosen informally by consultation among the oligarchs, thus setting a precedent for the method of selecting the premier. Yamagata (Choshu) was succeeded by Masayoshi Matsukata (Satsuma) and thus began the practice of alternating the premiership between members of the two dominant factions of the oligarchy. Experiencing the hostility of the parties when he took the initiative to seek more funds (and more taxes) for navy shipbuilding (a Satsuma preserve) and to nationalize the railways, Matsukata did what Yamagata had wanted to do: he dissolved the lower house in December 1891. The elections, called for February 1892, were preceded by Home Ministry directives to all prefectural governors and police to support the government's candidates. Police in some areas literally intimidated voters with drawn sabers. The result was the bloodiest election in Japan's history: 25 dead, nearly 400 wounded. Yet the government still controlled only one-third of the lower house seats.

The Third Diet (May 1892) opened with a lower house resolution of no-confidence censuring the government for its tyrannical election interference. It failed by three votes. Matsukata refused to resign and prorogued the lower house for a week. The house retaliated by cutting the budget by one-third, so Matsukata sent it to the House of Peers where the funds were restored, thus creating a controversy as to whether the upper house had such powers. The emperor referred the question to the Privy Council, which ruled in favor of the premier. In the absence of constitutional competency of the Supreme Court to decide such matters, the Privy Council became the interpreter of the constitution. Cognizant of the intransigence of the parties and their ability to obstruct government programs, Matsukata disciplined some prefectural governors guilty of the most blatant election interference. This act affronted the army and navy, whose ministers resigned, thus forcing Matsukata's resignation.

The *genro* then selected Hirobumi Ito (Choshu) to replace Matsukata. The lower house, undeterred in its efforts to overcome the power of the oligarchy, censured the Cabinet in November 1892 by honoring the throne and supporting the exalted status of the emperor. Ito reacted by bringing about an audience of Diet leaders and ministers with the emperor who ordered them to compose their differences. Overwhelmed by this calculated use of imperial prestige for political purposes, the party members caved in and approved the budget with little change.

In December 1893 the parties tried once more to cause the premier's dismissal, this time over revision of unequal clauses in various treaties. Fearful that such an action would endanger negotiations, the oligarchy held fast, dissolved the lower house, tightened regulations on public gatherings, suspended publication of newspapers that criticized the government, hampered the activities of all parties, and dissolved some political groups. Elections in March 1894 (this time carried out with practically no government interference) resulted in a lower house hostile to Premier Ito. It promptly passed a no-confidence resolution by a vote of 253 to 17. Ito refused to accept the resolution, did not reply to it. Faced with a completely obstructionist lower house, Ito dissolved it in June 1894, on the eve of war with China, an event which brought a striking change to oligarchy-party relations.

The parties rallied behind the government during the Sino-Japanese War (1894–1895) because the need for Japan to control Korea transcended all other interests. Japan's victory showed the weakness of Manchu China and the strength and unity of Japan. Deprived of the major spoils of war by the Tripartite Intervention of Russia, Germany, and France, the people of Japan and their government came to believe their future lay in greater material and spiritual strength, so military budgets passed easily. For ten years,

the Japanese persevered (*gashin shōtan,* "to lie on firewood and eat gall") for the sake of vengeance, which was gotten in the victory over Russia in 1905.

During this period there was no controversy about general policy direction for Japan, only about who would lead Japan, the oligarchs or the party leaders. The latter did not succeed in wresting control from the oligarchs for several reasons: (1) the Liberal party split over land reform and lacked a diversified base with urban commercial and industrial support; (2) party leaders were willing to abandon the democratic movement to take posts offered to them in government; (3) the movement produced no outstanding theorists, and indeed, there were no symbols to compete with the emperor; (4) nationalism, a passion shared by the oligarchy, the parties, and public alike, keenly aware that national strength and military preparedness were the keys to international respect; and (5) the ability of the oligarchs to make concessions without diminishing their own power.[19] Nevertheless, the oligarchy abandoned its theory that cabinets were transcendent, that is, "above party, on behalf of the emperor, for the nation." Ito accepted the presidency of the Seiyukai party (successor to the Kenseito) in 1900, and later Katsura and Saionji were drawn into party affairs. Parties did not become mass-based organizations, but they expanded their base to operate via the bureaucracy and, in some degree, as an extension of it. Thus, the parties moved from being "part of a protest movement" to "sharers in political power."[20]

PARTY GOVERNMENT

The second stage of political development under the Meiji Constitution was party government from 1918 to 1931. Japan emerged from World War I as a member of the victorious Allied coalition, able to expand economic, strategic, and political interests in former German areas of China and islands in the north Pacific Ocean. As supplier to the Allies and to former European markets in Asia, Japan had enjoyed a profitable wartime boom, and with it came inflation and eventually rice riots in 1918. Unable to cope with the crisis, the *genro* named as premier a commoner and party leader, Kei (Takashi) Hara. This appointment of a commoner symbolized the changes in the bases of power between 1890 and 1918. The lone *genro* survivor after 1922 was Saionji (1849–1940), and he supported party government. Power flowed to and was dispersed among important and diverse groups in addition to the successors to the oligarchs in high civilian positions: the higher ranks of the bureaucracy; the *zaibatsu;* the hereditary peerage who held posts in the Imperial Court, the Privy Council, or the House of Peers; leaders of the major conservative parties; and an increasingly specialized and self-conscious military officer corps.[21] This group of elites lacked the generalized and unified goals of the oligarchy, so the Diet and the party system served as the mechanism to balance interests. Furthermore, Japan shared, to some extent, in the worldwide postwar faith in cooperative internationalism, the equality of peoples, and reaffirmation of liberal principles of government. Party cabinets governed Japan for most of the time from the end of World War I through the Manchurian crisis, but never achieved the responsible Cabinet-Diet relationships hoped for in the then current expression "the normal course of constitutional government" (*kensei no jōdō*).

Liberalism   The record for these few "liberal" years is mixed. Universal manhood suffrage was granted in 1925, increasing the electorate from three to twelve million, but this act was preceded by other legislation which could be used to suppress the opposition's public activity critical of government. Japanese troops were withdrawn from Siberia, and major cuts were made in the military forces. At the same time the army strengthened its social base of support throughout Japan,[22] and the army and navy ministries maintained their special status. The period was not one of fundamental reform, nor did real power pass to the House of Representatives. This was because of constitutional limitations and because other elite groups successively contended for power, but also because the parties lacked wide appeal and were so distrustful of potential liberal allies in the socialist labor movement and among Marxist intellectuals that these groups were treated as roughly as during the oligarchs' rule.[23] Added to these considerations are the fundamental cultural characteristics of Japanese society, which discouraged the growth of individualism, a sense of personal responsibility, and a sense of self-confidence apart from that which derives from group relationship. Political relationships depended on the personal qualities of leaders, and parties depended on the alliance of factions. The situation is described aptly by a former mayor of Tokyo, Yukio Ozaki:

Here in the Orient we have had the conception of a faction; but none of a public party. A political party is an association of people having for its exclusive object the discussion of public affairs of state and the enforcement of their views thereon. But when political parties are transplanted into the East, they at once partake of the nature of factions, pursuing private and personal interests instead of the interests of the state—as witnessed by the face of their joining hands by turns with the clan cliques or using the construction of railways, ports and harbors, schools, etc., as means of extending party influence. Besides, the customs and usages of feudal times are so deeply impressed upon the minds of men here that even the idea of political parties, as soon as it enters the brains of our countrymen, germinates and grows according to feudal notions. Such being the case, even political parties, which should be based and dissolved solely on principle and political views, are really affairs of personal connections and sentiments, the relations between the leader and the members of a party being similar to those which subsisted between a feudal lord and his liegeman, or to those between a "boss" of gamblers and his followers in this country. A politician scrupulous enough to join or desert a party for the sake of principle is denounced as a political traitor or renegade.[24]

AUTHORITARIANISM

The liberal period of Japanese prewar politics gave way to a third stage (1932–1945) marked by a return to authoritarianism, renewed vitality of civilian and uniformed militarists and the eventual dissolution of the parties. These developments were accompanied by and reinforced a heightened sense of nationalism and international mission. To one Japanese scholar, Japanese nationalism was qualitatively identical to love of family or home surroundings. It was a concrete expression, not an abstract feeling characteristic of Western nationalism. Historically Japan had a sense of cultural distinctiveness and moral superiority stemming from the Confucianist point of view. This conception of the world was shattered in the late 19th century to be replaced by a view of the international scene as an arena of struggle where Japan was seen as weak, politically and militarily backward. To some degree then, nationalism came from fear of an international system into which the West forced Japan. Nationalism in Japan is also related to a pattern of political integration different from that of the West. Theoretically the modern state exercises power legitimized by the consent of the people, and the idea of political liberty as the right of citizens to participate in government is an important premise for political integration. In marked contrast, Japan's political integration from the outset proceeded on national lines, appealing to national uniqueness, racial homogeneity, and the absolute qualities of the emperor's personal role. The third characteristic of Japanese nationalism was the "particularistic idea of national mission." If Western nations had a concept of a universalistic value (humanity) which transcended themselves, the Japanese did not. The ultimate end of the national state for Japan was its own self-preservation through self-perpetuation and expansion. These characteristics contributed to the fusion of Japanese nationalism with militarism in the 1930s.[25]

The Manchurian Incident   The Manchurian Incident of September 18, 1931,[26] was symptomatic of these developments. Manchuria had been the focus of Japan's strategic aspirations since the 1890s, and the Russo-Japanese War was fought to deny Russia control of Manchuria. The three-cornered interests of Russia, China, and Japan in the status of Manchuria came into sharper focus after Chiang Kai-shek unified China in 1927–28. Japan's claims in Manchuria were strengthened by the residence there of several hundred thousand Koreans who had become Japanese citizens after Korea was annexed in 1910. The Manchurian Incident itself was manufactured by second-echelon officers of Japan's Kwantung Army who claimed falsely that their forces had been attacked by Chinese troops in Mukden. Thanks to well-laid plans, the numerically very inferior Kwantung Army seized key points in a few days and soon secured effective control of Manchuria. These military actions were taken unilaterally without the knowledge of the Foreign Ministry or of higher military headquarters in Tokyo, an arrogant example of "dual diplomacy." In early 1932, the last Manchu Emperor, P'u-yi, was named regent of the new state of Manchukuo. Direct action in

Manchuria was followed by direct action in Japan when the Blood Brotherhood League (*Ketsumeidan*) assaulted the government in the May 15th Incident, murdering Premier Tsuyoshi Inukai and bombing government agencies. The plot failed but the plotters gained wide public sympathy, and others continued to agitate for a more nationalistic, patriotic, and aggressive foreign policy. The most serious attempt to overthrow parliamentary government was the abortive uprising in Tokyo on February 26, 1936, by young officers who used assassination, terrorism, and military power to seize temporary control of much of Tokyo.

On the continent Japan expanded its control into northern China, then halted after the Tangku truce of 1933. During large-scale Japanese maneuvers near the Marco Polo Bridge (Liukuochiao) a few miles from Peking, fighting broke out between Nationalist Chinese (Kuomintang) and Japanese forces on July 7, 1937. The matter could not be adjusted locally, Japanese reinforcements arrived in a few weeks, and large-scale war began. Japan enjoyed early tactical military successes, occupying much of north China, the Yangtze Valley to Hankow, and the important city of Canton by the fall of 1938. For the next seven years, Japan was bogged down in a war it could not win.

The End of Party Government   Internally, the resignation of the party (Seiyukai) Cabinet in May 1932 following Premier Inukai's assassination marked the end of party government. The replacement Cabinet, which lasted two years, was a coalition of party members, bureaucrats, militarists, and peers. Thereafter nine Cabinets held office before Hideki Tojo became premier in October 1941, moderates losing ground all the way until a small group of militarist officers and bureaucrats gained control. Japan's goal of a new order in East Asia, that is, Japanese control and coor-

dination of Japan, Manchukuo, and occupied China, was announced in 1938. The parties rallied to the government, announced their own dissolution, and were reorganized as the Imperial Rule Assistance Association in 1940. Taking advantage of early German successes in Europe and of its Neutrality Pact with the Soviet Union (April 1941), Japan moved into southern Indochina in July 1941, Tojo gained supremacy among the small group of decision makers, and Japan attacked the United States in December 1941, ensuring its own eventual defeat.

Although the militarists remained in control for most of World War II, they did not alter the essential structure of government. There was a proliferation of all types of organizations to control munitions and industrial production, commercial activities, the labor market, and massive conscription, but the Diet continued to function. Unlike its major "ally" Germany, Japan developed no new ideology: national unity was rooted in family, and village loyalty extended to the state. There was no *Führerprinzip*, nothing to compare to the Nazi party, no SS or SA elites, and no new groups were added to the ruling elite. Japan did not become a totalitarian state, and even in greatest adversity, there were no attempts to alter the nature of the state.

Defeat and a New Ideology

The arrival of American combat troops at Atsugi airfield in late August 1945 to begin the Allied occupation of Japan was final and visible proof of the utter defeat of Japan. The occupation was called the "greatest gamble in history," for no one knew how Japan would react to this unprecedented humiliation, whether the million or so Japanese men still under arms would fight to the death, or whether the Japanese would peacefully accept the directives of the occupying force and cooperate with the victors. Nor was there any assurance that the Allies would be able to carry out the objectives of the occupation. These were stated in the directive to General Douglas MacArthur, who had been designated Supreme Commander for the Allied Powers (SCAP): (1) to ensure that Japan will not again become a menace to the United States or to the peace and security of the world; and (2) to bring about the eventual establishment of a peaceful and responsible government, one which the United States desired to "conform as closely as may be to principles of democratic self-government." The means included limitation of Japan's sovereignty to the major islands, complete disarmament and demilitarization of Japan, providing the opportunity for economic development to meet peacetime needs, and last, encouragement of the Japanese people "to develop a desire for individual liberties and respect for fundamental human rights, particularly the freedoms of religion, assembly, speech, and the press."[27]

RESISTANCE TO CHANGE

There was much in Japan's ideological heritage to discourage those who sought to remold, or, more accurately, to revolutionize, Japan's political structure and supporting value system. Chief among the impediments to democratization were (1) the official doctrine imputing divinity to the uniquely ancient imperial institution, (2) a lack of strong representative institutions, (3) a social structure based on loyalty, discipline, and submission to authority, (4) a lack of political and economic individualism, and (5) the acceptance of aristocratic and autocratic rule under theoretical monarchical absolutism. At the same time, other aspects of the political heritage would work for successful renovation of Japanese life: (1) the parliamentary system had been in

continuous operation since 1890, and proof of its utility was shown by Tojo's handpicking candidates for the 1942 Lower House elections; (2) some policies vital to the success of the occupation, for example, land reform and female suffrage, had been issues in the 1880s; and (3) organizations, such as unions and cooperatives, went back 40 to 50 years.[28] Japan's tradition of comprehensive borrowing from China in the 7th century and from the West in the 19th century coupled with the homogeneity of the population (no sharp cleavages along cultural, ethnic, or religious lines) eased the transformation of Japanese society envisioned by its conquerors. The characteristic of submissiveness to authority was called into play by the emperor's adjuration to his subjects to "endure the unendurable." Cooperation with the occupation authorities was generally willing and total.

The shock of defeat coupled with the realization that the nation's ideological underpinnings and national structure were totally inadequate to the goals pursued in the 1930s and 1940s left the Japanese bewildered and uncertain, receptive to change, and eager for firm leadership. The occupation provided both change and leadership in seeking the two major objectives of the occupation: demilitarization and democratization. Demilitarization, in its narrow sense, was accomplished quickly and efficiently by the surrender, disarmament, and demobilization of Japan's armed forces, the destruction of war material, and the destruction or conversion of arms factories to nonmilitary uses.

DEMOCRATIZATION AND THE
AMERICAN IMPACT

Democratization was approached on a wide front, because whatever form the "responsible and peaceful" government might assume, it could not endure unless the "principles of democratic self-government" were understood and supported by the people of Japan. Political prisoners were freed immediately. More than 200,000 politicians, officials, and teachers were purged from office in the government or large corporations because of wartime ultranationalism. Compulsory education was lengthened from six to nine years, textbooks were rewritten, and the entire system was decentralized to the control of elected local boards of education. Labor organizations were called into existence and given the right to bargain collectively. A thorough land reform was carried out, and the *zaibatsu* cartels were deconcentrated. The voting age was reduced from twenty-five to twenty years, and the franchise was extended to females. The highly centralized government was greatly decentralized, and lesser administrative units were granted many powers previously reserved to the central government. Social welfare, public health, and fair-trade regulations were promulgated over a broad spectrum. State Shinto was disestablished, and on New Year's Day 1946, the emperor stated that ties between the throne and the people of Japan did not rest on the "false conception that the Emperor is divine and that the Japanese people are superior to other races and fated to rule the world."

All of these reforms and many others were carried out by General MacArthur's directives working through the bureaucracy of the Japanese government. Conscious of the problems inherent in direct military government and in the allocation of zones of responsibility to its allies, the United States ruled indirectly and did not share, in effect, any powers with its allies, despite the organizational paraphernalia of the four-power Allied Council for Japan in Tokyo or the thirteen-power Far Eastern Commission in Washington.

Realizing that these reforms required expression in a new constitution if they were to endure, General MacArthur ordered Premier Kijuro Shidehara in October 1945 to deal with the reform of Japan's government. Dissatisfied with his efforts, MacArthur ordered the SCAP Government Section to draft a new constitution. The draft was widely discussed and criticized, especially by conservative Japanese officials who resisted changes in the imperial institution, and from the opposite direction by the Soviet Union and the Japan Communist party, which sought to abolish the throne and set up a people's republic. Without a plebiscite or a formal Diet review, the SCAP version of a new constitution was adopted in late 1946 and took effect on May 3, 1947.[29]

THE NEW IDEOLOGY

The new ideology eloquently expressed in the 1947 Constitution owes little to the traditional ideology of Japan. In fact, the American influence is unmistakable. The preamble reads:

We, the Japanese people, acting through our duly elected representatives in the National Diet, determined that we shall secure for ourselves and our posterity the fruits of peaceful cooperation with all nations and the blessings of liberty throughout this land, and resolved that never again shall we be visited with the horrors of war through the action of government, do proclaim that sovereign power resides with the people and do firmly establish this Constitution. Government is a sacred trust of the people, the authority for which is derived from the people, the powers of which are exercised by the representatives of the people, and the benefits of which are enjoyed by the people. This is a universal principle of mankind upon which this Constitution is founded. We reject and revoke all constitutions, laws, ordinances, and rescripts in conflict herewith.

While this new ideology appears to have been accepted by many Japanese, it is still not clear what will evolve from the mix of the old and the new. Traditional values remain deeply imbedded in Japanese culture, yet most recognize the need to adopt a modernized ideology attuned to the "democratic" spirit of the Japanese system. The structure that gives expression to this new ideology, the traditional values, and the major political actors are discussed in Chapter 13.

Summary

Japan has a lengthy, distinctive, and strongly unified cultural tradition. The preliterate native religious base of Shinto has shown remarkable tenacity despite being overlain by successive waves of alien thought. Buddhism entered Japan in the 6th century, and Japan has today the world's most important actively Buddhist population. Beginning in the 7th century, Japan received great infusions of Chinese culture, of which Confucianism was most important. The Seventeen Article Constitution is the earliest evidence of a considered body of government ideals, a combining of Buddhist and Confucianist concepts. Japan adapted much from China, but discarded the concept of a civil service based on merit, preferring its own traditional hierarchy based on birth. Nor did Japan embrace the mandate of heaven.

During the military dictatorship of the Tokugawa Period (1603–1868), Japan's ideology stressed the status quo, relying on Shinto to reinforce loyalty to the emperor, Buddhism to highlight the selflessness demanded of the ruling military class, and Confucianism to emphasize virtue, learning, and class responsibility for correct government. With the Restoration in 1868, the imperial myth was strengthened to make the emperor the focus of all loyalties previously diffused to the feudal lords. The system maintenance ideology was reoriented to "goal attainment." The Meiji oligarchy saw the danger of the highly competitive international state system of the West and determined to avoid China's fate. Sensing Japan's own weakness, Japanese leaders dismantled the feudal system and erected a constitutional parliamentary unitary state seeking economic development, a strong military force, and a recognition of its equality by the West. Under the Meiji Constitution (1890–1947), the oligarchy ruled in an authoritarian manner until the 1920s. For a few years, party government suggested more liberal trends with the expansion of the franchise to all males and the reduction of military expenditures. The third period (1932–1945) of Japan's prewar politics was marked by a return to authoritarianism, renewed vitality of civilian and uniformed militarists, military adventures in Manchuria and China, and eventual dissolution of the political parties.

In large measure, Japan's postwar ideology was dictated by the American government. The goals of the military occupation were to ensure that Japan would never again be a menace to the United States or to the peace and security of the world, and to establish in Japan a peaceful and responsible government that would "conform as closely as may be to the principles of democratic self-government." Japan's institutions were restructured to develop a desire for individual liberties, respect for fundamental human rights, for the freedoms of religion, assembly, speech, and the press. Despite those aspects of Japan's ideological heritage—divinity of the imperial institution, a lack of strong representative bodies, a social structure based on submissiveness toward authority, and a lack of political and economic individualism—the new ideology seems to have taken root.

NOTES

1. Ryusaku Tsunoda et al., *Sources of Japanese Tradition*, vol. 1 (New York: Columbia University Press, 1964), p. 34.

2. Ibid., p. 50.

3. Sir George Sansom, *A History of Japan to 1334* (Stanford, Calif.: Stanford University Press, 1958), pp. 56–60, 72–7.

4. Sansom, ibid., op. cit., pp. 68–69.

5. Tsunoda, op. cit., pp. 96–97.
   (Stanford, Calif.: Stanford University Press, 1963), pp. 7–8, 17–18.
   in Japan (Baltimore: Johns Hopkins Press, 1950), pp. 35–43.
   (Stanford, Calif.: Stanford University Press, 1963), pp. 7–8, 17–18.

8. Sir George Sansom, *Japan A Short Cultural History* (New York: 1943), p. 524.

9. Various translations of the Charter Oath are found in Paul M. A. Linebarger, Djang Chu, and Ardath W. Burks, *Far Eastern Government and Politics* (Princeton, N.J.: Van Nostrand, 1954), p. 584.

10. Nobutaka Ike, *The Beginnings of Political Democracy in Japan* (Baltimore: Johns Hopkins Press, 1950), pp. 35–43.

11. Robert A. Scalapino and Junnosuke Masumi, *Parties and Politics in Contemporary Japan* (Berkeley: University of California Press, 1962), pp. 4, 12. Italics in original.

12. Ike, op. cit., pp. 101–110; Chitoshi Yanaga, *Japan since Perry* (New York: McGraw-Hill, 1949), pp. 149–162.

13. Ike, op. cit., pp. 185–186.

14. Text of the constitution is found in Linebarger et al., op. cit., pp. 585–591.

15. Yoshio Matsushita, *Meiji Gunseishi Ron* (Tokyo: Yuhikaku, 1956), vol 2, pp. 295–296.

16. Joseph Pittau, *Political Thought in Early Meiji Japan 1868–1889* (Cambridge, Mass.: Harvard University Press, 1967), p. 190.

17. Hugh Borton, *Japan's Modern Century* (New York: Ronald Press, 1970), pp. 224–226.

18. Ibid., pp. 223–241, and Yanaga, op. cit., pp. 215–227. Paul H. Clyde and Burton F. Beers, *The Far East*, 6th ed. (Englewood Cliffs, N.J.: Prentice-Hall, 1975), pp. 275–285. George Akita, "Foundations of Constitutional Government," in *Modern Japan 1868–1900* (Cambridge, Mass.: Harvard University Press, 1967), pp. 77–89.

19. Ike, op. cit., pp. 190–191.

20. Scalapino and Masumi, op. cit., pp. 12–15.

21. Robert E. Ward, *Japan's Political System* (Englewood Cliffs, N.J.: Prentice-Hall, 1967), p. 12.

22. See Richard J. Smethurst, *A Social Basis for Prewar Japanese Militarism* (Berkeley: University of California Press, 1974).

23. Clyde and Beers, op. cit., pp. 323–324.

24. Yukio Ozaki, *The Voice of Japanese Democracy* (Yokohama, 1918), pp. 93–94, quoted in Tsunoda, op. cit., pp. 182–183.

25. Sannosuke Matsumoto, "The Significance of Nationalism in Modern Japanese Thought," in Scheiner, op. cit., pp. 135–139.

26. See Mark H. Peattie, *Ishiwara Kanji and Japan's Confrontation* (Princeton, N.J.: Princeton University Press, 1975), and Takehiko Yoshihashi, *Conspiracy at Mukden* (New Haven, Conn.: Yale University Press, 1963).

27. "United States Initial Post-Surrender Policy for Japan," prepared jointly by Department of State, War and Navy Departments, dated August 29, 1945, approved by the president, September 6, 1945.

28. Ike, op. cit., pp. 210–212.

29. See Theodore McNelly, *Contemporary Government of Japan* (Boston: Houghton Mifflin, 1963), pp. 36–46.

CHAPTER 13

JAPANESE POLITICAL ACTORS: POWER AND LEGITIMACY

Japan is a unitary parliamentary democracy with a wide range of political actors: political parties, government bureaucracies, labor unions, business and commercial circles, and a great number of highly diverse special interest and associational groups. Yet the importance of these political actors varies considerably.

Political parties, as a group, are the most important political actors in Japan. They exist to acquire political office and political power for their members, and do this by choosing candidates, articulating issues, and participating in elections. Under Japan's parliamentary system, the majority party of the House of Representatives selects the prime minister and Cabinet—in essence, the executive branch—and ideally provides a stable parliamentary majority to support the executive's legislative program. This function has been fulfilled by the Liberal Democratic party since 1955, despite increasing indications that it may soon lose the electoral strength to do so. Currently there are six political parties represented in the dominant House of Representatives.

The government bureaucracy plays an important role as the administrator of policy and in policy formulation by participating in drafting of various laws and regulations. High-ranking bureaucrats have close party ties and, at times, retire early to make new careers as party politicians.

Labor unions and business groups are organized to seek political, economic, and social goals by articulating issues, and by public support of and financial contributions to parties. Labor unions have been the main support of the Japan Socialist party while the Liberal Democratic party is the primary beneficiary of business groups.

A limited number of political influentials play an important role in the political system. Their influence coming primarily through business interests, these political actors have direct links with official institutions of government and political parties. Yet, it is their indentification with corporate structures that gives political influentials an important role as political actors.

Individuals as political actors are relatively less important in Japan. This is because the prime minister owes his position, not to victory in a nationwide election, but to his selection by parliamentary equals through a process of factional bargaining. Japanese political leaders do not have a large national following because political parties are not mass parties, but parliamentary parties. Second, Japanese social organization discourages the leader, emphasizing group decision and group action in almost all matters. Even when reaching a position of great influence through party activity, the leader cannot expect a long tenure of office because of factional jealousy and expectations that the prestige and fruits of office will be rotated among those who made him leader.

Legitimacy   Legitimacy is defined in the introduction to this book to mean "operating within the rules of the game," with the rules derived from the values and perceptions shared by the political actors. In a broader sense, legitimacy may connote general popular acceptance of the government in both its form and the ideological bases which mold its policies. At any given time, however, groups within the general population may advocate variant forms and ideologies and use unacceptable means to achieve them. Such groups have been active in Japan for the past century, but one still must conclude that, under our definition, the governments established under the Meiji Constitution and the 1947 Constitution have enjoyed a high degree of legitimacy, regardless of the fundamental differences in the ideologies undergirding two highly contrastive political entities. In part, this is due to Japanese acceptance of an authoritative central government as part of the natural order of things, be it Tokugawa feudalism, an oligarchic imperial bureaucracy, a military occupation, or a representative democratic constitutional monarchy.

On the other hand, neither of Japan's modern constitutions can be said to have legitimacy in the sense that some Western constitutions based on theories of a general will or social contract enjoy legitimacy. The 1890 Constitution was drafted in secrecy by a small group of leaders intent on preserving the essence of Japan's polity *(kokutai)* and graciously bestowed on a grateful citizenry by the emperor. The 1947 Constitution was drafted in secrecy by officials of a victorious occupation force and was accepted by Japan because no other course was possible. In general, the Meiji Constitution enjoyed a highly visible degree of support because the nation was united behind the political myths associated with the imperial institution and, by all criteria, Japan was a real "success story" from the 1870s until midway into World War II. Today Japan is perhaps less united in support of how the state and society have been "reconstituted" under the 1947 Constitution. This should not be surprising because of the freedom of intellectual and political activity which is part of Japan's search for enduring values to replace those which were discarded perforce after defeat in 1945. A dissatisfied minority left criticizes the government because it was externally imposed and a minority right advocates a return to imperial rule. All in all, the new Constitution is almost universally seen to be legitimate.

Institutions

THE EMPEROR

Throughout Japan's history the emperor has been the theoretically absolute ruler of Japan; but, as we have seen, his functions were essentially legitimizing and ceremonial. This was true even under the 1890 Constitution, although he combined in his "sacred and inviolable" person the "rights of sovereignty," legislative power, and other attributes of absolutism. Article 1 of the 1947 Constitution reads:

The Emperor shall be the symbol of the state and of the unity of the people, deriving his position from the will of the people with whom resides sovereign power.

The emperor performs ceremonial acts, such as the appointment of the prime minister and chief judge of the Supreme Court, but only in accord with instructions from the Diet and Cabinet, respectively. "On behalf of the people" and with the approval of the Cabinet, he convokes the Diet, dissolves the House of Representatives, proclaims general elections, and performs other matters of state. His duties are limited to those constitutionally decreed: "He shall not have powers related to government." Neither the 1890 nor 1947 Constitution clearly defined the emperor's status in legal terms. Perhaps it is more confused today. It is difficult to describe a symbol "of the state" or of the "unity of the people" when that symbol is a person. The emperor is more than a symbol: he is a living extension of the most ancient reigning family in the world today. For most Japanese he retains a degree of prestige undiminished from past generations, earning the respect of his people by his exemplary conduct, filling a vital function as a stabilizing influence in politics. Some conservatives would like to see his constitutional role change to that of chief of state, but that is unlikely for the present.

THE CABINET AND THE DIET

Sovereignty lies with the people (see Figure 13-1). Their elected representatives compose the National Diet, which is constitutionally designed as "the highest organ of state power" and the "sole law-making organ of the state." The Diet consists of the House of Councillors (252 members) and the House of Representatives (511 members). Both houses are now totally elective by nearly all Japanese, male and female, over twenty years of age.

The Prime Minister and the Cabinet The Prime minister is designated from among Diet members by a resolution of the Diet. Here, too, the lower house designation is the decision of the Diet in case agreement cannot be reached with the upper house. All prime ministers under the current constitution have been members of the House of Representatives. The prime minister appoints all Cabinet ministers who must be civilians and a majority of whom must be members of the Diet. In the exercise of executive power, the Cabinet "shall be collectively responsible to the Diet," and therefore is susceptible to a no-confidence resolution. If passed, it requires (1) Cabinet resignation en masse within ten days, or (2) dissolution of the lower house by the emperor on the advice of the prime minister, the calling of new elections within forty days of dissolution, and convoking the Diet within thirty days thereafter. Since the conservative parties united in 1955 to form the Liberal Democratic party, that party has held a majority in the lower house. A vote of no-confidence remains unlikely because the governing Liberal Democratic party has no incentive to vote itself out of office.

The Diet The upper house in Japan's bicameral Diet, the House of Councillors (*Sangi-in*), has a total membership of 252. Of these, 100 are elected from the national constituency, that is, by all voters in the nation, and 152 are elected from prefectural constituencies, each entitled to two to eight seats, depending on the population of the prefecture. The term of office is six years. Elections are held every three years for one-half of the members from each of the two types of constituencies. This permits structural continuity in the Diet. The House of Councillors is not subject to dissolution, but is "closed" when

Figure 13-1: Organization of the Government of Japan, 1977

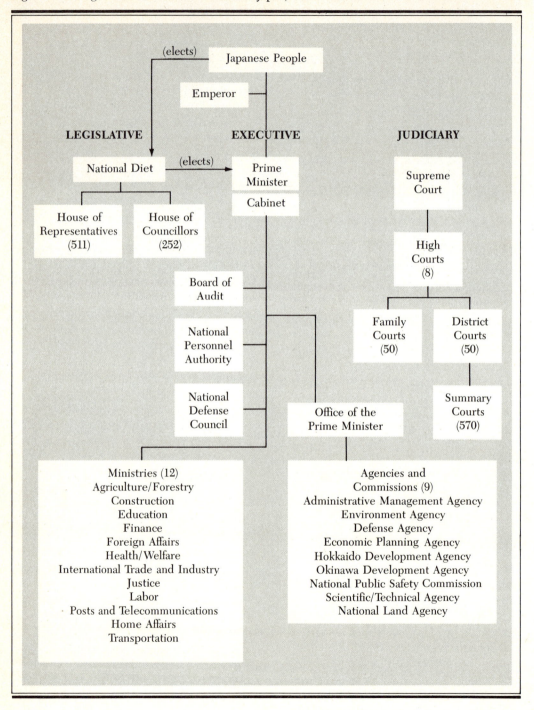

the House of Representatives is dissolved. In time of national emergency, the House of Councillors may be convoked in emergency session by the Cabinet, but it is clearly subordinate to the lower house, which must approve any actions taken by the House of Councillors during the national emergency.

The House of Representatives *(Shugiin)* is elected under the single-vote medium-size multimember constituency system, that is, Japan is divided into 130 election districts, each of which returns three to five representatives, depending on its population, except for the lone single-member island district of Amami Oshima south of Kyushu. Each voter is entitled to a single vote; thus, a given district may have eight candidates for four seats, but the individual voter may cast his ballot for only one candidate. The four candidates with the highest number of votes win the seats.

This system poses formidable problems for the major parties, candidates, and campaign managers. The party must predetermine its probable vote-getting ability to decide whether to run three, four, or five candidates. If it overestimates the vote and runs five candidates, seats may be lost to another party which concentrates its vote-getting on one or two candidates. If it underestimates the vote, it may run and elect two candidates when it could have elected more. Once the proper number of candidates has been determined, the party still faces the concrete problem of how to assure the optimal distribution of the vote. Generally the Liberal Democratic party has been successful in these calculations; nevertheless, Liberal Democrats have criticized the system because it encourages factionalism and disunity in the party, places a premium on local rather than national issues, and contributes to corruption and election abuses.[1] It is also argued that the system has a structural bias in favor of the smaller party which is not tempted, as is a stronger party, to run too many candidates. Election campaigns, although restricted to thirty days, are said to be too expensive, giving the advantage to candidates with access to larger funds, and reducing their independence after election.[2] This criticism applies equally to other systems, including our own.

Perhaps the most serious defect in the system, theoretically speaking, is the disparity in the value of the individual's vote. The current malapportionment of seats has resulted from the large-scale shifts of population in Japan over the past twenty-five years, primarily from rural to urban areas. The imbalance was partly redressed by redistricting in 1964, but serious inequities remain. Changes in the electoral system have been discussed for many years and more discussion, without important change, is likely. The Liberal Democratic party generally stands to benefit from the status quo, and electoral systems are extremely resistant to change.

The two houses have similar internal organizations, each provided with a secretariat, a legislative bureau, special committees, and sixteen standing committees with responsibilities parallel to those of the Cabinet ministries, plus budget, audit, house discipline, and management committees. The Diet is supported by a staff of about 4,000; the Cabinet has about 900 employees, and more than 30,000 civil servants comprise the office of the prime minister.[3]

THE JUDICIARY

The outline organization of the judicial system is shown in Figure 13-1. The system is fundamentally different from that under the Meiji Constitution, whose courts were subject to the control of the executive through the minister of justice. The Supreme Court is vested with "the whole judicial power," making it substantially equal to other branches of government, and is constitutionally charged with judicial review as "the court of last resort with power to determine the constitutionality of any law, order, regulation or official act." On three occasions the Supreme Court has found laws passed by the Diet to be unconstitutional, and none were of particular importance. On other occasions it has upheld the constitutionality of other acts, the most controversial of which was the Sunakawa decision of 1959, which held that stationing of American forces in Japan did not violate Article 9 of the constitution.[4]

The Supreme Court consists of 15 judges, all of whom must be 40 years of age and two-thirds of whom must have distinguished themselves as judges. The chief justice is designated by the Cabinet and is appointed by the emperor, a nicety of protocol symbolizing the coordinate status of chief justice and prime minister. Associate justices are appointed by the Cabinet with imperial attestation. Appointments are permanent, but judges can be recalled through the "review" of each appointee by the electorate at the first general election following the appointment, or by the decennial review required thereafter. To discourage further any packing of the court by the Cabinet, justices are also subject to recall by referendum. As of 1977, no justices had been removed by any of these procedures. Retirement is mandatory at age 70. Judges may be impeached by the Diet Judge Impeachment Court (the only special tribunal authorized by law).

Judicial autonomy for the Supreme Court gives it the power to establish rules of procedure, maintain internal discipline of the courts, set standards for attorneys, and generally exercise control of all matters except judicial deliberation within individual courts. All judges of lesser courts are appointed by the Cabinet from among nominees recommended by the Supreme Court.

Eight high courts located in regional cities throughout the nation have original jurisdiction in election disputes, petitions for habeas corpus, and cases of armed revolt. They also function as courts of appeal for criminal and civil cases. Fifty district courts have original jurisdiction in all criminal and civil cases except for petty offenses tried in the 570 summary courts, which function as small courts as justices of the peace function in the United States.[5] The fifty family courts were established in conjunction with the basic changes in the legal position of women and children under the 1947 Constitution (Article 24), which reads

With regard to choice of spouse, property rights, inheritance, choice of domicile, divorce and other matters pertaining to marriage and the family, laws shall be enacted from the standpoint of individual dignity and the essential equality of the sexes.

These are matters traditionally handled by the head of a family. A second area of responsibility for the family courts is juvenile crimes.

Courts in Japan generally play a less important role than that played by the courts in the United States. Traditionally the Japanese are not a litigious people, an observation highlighted by the fact that, on a per capita basis, American lawyers outnumber Japanese lawyers by about forty to one. Japanese prefer to settle disputes by the informal use of intermediaries, by conciliation, group decision, and consensus. Resort to litigation is unseemly and is usually undertaken only after other methods have failed.

THE BUREAUCRACY

The civil service has played a vital role in the government and administration of Japan since the early Meiji period. It is a target of interest groups because it is the part of the executive branch which carries out the day-to-day operations of the government and because it is the origin of much legislation. At the same time it is a powerful interest group itself, a highly educated, extremely competent, and self-conscious corps, jealous of its own power and resistant to the legislative branch of government. The prewar bureaucrat was regarded as a servant of the emperor whose attitude toward the public was crystallized in the phrase *kanson minpi*, "the officials are honored, the people are despised," and the average bureaucrat today probably does not really regard himself as a public servant.[6] The national bureaucracy (excluding military forces) increased from about 250,000 people in 1940 to 1,535,000 in 1955 to 1,698,355 in 1975. The number of local government employees in 1975 was 2,857,336, including 850,000 teachers and 189,000 police.[7] National and local government employees comprise about 9% of the total work force. Bureaucrats exert influence by control of the machinery of government, by participation in drafting bills, through the deference normally accorded them by lobbyists, petitioners and even Cabinet ministers, and by early retirement (age 50 to 55) followed by entry into political party activity and leadership positions in the business world from which they continue to pursue their conservative interests.

THE UNITARY STATE AND LOCAL GOVERNMENT

Until the end of World War II all governmental powers were concentrated at the national level, and local affairs were controlled through the Home Ministry. This ministry was abolished during the occupation and replaced by the Local Autonomy Agency (now again called Home Ministry), designed to oversee compliance with Chapter VIII of the 1947 Constitution. This provided for the establishment of local public entities based on the principle of local autonomy and for the direct popular election of chief executive officers and assemblymen. Implementing legislation required a "presidential" form in

contrast to the parliamentary cabinet form at national level and provided for the referendum, initiative, and recall.[8]

The first level of government below national level consists of 47 prefectures *(ken)* which include the metropolis *(to)* of Tokyo, the two urban prefectures *(fu)* of Osaka and Kyoto, and the regional prefecture *(do)* of Hokkaido. Organization of the prefectural administration is decided by the prefecture except for the five departments mandated by law: general affairs, finance, health, welfare, and labor. There is considerable variation in prefectural government organization, and the size of assemblies varies from 125 members in Tokyo (population 11,519,000) to 40 members in Tottori prefecture (population 575,000).[9] Each prefecture has a governor and a unicameral assembly, both elected for a four-year term. The governor and assembly have balancing powers: the assembly is empowered to pass a motion of nonconfidence; the governor may dissolve the assembly and call for a new election. If a new election results in a nonconfidence motion, the governor is required to resign. The governor may also be recalled by a petition signed by one-third of the voters.[10] The second tier of local government consists of 643 cities including the wards *(ku)* into which Tokyo, Osaka, and Kyoto are subdivided, and 2,620 towns and villages. All of these entities are self-governing units administratively independent of the prefecture and have elected councils and mayors or town and village heads.

Local governments are not sovereign entities because Japan is a unitary state. The American occupation authorities tried to decentralize the government to the local level in the belief that it would further democratization by making the government apparatus closest to the people most responsive to their needs. In general, the small geographical extent of Japan, the generations-old habit of depending on the central government, the lack of financial independence, and the need for prefectural officials to devote most of their energy to carrying out Tokyo's policies have made local autonomy a less powerful force than was anticipated.

Decision Makers

In the Japanese system, as in the other systems we have studied, decision makers as a group are political actors. The Japanese system resembles the American political system. Decision makers include both elected officials and appointed officials. In Japan, however, the clearly dominant House of Representatives provides opportunities for its key members to act as political actors, overshadowing the House of Councillors.

ELECTED OFFICIALS

Not all of the 763 elected members of the two houses are important political actors. Like the American system, the chairmen of standing committees and their key members are the decision makers. Committees have an absolute control over the flow of legislation. Equally important, committee hearings are controlled by the chairman and key members, who have already developed their strategy in secret session.

The House of Councillors (upper house) has generally followed the lead of the lower house. The power relationships and factional leadership of the lower house are usually reflected in the upper house, which is clearly the subordinate house. While in theory the upper house was to be independent of "politics" in the usual sense—similar to the old House of Peers—the upper house has become increasingly politicized and operates like the United States Senate. It does not have the power of the Senate, but does exercise more

power than the House of Lords in England. Here again, the major political actors are faction leaders and committee chairmen.

Because Japan's political system is a parliamentary system, the prime minister and Cabinet members are elected by the party controlling the parliament. Over the past 30 years, this has consistently been the Liberal Democratic party (although the elections in 1977 reduced the strength of this party in the Diet). Moreover, the prime minister and the Cabinet represent various factions within the party. Through party power and the power of their official positions, each of these Cabinet members, including the prime minister, is an important decision maker in his own right. Contrary to the American presidential system, each Cabinet member heads a "mini-party" or faction within the major party. Few decisions are made by the controlling party which do not incorporate agreement by all the factions.

APPOINTED OFFICIALS

As is true of the American system, key members of the bureaucracy are decision makers and political actors. While it would be difficult to identify all of these decision makers among the thousands of bureaucrats, some general observations are useful.

The parliamentary system of administration differs from the presidential system. Career civil servants in Japan occupy top posts immediately subordinate to Cabinet ministers. For example, the Cabinet minister is assisted by a vice-minister, who is generally a career civil servant, and the intra-ministry administrator. Day-to-day administrative duties are handled by a number of minister's secretaries. Such duties include matters confidential to the minister; appointment, promotion, training, and dismissal of ministry personnel; study of legislative statutes; and budgeting.

In addition, each minister has a number of other vice-ministers assisting him. These are party members who are appointed by the minister and who serve in a liaison capacity between the Diet and the ministry. Vice-ministers are also involved in interdepartment coordination.

Thus we can see that in each ministry there are important decision makers, aside from the minister himself, who are appointed officials. Contrary to the American system, where generally the highest civil servants in the federal bureaucracy are found below the level of assistant secretary, in Japan, civil servants are found at the vice-minister level and have a strong voice in decision making.

In this regard, the office of the prime minister has a number of appointed personnel who act as an extension of the office, similar to the White House staff in the American system. This inner bureaucracy does act as a decision maker by virtue of its close association with the prime minister. Moreover, its duties require oversight of various activities that are the responsibility of the prime minister.

Traditionally, the Japanese civil service has maintained a virtually autonomous status, providing a solid group against penetration by government politicians; however, in the most recent years, the bureaucrats have become increasingly like their American counterparts. They have, on occasion, bypassed their chain of command and established links directly with political parties and outside interests, suggesting that political forces outside the official structure have begun eroding the traditional bureaucratic cohesiveness against outside influences.

In the final analysis, there are clusters of decision makers, as is true of the American system, that are associated with the Diet, the prime minister, the Cabinet, and key members of the bureaucracy. The bureaucracy plays a more important role in the Japanese system than in the American system because of the administrative structure of Japan's unitary and parliamentary system.

Groups

Japan is an open, democratic, complex, and highly industrialized society composed of a wide variety of individuals and groups increasingly subject to the administrative regulation and bureaucracy that is part of modern society. These groups seek to improve their condition by political means, including personal contacts with dietmen and key bureaucrats, by active lobbying of Diet committees, by financial assistance in election campaigns, by hiring former bureaucrats and politicians, and by lavish entertainment. Sometimes violence, assassination, and other extraparliamentary means are used. A listing of these interest or pressure groups would, indeed, be lengthy.[11] However, the groups that are most important as political actors are easily categorized into political parties, intellectuals, labor unions, and business and student groups, with parties and business clearly the dominant political actors.

POLITICAL PARTIES

As we have seen, political parties were first organized in a tentative way as early as 1874 and thereafter played roles of varying importance until all were dissolved in 1941 to form the Imperial Rule Assistance Association. In the early days of the occupation, a wide variety of political organizations appeared, but the most important of them continued a prewar lineage. The postwar Liberal party was formed from among members of the *Seiyukai* and other major conservative groupings; the Progressive party, from the *Minseito*. The Socialist and Communist parties date from the 1920s, but neither was politically important until after Japan's defeat when all wartime political prisoners were immediately freed by order of SCAP. The purge of wartime politicians in 1945 and 1946 deprived the conservative parties of many of their leaders. The Liberal party leader Ichiro Hatoyama was purged by order of General MacArthur just prior to winning appointment as prime minister, a position he finally achieved in 1954. The purges depleted the ranks of experienced Diet members so that about four-fifths of those who gained office in the first elections in April 1946 were first-timers. Thereafter, more and more bureaucrats resigned to run for office, and in time, this created a major source of factionalism in the division between partymen *(tojin)* and bureaucrats *(kanryo)*, a rivalry that has persisted on the conservative side ever since.

Throughout the seven years of Allied occupation (1945–1952) real governing power was in the hands of SCAP officials; therefore, party activity was directed mainly toward securing control of the House of Representatives in anticipation of the early restoration of Japan's sovereignty. During this period party nomenclature and statements of policy were far less important than personal alliances constructed by the leading political figures. Table 13-1 shows the lower house seats won by the several parties participating in the five elections from 1947 through 1955. Only once (Liberal party in 1952) did any party achieve a simple majority of the seats. Yet the conservative parties as a group were able to control the government on a coalition basis, except for the eight-month premiership of Socialist leader Tetsu Katayama in 1947–1948. The conservative parties were riven by factionalism centering on personal loyalties, and the progressive parties by personalism and ideological preferences.

Having gained seats at the expense of the conservatives in the 1955 general election, the socialists composed their differences and formed the Japan Socialist party in October 1955. This act spurred the conservative groups to wind up months of negotiations, and they announced the formation of the Liberal Democratic party a month later. The current alignment of major parties dates from late 1955. These two major parties are treated individually below, along with the Japan Communist party, the Democratic Socialist party, a splinter group of right-wing socialists formed in 1959, and the Komeito, or Clean Government, party, a curious hybrid of religion and politics which first entered candidates in the general elections of 1967.

General Characteristics of Political Parties
Earlier we read Yukio Ozaki's statement: "Here in the Orient we have had the conception of a faction; but none of the public party." Writing fifty years later, Nathaniel Thayer wrote that "a sense of party is woefully lacking in Japan."[12] These observations highlight a persistent characteristic of all Japanese parties, factionalism, and it is not accurate to regard any party as a genuinely cohesive organization. A second characteristic is that no party in Japan has a mass membership. For instance, the Liberal Democratic party reported in 1970 a dues-paying membership of 745,000[13] out of a population of nearly 100,000,000, yet this estimate is generally judged to be excessive. Essentially the parties are parliamentary parties with the center of operations in Tokyo. At the national level, the parties have similar organizational structures, including a party congress, executive and policy boards, a secretariat, and prefectural organizations. The party system itself is not a two-party system in the sense that the Liberal Democratic party and the Japan Socialist party alternate in the exercise of power. The Liberal Democratic party has exercised preeminent control of the government since occupation days. Nor is it correct to regard it as a multiparty system under which other parties

Table 13–1: Distribution of Seats in Elections for the House of Representatives

	1947	1949	1952	1953	1955
Liberal Party	131		240		112
Democratic Party	121	69			185
Peoples Cooperative Party	29	14			
Liberal Democratic Party		264			
Progressive Party			85	76	
Hatoyama Liberal Party				35	
Yoshida Liberal Party				199	
Conservative Total	**281**	**347**	**325**	**310**	**297**
Socialist Party	143	48			
Left-Wing Socialist			54	72	89
Right-Wing Socialist			57	66	67
Labor-Farmer Party		7	4	5	4
Communist Party	4	35		1	2
Progressive Total	**147**	**90**	**115**	**144**	**162**
Minor Parties/Independents	13	29	26	12	8
Grand Total	**466**	**466**	**466**	**466**	**467**

share power in ruling coalitions. The most appropriate term is "one and one-half party system," which means governmental control by one party, the Liberal Democratic party, in the face of opposition by the Japan Socialist party, which has so far been incapable of assuming power. With these general characteristics in mind, let us examine each party in more detail.

The Liberal Democratic Party   A new era in Japan's politics began with the consolidation of the conservatives into the Liberal Democratic party (*Jiyuminshuto* or LDP), in late 1955. As the majority party, the Liberal Democratic party selects the prime minister and provides all Cabinet ministers[14] and chairmen of Diet committees. It decides what bills will become law and conducts Japan's foreign relations. For all practical purposes, therefore, the Liberal Democratic party is the government of Japan.

No law in Japan governs the organization of political parties, so the LDP operates under self-defined rules and regulations. The LDP is led by a president who, until 1960, was chosen by secret informal agreement among party faction leaders. In response to demands for "democratization," this selection process was changed to a secret ballot conducted at the party conference, and the term of office was fixed at two years. By 1971, Eisaku Sato had been elected president four times, and agreement was reached that year to check what looked like the potential for an incumbent president (who was also prime minister) to remain in office indefinitely. Rules were changed to extend the term of office from two to three years and to limit the number of terms to two (six years) unless the incumbent was endorsed for a third term by two-thirds of the LDP dietmen.[15] The procedure was further modified in 1977 to provide for a primary system in which local LDP members would take part.[16]

The party conference (450 to 500 members) is composed of all LDP Diet members and four delegates from each prefectural federation, but it is clear that dietmen run it. It is not "the supreme organ of the party" as party rules term it; rather, it is a "parliamentary club."[17] Regularly convened annually in January, the party conference serves as an assembly for dietmen and prefectural notables to be briefed on LDP plans, policies, and pending legislation. Special sessions are held to elect a new party president just prior to a change in prime minister. Other major offices include the vice-president, the secretary-general, and the chairmen of the LDP's two most important bodies, the Executive Council and the Policy Affairs Research Council (Policy Board). The party president appoints these officials. Considered a stepping-stone to the presidency, the position of secretary-general carries with it power to control the party purse; to appoint the twenty parliamentary vice-ministers (an average of fifteen from the House of Representatives and five from the House of Councillors), whose main duty is to guide bills from their ministries through the legislative process; to appoint the chairmen of standing and special committees of the House of Representatives; to oversee LDP endorsements for candidates; and to act generally as spokesman for the party.[18]

Fifteen divisions make up the LDP Policy Board, and every LDP dietman serves in at least one division. These divisions correspond roughly to the Cabinet ministries and the standing committee organization of both houses of the Diet. Public policy originates in the LDP divisions, which maintain contact with the ministries which draft most of the legislation. The Executive Council, as a body, is not involved in LDP elections, does not allocate funds, and is not involved in daily operations of the party. Consisting of thirty Diet members—fifteen from the House of Representatives, seven from the House of Councillors, and eight appointed by the party president—the Executive Council serves two main functions: (1) to approve some two

hundred appointments to party posts, and (2) to serve as the screening body for Policy Board recommendations, which must gain Executive Council consent. Each prefecture has an LDP "federation" in its capital city with branches in most of the local political subdivisions, many of which are closely identified with local interest groups.

Factions are the focus of Japanese politics.[19] Factions are not a result of the political system, nor have the factions produced the political leaders. On the contrary, factions have been created by the political leaders. Their modern origin in the mid-fifties results from the multiplicity of leaders of those conservative "parties" which came together to form the LDP. Political factions existed earlier in Japan, and the relationship between faction leader and faction member with mutual obligations of a long-enduring nature are compatible with traditional Japanese social concepts. The number of LDP factions has varied from about a half-dozen to twelve or thirteen, and the size of individual factions, from four members to more than one hundred. Most factions are formal entities with a headquarters, regular meetings, and firm discipline within a factional hierarchy, and all are composed of members whose factional loyalties are well known to the press and the attentive public.[20]

Six major LDP faction leaders in the 1973 House of Representatives controlled 240 of its 281 LDP members (see Table 13-2). Three lesser faction leaders controlled 32 other members. Only nine LDP dietmen were not affiliated with a faction. Each faction leader was a formidable and experienced politician in his own right. Tanaka had earlier held three different Cabinet posts and served in two top LDP posts, those of Policy Board chairman and secretary-general. Miki had held six Cabinet portfolios and served as LDP Policy Board chairman and LDP secretary-general. Ohira, Fukuda, and Nakasone had also held important Cabinet portfolios. At one time or

Table 13–2: Major Liberal Democratic Party Faction Leaders in the House of Representatives, 1973

Factional Leader (Age)	Position	Times Elected	Number in Faction
Kakuei Tanaka (54)	Prime Minister	11	47
Masayoshi Ohira (62)	Minister of Foreign Affairs	9	44
Takeo Fukuda (67)	Director-General, Administrative Management/Agency	9	53
Takeo Miki (65)	Deputy Prime Minister, Director-General Environment Agency	14	39
Yasuhiro Nakasone (54)	Minister, International Trade and Industry	11	39
Etsusaburo Shiina (74)	Vice-President, LDP	7	18

Source: Adapted from Hans B. Baerwald, *Japan's Parliament* (Cambridge, England: Cambridge University Press, 1974), pp. 60, 62, 67.

another, both Ohira and Fukuda served as foreign minister and LDP Policy Board chairman. Arithmetically, the cooperation of several factions is required to form a majority of the LDP Diet members, a matter that is especially crucial to the election of the prime minister. For example, when Tanaka was forced to resign in December 1974 as prime minister because of scandals during his administration, he was replaced by Takeo Miki, whose faction ranked fourth in size. When Miki organized his Cabinet, four factions got three Cabinet posts each. Fukuda, who had refused to permit his followers to serve in Tanaka's Cabinet, received, in return for support of Miki, the prestigious post of deputy prime minister, replacing Miki, who had held that post under Tanaka. Nakasone's faction got only one portfolio, but Nakasone himself moved to occupy the very powerful position of LDP secretary-general. Such bargaining is the process by which a prime minister is made, and the hope of them all is to negate its power because it is how a prime minister is unmade.

For two decades LDP leaders have called for the dissolution of factions. After the steep drop in LDP vote-getting power in the December 1976 elections, Fukuda was elected prime minister with the barest majority (see Tables 13-3 and 13-4). Fulfilling a campaign promise to do what he had been advocating since 1960, Fukuda proceeded to dissolve his faction in March 1977 and the leaders of the two other large factions, Tanaka and Ohira, did the same. However, these actions are regarded as camouflage because each faction is converting itself into a "policy study group," and each group decided to handle its own candidates for the July 1977 House of Councillors election. At the same time, new legislation controlling political funds makes it less likely that large factions can continue to exist in their traditional role as "combat units to win the premiership."[21] Faction activity, in one guise or another, is likely to remain a prominent characteristic of the political scene.

Thayer summarizes the rationale for the factional system, listing five "essential party and national goals" that are achieved by the

Table 13–3: Results of Elections for House of Representatives Since 1958

	May 1958	November 1960	November 1963	January 1967	December 1969	December 1972	December 1976
Liberal Democratic Party	287	296	283	277	288	271	249
Japan Socialist Party	166	145	144	140	90	118	123
Japan Communist Party	1	3	5	5	14	38	17
Komeito				25	47	29	55
Democratic Socialist Party		17	23	30	31	19	29
Others	13	6	12	9	16	14	38[a]
Vacancies						2	
	467	467	467	486	486	491	511

[a]Includes 17 seats won by the New Liberal Club (NLC), a group of 6 conservatives who bolted the LDP in the summer of 1976. Also includes 21 independents, 8 of whom lined up with the LDP to give that party 257 seats.

Source: Adapted from Donald E. Whitaker et al., *Area Handbook for Japan*, 3rd ed. (Washington, D.C.: U.S. Government Printing Office, 1974), p. 346.

Table 13–4: Results of General Elections for House of Representatives Since 1958 (percent)

	May 1958	November 1960	November 1963	January 1967	December 1969	December 1972	December 1976
Liberal Democratic Party							
Seats	61.5	63.4	60.6	57.0	59.3	55.0	48.7
Votes	57.8	57.6	54.7	48.8	47.6	46.9	41.8
Japan Socialist Party							
Seats	35.5	31.0	30.8	28.8	18.5	24.0	24.1
Votes	32.9	27.6	29.0	27.9	21.4	21.9	20.7
Japan Communist Party							
Seats	0.2	0.6	1.0	1.0	2.9	7.7	3.3
Votes	0.3	0.3	0.4	0.5	0.7	10.5	10.4
Komeito							
Seats				5.1	9.7	5.9	10.8
Votes				5.4	10.9	8.5	10.9
Democratic Socialist Party							
Seats		3.6	4.9	6.2	6.4	3.9	5.7
Votes		8.8	7.4	7.4	7.7	7.0	6.3
Other							
Seats	2.7	1.3	2.5	1.9	3.3	3.3	4.1
Votes	6.7	3.2	4.9	5.8	5.5	5.3	5.8

Source: Donald E. Whitaker et al., *Area Handbook for Japan*, 3rd ed. (Washington, D.C.: U.S. Government Printing Office, 1974), p. 348.

factions: (1) the LDP chooses its leaders through the faction; (2) most party funds are raised and disbursed through the factions; (3) factions determine who occupies the major government and party posts; (4) individual candidates for office get most of their campaign support through the factions; and (5) the factions serve profound psychological needs of the dietmen.[22] Thayer has also observed that, without factions, Japan would have Cabinets whose members rarely change, Cabinets chosen mainly on the basis of age and seniority within the party, and Cabinets chosen primarily to advance the private political interests of the prime minister.[23]

Stated somewhat differently, the LDP factions determine Cabinet-level leadership for Japan. Usually Cabinet members are co-opted into the Cabinet as a result of group associations, so the Cabinet becomes, to some degree, a composite of the factions. This integration of group elites is a rational means to secure intergroup communication; hence, the Cabinet is simultaneously a "high level communication network as well as a decision-making body."[24] There were more than two dozen Cabinets from 1945 to 1977, but prime ministers tended to remain in office while shuffling Cabinets almost annually as a means of repaying past support and assuring future support. More than half of the postwar Cabinet ministers served less than one year, and more than three-quarters had a tenure of less than two years.

Nearly 300 politicians from every prefecture in Japan have served as Cabinet ministers. Of 249 whose educational background was known, 117 graduated from Tokyo University, 20 from Kyoto University, and 19 from Waseda University in Tokyo. With reference to prior occupation, nearly half (45.8 percent) are career politicians, with business (18.7 percent) and the bureaucracy (17.5 percent) forming important increments. Politicians have tended to increase their percen-

tage, although it is difficult to differentiate the bureaucrat from the politician, for many leaders pursue both careers. Appointment to the Cabinet usually occurs when the member is 51 to 55 years old; for prime ministers the age at appointment generally is between 56 and 65 years. Professor Cheng concludes that his aggregate data show that the path to the top leads from Tokyo's prestigious First Higher School through the Tokyo University Law Department into the higher ranks of the national bureaucracy to the Cabinet.[25]

LDP policies have been the policies of the government of Japan since 1955 and are discussed in Chapter 14. In broad outline, the LDP's economic program has been to develop fully private enterprise with government assistance and protective regulation. It has sought a constant expansion of production, an increase in the standard of living at home, and increased competitiveness in international trade. Domestically, the LDP has sought to deal with problems common to other industrialized nations: campus unrest, inflation, pollution, a lack of adequate housing, and the variety of problems associated with the fourfold increase in petroleum prices since 1973. Externally the LDP has made the relationship between the United States and Japan the cornerstone of its foreign policy. Japan supports the United Nations, which it joined in 1956, and plays a prominent role in many important international agencies.

LDP control of the machinery of government has been firm, but the party's ability to continue in power is now less certain than ever before. The number of seats held by the LDP in the House of Representatives has declined both absolutely (see Table 13-3) and as a proportion of seats (see Table 13-4). Since 1967, the LDP has controlled the government with less than a majority of the popular vote, and the plurality dropped markedly in December 1976. Some basic reasons for continuing LDP control are the malapportionment of electoral districts, the advantages naturally accruing to the party in power, and the inability of the opposition parties seriously to challenge the LDP, either singly or as a coalition.

Japan Socialist Party   Socialists played no important role in prewar Japanese politics, but emerged during the occupation to become and to remain the most important party in opposition to the LDP. Winning the largest number of lower house seats in the 1947 elections (Table 13-1), the Japan Socialist Party (*Nihon Shakaito*, or JSP) formed the short-lived coalition Cabinet under Tetsu Katayama, the only socialist Cabinet in nearly ninety years of parliamentary government. A bribery scandal almost destroyed the JSP in the 1949 elections when its Lower House representation dropped from 143 to 48 seats (from 31 to 10 percent of the total). Two years later, the JSP split into separate Left-Wing and Right-Wing parties over ideological issues. Four years later the JSP was once again unified and scored its greatest victory in the 1958 general election, winning 166 seats and slightly more than one-third of the popular vote. Some observers speculated that the gradually increasing strength of the JSP would enable the Socialists to overthrow the LDP within a few years. At the party conference the following year, the JSP split over leftist denunciation of a right-wing JSP member who suggested that the U.S.-Japan Security Treaty, susceptible to revision in 1960, was vital to Japan. Having been rebuffed for opposing the mainstream leftist JSP view that the treaty ought to be abrogated, Suehiro Nishio and about forty dissidents defected to form the Democratic Socialist party in 1960.

Factionalism characterizes the JSP, as well as the LDP, differing mainly in that the ideological commitments in the JSP are much stronger.[26] The major factional groups, all about the same size, are leftist, rightist, and centrist. The leftists, led by Kozo Sasaki, are

orthodox Marxist and more radical and doctrinaire than socialist parties in Europe, advocating revolutionary overthrow of capitalism and opposition to American imperialism. On the other end of the spectrum, former vice-chairman of the JSP and leader of the right-wing faction, Saburo Eda, proposed a "new socialism" in July 1976,[27] and then broke away from the JSP shortly before his death in May 1977. Calling for a socialism based on individual freedom and a more varied and free society, Eda castigated the pro-Soviet JSP left wing for continuing to adhere to "bankrupt" Marxist-Leninist dogma, a policy he felt would lead the people of Japan to foresake the JSP. This "Eda thesis" is a continuation of the basic ideological argument of the past many years: whether the JSP ought to be a mass party or a class party, whether to be a parliamentary party or a revolutionary party.

Domestic policy objectives sought by the JSP include: price stabilization; improved social welfare programs for social insurance, old age, and medical care; farm price supports; elimination of tax advantages for big business and the rich; elimination of pollution; and "clean politics." The JSP has consistently opposed the U.S.-Japan Security Treaty, demanding its abrogation and the conversion of Japan's military forces into an organization the JSP would call the Peaceful Land Construction Force. In the JSP view, Japan's security should be sought in unarmed neutrality, a unilaterally disarmed Japan safe in a new security system in Asia, embracing a unified Korea and guaranteed by nonaggression treaties between Japan and the People's Republic of China and Japan and the Soviet Union.

The JSP is led at the national level by the chairman of the Central Executive Committee (24 members) and the secretary-general, who are elected by the party convention (about 500 participants) with delegates from local units and affiliated organizations. The top leadership is assisted by a number of committees. Although the JSP got about 16,000,000 votes in the 1976 general elections, its membership base was estimated to be about 50,000 in 1974.[28] This lack of local organization is made up by *Sohyo* (General Council of Japanese Trade Unions), a four-million-member labor federation which bestows its support solely on the JSP and sponsors most of the JSP candidates.

A Japanese politician has said the JSP is "the cat who can't catch the mouse."[29] This colorful expression means the JSP is unable to achieve one-third (171) of the votes in the House of Representatives, the number necessary to obstruct effectively LDP Diet operations. JSP strength peaked in 1958 and apparently bottomed out in 1969, when JSP candidates got only 90 seats of 468. Recovering in the 1976 elections, the JSP managed to obtain 123 seats (24.1 percent) while its popular vote dropped slightly to 20.7 percent. Unable to cooperate effectively with other opposition parties, the JSP remains deeply divided, threatened most recently by the *Kyokai-ha* (Socialist Study Association faction). Organized in 1951 with the mission "of adapting Marxism-Leninism to the history of Japan and achieving a socialist revolution in Japan," this group (with only four Lower House members) reportedly controls the 350,000 member Socialists' Youth Federation and will enter its own candidates in prefectural elections to oppose JSP-endorsed candidates. Sasaki, left-wing leader of the JSP, says the Kyokai-ha is more radical than the Japan Communist party and a "minus to the JSP."[30]

The JSP will continue to get the vote of much of organized labor, the intellectuals, and of many urban residents, but neither its domestic nor its international policy statements are supported widely by the Japanese public. Ideological struggle and controversy continue to deprive the party of internal cohesion and have so far made it impossible to cooperate effectively with other opposition parties to form the national coalition government by the end of the 1970s as called for in the 1974 party program.

Japan Communist Party Formed in 1922, the Japan Communist party *(Nihon Kyosanto,* JCP) was immediately declared illegal. Its leaders, released from prison in October 1945 by SCAP, reorganized the JCP and infiltrated the labor movement. They harassed the occupation by voting against the Constitution and organized a general strike in 1947 to overthrow the government of Prime Minister Yoshida, hoping to replace it by a united front in which they would take part. General MacArthur forced cancellation of the planned strike and avoided a worse crisis. Under the leadership of Sanzo Nosaka, who returned to Japan after spending the war years in Yenan, the JCP concentrated on "peaceful revolution" to achieve socialism and saw its lower house representation jump from 4 to 35 seats in 1949 (Table 13-1). Nosaka was sharply criticized by the Cominform for supporting American imperialism and the heretofore quiescent factionalism in the JCP erupted openly. Some violence against American personnel and property occurred during the JCP campaign against American imperialism, several Communists were arrested, and in early June, 1950, SCAP purged from public life the entire Central Committee of the JCP. The leadership went underground, having alienated the people of Japan to the extent that they lost all 35 representatives in the 1952 elections.

By the mid-1950s, the JCP leadership was pretty well reconstituted by the return of those purged in the few weeks prior to the Korean War, but Diet representation increased very little until 1969 (see Tables 13-3 and 13-4). From the mid-fifties to the mid-sixties, the JCP was plagued by ideological factionalism represented by a pro-Moscow group, a pro-Peking group, and a "nationalist" group. In 1958, leaders of the JCP-sponsored national student organization (*Zengakuren*) were expelled for "left-wing adventurism," for being too radical. The Sino-Soviet dispute and the Great Proletarian Cultural Revolution in China further exacerbated intra-JCP tension. In 1966, the mainstream JCP faction adopted a policy of "autonomy and independence," a policy strengthened by the pro-Peking faction's disapproval of the Cultural Revolution and the pro-Moscow faction's dislike of the Soviet military occupation of Czechoslovakia in 1968. The JCP remains neutral in the Sino-Soviet dispute.[31] This policy paid handsome dividends at the polls until the 1976 elections.

JCP domestic policy is directed toward establishment of a mass vanguard party to carry out a people's democratic revolution against domestic reactionaries, to organize a "democratic" united front in Japan, and to free Japan from American imperialism. In electoral campaigns, the JCP advocates internal policies generally indistinguishable from those of the Socialists. In foreign policy, it is adamantly anti-American, opposes U.S.-Japanese economic cooperation; demands abrogation of the U.S.-Japan Security Treaty and peaceful neutrality of Japan; seeks complete withdrawal of American military forces from Asia, the establishment of some sort of collective security system in Asia, and the immediate dissolution of Japan's military forces.

Democratic centralism is the organizational principle of the JCP. The All-Japan Communist Party Congress meets biennially and formally has supreme power in the party. When not in session, its duties are delegated to the 110-member Central Committee under longtime chairman Sanzo Nosaka. Real power lies with the seven-member standing committee led by Kenji Miyamoto, also president of the 31-member Presidium of the Central Committee. JCP national organization is

fleshed out with prefectural and district committees and many primary organizations (cells) embracing a membership of perhaps 350,000 members in 1973 able to get out 7,800,000 votes in 1976. Under Miyamoto's leadership the JCP has been able to avoid intra-party dissension, to improve greatly its public image and to increase its Diet strength. Unchallenged as the leader of the JCP, Miyamoto is unique among national political leaders because he has never held a Diet seat.

The JCP is well-financed (second only to the LDP) and carries its programs with considerable success to millions of Japanese through its extensive publications which appear daily, *Akahata* (Red Flag), and monthly *Zenei* (Vanguard). Whether the creation of the image of a "Nationalist" Communist party will result in renewed gains and greater influence for the JCP remains to be seen.

The Democratic Socialist Party   The dissident right-wing of the JSP led by Suehiro Nishio established the Democratic Socialist party (*Minshu Shakaito*, or DSP) in January 1960 to satisfy, in its words, "an urgent desire in Japan for a democratic socialist party which, while abiding by parliamentarianism, will fight both extreme leftists and rightists, and promote the general welfare of all sections of the working people, without special favor or partiality to labor unions." Nishio believed the JSP erred in thinking a Marxist revolution was possible in Japan, and he thought the LDP was too concerned with big business interests.[32] The DSP was to chart a course of gradual and moderate change by parliamentary means through the middle ground between the LDP and the JSP.

Entering their first general election in late 1960, the forty-odd DSP dietmen suffered severe defeat, emerging with only 17 seats, although their percentage of the total vote (8.8 percent) was more than double their percentage of seats won (3.6 percent, see Table 13-4).

Modest gains followed until 1972, when the party dropped from 31 to 19 seats, only to rise to 29 seats in 1976.

DSP domestic policy does not differ importantly from that of other parties. Internationally it seeks some approach between that of the LDP, which is too pro-American, and that of the JSP, which is too anti-American and too pro-communist. Currently under the leadership of fifth-term Chairman Ikko Kasuga, the DSP favors a three-stage dismantling of Japan's military, but not until some collective system can be devised to ensure Japan's security. From time to time the DSP has supported LDP policies in opposition to the JSP, for example, the formalizing of diplomatic relations with the Republic of Korea in 1965.

Organizationally and financially weak, the DSP relies for its support mainly on the two-and-one-quarter-million-member *Domei* (Confederation of Japanese Labor). With about 40,000 members, the DSP has had little success in attracting young voters or building grass roots support. The long-term outlook for an influential role is not encouraging for those who expect the DSP to present clear-cut alternatives to LDP or socialist programs. The 1977 DSP action policy anticipates that the LDP will lose power and seeks a "centrist progressive coalition" with the JSP, Komeito, and conservative forces.[33]

The Komeito The newest political party is the Komeito (Clean Government party, or KMT) founded in 1964 as the political arm of the *Sokagakkai* (Value Creation Society). The Sokagakkai was established in the 1930s by an obscure school teacher named Tsunesaburo Makiguchi who believed man's universal goal was happiness achieved by his own efforts to create the "values" of benefit, beauty, and goodness. Makiguchi made the Sokagakkai the lay missionary society of the aggressively evangelical Nichiren Sho, a native Buddhist sect founded in the 13th century. Revived as a "new religion" in the postwar years, the Sokagakkai has enjoyed tremendous growth into a well-financed, highly disciplined, hierarchical national organization of ten to fifteen million members.

Sokagakkai first entered politics in 1955 by successfully sponsoring "independent" candidates in several local elections where it could concentrate its vote. In 1959 it elected all 76 of its candidates to the Tokyo ward assemblies and all six candidates for the House of Councillors national constituency seats. In 1964 the Sokagakkai established the Komeito as a full-fledged political party and ran an effective campaign in its initial bid for seats in the House of Representatives, winning 25 of the 32 seats it contested. Komeito lower house representation nearly doubled, to 47 seats, in the 1969 general elections to make it the third strongest party.

The general public has long been generally distrustful of the intent and methods of the Komeito. Fears of a Buddhist-based state religion were heightened by authoritarian tendencies within the party and the reported intimidation of those seeking to publicize the inner workings of the party. Komeito leaders responded to criticism of its religious connections by proclaiming the separation of the party from Sokagakkai in 1970. Nevertheless, this declaration was not taken at face value, and the Komeito suffered its first major defeat in the 1972 general elections, dropping from 47 to 29 seats in the lower house, but recovered to win 55 seats in 1976.

The Komeito has consistently promised to offer a genuine Japanese alternative to the values and institutions of the foreign ideologies of the Western liberal democracy and Marxism that guide Japan's two major parties. Faithful to its name, the Komeito's 1972 platform called for purification of government and politics in Japan, tax revision to aid the poor, increased welfare payments, and opposition to any constitutional revision that might lead to revived militarism. In foreign policy, the Komeito advocated neutrality for Japan, a universal collective security system, and termination of U.S.-Japan security arrangements.[34]

Yoshikatsu Takeiri is the nominal leader of the Komeito, but Daisaku Ikeda, founder of the party and still president of the Sokagakkai, is acknowledged to be the driving force behind the party. The KMT is tightly organized at the grass roots level and appeals mostly to youth, women, and newer urban residents who are less well-educated and belong to the lower economic brackets. Formal party membership is probably about 250,000; so the party depends on the Sokagakkai for its electoral support. Many Japanese regard it as a lower-middle-class neo-fascist organization and resent its religious affiliation. Several years ago, its leader stated, "Religion rescues the individual; politics rescues the society,"[35] an assertion not widely appealing to Japanese. Whether the 1976 election victory is the beginning of a permanent increase in strength is doubtful. But if the KMT can emerge as a pragmatic political party, it may be able to influence Japanese politics at the national level, perhaps as a coalition partner.

OTHER GROUPS

Intellectuals   The intellectuals are a potent opinion-making group in Japan, and generally this group encompasses academicians, university students, media personnel, or anyone involved in literary and artistic endeavors. Intellectuals can influence public opinion, in part, because Japan is the most literate nation in the world, ranks first in the world as producer of motion pictures, has the world's third largest daily newspaper circulation, and 89 percent of Japanese households have a TV set. About 1,800,000 young Japanese are enrolled in colleges and universities.[36] As a group, the

intellectuals are not generally susceptible to manipulation because of the diversity of views. Yet a large number of them tend to be Marxist and anti-establishment, and therefore tend to vote with the JSP or JCP. At the same time, they resist recruitment by these parties.

The intellectuals consider themselves to be the guardians of civil liberties and strongly oppose any changes in the 1947 Constitution. In the past ten years, their prescription for the Japanese economy has shifted, as also reflected in intra-JSP arguments, from a demand for fundamental alternation to "structural reform." University students have had good cause for dissatisfaction with their lot, and this dissatisfaction was joined to the leftist and anti-establishment orientation of most of the faculty to produce large-scale and often violent demonstrations well before such things occurred in the United States. Student activity in 1960 opposing renewal of the U.S.-Japan Security Treaty was responsible for the cancellation of President Eisenhower's visit to Japan. In the late 1960s, as many as a hundred campuses were disrupted at the same time, and Tokyo University required police assistance to put down the considerable violence. The Japanese public strongly disapproves of student violence, and it has embarrassed the political parties—the LDP for being unable to control it; the JCP, whose *Zengakuren* was so violent their leaders were expelled from the party; and the JSP, whose loss of 50 of its 140 Diet seats in 1969 has been attributed to the campus violence of members of its Youth Association. Student support is a minus for the parties, and organized labor has no desire to be associated politically with students whose basic interests they perceive as incompatible with those of labor.

Labor Unions   Organized labor was roughly handled by the Japanese government in prewar days. On the premise that an active and responsible labor movement is conducive to the development of democracy, the occupation gave labor the rights to organize, to strike, and to bargain collectively. By 1975 there were 65,400 unions with a total membership of twelve million,[37] or about one-sixth of the total electorate. The major labor federations and selected large affiliates are shown in Table 13-5.

Sohyo, the largest federation of unions, has been associated closely with the Japan Socialist party. It is the major organized element of JSP strength, its primary source of financial backing, and has nominated many JSP Diet candidates. Sohyo's major affiliates include local and municipal government workers, and teachers, telecommunication workers, and railway workers who are also government employees. Union leaders have tended to emphasize political struggle to the detriment of economic or livelihood struggles. Sohyo's proportion of organized labor declined in the 1960s, and the leadership has reiterated, under pressure, the policy of stressing material benefits for its membership. Despite the great potential for mobilization, Sohyo's members are not especially politically conscious; however, Sohyo does promote its interests through strikes and mass demonstrations by its members, and more important, through JSP Diet members who owe their election and political careers to Sohyo support.

Domei is the second most powerful labor federation and is composed mostly of workers in private industry. Emphasizing the economic welfare of its members and cooperation with management, Domei supports the Democratic Socialist party. The other two labor federations are not identified with a political party.

Business Business is by far the most powerful interest group in Japan. The power of the prewar *zaibatsu* was blunted by occupation policies that broke up the giant cartels, but the major firms belonging to the zaibatsu have returned to prominence. Today, however, they are operated by a new professional managerial class. Ownership and management are generally separate, and stock ownership is widespread among the middle class. Big business now has a new name, *zaikai*, the "financial world." The four most important business interest groups are *Keidanren* (Federation of Economic Organizations), *Nikkeiren* (Japan Federation of Employers' Association), *Keizai Doyukai* (Committee for Economic Development), and the Japan Chamber of Commerce and Industry. The Chamber of Commerce dates from 1878; the other organizations were formed in the late 1940s. Keidanren is the authoritative body for big business, excluding medium and small enterprises from its membership, but embracing about 750 major corporations and 100 national trade associations.[38] It maintains staff committees dealing with a wide range of economic matters, and its reports and recommendations enjoy a good reputation in the government and bureaucracy with which it is continuously in contact. These associations, the LDP politicians, and the bureaucracy are mutually interdependent and cooperate overtly and covertly in pursuit of common interests, but not without many examples of bribery and corruption. The most recent and potentially most damaging scandal is that involving the Lockheed Corporation's alleged illegal activities with a number of Japanese politicians and business elites and its behind-the-scenes manipulations. The LDP is Japan's best-financed political party, and business provides its financial support, not mainly for the party's general funds, but for the support of selected factions and individual members.

Of the major interest groups considered here, the intellectuals and organized labor remain leftist, anti-establishment, and oppose the LDP. Even if ideological differences could be put aside, the LDP would have no incen-

Table 13–5: Major Labor Federations and Major Affiliated Unions

	Number of Unions	Membership
General Council of Japanese Trade Unions (*Sohyo*)	22,367	4,320,084
National Council of Local Municipal Government Workers Union (*Jichiro*)	3,811	1,065,453
Japan Teachers Union (*Nikkyoso*)	1,738	590,926
National Telecommunications Workers Union (*Zendentsu*)	1,607	308,138
National Railway Workers Union (*Kokutetsu*)	2,314	223,545
Japan Federation of Iron and Steel Industry Workers Union (*Tekkororen*)	130	196,967
Confederation of Japanese Labor (*Domei*)	11,600	2,263,122
National Federation of Textile Industry Workers Union (*Zensendomei*)	2,589	538,600
National Federation of Metal Industry Workers Union (*Zenkindomei*)	1,300	298,406
Japan Confederation of Shipbuilding and Engineering Workers Union (*Zosenjukuroren*)	86	214,085
Japan Federation of Automobile Industry Workers Union (*Jidosharoren*)	492	178,107
Federation of Independent Unions (*Churitsuroren*) and others	3,869	1,352,084
Federation of All-Japan Electric Machinery Workers Unions (*Denkiroren*)	538	533,287
National Federation of Free Labor Unions (*Zenjiroren*)	851	476,626
National Federation of Life Insurance Workers Unions (*Zenseiho*)	1,335	306,633
Federation of City Bank Workers Unions (*Shiginren*)	349	168,558
National Federation of Industrial Labor Unions (*Shinsanbetsu*)	207	69,974

Source: The Oriental Economist, *Japan Economic Yearbook 1974* (Tokyo, 1974), p. 247. Data as of June, 1973.

tive to cooperate with these interest groups because of the continuing mutual support, general cohesion, and shared attitudes and values among the bureaucracy, big business, and the LDP.

Political Influentials

Although there are a number of political influentials in the Japanese political system, these are primarily associated with the formal institutions of government. There are a number of prominent businessmen who, as representatives of corporate interests, are political actors. However, most such political influentials tend to operate out of the public eye: they prefer low visibility and informal links with political parties and government officials. There is no question that there is a close connection between the bureaucracy, government, and business interests. Equally important, there is a close tie between the majority LDP and business interests.

On the other hand, there have not developed in Japan, as yet, clusters of individual academicians, individual intellectuals, mass media personalities, or individually wealthy persons who are political actors in their own right. It would appear that the Japanese tradition of group action and group loyalty has continued to subdue the rise of such individuals. While the media has developed into an independent and severe critic of government, it still lacks the tradition conducive to developing political influentials.

Perhaps the most singular aspect of the Japanese political system is the emperor. Theoretically the emperor does not have key state duties, that is, decision-making functions. Yet, the symbolic power of his office does have indirect affect on general political attitudes. Representing continuity with the past and a symbol of Japan as a nation, the emperor is revered by many Japanese. This is particularly true of the conservative politicians and their constituency. In this respect, the emperor is a political influential who can, through his own discreet behavior, affect Japanese politics.

Individuals

In modern Japan, the individual has played an increasingly important role. The electoral process and the establishment of a parliamentary system based on a democratic electoral process have made the individual important in establishing the legitimacy of government and in deciding what parties will control the system. To be sure, this does not make the individual Japanese an important political actor, but it does create an environment in which individual autonomy may be pursued. Nevertheless, the prevailing tradition in Japan remains group action and group loyalty.

Individual rights and liberties remain completely subordinated to the group, be it a corporation, labor union, or governmental institution. Modern type movements, such as Women's Liberation, which could place a premium on individual rights, are still inconsequential threads in Japanese society.

In the Japanese political system, more so than the American political system, the individual rarely is a political actor in his own right. Only through group action can the individual achieve any sense of political impact. What compounds the problem is that this group action remains linked to traditional behavior patterns. In the main, the Japanese political system operates on pressures exerted primarily by other political actors. While this is similar to the American political system, the "average" Japanese has not been socialized into a political culture that accepts the idea that the individual can challenge the system. While the Japanese have developed the necessary structures and ideological principles to establish a democratic system, it is still not clear whether a civic democratic culture has developed as an underpinning of this system. Moreover, it is not clear into what final form the democratic system will evolve. To be sure, there is a distinct American flavor to the entire structure, but the Japanese view of politics and the amalgam of the old and the new may develop a civic culture that is not "Americanized" to a degree that the MacArthur Constitution envisioned. Constitutional monarchy, a strong cabinet system, and a dominant one-party system are possibilities that are not in the tradition of the American style of democracy. The Japanese system may evolve into its own form of democracy which can be as effective as any American-imposed system. As students of comparative politics, we should be aware of a number of democratic political systems that resemble but operate in a fashion different from the American system, for example, those of Sweden, Canada, Norway, France, Germany, and Great Britain.

Summary

Japan has a wide range of political actors: government organs and the bureaucracy, political parties, labor unions, business and commercial circles, and a large number of highly diverse special interest and associational groups.

Sovereignty lies with the people and is exercised through the National Diet, the highest organ of state, a bicameral body elected by universal adult suffrage. The lower house is dominant, able to override upper house disapproval of a bill. It designates the prime minister who appoints the Cabinet. Nearly all bills are sponsored by the Cabinet and originate in the ministries with the backing of the majority party and the bureaucracy. The prime minister and Cabinet are the executive, so there is no executive veto. The judiciary is autonomous.

The major political parties represented in the lower house are essentially parliamentary parties, lack a mass membership, and consist of factions organized around individual leaders. Factions are the focus of politics in Japan. They are not a result of the political system, nor have the factions produced leaders. On the contrary, the leaders have created the factions. Coalesced factions are the party. The party system is not a two-party system in the sense that the LDP and JSP alternate in the exercise of power, for the LDP has controlled the government since the end of the occupation. The LDP has governed Japan with less than a majority of the popular vote for more than a decade. The major opposition party, the JSP, has seen its proportion of the vote drop to about one-fifth, with the remaining 37.5 percent going to four minor parties and independents.

Labor unions have a total membership of about 12,000,000 (one-sixth of the electorate). The largest labor union federation, Sohyo, has organized local and national government employees and is the main support of the JSP. Domei, composed mostly of workers in private industry, lends its support to the Democratic Socialist party.

Business is the most powerful interest group in Japan and is represented by four major organizations, including Keidanren, the authoritative body for big business. Keidanren embraces 750 major corporations, maintains staff committees to deal with a variety of economic concerns, and has close contacts with government ministries and LDP politicians.

Decision makers as political actors in the Japanese political system are similar to those in the American political system; that is, there are elected officials and appointed officials that are political actors in their own right. Political influentials exist in the Japanese political system, but their role is not clear, since such individuals are influential primarily as a result of their corporate positions in business. Political influentials do not exist in the same wide scope and variety apparent in the American system. Individuals in Japan occupy a more anomalous position than they do in the American system. While sovereignty lies with the people, rarely can the individual exercise power as a political actor. The ideology in Japan is not yet conducive to the development of a concept of individual rights and liberties as the basis for the exercise of individual political power.

NOTES

1. Robert E. Ward, *Japan's Political System* (Englewood Cliffs, N.J.: Prentice-Hall, 1967), pp. 54–55.
2. Hans B. Baerwald, *Japan's Parliament* (Cambridge, England: Cambridge University Press, 1974), pp. 126–127. The author reports that in 1969, a Diet member's monthly pay was about $900, and that Japanese newspapermen estimated a successful candidate needed to spend about $280,000 for his cam-

paign and that a candidate who spent about $200,000 might well lose. See Nathaniel B. Thayer, *How the Conservatives Rule Japan* (Princeton, N.J.: Princeton University Press, 1973), pp. 139–144, for details of some of these arguments.

3. Figures are for 1975. Bureau of Statistics, Office of the Prime Minister, *Statistical Handbook of Japan* (Tokyo, 1975), p. 146.

4. Theodore McNelly, "The Constitutionality of Japan's Defense Establishment," in James H. Buck, ed., *The Modern Japanese Military System* (Beverly Hills, Calif.: Sage Publications, 1975), p. 102.

5. See Donald P. Whitaker et al., *Area Handbook for Japan* (Washington, D.C.: U.S. Government Printing Office, 1974), pp. 305–309.

6. Robert E. Ward, *Japan's Political System* (Englewood Cliffs, N.J.: Prentice-Hall, 1967), pp. 96–97.

7. Bureau of Statistics, Office of the Prime Minister, *Nihon Tokei Nenkan 1975* [Japan Statistical Yearbook 1975], pp. 594–595.

8. Ardath W. Burks, *The Government of Japan* (New York: Crowell, 1961), p. 198.

9. *Nihon Tokei Nenkan 1975*, p. 596.

10. Whitaker, op. cit., pp. 312–313.

11. For an especially competent discussion of interest groups in Japan, see McNelly, op. cit., pp. 45–81.

12. Thayer, op. cit., p. 179.

13. Theodore McNelly, *Politics and Government in Japan*, 2nd ed. (Boston: Houghton-Mifflin, 1972), p. 93.

14. The only Cabinet minister chosen from outside the Diet was Michio Nagai, an editorial writer for the *Asahi* newspaper, who was appointed minister of education by Prime Minister Miki in December 1974.

15. Thayer, op. cit., p. 179.

16. *Japan Times Weekly*, April 30, 1977, p. 1.

17. Thayer, op. cit., pp. 241, 247.

18. Ibid., pp. 279–294.

19. Ibid., p. 41.

20. See ibid., pp. 323–332, for listing by faction of LDP members of the House of Representatives as of July 1968, by electoral district, age, occupation, education, and number of times elected. See also Baerwald, op. cit., pp. 30–73, for charts showing lineages of factions (1962–1973) and biographical data on faction leaders.

21. Minora Shimizu, "LDP and Dissolution of Its Factions," *Japan Times Weekly*, March 27, 1977, p. 5.

22. Thayer, op. cit., p. 17.

23. Ibid., p. 55.

24. This paragraph is based on Peter P. Cheng, "The Japanese Cabinets, 1885–1973: An Elite Analysis," *Asian Survey*, vol. 14. no. 12 (December 1974), pp. 1055–1071.

25. Ibid., p. 1070.

26. Minoru Shimizu, "JSP's Factional Struggle Escalates," *Japan Times Weekly*, February 5, 1977. See Baerwald, op. cit., p. 67; for a chart tracing the lineage and strengths of JSP factions, see pp. 68–69.

27. *The Japan Times Weekly*, July 3, 1976, p. 1.

28. Ibid., December 14, 1974, p. 11.

29. Thayer, op. cit., p. 13.

30. Minoru Shimizu, "Deep Internal Divisions in the JSP," *The Japan Times Weekly*, January 31, 1976, p. 4.

31. McNelly, op. cit., pp. 112–117.

32. Ibid., pp. 106–107.

33. *Japan Times Weekly*, April 2, 1977, p. 3.

34. Whitaker, op. cit., pp. 334–336.

35. Laurence Olson, "The Value Creation Society," *American Universities Field Staff Reports Service*, vol. 11, no. 6 (Japan), 1964, p. 21.

36. *Statistical Handbook of Japan*, pp. 138, 140, 142.

37. Ibid., pp. 117–118.

38. McNelly, op. cit., p. 75.

CHAPTER 14

JAPANESE POWER AND POLICY

The previous chapter outlined how Japan's political system is organized, described the major political actors, and showed that the political system seems to enjoy a rather high degree of legitimacy and acceptance among the people. The conservative politician–big business career bureaucrat coalition led by the Liberal Democratic party (LDP) has dominated the "one-and-one-half-party" system for nearly three decades. On the surface Japan seems to have developed one of the most stable political systems of any modern, industrialized democratic society. This has been achieved during a period of really extensive domestic social and economic change. While the apparent political stability is remarkable, the image of Japan's political stability tends to obscure the potential for the emergence of a political system pursuing policies of a different nature and using power in new ways.

The policy process in Japan is similar to the process discussed in the chapter on the American policy process; that is, the phases of the process are generally categorized through the various activities of the political actors. Moreover, the official institutions of government in both the United States and Japan parallel each other in their policy roles. For example, the Diet plays an important role in the approval phase with its representative function and its control of the purse strings. However, since the Japanese system is a cabinet-parliamentary one with the ruling party controlling the executive and legislative process, there are some differences. Moreover, the emergence phase is marked by limited activity on the part of political actors outside the official structures, except for the linkage between business and government. And as we shall also see, the individual Japanese can respond in times of crises and well-articulated issues, but generally has little influence on policy except in the aggregate. In the main then, the emergence, identification, and approval phases, while following similar lines in Japan and in the United States, reflect a narrower involvement of political actors, primarily those within the party, business, and official institutions of government.

The important point in studying the policy process is that the major political actor in all phases, except feedback, is the Liberal Democratic party. Selecting the prime minister and filling all Cabinet posts, the LDP operates almost as a closed corporation. Consensus building takes place within and between the various factions in the party, generally hidden from public scrutiny. *Zaikai* (business groups), in the bureaucracy, and the LDP form the "establishment." As a result, political actors who are not part of the establishment (for example, labor unions and student groups) tend to be excluded from all policy phases with the exception of feedback. As a result, they are most vocal in the feedback phase.

The higher bureaucracy in Japan is deeply involved in politics and acts as an important political actor in the policy process. This is a reflection not only of the bureaucratic tradition, but also of the common problems associated with a large legislative body. The Diet, similar to the United States Congress, passes general guidelines and expects the bureaucracy to apply its expertise for the specific rules and regulations and day-to-day administration. Moreover, there is a close relationship between the bureaucracy, the ministries, and the LDP. Thus, after retirement from civil service, it is not unusual for bureaucrats to run for political office based on the close ties established earlier.

Another major characteristic of the policy process that is common to most of the phases is the relationship between various political actors and the Cabinet. Generally speaking, the rate of turnover in the Japanese Cabinet is very high; that is, Cabinets come and go as the government is reshuffled over policy issues. Nonetheless, usually the prime minister has a greater longevity, in order to provide rewards for political allies and various faction members. Ministerial status is viewed as a characteristic of major political figures in Japan.

As a result of the relatively frequent shifts in Cabinet members, except for the prime minister and foreign minister, much of the continuity of administration lies with the prime minister, leaders of the various factions of the LDP, the higher ranks of the bureaucracy,

and the business leaders who provide financial support of the LDP.

Emergence

Although the people are sovereign, it is difficult to link policy that emerges from the people. Given the nature of the Japanese political system, policy emergence generally evolves from interaction of groups, from within the official institutions of government, and through the political parties—particularly the factions within the LDP. The emergence of policy in the United States is an unstructured process generated by political awareness and interaction among political actors generally outside the official structures. While the emergence phase is somewhat similar in Japan, the major structures outside government are the mass media and labor unions. On the other hand, circles (financial interests) are deeply involved in the emergence phase. Yet, the process does not have the dynamism or the grass roots level impetus it has in the United States. This more-or-less structured process focusing on elite or leaders, or organized groups, tends to make the Japanese emergence and identification phases overlap considerably.

Generally, it is only as a result of some reaction to policy (feedback) that policy emerges from the people. This is particularly true with respect to the domestic implications of Japan's Security Treaty. This treaty has been a continual source of policy decisions and reactions since its inception. In this respect later we shall briefly examine the Security Treaty to learn of the intermingling of some phases and the role of political actors in the process.

The parliamentary structure under control of the LDP effectively excludes many political actors from this phase. Moreover, given the nature of Japanese political attitudes and group orientation, there is lacking the "open-ness" and policy scrutiny characteristic of the American political system.

Identification

This phase is generally dominated by the activities of the major political parties. The LDP, the ruling party (through the interactions of its various factions), and the Cabinet, usually place themselves in a position to support or oppose a particular policy. Support of a particular policy usually means that emergence has developed primarily through the conservative groups and alliances within the government structure and bureaucracy. Policy positions are generally established through official structures, that is, the Cabinet and ruling party in the Diet. Invariably, the opposition, led primarily by the Japanese Socialist party, will place itself on the opposite side of the LDP. It is through the articulation of policy by these official institutions and groups (parties, labor unions, business interests) that policy passes through the identification phase.

Approval

As is true in the United States, approval generally takes place in the legislature, the Diet. What is significantly different, however, is that the ruling party, the LDP, controls the Diet as well as the executive. Given the nature of parliamentary systems (party cohesion, and the fact that a defeat on major policy brings the government down, to include the lower house), the LDP can pass virtually any type of legislation through the Diet, even against vocal and organized opposition.

Let us examine the Japanese legislative process in more detail. The House of Representatives (lower house) is the dominant house. The budget must first be submitted to the House of Representatives and, where the House of Councillors (upper house) decides differently and no agreement can be reached even through a joint committee of both houses, the decision of the House of Representatives becomes, after thirty days, the decision of the Diet. Normally a bill becomes law on passage by both houses, but a bill passed by the House of Representatives alone becomes law when (1) the House of Councillors takes no action within sixty days; or, (2) the House of Councillors disapproves a bill and the House of Representatives overrides their disapproval by a two-thirds majority of members present.

The close relationship between Diet committees and Cabinet ministries in Japan is essentially a reflection of the enormous complexity of government. This connection provides the opportunity for bureaucrats or civil servants to play an important role in the preparation of legislation not unlike that in the United States where elected representatives also lack the resources, the expert knowledge, and wide experience to deal, by themselves, with the vast range of needs of the political system and must be content to deal with policy in its broad outlines.

Legislative initiative lies with any member of the Diet, but individuals must have the support of other members (twenty in the lower house and ten in the upper house) to introduce a bill. In practice, nearly all bills are sponsored by the Cabinet, originate in one of the ministries, and are backed by the leadership of the majority party and the bureaucracy. Bargaining among factions of the LDP and bargaining at the second echelon in interested ministries may result in a consensus after which the bill reaches the Cabinet for approval. If presented to the Diet, the bill is presumed to have full support of the bureaucracy and the majority party. This process "takes place behind closed doors and access to the proceedings is limited."[1] The legislative opposition is made aware of the government's general intent and has an opportunity to determine a position. What is important about it all, writes Professor Baerwald, is that the positions to be taken are decided before the Diet begins, that these positions result from factional disputes in the LDP and perhaps interparty struggles among the opposition, and that group loyalty to these decisions makes compromise virtually impossible. Therefore, he adds, "the fate of a particular legislative proposal is completely predetermined even before a Diet session begins—assuming that one side has an absolute majority in both chambers, as has been the case for the LDP since 1955."[2] This does not mean negation of the Diet's constitutional mandate to legislate; it does mean the method lacks much flexibility.

LDP dominance of the government for the past two decades and the inflexibility of the legislative process, coupled with the general polarization of Japanese politics into opposing camps (the LDP versus a disunited opposition of socialists, communists, and others), has meant that the opposition role is limited to criticism, delay, and obstructionism. Unlike the United States, Japan has no executive veto because the prime minister and Cabinet are the executive and introduce the legislation the LDP desires. Nor is there ever any question of state's rights, for Japan has a unitary, not federal, government. The Japan Socialist party, the LDP's main opposition, has used a variety of techniques to ameliorate the "tyranny of the majority." This "tyranny" is the willingness of the LDP to "ram through" bills it sponsors without regard for the traditional general consensus-making characteristic of Japanese group decision making, and to do so without due regard for the interests of the minority. LDP tactics arouse the opposition to emotional heights. The opposition uses the filibuster in committee and on the Diet floor. On some occasions, opposition Diet members try to delay legislative action until the expiration of a Diet session by dilatory balloting, or by physically blocking halls of the Diet building. In 1960 they even locked the Speaker of the House in his office so that he could not chair the debates on revision of the Security Treaty with the United States. The LDP has retaliated by altering the agenda at the last moment, or by calling in regular police (in 1960) to bodily remove the opposition from the Diet floor one by one. Such action, of course, places the LDP in an awkward position with the press and public. On other occasions the opposition has boycotted Diet sessions, but they are not numerous enough to prevent a quorum, so the LDP has passed legislation without their presence, clear proof of the "tyranny of the majority."

In sum, the ruling party in the Diet is assured of support of its legislative program. Thus, what is identified as policy by the prime minister and Cabinets is, in essence, virtually assured of approval. The fact that the LDP has the support of much of the bureaucracy and business interests also links the approval phase with implementation. While the legislature plays an important role in approval, it is apparent that the prime minister and Cabinet play the dominant role.

There is another institution that has the potential of becoming involved in the approval phase. The Japanese Supreme Court, while having the authority to undertake judicial review, similar to that undertaken by the Court in the United States, has not established a strong tradition in this respect. The legal profession, the reliance primarily on written laws, and the legal system in the policy process is only now emerging. Thus, the Japanese Supreme Cort does not play as important an approval role as that played by the Court in the United States. Nevertheless, like many facets of the Japanese political system, the potential is there.

Implementation

The bureaucracy is the major political actor in implementing policy. As is true in the United States, the bureaucracy devises the specific rules and regulations for implementing policy and, therefore, implicitly makes policy. In Japan as contrasted to the United States, the bureaucracy plays a more direct role in decision making at the highest levels. This fact, and coupled with the tradition of Japanese bureaucracy, gives the bureaucrats a commanding position in dealing with the people. While not as entrenched or pervasive as the bureaucracy of the Soviet Union, the Japanese bureaucracy does have a significant day-to-day impact on the Japanese people. Because the Japanese political system is a unitary one, there is a tendency for strong centralization and decision from the center. This tendency makes the bureaucratic structure more immune from the "democratic" pressures that may arise from the people.

The characteristics of bureaucratic structures in general and the power of the bureaucracy as discussed in Chapters 3 and 4 generally apply to the Japanese bureaucracy. A few additional points need to be made. The bureaucracy in Japan is not as susceptible to external political actors as is the bureaucracy in the United States. To be sure, the Japanese bureaucracy is increasingly becoming infected by "democratic" forces. Still, the fact remains that the Japanese bureaucracy has a long tradition of immunity from the politics of outside groups. Thus, its roles as a political actor and its domination of the implementation phase are quite visible and reflect its relative autonomy and its own values and perceptions.

Feedback

The feedback process in the Japanese system is perhaps the most vociferous and dynamic of all the phases, attracting activity by many political actors—even more so than in the United States. The politicalization of labor unions, the strong oppositional mentality that has developed in the opposition parties in Japan, the outspoken and highly critical role played by the mass media—all serve to mobilize segments of the Japanese populace to respond to government policies. Attacks against government represented by the LDP policy are particularly harsh in matters of thermonuclear policy and national security issues. Because Japan was defeated in World War II and is the only country to have suffered through nuclear attack, the Japanese are particularly sensitive to government policies that support nuclear armaments and make Japan dependent upon the United States.

In the main, feedback from political actors within the government and through the business-LDP coalition (with bureaucratic support) is usually always for the established policy. Indeed, such feedback generally attempts to reinforce the policy already approved by the LDP.

The policy phases can be illustrated by briefly examining the Japanese Security Treaty, Japan–United States relations, and the various phases and their impact on Japanese domestic politics and policy.

Policy Process: The Security Treaty

The 1960 Security Treaty crisis has been called the "greatest mass movement in [Japan's] political history."[3] This series of events concerns the specifics of Japan's relationship with the United States in security matters, so it might be regarded as foreign affairs. But it was at the same time the most important and vociferously contested LDP political decision. This crisis illuminated the policy process and the interaction of domestic politics and foreign policy. The issue emergence is traceable to the occupation period.

EMERGENCE AND IDENTIFICATION

Japan really had no foreign policy from 1945 until 1952. It was an occupied enemy nation under effective United States control and had no foreign relations outside that framework. Midway in the occupation it was apparent to the United States that the Grand Alliance of World War II had been more effective in defeating Japan and the Axis powers than it would be in preserving international peace under the United Nations in the postwar world. Communist successes in China destroyed any hopes that postwar Asia would be stabilized by a nonaggressive non-Communist China. The Soviet consolidation of East Europe, the Berlin Blockade, Soviet acquisition of a nuclear capability (1949), and the seemingly intractable problems of a Korea "liberated" from Japan but divided into two increasingly hostile governments—all led United States policy makers to reconsider Japan's future role. A second factor in this decision was the increasing confidence and self-assertiveness of Japan's conservative political leaders. Japan changed from enemy to ally with the simultaneous coming into force of the Peace Treaty with Japan and the Japan–United States Security Treaty on April 28, 1952.

Although the occupation lasted six and one-half years, General MacArthur first called publicly for a peace treaty in March 1947, only seventeen months after Japan's surrender. SCAP feared that prolonging the occupation would intensify Japanese resistance to it. Others opposed an early treaty because the work of the occupation was incomplete, or Japan was too weak, or because the United States needed military bases in Japan to handle the increasing tensions in East and Northeast Asia. For the Japanese side, up to 1947, Premiers Shidehara and Yoshida (and General MacArthur as well) favored permanent neutralization of Japan. By June, however, Japan proposed to SCAP that Japan's security be entrusted to the United States in exchange for United States bases on Japanese soil. Three months later Japanese leaders proposed that Japan would depend on the United States for defense against external aggression (until the United Nations could handle it) and that a national police force should be organized to prevent civil insurrection. Both overtures were ignored.[4] Nevertheless, the Japanese government had decided that a "United States–Soviet conflict was inevitable," that it was not practical to rely on the United Nations for its security, and therefore that Japan ought to "cast its lot" with the United States since it was already under an American-run occupation.[5] Initial conversations among the Allies for a peace treaty with Japan broke down in 1948 but were resumed with vigor three months after the Korean War erupted.

APPROVAL

The treaty was signed at San Francisco on September 8, 1951, by forty-eight nations which did not include the People's Republic of China, the Soviet Union, Poland, Czechoslovakia, or the Republic of China. Therefore the technical state of war between Japan and Russia and China continued. Japan agreed to recognize the independence of Korea; renounced all claims to Formosa, the Pescadores Islands, the Kurile Islands, and the southern half of Sakhalin; and agreed to United States administration of the Ryukyu and Bonin Islands. Japan agreed to apply for admission to the United Nations. The treaty signatories recognized that Japan possessed the "inherent right of individual or collective self-defense" as specified in Article 51 of the United Nations Charter. This specific provision was opposed by the Soviet Union as a danger to peace in East Asia. The Peace Treaty legitimized United States occupation of the Ryukyu Islands, the continued existence of United States bases in Japan, and the Security Treaty, which was signed the same day.

Japan's right of "individual and collective" self-defense was recognized by the United Nations Charter and the Peace Treaty, but the 1947 Constitution (Article 9) stated:

Aspiring sincerely to an international peace based on justice and order, the Japanese people forever renounce war as a sovereign right of the nation and the threat or use of force as a means of settling international disputes.

In order to accomplish the aim of the preceding paragraph, land, sea, and air forces, as well as other war potential, will never be maintained. The right of belligerency of the state will not be recognized.

IMPLEMENTATION AND FEEDBACK

Despite this apparent constitutional prohibition, SCAP authorized Prime Minister Yoshida in July 1950 to establish the paramilitary 75,000-man National Policy Reserve (NPR) to assure Japan's internal security. The NPR replaced United States Army occupation forces moved to Korea to repel North Korean aggression. During the negotiations for the Security Treaty, United States Special Ambassador John Foster Dulles urged conversion of the NPR to a 350,000-man army capable of defending Japan against invasion by a rather large-scale conventional force, such as that of the Soviet Union. In contrast, Yoshida wanted a small force for internal security, believing United States forces in Korea and Japan would deter any invasion. So the Security Treaty was a compromise. Japan promised to "increasingly assume responsibility for its own defense against direct and indirect aggression." The United States got bases in Japan to "contribute to the maintenance of international peace and security in the Far East and to the security of Japan against armed attack from without." Thus Japan's role in the emergence and identification of the appropriate policy for its own defense was subordinated to American policy needs.

Security arrangements have been the most persistent problem in United States–Japanese relations. The 1951 Security Treaty, aside from being urged on Japan as part of the price for restoration of her sovereignty, had important impact on domestic politics. It derogated Japanese sovereignty in two respects: it gave the United States a veto over any third power's right to garrison, maneuver, or transit military forces in Japan, and give the United States the right to use its forces to "put down large-scale internal riots or disturbances in Japan caused by an outside power." The 1951 Treaty had no termination date, so Japan, in effect, accepted United States bases for an indefinite period. Nor was there any firm commitment by the United States to defend Japan. For its part, Japan established a triservice Self-Defense Force (SDF) in 1954 with an authorized strength of 152,000 personnel. Through a series of five-year defense plans, Japan concentrated on qualitative improvements and increased SDF strength to about 250,000.

Following this policy throughout the 1950s, the LDP resisted both external pressures to increase the SDF entirely. The bureaucracy and big business generally supported the "middle-road" policy. Because it dominated the government, the LDP was able to proceed despite the disapproving feedback and constant criticism by the media and the opposition political parties, generally under the rubric of the "base problem." Large numbers of American servicemen and families enjoyed an obviously higher standard of living, with extraterritorial privileges, near or in the midst of many of Japan's great cities. The bases themselves used land the Japanese wanted for other purposes. The usual military base–related nuisances of bars and prostitution offended many Japanese.

THE REVISED TREATY

Emergence and Identification In 1959 Prime Minister Nobusuke Kishi negotiated a new Treaty of Mutual Cooperation and Security between the United States and Japan. The renegotiated treaty embodied important changes in response to feedback from his own LDP and from opposition groups: namely, (1) United States forces would have no role in domestic disturbances; (2) the United States made a slightly stronger commitment to defend Japan in case of an armed attack against either on Japanese territory; (3) "joint consultation," which was understood in Japan to mean that the United States would get the prior approval of Japan to use bases in Japan for operations elsewhere; and (4) the treaty would remain in force for ten years, susceptible to termination by either party on one year's notice. The LDP wanted the revised treaty because it removed some earlier causes of friction. In a positive way, it reaffirmed the LDP belief that Japan should not be neutral and had a moral responsibility to assist the United States in keeping a reasonable level of noncommunist power in Asia. Besides that, there were obvious political and economic advantages in continued cooperation. Indeed, Japanese leaders anticipated greater independence in foreign policy in the framework of cooperation with the West.

These views favorable to the renegotiated treaty carried no weight with those in opposition. To them, the overriding concern was not to improve current security arrangements; it was to eliminate them entirely. The socialists and others considered United States bases highly visible evidence of Japan's subservience to the United States in what was essentially a continuation of the occupation. This sign of nationalism is part of the neutralism, at home and abroad, espoused by the JSP. The socialist position had rather wide public support reinforced by Japan's so-called atomic allergy and the popular preference for pacifism. The opponents argued that the security treaty posed a great danger to Japan, which might easily be drawn into American military adventures in east Asia.

Approval Kishi signed the revised treaty in Washington and introduced it in the House of Representatives on February 4, 1960. The opposition debated it for the next hundred days until it was finally forced to a vote in the May 19th Incident. The opposition had some factors working for it. The stationing of United States forces in Japan under the Security Treaty was ruled by the Tokyo District Court in March 1959 to be in violation of Article 9 of the constitution. (This so-called Sunakawa case decision was not reversed by the Supreme Court until December 1960.) Early in May an American U-2 reconnaissance aircraft was shot down over Soviet territory. Thereupon, the socialists charged that the United States had flown U-2s from Japanese bases over North Korea, the Soviet Union, and Communist China. The Soviet Union withdrew its invitation to President Eisenhower to visit Moscow. Ike's itinerary for his June 1960 visit to Japan was changed so that he would arrive in Tokyo on June 19 after visiting American allies in Asia and not, as was originally planned, fresh from a tension-easing visit with Khrushchev. Kishi decided to force a vote on the treaty which, under the constitution, would automatically come into effect thirty days after lower house approval and thus coincide with Ike's arrival in Tokyo. Late in the evening of May 19, the special committee of the House of Representatives to consider the revised treaty was being filibustered by the Socialists, who hoped to prevent action until midnight, at which hour the Diet session would end. At 10:25 P.M. a special plenary session was called. The Socialists locked the Speaker of the House in his office, barricaded it with furniture, and physically blockaded the halls of the chamber by a sit-down. About 500 police entered the Diet building, forcibly removed the human blockade, and escorted the Speaker to the rostrum. He called the House to order although members of the JSP, the DSP, and some LDP dietmen were absent. The House immediately voted to extend the session for fifty days, adjourned at 11:52 P.M., reopened at midnight, and at 12:18 A.M., without debate and with only LDP members present, approved the Security Treaty.[6]

Feedback (Implementation) In this case, implementation and feedback were compressed into one because the very act of negotiations over the treaty and the eventual approval by the Diet (LDP) encompassed implementation. As a result, the treaty signing immediately touched off feedback activities.

This "forced passage" on an absolutely critical relationship in Japan's foreign policy, taken in the face of the opposition parties' boycott of the Diet session, is a prime example of the interaction of domestic and foreign policy. It exemplifies the tyranny of the majority, and re-emphasizes the fact that foreign policy is not a bipartisan matter in Japan. The approval of the treaty was an application of Western majoritarianism to a society which questions the validity and the morality of its content. Although the policy issue at stake was the United States–Japanese defense relationship, the vehement, all-around criticism of the May 19 Incident was directed mainly at Kishi and "antidemocratic" factions in the LDP. Professional agitators in the student organization *Zengakuren* (whose leadership was so far left as to be expelled by the JCP) led mass street demonstrations, but they were joined by thousands and thousands of nonradical students. On June 4 a reported five and one-half million communication workers conducted a work stoppage. Thirteen million people signed petitions demanding Kishi's resignation, dissolution of the Diet, and undoing of the Security Treaty. When James Hagerty, President Eisenhower's press chief, arrived in Tokyo to make final plans for the

visit, he and United States Ambassador Arthur MacArthur were immobilized by demonstrators at the airport and escaped by U.S. Marine Corps helicopter.

The first violence in this series of protests erupted on June 15, resulting in the death of a coed and injuries to hundreds of police and student demonstrators. The following day, fearful for Eisenhower's personal safety and wary of any potential political involvement of the emperor, Kishi secured cancellation of what would have been the first visit by an American president in office. The revised treaty was to take effect at midnight on June 19; three hundred thousand demonstrators gathered at the Diet in a vain vigil. Ratifications were exchanged on June 23. Although the LDP possessed and used its majority in the lower house, Premier Kishi was forced to resign at a critical stage and after he had secured the government's goal of a revised Security Treaty. The reason lies in LDP factional politics. Kishi governed with the support of five other factions. Some of them deserted him during the crisis, partly because of his tactics, that is, because some LDP factions were not informed of his strategy for the May 19 forced vote. But mostly they deserted him because he had governed long enough and "they wanted to oust Kishi, supplanting him with one of their own leaders,"[7] Hayato Ikeda.

The important points about these events are that (1) the Socialists were willing to use force in the Diet, (2) the LDP responded in kind by resorting to regular police to clear the Diet and then force ratification of the Security Treaty with opposition party members absent, (3) the millions of Japanese who engaged in political activity in May and June 1960 did so mostly outside the framework of the party structure, and (4) that in the final days, both the right and left resorted to violence, a strong underlying potentiality in modern Japan's history. Despite the strength of the political activity to oust Kishi, his resignation did not result mostly from public disapproval, nor did it result from a compromise between major parties in the Diet. It resulted from compromise among LDP factions. In the November 1960 general elections, the LDP did well, winning absolute majorities in the total vote and in Diet seats. Opposition political elements continued to criticize the security treaty and, as 1970 (the year it could be terminated with one year's notice) approached, some observers feared a rerun of 1960. Premier Eisaku Sato's government decided to let the treaty continue in force automatically. The Socialists and Communists mobilized hundreds of thousands of demonstrators in Tokyo on the tenth anniversary (June 23, 1970) of the treaty, but the government's policy remained unchanged.[8] This single, most persistent and troublesome policy in domestic politics has, in essence, been formulated and approved without the consent of important opposition elements. It has been carried out in the face of highly critical feedback that concerns not only policy substance, but the policy process itself.

Foreign Affairs and National Security Policy

Japan has achieved a great deal in pursuit of its two major domestic objectives: (1) economic development, which brought to the Japanese people the material affluence of a highly industrialized, technologically advanced, and internationally competitive economic system; and (2) political and social development, which have provided visible fruits of the liberal democracy decreed by the occupation and carefully nurtured thereafter by the Japanese themselves. These results could not have been achieved had not Japan been able to remain isolated from the threateningly dangerous and costly politicomilitary competition which has made heavy demands on the energies and resources of most of the major world states since 1945.

For the most part, Japan's foreign policy has been passive, adaptive, reactive to outside pressures, and characterized by a "low-risk low posture" approach to the political and military problems of the rest of the world. Japan's overall foreign policy has been guided by three basic principles: (1) support of United Nations to promote international cooperation and contribute to world peace; (2) promotion of foreign trade and a generally free international economic system to serve Japan's own economic purposes; and (3) close cooperation with the United States for economic development and for reasons of national security. The Japanese–United States treaty relationship has overshadowed the others.

This treaty arrangement brought forth a strange anomaly in domestic policy. To carry out its part of the treaty responsibilities, Japan has created the Self-Defense Force (SDF) which is charged to defend the very constitution that prohibits the existence of the SDF as a military force. Unlike the People's Liberation Army in China, the triservice SDF has not been a political actor, although it has been a focal point for anti-LDP activity. Its status reflects important attitudinal changes on the part of the Japanese and illustrates procedural restraints in the policy process related to both domestic and external security matters.

The SDF differs fundamentally from the prewar forces in that its mission is purely defensive and that it is clearly integrated into a civilian control system existing at every planning and policymaking stage (see Figure 14-1). The Diet, Cabinet, prime minister, National Defense Council members, and Defense Agency dirctor-general are required to be civilians. All bureau chiefs and chief executives of the auxiliary organs (National Defense College) are also civilians. The Joint Staff Council (JSC) is the highest military advisory body in the Director-General and is the executive body for carrying out orders of the director-general.[9] The prime minister is

Figure 14-1: Organization of the Japan Defense Agency

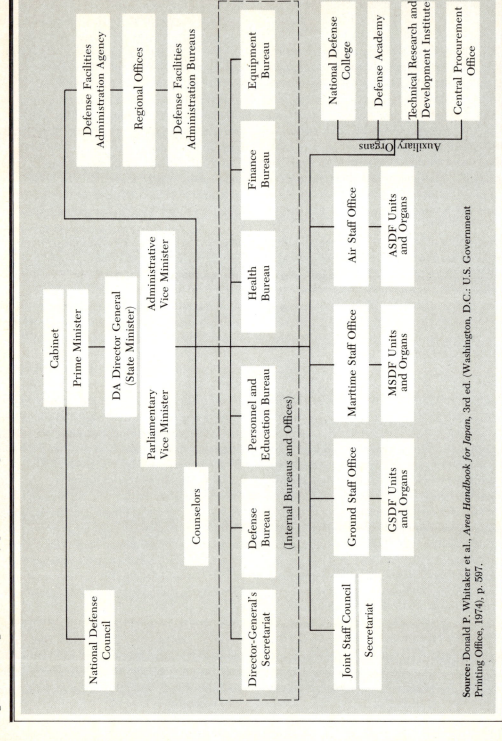

Source: Donald P. Whitaker et al., *Area Handbook for Japan*, 3rd ed. (Washington, D.C.: U.S. Government Printing Office, 1974), p. 597.

the single public official with the right to mobilize the SDF for a defense operation and he must, by law, prior to mobilization, consult with the National Defense Council, then with the Cabinet, and finally receive Diet approval. If an emergency arises when the lower house is dissolved, he may convoke the House of Councillors (which is never "dissolved" but is "closed" when the lower house is dissolved) and take action only with that body's consent. Even this action is provisional until full Diet approval has been received.

The Japanese public is ever mindful of the high-handedness of the prewar military leaders and the devastation of defeat, and is uncertain about Japan's future role in world affairs. Beset by lingering doubts about the constitutional status of the SDF, the public has been slow to give wholehearted support to Japan's armed forces. In view of recent trends in international politics, this reluctance seems to be changing. A recent poll showed that 79 percent of those polled recognized the need for having the SDF, although a minority of Japanese strongly oppose the SDF[10] and call for its dissolution.

Since World War II Japan has depended on the United States for its security, wisely pursuing a "go-slow" policy. Although its absolute defense expenditures have multiplied in the past two decades, the recent annual (1975–76) cost of the SDF ($4.5 billion) is 0.9 percent of the GNP and 6.22 percent of the national budget. (For 1955, the percentages were 1.78 percent of the GNP and 13.61 percent of the budget.)[11] Thus the SDF has absorbed a smaller and smaller portion of available resources. This enables Japan to spend relatively more for economic development, social welfare programs, education, and the general raising of living standards. This policy has the added advantage of not alarming Japan's neighbors and of reinforcing Japan's self-image as a major contributor to world peace through economic development. As Nobel Peace Prize Winner and former Prime Minister Eisaku Sato phrased it in 1970, Japan is trying "to give history an unheard-of challenge by aiming at a new utopia where top priority shall be given to social welfare and world peace."[12]

Japan's defense policy and its views of the Security Treaty which undergirds that policy have shifted in response to United States moves following announcement of the Nixon Doctrine. As a result of Nixon's visit to China (with no prior consultation or notification to the vitally interested Japan), the reduction of American forces in Korea, the total disengagement from Vietnam, and the active pursuit of détente with the Soviet Union, some Japanese commentators have openly questioned whether any American president would dare risk American lives in the crisis involving her ally Japan and whether the United States has lost its moralistic commitment to contain communist expansion.[13] Others have argued that it is not possible for Japan to depend decisively on the United States for any length of time in the new multipolar world.[14] The contrary case is that, while it may be unreasonable for one nation (Japan) to depend on one other nation (United States) for peace, it may also be dangerous to rely on a regional balance of power for the simple reason that local balances do not have real autonomy, and this is true of northeast Asia. It is also true that United States–Japanese security arrangements are based on a community of interests, such as a stable international order, preservation of peace in northeast Asia, and economic cooperation, and on the community values associated with representative democratic government and peaceful interstate relations among equals.[15]

In mid-1976, Japan issued a comprehensive statement of its security policy. Japan will continue to follow its three nonnuclear principles of no manufacture, no possession, and no introduction of nuclear weapons into Japan. This declaratory policy was not wholly believed by those who feared or favored nuclear armament by Japan, partly because Japan had failed to ratify the Nuclear Nonproliferation Treaty, which Japan signed in February 1970. This doubt was resolved when Japan became the ninety-sixth country to ratify the treaty in May 1976. All parties voted for ratification except the Communist party, which opposed it on the grounds that it endorsed a "nuclear monopoly" by a few powers.[16]

Recognizing that the constitution restricts the SDF to purely defensive purposes, Japan's defense capability is a "demonstration of its people's will and responsibility to defend their freedom, independence and security, and to uphold peace, progress and prosperity." Japan explicitly will "depend on the credibility of the American nuclear deterrent." The purpose of the SDF capability is not so much to fight as it is to function for the maintenance of peace; thus the United States provides the nuclear deterrent, Japan provides the conventional deterrent; each is the reification of the Nixon Doctrine in Japan. The SDF must meet the requirements of a basic standing force: "basic" in that it is the minimum force any independent nation needs; "standing" in that it is required at all times. To carry these concepts into practice, it is critically important to have smooth operational coordination with United States forces.[17] Future defense policy will continue to seek qualitative improvements in the SDF and closer coordination with the United States barring any abrupt and substantial changes in the distribution of power in East Asia.

JAPANESE-SOVIET RELATIONS

Relations between Japan and Russia have never been cordial. Competition in Manchuria and Korea led to Japan's defeat of Rus-

sia in 1905. Japan increased its influence in East Asia to the detriment of Russian interests by annexing Korea in 1910, establishing Manchukuo in 1933, and aggression in China after 1937. The Soviet Union unilaterally violated the 1941 Soviet-Japanese Neutrality Pact by attacking Japanese forces only a week before the war ended in 1945 and occupying Manchuria, the north half of Korea, and all of the Kurile Islands. Soviet perfidy is well-remembered by the Japanese, whose public opinion polls consistently rank the Soviet Union among the least liked foreign countries.

The Soviet Union refused to sign the 1951 Peace Treaty with Japan, and the two countries remained in a technical state of war as of late 1976. The Peace Treaty provided that Japan would seek admission to the United Nations, but its admission was blocked by the Soviet Union until after the Soviet-Japanese Joint Declaration of October 19, 1956, by which the two agreed to restore diplomatic relations and to negotiate a peace treaty. The major outstanding issue is territorial and concerns the status of the islands of Etorofu, Kunashiri, Shikotan, and the Habomai group, those islands in the Kurile Archipelago nearest to Japan's northernmost island of Hokkaido. Japan insists on the return of all of them, which Russia recognized as Japanese territory in a treaty of 1855 and reaffirmed in the 1865 Russo-Japanese Treaty in which Japan gave up claims to Sakhalin in return for Russia's relinquishing its claims to the Kuriles, specified as those islands north of Etorofu.[18] Japan's case is supported consistently by official United States statements and by Peking. But the Soviets hold the territory and a Soviet-Japan Peace Treaty ending World War II seems distant since neither side has much to gain by conceding the other's position. The Soviet Union continues to seize Japanese fishing boats and intern the crews temporarily and has yet to explain the whereabouts of thousands and thousands of World War II Japanese prisoners-of-war.

Over the past ten years, Soviet-Japanese contracts have expanded considerably. Two-way trade increased from $408 million in 1965 to $1.162 billion in 1973, a total, however, less than that of two-way trade with Communist China, the Republic of Korea, or Taiwan.[19] From time to time, multibillion-dollar Japanese aid in the economic development of Siberia has been explored, but Japan is reluctant and such projects are viewed askance by Peking. Soviet-Japanese relations will probably remain less than cordial. Both sides are adamant on the territorial issues, and Japan is very conscious that Soviet policy seeks to loosen Japan's ties with the United States and to prevent closer ties with Peking.

SINO-JAPANESE RELATIONS

Until 1945, Japan's policy toward China had been aggressive, domineering, and supported by superior military force. Japan decisively defeated China in the war of 1894–1895 and thereafter pursued unremittingly policies designed to secure special privileges in China, to transfer Chinese territory to Japan, and ultimately, to gain military control of China (1937–1945) to incorporate it into a Greater East Asian Co-Prosperity sphere controlled by Japan. Since 1945 Japan's relations with "China" have been complicated. Japanese forces in China surrendered to the Nationalist forces; but by the time peace treaty negotiations began, the People's Republic of China had firm control of mainland China and the Nationalists had moved the Republic of China to the island province of Taiwan. In the peace treaty, Japan renounced all claims to Taiwan, which had been incorporated into the Japanese Empire in 1895, but no statement was made as to which "China" was to receive the regained territory. The allies disagreed

over whether the Communist or Nationalist China should sign the San Francisco Peace Treaty, so neither did. Japan did, however, simultaneously sign a separate peace treaty with Nationalist China in deference to United States wishes.

For the next twenty years, the government of Japan officially supported United States policy toward the Republic of China, which held that the Nationalists were the sole legitimate government of China. Acceptance of this policy, even in the mid-fifties, was confined mainly to the more conservative elements of the LDP and did not accord with the views of most Japanese, who acknowledged the People's Republic of China's de facto control of the country, were highly conscious of the cultural ties, and saw the potential for trade. Japanese communists, socialists, intellectuals, labor and trade organizations, and powerful elements of the LDP favored "normalization" of relations with Communist China.

When Nationalist China was expelled from the United Nations and Communist China was admitted in September 1971, and when President Nixon made overtures to Peking without prior consultation, Japan prepared for a new policy toward the People's Republic of China. Matters moved rapidly when Kakuei Tanaka assumed the premiership on July 7, 1972. Diplomatic relations were established on September 19, 1972.[20] Factors contributing to Peking's sudden readiness to negotiate included re-evaluation of its international posture emerging from the Cultural Revolution, the apparent Soviet–United States rapprochement in early 1972, the dispatch of Soviet Foreign Minister Andrei Gromyko to reopen negotiations for a Soviet-Japanese peace treaty, continuing fear of Soviet intentions toward China, the need for increased foreign trade, and the recognition that Japan—the world's third leading economy—had the potential to develop much stronger military forces. For Japan, normalization of relations removed the China issue as a domestic and intra-LDP problem and offered the opportunity for greatly increased trade on an enlarged sphere of political activity. The People's Republic of China was acknowledged by Japan as "the sole legal Government of China." Japan noted but did not "recognize" that "Taiwan is an inalienable part of the territory of the PRC." The joint communiqué did not mention the United States–Japan Security Treaty, the abrogation of which had been consistently demanded by leftists in Japan and, a few years earlier, would have been a vital part of the negotiations. The United States withdrawal from Southeast Asia and Nixon's visit to China probably convinced Peking that the Security Treaty would act as a deterrent to the Soviet Union on the one hand, and, on the other hand, tend to restrain any Japanese tendencies to build a stronger military force so long as United States forces had bases in Japan.

The Nationalist Chinese reaction to the normalization of relations with Peking was the immediate severence of diplomatic ties with Tokyo; nevertheless, both nations have organized nongovernmental organizations to continue the usual functions of diplomacy, such as issuing visas and trade licenses and protecting interests with government and business subsidies.[21] All in all, Japan seems to have benefitted domestically and internationally under the new arrangements, but must, in the future, plan "very cautiously" its diplomacy with China "particularly in connection with U.S.-Japanese and Soviet-Japanese relations."[22]

JAPANESE-KOREAN RELATIONS

Since early Meiji times, Japanese leaders have considered Korea to be of prime strategic importance, an area which, in hostile hands, would be a serious and immediate threat to Japan, a "dagger pointed at the heart of Japan." Mastery of Korea was the goal of the Sino-Japanese War (1894–1895), the Russo-Japanese War (1904–1905), and the Korean War (1950–1953). Today influential Japanese believe "Korea is the key to the power balance of Asia."[23]

Annexed by Japan in 1910, Korea was "liberated" in 1945 and divided at the 38th parallel into Soviet (north) and United States (south) zones of occupation, which were converted in 1948 to the Democratic People's Republic of Korea (DPRK) and the Republic of Korea (ROK), respectively. DPRK aggression against the ROK in June 1950 was reinforced by massive Chinese military intervention later that year, but the military unification of all Korea under a communist government was prevented by the United Nations Command. An armistice was signed in 1953, and a Demilitarized Zone (DMZ) was established roughly along the 38th parallel. Chinese forces were withdrawn in 1958, but the United Nations Headquarters and United States forces remain in South Korea. The People's Republic of China and the Soviet Union support the Democratic People's Republic of Korea, while the United States has a Mutual Defense Treaty (1954) with the Republic of Korea. No progress has been made toward a peace treaty to end the Korean War, and none has been made toward unification of the peninsula.

Japan gave up all claims to Korea in the 1952 Peace Treaty, and neither government in the peninsula was a party to that treaty. Post-treaty relations between Japan and South Korea were acrimonious, made so by Japanese disdain and contempt for Koreans and their culture, and by Korean hatred and resentment of thirty-five years of imperial Japanese rule which sought to destroy the Korean language and culture. Strong emotions enveloped real issues including Korean demands for war reparations and the touchy problems related to the status and activities of several hundred thousand Koreans resident in Japan, the majority of whom are linked to the DPRK-oriented political organization, the *Chosen Soren.*

Diplomatic relations were finally established in 1965, despite student riots in Korea which had to be quelled by the ROK Army, and in the face of large-scale demonstrations in Japan which required a "surprise midnight vote, strongly reminiscent of the 'forced passage' of the Security Treaty five years earlier."[24] Korean dissidents opposed any rapprochement with their former colonial oppressors and feared a new Japanese economic imperialism as much as they hated the earlier political and cultural imperialism. Leftists in Japan opposed the treaty, arguing that the United States wanted to lead Japan into an anticommunist league with the Republic of Korea and Nationalist China and that Japan would be dragged, against its will, into any new war in Korea.

The Japan-ROK Treaty of 1965 and supplementary agreements recognized the Republic of Korea as the only legal government of Korea and provided for about a half billion dollars in good, services, and loans to foster the development of Korea's economy, which was then well into its first Five-Year Plan (1962–1966). By the mid-1970s Japan had become the largest foreign source of private investment capital for the Republic of Korea, as well as its major trading partner. Political relations have been marred by such unfortunate incidents as the South Korean CIA kidnapping from Japan and forcible return to Korea of a major political figure in self-imposed exile, and by the assassination of South Korean President Park's wife by a Korean resident of Japan. More amicable South Korean–Japanese relations are hindered by the continuing Japanese dislike of Koreans, who are always rated, along with residents of North

Korea and the Soviet Union, as the "least-liked" in public opinion polls, and by the South Korean belief that it is threatened by subversive activities carried out from the "sanctuary of Japan."[25]

Japan does not have diplomatic relations with North Korea, although a variety of limited commercial and individual political contacts have occurred. The Democratic People's Republic of Korea is the most closed, tightly organized, and highly disciplined of all socialist societies, and has pursued a militant policy of subversion against South Korea, taking the position that it is the only legitimate government of Korea. It demands abrogation of Japan's 1965 treaty with the Republic of Korea as a condition for establishment of diplomatic relations.

Accomplishments and Prospects

Japan has yet to realize for all of its people all of the ideals embodied in the United States-inspired 1947 Constitution, but these ideals have generally been embraced by the government and people alike. Japan has dealt competently with matters of public health, social security, unemployment insurance, and other welfare areas. At the same time, the whole range of problems attendant to a highly industrialized urban society afflict Japan—air and stream pollution, overtaxed transportation systems, housing shortages, and the lack of public recreation areas.

Yet, there is no question that Japan has had a remarkable history over the past thirty years. Its major accomplishments are in Japan's economic development, political stability and democratization, and world affairs. Rising out of defeat in World War II and its disastrous experience of nuclear attack, Japan has been able to develop a society that appears to have adapted well to the democratic idea, to parliamentary structure, and to the demands of an advanced industrial society. Yet all of these are also linked in Japan's prospects and fears for the future. It is with this in mind that we briefly assess Japanese accomplishments, prospects, and problems.

ECONOMIC DEVELOPMENT AND VULNERABILITY

Economically prostrate in 1945, Japan did not show remarkable signs of economic growth until the mid-1950s. By the late 1960s, Japan had become the third ranking national economy in the world. Some factors contributing to this include Japan's prewar prominence as the only advanced industrial society in Asia, the political and fiscal stability provided by the LDP along with the mutually supportive government-business relationship, the high level of education and skills of the work force, the strong propensity for deferred consumption among the Japanese, and a national security policy that enabled Japan to avoid high defense costs. Japan has shown that a resource-poor island nation distant from major world markets can become an economic superpower; nevertheless, it is the most vulnerable major economy in the world, heavily dependent on imports for food, for nearly all of its iron ore and petroleum, for half of its coal and wood, and for all of its bauxite.

For several years, Japan has been the third largest national economic unit in terms of total GNP (Gross National Product). From about $10 billion in 1950, the GNP rose to $200 billion in 1970, and to over $400 billion in the mid-1970s. In 1973 the prestigious Nomura Research Institute was predicting that Japan's per capita GNP would soon draw within a few hundred dollars of that of the United States.[26] Growth has slowed markedly since then, and Japan faces the prospect of reduced growth because of higher energy costs, upward revaluation of the yen, and increasing

domestic labor costs. While Japan's economic health remains vulnerable to a number of problems, its remarkable growth has lent stability to the political scene. Politics has fostered economic growth to the point where the average Japanese enjoys a standard of living surpassed by very few and unmatched in any socialist state in the world.

It must not be forgotten that even before the war Japan was an advanced industrial society. It was, and remains, the only Asian nation to become a major world economy. Its astounding growth since World War II was given great impetus by its role of supporting the United Nations war effort in Korea in the early 1950s, but some underlying permanent factors must be outlined.[27] The Japanese people have the necessary education, technical competence, and capacity for hard work. The government has provided political and fiscal stability. Japan's shipbuilding industry has manufactured an enormous fleet of supertankers to provide economically the vast oil resources required. The government has effectively increased industrial hydroelectric power and is a world leader in the development of nuclear power generation. Although Japan lost its overseas empire in 1945, it was also relieved of the economic burden of defending and expanding it. Japan habitually spends less than one percent of its GNP on defense, while its economic competitors spend five to ten times as much proportionately, leaving a much larger margin for capital investment. This has been possible because of Japan's reliance on the United States for deterrence of external attack. The special United States–Japanese relationship in foreign trade, a logical concomitant of political relations forged in the occupation, continues.

Economic development in post-Treaty Japan has often been judged a "miracle." We have seen, however, that Japan's prewar status as an advanced industrial society, the managerial and technical competence of its people, and wise government encouragement of a profit-oriented capitalist system in a favorable global environment all contributed to Japan's rise to become the world's third largest national economy unit. Now a global economic power, Japan trades more with North America than with Europe, more with Europe than with Asia. Its future economic well-being depends on assured, timely, and economical access to a variety of essential industrial raw materials, and to markets for its manufactured goods. International political stability is absolutely essential to Japan's prosperity, but Japan lacks the military power and diplomatic prestige to influence the political acts of other states that may destabilize international relations and thus thwart Japan's economic objectives, both domestic and international. Fundamentally strong, well-managed, and resilient, Japan's economy is destined to remain vulnerable to disruption by factors beyond its control, a possibility we must always keep in mind when judging the prospects for continuing domestic political stability.

POLITICAL STABILITY, INSTABILITY, AND DEMOCRATIZATION

The most striking fact about postwar Japan's political system is that the conservative Liberal Democratic party (LDP) has monopolized control of the government in what we have called a "one-and-one-half-party system" which has given Japan a remarkable continuity in government. Political stability has been achieved in a domestic environment favorable to continuing economic growth and preservation of social and political ideals and in an international environment which permitted Japan to follow its low-risk low-posture diplomatic policies. Yet none of Japan's political parties has a mass membership or a mass

following; nor do most Japanese identify with a political party. There are large numbers of elected local officials without a party affiliation, although most are conservative in political preference. The parties are really parliamentary parties, located in and focused on the capital, separated from the people. Policy compromises occur between factions within parties, not between parties. As Professor Scalapino sees it, Japan is a paradox of "an open society made up of closed components [which] must be ended." Japan, he states, is approaching the status of a mass society, but mass participation in politics must not be left to the extraparty activities, such as occurred during the Security Treaty crisis of 1961.[28]

One outstanding Japanese scholar has suggested that the "stability" in postwar politics may really be "immobilism."[29] Immobilism derives from the lack of national consensus about fundamental policy issues; for example, the LDP has yet to gain, if it ever will, full active support of the Security Treaty from the public and the opposition parties. In fact Japanese politics has seen a multipolarization accompanying the decline in LDP strength: Japan Socialist party and the Democratic Socialist party have failed to gain strength, and the Komeito and Communists have profited therefrom in varying degrees. The LDP remains in power because it deals effectively with constituents' needs, and not because of support in foreign policy. Consensus decision making has several advantages, but it is a process that is time-consuming, can be delayed by a stubborn minority, and encourages a "system of mutual irresponsibility" in which the "responsibility and competence of the leaders and those being led is not clearly defined." Government decisions must be coordinated among business, the LDP and the bureaucracy, all three of which must develop an internal consensus, complicated by factionalism in the latter two. Imaginative policies are hard to come by. Japan has demonstrated remarkable skill in adapting and reacting to outside pressure. The concern is that Japan "remains in a disadvantageous position should any destabilization demand a rapid decision,"[30] especially in international affairs.

Japan's international role will be profoundly influenced by its domestic situation. If the LDP loses its majority, the most likely result would be confusion, a series of coalitions and the emergence of new political forces, the nature of which is not predictable.

FOREIGN RELATIONS: SECURITY
AND DEPENDENCE

Japan has arrived in the late 1970s generally untouched in adverse ways by the tumultuous events in East Asia since 1945. The low-posture, passive, reactive foreign policy followed by Japan since 1952 seems not to be altered appreciably. Some steps have been taken to develop a more "autonomous" diplomacy to complement its heavy dependence on the United States, for example, the exchange of diplomatic recognition with the People's Republic of China, but this, too, was reactive to United States initiatives. In the late 1970s, Japan confronts serious problems because, willing or not, she has emerged as a principal in the evolution of great power rivalry in East Asia where the interests of Japan, the United States, the Soviet Union, and China converge in a uniquely complex and shifting pattern. Less and less can Japan avoid the political commitments it has sidestepped for so long. Observing that "no region in the world is more dynamic, more diverse or more complex than Asia," Secretary of State Henry A. Kissinger compared the problems of security in Europe and Asia.[31] In Europe two alliance systems confront each other directly across a clear north-to-south line through the European continent. The major danger is external attack, and the strengths and weaknesses of the two sides are roughly calculable. In Asia, he continued, the balance is multiple, more fluid, involves the possibility of armed attack across a border in Korea, but is especially complicated by contention between the two major communist powers in the world.

Japan has sought successfully to project the image of an economically powerful, militarily weak, politically stable democracy devoted to world peace and economic development. It now seeks a more "autonomous" diplomacy, that is, one less dependent on the United States. The technique is capsulized, for East Asia, as keeping "equidistant" from China and from the Soviet Union. But this is increasingly difficult to do because Japan, in its search for autonomy, cannot escape pressure from the Soviet Union and China, or from North and South Korea. In security matters, Peking has supported (contrary to Japan's domestic socialists and communists) continuation of the United States–Japan Security Treaty because it deters the Soviet Union and discourages a substantially enlarged SDF. For its part, the Soviet Union has insisted that Japan give up islands that historically have been recognized as Japanese territory before a World War II Peace Treaty can be signed. To assure peace in East Asia, Moscow advocates a collective security system of some type for the purpose of gaining an active major foothold in northeast Asian politics—something it now lacks and which China wishes to deny it. With regard to North Korea, both China and the Soviet Union support it diplomatically and probably have considerable leverage in restraining its excessive militancy, although this is by no means certain, nor is it guaranteed in the future. On the other hand, Japan and the United States are committed to support the Republic of Korea, although the nature, amount, and dependability of their support is problematical. North Korea insists that Japan abrogate its Security Treaty with the United States as a condition for establishment of diplomatic realations. South Korea's relations with Japan are troubled by the large leftist Korean minority in Japan which supports Pyongyang, and the Republic of Korea strongly protests any indications that Japan may move to recognize the Democratic People's Republic of Korea. The cross-currents of conflicting objectives in northeast Asia stemming from détente and the recent redistribution of power in the area seem to have been beneficial to United States interests. The United States has succeeded in cooperating, to some extent, with the Soviet Union in Europe while excluding it from a major role in Asia. In Asia, the United States has chosen to cooperate with the People's Republic of China, which is clearly the most important of the two for stability in Asia. So long as it feels threatened by the Soviet Union, China will accept some United States cooperation because it is an element of strength for China in its competition with the USSR.

Japan's long-standing policy is that the United States–Japan Security Treaty is the "cornerstone of peace and stability in East Asia," a view publicly shared by recent United States presidents. Secretary Kissinger said in mid-July 1976, "No relationship is more important to the United States than our alliance with Japan."[32] He has also reminded us that, "as maritime trading nations with complementary economies, the U.S. and Japan account for 52 percent of the production and 26 percent of the trade of the entire non-Communist industrialized world"[33] and that two-way trade in 1974 was $25 billion. But the ties are based on more than economic interests: shared values are at least as important.

For the first quarter century following the end of the Allied occupation, Japan adapted successfully to a series of important events she could not influence—the war in Korea, nuclear proliferation, the war in Vietnam, and the oil crisis. Northeast Asia is the only area in the world where the interests of China, the Soviet Union, Japan, and the United States converge

geographically, so it is not unreasonable for Japanese to state that "there is no more important issue than the Korean problem for U.S.–Japanese relations in this latter half of the 1970s."[34] How this issue is handled depends on events not subject to Japan's influence: the relations between the ROK and DPRK, UN actions, the sequelae to Mao's replacement, Soviet initiatives, and perhaps most importantly, on domestic opinion in the U.S. as reflected in congressional action. As Japan moves toward greater participation in East Asian politics, the adaptive capacities of its political system may be subjected to severe tests.

Summary

The exercise of power throughout the policy phases is primarily by political actors officially connected with the ruling government structures. The peculiarities of the parliamentary system, the nature of Japanese society, and the unitary administrative system provide the power base for the ruling party, the LDP, to take the primary role in virtually all phases of the policy process. The close link between business interests, the conservative factions in the LDP, and the bureaucracy provide a coalition that has demonstrated a capacity to rule, even against outspoken criticism and forceful negative feedback from political actors outside of the government structure. The Japanese policy process demonstrates a particular tendency to be controlled by an elite of conservative businessmen and bureaucrats, supported by a conservative "Japanese middle class." Nevertheless, the "democratic" environment has the potential to develop the wide range of political actors and impact on policy that is now apparent in the presidential system in the United States.

The most persistent troublesome policy in domestic politics has been United States–Japan security relationships. The policy of cooperation emerged during the occupation. It resulted from shared perceptions and common interests in providing means to contribute to stability and future peace in East Asia which was threatened by the Communist victory in China and by the North Korean aggression in 1950 backed by the People's Republic of China and the Soviet Union. The Security Treaty formalized the relationship when autonomy was restored to Japan in 1952. Implementation and approval of the policy came from the LDP despite widespread opposition. Revision of the treaty in 1960 called forth the greatest mass movement in Japan's political history. The LDP forced approval of the revision in a Diet session which included LDP members only. The approval process showed that the Socialists and the LDP were both willing to use force. Millions of Japanese who engaged in political activity in the weeks prior to approval did so mostly outside the framework of the party movement. This policy, of overriding importance in both domestic and external politics, has been formulated and approved without the consent of important opposition elements. It is carried out in the face of highly critical feedback which concerns not only policy substance, but the policy process as well.

Japan's foreign policy has been passive, adaptive, and reactive to outside pressures and characterized by a "low-risk low-posture" approach. Its basic principles are cooperation with the United Nations and close cooperation with the United States for economic development and national security. Japan seeks to project the image of an economically powerful, militarily weak, politically stable democracy devoted to world peace. Having moved toward a more autonomous foreign policy and greater participation in East Asian politics, the adaptive capacities of the political system may be severely tested.

Japan's remarkable progress over the past thirty years has resulted in political stabil-

ity, democratization, and economic development. Yet Japan has faced important problems in foreign policy and national security policy. Each of the accomplishments has inherent problems for the future. The Japanese system, although democratic, has not as yet developed the "openness" in its policy process or the range or effectiveness of political actors outside government structures generally associated with democratic systems.

NOTES

1. Hans H. Baerwald, *Japan's Parliament: an Introduction* (Cambridge, England: Cambridge University Press, 1974), p. 123.
2. Ibid., p. 124.
3. Robert A. Scalapino and Junnosuke Masumi, *Parties and Politics in Contemporary Japan* (Berkeley: University of California Press, 1962), p. 125. This account is based mainly on this work, pp. 125–153.
4. Ikuhito Hata, "Japan Under the Occupation," *Japan Interpreter*, vol. 10, no. 3–4 (Winter 1976), Tokyo, p. 375.
5. Martin E. Weinstein, "The Evolution of the Japan Self-Defense Force," in James H. Buck, ed., *The Modern Japanese Military System* (Beverly Hills, Calif.: Sage Publications, 1975), p. 41.
6. Theodore McNelly, *Politics and Government in Japan*, 2nd ed. (Boston: Houghton Mifflin, 1972), p. 221.
7. Scalapino and Masumi, op. cit., p. 141.
8. McNelly, op. cit., p. 223.
9. Boei Nenkan Hankokai, *Boei Nenkan 1974* [Defense Yearbook 1974] (Tokyo, 1974), pp. 201–202.
10. Japan Defense Agency, *Defense of Japan Defense White Paper (Summary)* (Tokyo, June 1976), p. 14.
11. Ibid., p. 20.
12. Quoted in Japan Defense Agency, *The Defense of Japan* (English translation), Tokyo, October 1970.
13. See Kimio Muraoka, *Japanese Security and the United States*, Adelphi: Paper 95 (London: International Institute for Strategic Studies, February 1973).
14. See Kiichi Saeki, "Japan's Security in a Multipolar World," *East Asia and the World System Part II: The Regional Powers*, Adelphi Paper 92 (London: International Institute for Strategic Studies, November 1972).
15. Masataka Kosaka, "Dentente and East Asia," Discus-

sion Paper No. 60, California Seminar on Arms Control and Foreign Policy, Santa Monica, California, 1975, pp. 6–7.

16. *The Japan Times Weekly*, Tokyo, May 26, 1976.

17. James H. Buck, "Japan: The Problem of Shared Responsibility," in W. W. Whitson, ed., *Foreign Policy and U.S. National Security* (New York: Praeger, 1976), pp. 166–178.

18. For details with maps, see *The Northern Territorial Issue*, Japan Reference Series No. 5-68 (Tokyo, Japan: Ministry of Foreign Affairs, 1968).

19. *Statistical Handbook of Japan 1975*, pp. 88–90.

20. See Tadao Ishikawa, "The Normalization of Sino-Japanese Relations," in Priscilla Clapp and Morton H. Halperin, *United States-Japanese Relations: The 1970s* (Cambridge, Mass.: Harvard University Press, 1974), pp. 146–163.

21. Lee W. Farnsworth, "Japan 1972: New Faces and New Friends," *Asian Survey*, vol. 12, no. 1 (January 1973), p. 118.

22. Ishikawa, op. cit., p. 163.

23. Kosaka, op. cit., p. 13.

24. McNelly, op. cit., p. 236.

25. Kosaka, op. cit., p. 16.

26. *Japan Times Weekly*, June 9, 1973.

27. Edwin O. Reischauer, *The United States and Japan*, 3rd ed. (Cambridge, Mass.: Harvard University Press, 1965), pp. 291–304.

28. Scalapino and Masumi, op. cit., p. 153.

29. See Masataka Kosaka, "Political Immobility and the Uncertain Future," in Priscilla Clapp and Morton H. Halperin, eds., *United States-Japanese Relations: The 1970s* (Cambridge, Mass.: Harvard University Press, 1974), pp. 19–34.

30. Ibid., p. 30.

31. Bureau of Public Affairs, U.S. State Department, "America and Asia," speech by Secretary Henry A. Kissinger in Seattle, Washington, July 22, 1976.

32. Ibid.

33. Henry A. Kissinger, "The United States and Japan in a Changing World," a speech before the Japan Society, New York City, June 18, 1975.

34. Yukio Matsuyama, "Misunderstanding in U.S.-Japan Relations," a speech to the Chicago Council on Foreign Relations printed in Japan Society, Inc., *Japan House Newsletter*, June 1976.

CHAPTER 15

CHINA AND JAPAN: CONCLUSIONS

In an earlier concluding chapter comparing the American and Soviet systems, we discussed the reasons behind grouping the two systems in a concluding chapter. Similar reasoning applies to this concluding chapter comparing China and Japan. Aside from the rationale presented in the preface, it is clear that the Chinese and Japanese systems represent a similar cultural heritage and, in a number of instances, an experience similar to that of the West. Even though Japan's defeat in World War II opened the door to deep Americanization, it did not erase Japan's centuries-old cultural heritage. Indeed, it is more likely that both the American impact and the traditional culture have influenced each other into a uniquely Japanese modern system. Similarly, Maoism and Communist ideology, though of longer impact on China, have not erased the traditions of the thousands of years of Chinese culture, even with concerted attempts to do so by the Communist elites.[1]

In brief, neither nation entered the post-World War II era with a clean slate, but both were able to make something of a fresh start, a change in direction facilitated, ironically enough, by the heavy physical and psychological damage of extended warfare, by disen-chantment with traditional institutions, and ways of thought and behavior, by the failures of earlier leadership, and in Japan, at the explicit direction of the occupying power.

Ideology

A vital difference between Japan and China is found in ideology, even though the Japanese generally consider China to be their "cultural mother and father." In the past century, Japan has changed from a decentralized military feudalism based on Confucian orthodoxy to a centralized theoretically absolute constitutional monarchy heavily indebted to the Prussian model and latterly dominated by militarists, to an open democratic representative constitutional monarchy imitative of the mainstream of Western European and American democracy. China passed from traditional Confucian imperialism to republicanism, warlordism, Confucian revival, and to a new type of socialist state, powered ideologically by Maoism, a Marxist-Leninist offshoot of 19th-century European intellectual activity.

The ideology of the People's Republic of China derives from Marxism-Leninism, modified and elevated to a higher level by China's revolutionary experience under Mao Tsetung's leadership. This ideology is the source of the party's authority and leadership over all segments of China's society. The party is the sole arbiter of ideological orthodoxy. Although power theoretically resides in the people, the party is the vanguard of the proletariat, a self-perpetuating elite of about 3 percent of the population. Ideology requires party leadership by a small oligarchy operating through a rigid hierarchy. The party determines the goals and the direction of the political system. Ideology emphasizes the good of the collectivity over individual rights and liberties, a concept with no place in the Chinese scheme of things. Nor is there any concept of responsibility or accountability of officials to the individual. The link between ideology and party is all-encompassing and unbreakable; each lives on the other. For this reason, ideological relevance is a major concern of the party and is sought through the mass line, the constant interaction between the masses and the Chinese Communist vanguard.

In Japan there is no specifically formulated unchallengeable orthodox ideology. What Japan does have is a commitment to a set of democratic ideas and ideals. Sovereignty lies with the people who regularly, and in large numbers, exercise their right to elect and to dismiss officials at all levels of government, the essence of democracy. Elected officials are directly responsible to and accountable to the electorate. The basic constitutional principle is that the government is a sacred trust of the people (not a party), the authority for which is derived from the people (not from the wisdom of a Mao Tse-tung), the powers of which are exercised by the people (not a party cadre), and the benefits of which are enjoyed by the people. Individual rights and liberties are exercised freely under constitutional guarantees.

Maoist ideology is the Chinese Communist party's prescription to cure the evils of the human condition. Without specifying the nature of the future, the Chinese Communist party (CCP) claims it will lead the Chinese people and all mankind to emancipation by eliminating everywhere the exploitation of man by man. The process is "permanent revolution" determined by the inevitability of never-ceasing class struggle, a struggle that will continue even after the achievement of a socialist society. Maoist ideology is aggressively conflict-centered and explains politics in terms of "contradictions" that set person against person, group against group, generation against generation, and class against class in their external resolution. The goal of Maoist activity is not simply the creation of a "powerful modern socialist society," but the creation of a "new man."

Japan's ideology is not genuinely prescriptive; rather, it suggests the broad outlines of a process, one way of conducting politics to resolve value conflicts within the society. It provides the rules of the game. These rules allow for orderly and relatively frequent transfer of government power, the participation of a large number of groups, the diffusion of authority, and a maximum of individual participation. Goals of the society are determined more or less openly and subjected to vigorous public challenge in the Diet and the media. Not all Japanese agree with the adversary process as reflected in Diet deliberations; but except for minority parties, which decry the "tyranny of the majority," the process is generally accepted. Japanese ideology does not seek to create a "new man"; it seeks fulfillment of the individual in the matrix of complex competitive politics.

Chinese Communist ideology holds that its basic principles are immutable, "scientific," deterministic, and universal. The Chinese Communist party is optimistic in the unshakable belief in the inevitable victory which will produce an abundant and peaceful life for all. Japan's Constitution (reflecting American authorship) states that it is based on a "universal principle of mankind" and is similarly optimistic in terms of hope for the future. Yet it does not speak of inevitable victory, for democracy is recognized for the fragile process that it is.

While the ideologies of both Japan and China seek better lives for their peoples, the means to this goal are fundamentally opposed: freedom versus regimentation, individual rights versus group needs, real political participation versus mass political activity, cooperation versus conflict, dissent versus repression, and evolutionary change versus continuous revolution.

LEGITIMACY

The degree to which the political systems in China and Japan are regarded as legitimate depends on the perceptions regarding ideology. In China political actors constantly refer to and link their exercise of power to Mao Tse-tung Thought. The range of linkage is limited because the body of reference consists of a restricted set of political views determined by a small co-optive group which is selected on merit defined by mastery and manipulation of the orthodox ideology. This Communist party elite rules by monopolizing the truth, exemplifying morality, and encouraging all to struggle selflessly for the common good. This group directs the major institutional political actors, so there is, in fact, a closed circle for the interpretation and application of ideology. Mao has been the interpreter par excellence of Chinese Communist ideology. Even in death, this role continues. The CCP Central Committee, headed by Chairman Hua Kuo-feng, issued posthumously Volume V of Mao's *Selected Works* (May 1977). Mao's thoughts will remain the criterion of ideological correctness, for none of his

colleagues even approached his stature as the "Pole Star" for all Chinese. At the same time, ideology will be reinterpreted both to rationalize past policy and to justify current and future policy. Mao's role as the source of ideological legitimacy is strikingly symbolized by the magnificent Chairman Mao Memorial Hall in T'en An Men Square. Completed in six months by 700,000 volunteer laborers, the classic colonnade structure is 350 feet square and over 100 feet high, and enshrines Mao's corpse in a crystal sarcophagus.

In Japan, ideology is not a closed circuit of interpretation and application of a fixed body of limited alternatives for political action. It encompasses the rules of the game in an increasingly pluralistic social and political environment. Ideology does not limit access to positions of power; rather, it encourages a variety of both private and public activity to that end. Such activity is considered legitimate so long as the rights and freedoms of individuals and groups are not infringed.

Ideology may prescribe the range of legitimate political activity, but in both China and Japan, ideologically impermissible actions do occur. A recent instance in China began with the large-scale riot by 100,000 people in Peking in April 1976 touched off by the removal from a monument in T'en An Men Square of memorial wreaths to Chou En-lai. It was followed over the next few months by serious disturbances in half of China's provinces with the deaths of hundreds or thousands reported.[2] In Japan, the Security Treaty Crisis of 1960 is the prime example of political activity in violation of the rules of the game. Yet in both nations, the ideology remains the guideline for acceptable political activity.

Political Actors

Political actors in the People's Republic of China have been within the party-state-military bureaucracy. The scope and type of political activity has been defined by the party. Although the People's Liberation Army has operated at times in a quasi-autonomous manner, the activity has been rationalized by ideology. Institutional groups are the major political actors, and it seems unlikely that associational or interest groups will play a role outside the institutional framework. The party will continue, with considerable success, to try to dominate all rivals for power. Intra-party politics and party-state-military politics will be the major focus of activity.

In Japan there is a wide range of activity open to many political actors, both in and out of government. Political parties are vital to the political process, but they represent only one type of political actor. One party (the Liberal Democratic Party, LDP), it is true, has been dominant in the national Diet. Yet other parties have competed successfully for power at lower levels of government. At the lowest level of elective office, most officeholders are not even affiliated with a particular party, but gain office as independents. At the national level, the power of the dominant LDP is constantly challenged, and the substance of its policy, restricted by the increasing power of its opposition. Government power is also limited by the influence of powerful interest groups. Business circles influence the LDP by assisting or not assisting candidates for office, but also by its contacts with government ministries such as Finance and International Trade and Industry. Large labor federations use their close linkage with the opposition political parties to restrict governmental power. A variety of associational groups that seek to ban the bomb, decrease pollution, or oppose the United States–Japan Security Treaty all exert varying degrees of influence by public debate, demonstrations, and through the media.

In China the party guards jealously its role as the sole repository of ideological orthodoxy, insisting that the one party alone can guide the Chinese people to socialism. Composed of an elite of about 3 percent of the population, the party leads, and requires obedience from, the six sectors of Chinese society: industry, agriculture, commerce, culture and education, the People's Liberation Army, and the government. The National Party Congress is the "highest leading body" of the Chinese Communist Party. It legitimizes party decisions made by its organizationally "subordinate" organs, which actually are functionally "superior" organs: the Central Committee, the Politburo, and the Standing Committee of the Politburo, the real decision-making elite of five to a dozen top leaders. The Central Committee, which functions for the National Party Congress when it is not in session, is essentially an assembly of leaders from all parts of China and all major functional organizations. It is the link between the small Peking-based group of leaders (Politburo) and the varied functional and geographic interests of the party.

The second major political actor, the state apparatus of the People's Republic of China, is a creation of the party, given formal status by the state constitutions of 1954 and 1975. In theory, all power belongs to the people, and this power is exercised through the 2,800-member National People's Congress, the "highest organ of state authority." Nevertheless, the National People's Congress is explicitly "under the leadership of the CCP." The National People's Congress has a 167-member Standing Committee, but the major operating element of the People's Republic is the State Council, which consists of a premier, 12 vice-premiers and the heads of 29 ministries, and collectively directs the affairs of state and oversees the operation of local state organizations. The position of chairman of the People's Republic of China was eliminated by the 1975 Constitution. As a rule, the most powerful offices in the state apparatus are occupied concurrently by members of the party Central Committee, the Politburo and its Standing Committee. These interlocking directorates assure coordination of party policy formulation and state policy execution.

The third major political actor is the 3,250,000-member People's Liberation Army (PLA). Since the party's founding in the 1920s, its military forces have been subject to party control: "The Party commands the gun, the gun must never be allowed to command the Party." PLA missions include the normal military missions to defend the sovereignty and territorial integrity of the state, but also to safeguard the accomplishments of the socialist revolution and to guard against imperialist subversion. Command of the PLA was vested in the chairman of the People's Republic of China (Mao until 1959, and Liu until the Cultural Revolution), but the 1975 PRC Constitution explicitly assigns overall command of the PLA to the chairman of the Central Committee. This step was meant to assure PLA subordination to the party, and to prevent a return of Bonapartism. However, it is possible that the PLA may some time seize a more autonomous role when its interests diverge from those of the party.

The triad of political actors, party, state apparatus, and PLA, that supports China's society—and its revolution—has all been affected enormously by the towering genius of Mao Tse-tung, probably the most powerful individual in any nation's history in terms of the temporal span of his influence and the portion of humanity directly affected by his political ideas. But Mao was not always in firm control, nor has the Chinese Communist party escaped serious challenge by the other actors. We have seen that China is a nation in conflict with herself, seeking the appropriate balance (or higher synthesis) in the contradictions between democracy and centralism, agriculture and industry, socialism and capitalism, region and center, red and expert; and that these conflicting views exist not only among the membership of a given institutional political actor, but also, when aggregated, among the party, the state, and the military. When Mao and the party pushed the

Great Leap excessively, the military and the state apparatus slowed it and then reversed course. When the Cultural Revolution began, Mao and Communist party radicals created a new short-lived political actor, the Red Guard, only to appeal to the People's Liberation Army to restore order and save the party when the Red Guards got out of hand. When the PLA threatened to displace the party as the principal actor, Mao resorted to a party and state coalition to reduce its power, narrowly averting his own assassination, and perhaps "saving" China from a military dictatorship.

In Japan political parties existed in rudimentary form a century ago, but genuine party government did not become a reality until after World War II. The current party alignment dates from late 1955 and the emergence of the conservative Liberal Democratic party (LDP) and the Japan Socialist party (JSP), as the two largest parties. Factions are the focus of Japanese politics. The current factions were not produced by the political system: they have been created by political leaders who led the various conservative and leftist "parties" which formed the LDP and the JSP in the 1950s. The dominance of factions has strong historical and social roots in Japan and is likely to continue simply because there seems to be no workable alternative. No party has a mass membership, and all political parties are essentially parliamentary parties with their attention and activity focused in Tokyo.

As the dominant and governing party for more than twenty years, the LDP has accomplished the purposes of a political party: to win elections, form governments, and carry out its policies. The JSP has been the major opposition party, but has not been able to acquire national power and form a government. As a doctrinaire Marxist party, the JSP advocates unrealistic and impractical policies in international affairs, and the LDP has skillfully pre-empted some of its domestic policies. The JSP is deeply divided internally and unable to cooperate with other opposition parties to deprive the LDP of power. Its major role has been to oppose LDP initiatives, delay legislation, and infrequently to prevent its enactment. None of the minor parties is likely to increase markedly in power, but they may be able to influence national politics as coalition partners.

Four of the most important interest groups in Japan are the civil service bureaucracy, the intellectuals, labor, and business. The civil service is a highly educated, very competent and self-conscious corps d'élite, jealous of its power and resistant to the legislative branch of government. Bureaucrats are powerful because they control the machinery of government, participate in drafting legislation, and some of them move into political party activity and business where they continue to pursue their conservative interests in general support of the LDP. Intellectuals are a potent opinion-making group and exercise their influence through the educational system and the prolific mass media. They show a wide diversity of viewpoints, but are generally Marxist and anti-establishment. At the same time, they resist recruitment by political parties and concentrate on their self-appointed role as the guardians of civil liberties. Student activity was crucial in the 1960 Security Treaty crisis and was disruptive in the late 1960s. The students are not courted by either the political parties or labor unions. Organized labor, about one-sixth of the electorate, has engaged in political activity through strikes, political contributions, and support for specific candidates. The JSP, sole recipient of the support of Sohyo, Japan's largest federation of unions (4,320,000 members), has been the major beneficiary of union activity. The second largest federation, Domei (2,260,000 members), supports the DSP. Business is by far the most powerful interest group, exerting its influence through very large, well-organized groups, such as the Federation of Economic Organizations, whose membership includes 750 major corporations and 100 national trade associations. *Zaikai* organizations have competent staffs who prepare authoritative reports and recommendations on economic affairs which are carefully studied by officials with whom it is constantly in contact. These associations, the LDP politicians, and the bureaucracy are mutually interdependent and cooperate effectively in the pursuit of common goals.

The political parties are univerally recognized in Japan as legitimate organizations to serve as the vehicles by which the people exercise the constitutional right of sovereignty. The interest groups noted above and hundreds of others pursue lawfully the aggregation and articulation of interests of specialized groups. In general, all operate within the rules of the game, and the public accepts the government in form, ideology, and operating process.

China and Japan differ importantly in major political actors. China is a one-party society. Although other "parties" are permitted to exist, they are of no consequence. Japan is a one-and-half-party political system, by which we mean the LDP (or predecessor conservative groups) has controlled the government almost continuously since World War II and that the JSP (one-half party) has served as the major opposition. Japan is not a true two-party system because there has not been alternation of power between the two major parties. Some observers see Japan's moving toward a multiparty system where power may be exercised by coalitions involving two or more of the five or six national parties. The fact that power has not alternated is not the result of a defect in the system: it results from the JSP's inability to develop widely attractive policy alternatives and to gain enough votes to form a majority in the House of Representatives.

The People's Republic of China has a variety of organizations (for example, labor unions, lower- and middle-class peasant organizations, and the Little Red Guards) that are listed in the Communist party constitution and must obey the party. Such groups should not be equated to the literally thousands of voluntary associations found in Japan which "politick" for their particular interests. Pressure groups play a vital role in Japan, as they do in other open, democratic, and highly industrialized societies. In Japan, parties and pressure groups provide a systematic means for articulation of diverse demands on the government, and the election system provides for direct popular participation in elections. In China the process depends on the mass line and elections, which provide no alternatives and take place within the hierarchy of Chinese Communist party and state congresses. As we have seen, the People's Liberation Army has played a very important role in Chinese politics. It is "the honorable obligation of citizens" to serve in the conscript PLA, which has been a vast school for millions of peasants and, at times, a model for the entire society. The PLA is lauded as the defender of the revolution. In contrast, Japan's Self-Defense Force has no role as a political actor, is a volunteer civil service force, and it is not held in high repute.

The role of the individual in the political systems of Japan and China is a solid indicator of the nature of the system and its political actors. In China the individual is clearly subordinated to the major institutional political actors in political and economic matters. Although the standard of living has risen and the distribution of available goods is more equitable, the individual plays no role in decisions concerning what to manufacture, or where, or how much. Price is not a function of supply and demand; and in the command economy, the individual is neutral as both worker and consumer. The small entrepreneur has no role. Politically the individual Chinese has little say about who rules or on what policies are made. He may be mobilized for a variety of political or economic or social objectives, but only within party-approved parameters. He does not vote to choose his leaders, nor does he take part in policy formulation or approval, except symbolically. The "mass"

media are scanty and do not provide policy alternatives for public or other discussion. Meaningful individual political activity derives from the party membership enjoyed by the very few. In general, individual participation in the political process is determined from above, and Chinese are denied the basic human rights so highly valued elsewhere.

In Japan, the role of the individual is almost diametrically opposed to that in China. In economic matters, the individual Japanese, through aggregate demand working in a consumer-oriented economy, has a great deal to say about the type, quality, and number of goods produced. Although the *zaikai* has tremendous power and influence, large numbers of Japanese are stockholders in all sizes of corporations and share in the profits of the capitalist system. The individual small and medium-size entrepreneur is a vital segment of the economy. Politically, the individual Japanese plays a small role, except in the aggregate. Elections do determine who shall rule, and voter participation under universal suffrage is much higher at all levels of government than in the United States. The competitive party system, freedom of assembly, and freedom of the press, coupled with highly developed information media and well-educated population, provide the opportunity for individual participation. There is really no limit to organizing for political activity. The constitutional guarantees of individual human rights and freedom have effectively protected individuals and groups from governmental suppression.

Power and Policy

The policy process and decision-making procedures in China and Japan are markedly different. On a level of broad generalization, both states pursue similar goals, for example, the security of the society and the state, a higher standard of living and expanded social services. Yet we have seen that the substance of policy differs greatly, for instance, in the economic field because of the application of highly contrative ideologies to widely disparate economic systems. The command economy of China seeks modernization in an overwhelmingly agrarian nation with a low standard of living. The relatively free capitalistic system of Japan, already having produced a very high standard of living, seeks to meet the social as well as the economic demands of a modern industrialized society. China stresses self-reliance, if not complete autarky, with limited foreign trade used as a political tool; Japan seeks worldwide interdependence through expanded foreign trade in a competitive international trading system. The process differs not only because of variant ideology and policy substance, but because the bases of legitimacy, the political actors, and their styles also differ.

The Politburo (or its Standing Committee) of the Central Committee of the Chinese Communist party is the focal point of the policy process in the People's Republic of China. It clearly derives its political authority from the party constitution. Deliberations are secret, but it is likely that the Politburo approves all major policy measures and initiates many of them. This does not mean that these policy decisions are made solely from the collective viewpoint of the party without regard to the interests of the People's Liberation Army and the state, for the Politburo members have vital functions in their individual capacities which are organizationally differentiated from the party. What appears as a Politburo decision may be, in fact, a synthesis of the viewpoints of the interlocking leadership of all three major political actors. If there is near unanimity on a given issue, policy is decided in the Politburo. When there is substantial disagreement within that group, the base for decision making is expanded, as we have seen in the Lushan meeting of 1959, when an expanded Central Committee plenum that included nonparty personnel was used.

The PRC constitution gives important powers to the state structure, but these are inferior to party powers. The essential function of the National People's Congress, like that of the National Party Congress, is to legitimize and secure active support for policy decisions made by the intra-party elite. The State Council and various ministries have had vital input to party decisions in economic and military matters, and have served as the primary organs to translate policy into action. At times extra-Constitutional groups such as the Red Guards have been used to execute policy. The mass media are rudely developed as compared to those of Japan. Its major role has been to inform the people of decisions made and to mobilize support for policy. The primary extra-party means for policy input is the mass line, which is most useful for refinement of policy already decided.

Policy is made by a small group within the party, heavily influenced by an ideology which points the direction for policy and requires the perpetuation of leadership by a small, closed elite providing firm leadership to the party and the state structure, each of which is supported by a strong hierarchical organization.

The focal point of the policy process in Japan is the Liberal Democratic Party (LDP), which has continuously controlled the Diet, "the highest organ of state power" and "sole law-making organ of the state." The LDP selects the prime minister and fills all Cabinet posts. Nearly all legislation originates in one of the ministries and is sponsored by the Cabinet after it has been approved by the bureaucracy and the LDP organs charged with policy approval. The consensus-building process is generally hidden from public view.

Consensus results from bargaining among interested ministries and LDP divisions organized parallel to Cabinet ministries. Factional bargaining is vital to the policy process and takes place within the LDP because that party has an absolute majority. Bargaining does not take place between or among the political parties. Once consensus is achieved within the bureaucracy and the LDP, passage of the legislation is a foregone conclusion.

The most influential interest group is the *zaikai*, which cooperates closely with the LDP and the bureaucracy, providing organized and systematic input into the policy process. The other political parties in Japan have so far been no more than a vocal, but disunited, opposition to the government, capable only of delay and criticism of the LDP decision-making process. The mass media are far more influential in Japan than in China, tending to be antigovernment and highly critical. Labor unions support the socialist parties single-mindedly and therefore have not been able to influence LDP policies significantly. Disruptive student activities have been widely publicized, but such groups have little leverage with the LDP. Personal leadership in Japan is much less important than in China. Prime ministers serve at the pleasure of other factional leaders, and no LDP leader has the individual political strength necessary to form a government. Every prime minister is thus subject to powerful restraints on his power by rival factional leaders.

China has been pre-eminently occupied with internal development since 1949, with power being used simultaneously to enhance and consolidate Communist party control over the entire Chinese society and to bring about the economic development of China. The goals have not always been complementary, and shifts in emphasis have caused great social stress. From accession to power in 1949 through 1952, China's leaders established political control over the countryside. Land reform to eliminate landlords and rich peasants was carried out with considerable loss of life. The first Five-Year Plan (1953–1957) was based on the Soviet model ("leaning to one side") and gave priority to the development of basic industry by forced-draft industrialization and maximum fixed capital formation. At the same time, rural collectivization was undertaken and 97 percent of peasant households were included by October 1957. Buoyed by the impressive economic gains made by 1957, Mao decreed the Great Leap Forward (1958–1960). This was an intensive political mass mobilization to transform China's social and economic organization by forming some 26,000 communes (the new basic unit of Chinese society) to realize the principle of "politics in command" and to "merge the Party and Commune into one." The Great Leap had several faults and led to a reduction in GNP; grain output fell to the 1953 level. Serious economic dislocations resulted from decentralized planning and inefficient efforts toward regional self-sufficiency.

Mao's economic policies were severely criticized by People's Liberation Army leaders at the Lushan plenum in 1959. Although Mao purged his PLA critics, he was forced to accept the fact of economic crisis, and China embarked on a period of readjustment (1961–1965) relying on economic rationality and a return to centralized planning and administration. The economy was effectively managed during this period, and new highs in GNP, industrial production, and agricultural production were achieved by 1965. The Great Proletarian Cultural Revolution (1966–1969) was a return to Maoist principles, successfully pitting "red" against "expert," party revolutionaries against the technical and managerial elites. The main target of the enormously tumultuous Cultural Revolution was the "capitalist roaders," the technicians and managers in the party and government bureaucracy. A new political order was formalized by the Chinese Communist party's Tenth Congress in 1973 and the adoption of a new Chinese Constitution in 1975. Genuine economic advances have been made since 1953:

tripling of the GNP, doubling of the per capita GNP, and an eightfold increase in industrial production. China remains a primarily agrarian society with a higher standard of living than ever before, but still low in comparison to Japan, the Republic of China, or the Republic of Korea.

Japan has been predominantly occupied with economic growth since the end of the occupation. This growth is due to several fundamental characteristics of Japan's society and government. The government has provided political and fiscal stability and a congenial atmosphere for the expansion of capitalist enterprise based on the profit motive. The people of Japan possess the required education, technical competence, and capacity for hard work. The paternalism of Japanese corporations has encouraged a high level of productivity. Government planning assistance has permitted Japan to be internationally competitive in a variety of product fields emphasizing high technology and labor-intensive industries. Relieved of the burden of defense expenditures common to industrialized states, Japan has had an unusually high share of fixed capital investment. Japan has multiplied its GNP from about $10 billion in 1950 to about $400 billion in 1973 and its per capita GNP promises soon to rank with the world's highest. In becoming the world's third most productive national economic unit, Japan has shown that a resource-poor, geographically isolated nation can develop into a global economic power. Nevertheless, Japan is the most economically vulnerable industrialized state: its prosperity demands assured access to both raw materials and trading partners. This economic growth has not been without its social costs. Japan has been transformed from one-third urban and two-thirds rural to two-thirds urban and one-third rural over a period of a quarter century. Displacement of millions of Japanese from a familiar life-style has brought with it psychological problems attendant on urban crowding. Pollution and similar problems abound, and many Japanese are disenchanted with economic growth as an end in itself.

Foreign Policy

The foreign policy process and goals of China and Japan reflect the differences in ideology and governmental processes. The approach in China is high in ideological content and apparently monolithic in execution. Undoubtedly it is the party elite alone that determines foreign policy goals and the appropriate measures to achieve them. In Japan the executive is very susceptible to pressures from within his own party, from the political opposition, the *zaikai*, and other interest groups. The prime minister is far less independent in the foreign policy process than is the executive in a presidential system. Foreign policy results from consultation, public debate, and compromise among many interested groups.

In international affairs, China has sought to protect its socialist revolution and ensure territorial integrity, to gain international acceptance, to assure that states on its periphery remain neutral if not friendly, to restore its historical influence in Southeast Asia, and to help write some of the rules of interstate intercourse. In pursuit of these goals, China relied heavily on Soviet diplomatic, military, and economic support throughout the 1950s. China intervened massively in the Korean War after the defeat of North Korean forces in October 1950, participated in the armistice negotiations, and in 1958 withdrew the PLA from Korea, apparently assured that her interests were protected in northeast Asia. In the mid-1950s, China participated in the Bandung Conference and has since subscribed to the five principles of "peaceful coexistence": mutual respect for each other's territorial integrity and sovereignty, mutual nonaggression, mutual noninterference in each other's affairs, equality and mutual benefit, and peaceful coexistence. In the early 1960s, China shifted to a more self-assertive policy required by the disruption of relations with the Soviet Union. During the Cultural Revolution, China effectively isolated itself from world affairs but continued to support Hanoi in its struggle to seize all of Vietnam while relations with Moscow deteriorated to open border conflict in 1969. Convinced that the United States would withdraw its military forces from Southeast Asia, China accepted United States initiatives to thaw Sino-American relations as a means to counter the Soviet Union and to prevent closer "collusion" between the United States and the Soviet Union. The Nixon-Chou communiqué of February 27, 1972, outlined the areas of agreement and is the basis of Sino-American relations. China has protected its sovereignty, expanded its role and prestige in international affairs by gaining Nationalist China's permanent seat in the United Nations Security Council, "normalized" diplomatic relations with Japan and all countries in Southeast Asia, protected its interests in Northeast Asia, and gained leverage in its relations with the Soviet Union. Nevertheless, China continues to regard the Soviet Union as the major threat to its own security. The two nations are locked in an ideological struggle with worldwide implications.

Japan's international posture has been conditioned strongly by its close ties with the United States which are rooted in deeply shared democratic values and essentially similar views of what is necessary for global economic activity and a peaceful, relatively stable world order. In addition to close cooperation with the United States, Japan's foreign policy is guided by (1) support of the United Nations and (2) promotion of foreign trade and a generally free international economic system. Japan's general approach to world problems has been "low posture," mainly passive, adaptive, and reactive to outside pressures, avoiding any potentially costly political involvement.

Japan's close ties with the United States derive from the special relationship during the occupation and are symbolized in the revised Security Treaty of 1960. This treaty provides that an "armed attack against either Party in the territories under the administration of Japan would be dangerous to its own peace and safety" and declares that "it would act to meet the common danger in accordance with its constitutional provisions and processes." Some Japanese view the treaty, and especially United States military bases in Japan, as a derogation of their sovereignty and as visible evidence of Japan's subservience to the United States. Nevertheless, the treaty seems to have served well the interests of both parties. It is likely to continue to be the cornerstone of United States–Japanese relations so long as the Liberal Democratic party remains in power.

Historically Japan has not had amicable relations with any of its closest neighbors in Asia—China, Korea, and the Soviet Union. It has recognized the People's Republic of China, a step that caused the Republic of China to sever ties, although relations continue with Taipei much as before. It recognizes the Republic of Korea, which has a mutual security treaty with the United States. But it does not recognize the Democratic People's Republic of Korea, which has close relations with the People's Republic of China and with the Soviet Union. Diplomatic relations have been "normalized" with Moscow, but territorial issues have prevented a peace treaty formally ending World War II. As Japan seeks to develop a foreign policy that is more autonomous (less dependent on the United States), and looks for ways to use its economic power and diplomatic influence, it will become increasingly difficult for Japan to avoid political involvement. Japan is emerging as a principal actor in the great power rivalry in East Asia where the interests of the United States, the Soviet Union, China, and Japan converge in a complex and shifting pattern. Having projected successfully the image of a politically stable, democratic, but militarily weak economic superpower, Japan is testing its new policy of remaining equidistant from its two great communist neighbors, China and the Soviet Union. Whether Japan can adapt to the new regional political environment depends mostly on events it cannot control, but to which it must react wisely, and the ability to react depends on continuing domestic economic and political stability.

Sharing the ancient humanitarian Confucian tradition for hundreds of years, China and Japan have departed from that tradition and developed politics probably as different as those of any two major nations in the world today. In the nonpolitical sector, China is mostly rural and agrarian, with a low level of gross and per capita national product, a relatively low level of specialization in social organization, and a relatively low level of literacy, as measured in terms of mass media circulation. High education of dubious quality is restricted to very few. In contrast Japan is highly urbanized and highly industrialized, with the world's third largest GNP and a high per capita GNP, a high degree of social specialization. Japan is a world leader in literacy, as measured by mass media circulation, and is second in the world in annual number of college graduates. In the political sector, China is a mobilized authoritarian state directed by the Chinese Communist party, a small elite of 3.5 percent of the population who control the making and carrying out of policy. Japan is a free, open, and democratic representative political system where sovereignty lies with the people and is exercised by regular elections in which opposing parties with alternative programs compete for popular favor.

Summary

We can only conclude that the political systems and ideologies of China and Japan differ fundamentally. Both countries may be entering periods of unusual stress. After decades of service as China's leader, Chairman Mao has been replaced by Chairman Hua, whose principal claim to legitimacy is a note written to him by an ailing Mao, "With you in charge, I'm at ease."[3] Whether the extraconstitutional succession can withstand challenges other than those already repulsed is unknown. Change, not order, will be sought in China. As "Chairman Hua has rightly pointed out: 'Chairman Mao's great theory [continuing revolution] has provided the solution to the most important issue of our time, consolidating the dictatorship of the proletariat and preventing capitalist restoration. . . .' "[4] Japan's political system must adapt to the changing realities of international politics while seeking to solve the problems attendant on highly industrial, high mass consumption urban societies. The national political dominance of the Liberal Democratic party is tenuous at best, made so by scandal, internal factionalism, and aggressive opposition. Japan's commitment to the future is concisely stated in Premier Miki's "Greetings to the American People on the Bicentennial of Their Independence."

Through three decades of vigorous testing, the Japanese People have also confirmed that democracy may not be tidy, because it thrives on diversity, but that it is the most creative and rewarding of political systems precisely because it relies on individual initiative and citizen responsibility.

The meaning of America's two hundred years, and of Japan's own experience, is that freedom with equality is both the goal and the means for human fulfillment in all its diversity and richness.

Both China and Japan have been heavily influenced by Western concepts: one, by an authoritarian ideology stressing the class struggle and ultimate victory of the proletariat, the other, by an ideology stressing individual rights and government accountability to the people. Both countries suffered serious internal disruptions during World War II, and China also experienced a revolution. Both systems appear to be following the major guidelines of their professed ideologies. One thing seems to be clear, however: in both systems the pull of tradition remains strong; neither China nor Japan will develop into a Far Eastern Russia or a Far Eastern America. Finally, both systems have yet to be truly tested in terms of the institutionalization of "new" ideologies. The Chinese concern with development and internal security is equally matched by Japan's heavy dependence on foreign trade and American nuclear umbrella. Both systems have yet to fully mobilize state power in terms of their own ideological goals. The Chinese are struggling to ensure that the party remains dominant and that its highest leadership resolves internal conflicts without disrupting the administrative and political process. The Japanese must ultimately face the possibility of the evolution of strong political actors challenging the existing factional leadership and the fragile position of the Liberal Democratic party.

NOTES

1. For discussion of some of these points, see John K. Fairbank and Edwin O. Reischauer, *East Asia The Great Tradition* (Boston: Houghton Mifflin, 1960), pp. 669–673, and W. W. Lockwood, "Japan's Response to the West; the Contrast with China," *World Politics*, no. 9 (1956), pp. 37–54.
2. *Newsweek*, January 17, 1977, pp. 33–34.
3. Fox Butterfield, "China: Unraveling the New Mysteries," *New York Times Magazine*, June 19, 1977, p. 54.

4. Lin Chin-jan, "A New Brilliant Concept, A New Great Constitution—Studying the concept of continuing the revolution under the dictatorship of the proletariat in Vol. V of the 'Selected Works of Mao Tse-tung,'" *Peking Review*, no. 25 (June 17, 1977), p. 12.

Further Readings

CHINA

Barnett, A. Doak. *Cadres Bureaucracy and Political Power in Communist China*. New York: Columbia University Press, 1967.

Clubb, O. Edmund. *Twentieth Century China*. New York: Columbia University Press, 1964.

Creel, H. G. *Confucius: The Man and the Myth*. New York: Day, 1949.

Fairbank, John K. *The United States and China*. 3rd ed. Cambridge, Mass.: Harvard University Press, 1971.

Fairbank, John K., Edwin O. Reischauer, and Albert M. Craig. *East Asia Tradition and Transformation*. Boston: Houghton Mifflin, 1973.

Fitzgerald, C. P. *China: A Short Cultural History*. 3rd ed. New York: Praeger, 1961.

Hinton, Harold C. *China's Turbulent Quest*. New York: Macmillan, 1970.

Lifton, Robert J. *Thought Reform and the Psychology of Totalism: A Study of "Brainwashing" in China*. New York: Norton, 1961.

Payne, Robert. *Mao Tse-tung*. New York: Abelard-Schuman, 1962.

Schram, Stuart. *The Political Thought of Mao Tse-tung*. New York: Praeger, 1963.

Schurmann, Franz, and Orville Schell. *People's China*. New York: Random House, 1974.

Snow, Edgar. *Red Star Over China*. New York: Random House, 1938.

Solomon, Richard H. *Mao's Revolution and the Chinese Political Culture*. Berkeley: University of California Press, 1971.

Townshend, James R. *Political Participation in Communist China*. Berkeley: University of California Press, 1968.

Yang, C. K. *Chinese Communist Society: The Family and the Village*. Cambridge, Mass.: M.I.T. Press, 1965.

JAPAN

Beasley, W. G. *The Modern History of Japan*. 2nd ed. New York: Praeger, 1973.

Borton, Hugh. *Japan's Modern Century*. 2nd ed. New York: Ronald Press, 1970.

Butow, Robert J. C. *Japan's Decision to Surrender*. Stanford, Calif.: Stanford University Press, 1954.

Brzezinski, Zbigniew. *The Fragile Blossom Crisis and Change in Japan*. New York: Harper & Row, 1972.

Dore, Ronald P. *City Life in Japan: A Study of a Tokyo Ward*. Berkeley: University of California Press, 1972.

Duus, Peter. *The Rise of Modern Japan*. Boston: Houghton Mifflin, 1976.

Emmerson, John. *Arms, Yen and Power: The Japanese Dilemma*. New York: Dunellen, 1971.

Feis, Herbert. *The Road to Pearl Harbor*. Princeton, N.J.: Princeton University Press, 1950.

Kahn, Hermann. *The Emerging Japanese Superstate Challenge and Response*. Englewood Cliffs, N.J.: Prentice-Hall, 1970.

Kawai, Kazuo. *Japan's American Interlude*. Chicago: University of Chicago Press, 1960.

Nakane, Chie. *Japanese Society*. Berkeley: University of California Press, 1972.

Nobutaka, Ike. *Japanese Politics Patron-Client Democracy*. 2nd ed. New York: Alfred A. Knopf, 1972.

Reischauer, Edwin O. *Japan: The Story of a Nation*. Rev. ed. New York: Alfred A. Knopf, 1974.

Scalapino, Robert A. *The Japanese Community Movement 1920–1966*. Berkeley: University of California Press, 1966.

Vogel, Ezra F. *Japan's New Middle Class*. Berkeley: University of California Press, 1971.

PART 6 Conclusions

CHAPTER / 16

FOUR POLITICAL SYSTEMS

Comparison is rarely complete without some analytical sense of the differences and similarities of political systems and processes. The discussions throughout the book have focused on the organizing concepts defined earlier and have, in themselves, provided the analytical base for comparison. While we are inclined to let these assessments speak for themselves, we feel it necessary and useful to review and highlight such matters. Doing so will not only help the student understand the comparative method, but will also once again bring into focus the major question in this book: How well do the political systems of the United States, the Soviet Union, China, and Japan perform in accordance with their own ideologies?

It is clear from our study that one of the most important characteristics of ideological relevance is the ability of the political system to maintain relative stability. While stability is a reflection of a number of processes and institutions, there are, in our view, at least four that are essential. The system must allow for a peaceful change of the ruling elite. Moreover, any elite assuming power must do so more or less in accord with accepted principles of the ideology. In addition, the function of the ruling elite (that is, how they operate while they are in power) must conform to generally accepted ideological principles. From the point of view of the individual, ideological relevance presumes that the general principles of the political system do not violate the existing attitudes and values held by most of the people in society. The conduct of the political system must also be in accord with the generally accepted interpretations of the ideology of the most powerful groups in society. That is, the processes of the system, how decisions are made, the relative role of various groups and their exercise of power, must generally be accepted by the major power holders in the system. In sum, the ideology must provide for the perpetuation and growth of the system as perceived by the major actors in society.

In our discussions we noted that the concept *political system* is a theoretical abstraction; that is, it is difficult to "see" a political system—its shape and its functioning. What does give it shape and direction are political actors (power holders) who make decisions in the name of the system. In doing so, political actors must not only reflect the ideology of the system, but they must also perform roles and function within the generally accepted values and attitudes of the mass of people in society.

Finally, the policies that evolve from a political system must support and perpetuate the ideology. Thus, not only must the political process be legitimate, but the policies that evolve and the political actors who influence the process and the policies must follow generally accepted ideological principles. If a political system is operating within this ideological framework, we can presume that it is performing relatively well.

As is clear from our discussion thus far, we have freely used such qualifying phrases as "reasonably well," "generally acceptable," and "more or less." This is deliberate. We recognize that it is not possible to scientifically categorize political system performance. While this can be done in terms of economic criteria (for example, gross national product), it is usually quite difficult and often impossible to do according to political and social criteria. Nevertheless, making comparisons according to general descriptive categories is an essential preliminary step in developing more precise and scientifically based comparisons. And it is this that we have attempted to do in this book and will synthesize in this concluding chapter.

Before we begin, however, we need to review some of the major economic and population characteristics of the four political systems. Table 16-1 shows five major characteristics. It is interesting to note that Japan has the highest economic growth, lowest expenditures on the military, and the smallest number of men in the armed forces of all four systems.

Ideology

The clearest conclusion is that each of the systems has maintained its ideology and political style for at least one generation (25 years): the United States, for over 200 years; the Soviet Union, over 60 years; Japan, over 30 years; and China, for just short of 30 years. While we must be careful in equating time with effectiveness, there is no question that, in each of the systems, there has been an institutionalization of the ideology. While we can question the extent of this institutionalization in China and, to a lesser extent, in Japan, the Maoist ideology in China and the traditional-modern intermix in Japan have served as the basis for political legitimacy during some turbulent times, particularly if one recalls the tremendous problems associated with the shift from a Nationalist regime under Chiang Kai-shek to Maoism in China. This was compounded by the economic and social shambles in China after almost 30 years of warfare. Similarly, Japan, though defeated in World War II, has managed to develop a cohesion and economic productivity that has placed it in the top category of industrial and commercial states in the world.

An important indicator of the institutionalization of ideology is the manner in which power is transferred from one leader to another, or from one group to another. Generally speaking, over the past generation, there has been a relatively peaceful transfer of power in all the systems. The United States is particularly effective in this respect. The Watergate affair demonstrated the strength of the system and the commitment to the values of legitimacy and peaceful resolution of conflict. In the Soviet Union, it appears that the "blood letting" days of the Stalinist era have succumbed to relatively peaceful transfers of power within the elite. This does not mean no conflict, but conflict that is controlled within the top echelons of the party. In China, the

Table 16–1: Population and Economic Data

	United States	Soviet Union	China	Japan
Population	215,000,000	253,300,000	900,000,000	110,500,000
Total Armed Forces	2,130,000	3,575,000	3,250,000 (excluding militia)	240,000
Gross National Product (GNP)	$1,500 billion	$780 billion	$230 billion	$500 billion
Annual Military Expenditures	6% of GNP	11% of GNP	9.3% of GNP	.1% of GNP
Growth Rate 1970–1974	3.2%	4.8%	4.7%	6.0%

Source: The data shown here are generally based on the period 1970–1974. Major sources used for this information are *The Military Balance 1975–1976* (London: International Institute of Strategic Studies, 1975; Ray S. Cline, *World Power Assessment* (Washington, D.C.: Georgetown University, 1975; T. N. Dupuy *The Almanac of World Military Power* (Harrisburg, Pa.: Stackpole Books, 1970).

transfer of power is still based on internal struggles within the Communist party with ramifications extending out to the rural areas and various regions. Yet, there has been no massive armed struggle. In Japan, power remains in the hands of the Liberal Democratic party, and transfers of power normally take place within the party with consensus of the various party factions.

While the political systems of the four countries studied here have been shaped by important aspects of their history, those of the United States and the Soviet Union show this influence most clearly. The United States developed out of an Anglo-Saxon and English heritage with its emphasis on law and rights. The Soviet Union reflects the absolutism of the tsars with its focus on centralization and control. The Chinese and Japanese systems, on the other hand, appear to have developed distinctly modern themes intermingled with the past. In China, the traditional dynasties and the Confucian value system reinforced a unitary and centralized system. Maoism, while steeped in modern values, does link strongly with the past in terms of dynastic ruler and centralized control. Japan probably is unique in this respect. Its ideology, based on Shintoism and Buddhism, has been the

dominant theme for centuries, with a government structure centered around the emperor and the shogunate system, combined with a system of inner and outer lords. Even with some experience in the 19th century with a parliamentary and party system, the imposition of a democratic constitution by the conquering Americans was a unique phenomenon. The important roles played by political parties in modern Japan and the cabinet-parliamentary system of government have provided a distinctly democratic experience.

In sum, in each of the political systems, there is a reasonable correlation between the political system, the ideology, and the character and power of political actors. To be sure, a gap remains between the actual working of the systems and their ideologies. Yet, in the systems studied here, it appears that the ideologies are adequately institutionalized, that is, accepted by the major political actors. As we learned, however, the similarities between the systems stop here. In each system, there are distinct differences in how the political actors pursue their goals.

Comparing the general ideological principles, we can see that the systems can be categorized in accordance with the relative degree of ideological openness. If an ideology provides for a legitimate and meaningful involvement in decision making by a wide variety of political actors and has a relatively wide base of legitimacy (that is, there are allowances for a variety of interpretations of ideology), then it is "open." Obviously a "closed" system is the opposite (see Figure 16-1).

Political Actors

The types of political actors, their methods of operation, and their degree of power generally reflect the political style that evolves from the system's ideology. Thus, the number of political actors and how much power they exercise in the political system is, at once, a function and measure of its ideological openness. In the American system there is a great variety of political actors, exercising a wide range of power. Institutional groups, such as Congress, and voluntary groups, such as labor unions, exercise varying degrees of power. The important point is that such groups are meaningful in terms of examining the political process. In the Soviet Union, the primary political actor and the one that is the basis of all legitimacy is the Soviet Communist party. Labor unions in the Soviet system have little, if any, political significance. Thus, while other groups exist, they are primarily arms of the party, or are supportive of it. To be sure there are groups based on dissent and some are antiparty oriented, but these are on the fringes of legitimacy and wield little political power. In China, as in the Soviet Union, the party is the primary actor. While China is communist, the system tends to be influenced by regional groups to an extent not seen in the Soviet Union, although these groups lack specific structures or clear purposes. The Cultural Revolution in China, for example, showed the degree to which local peasant groups, aligning themselves with local army units, could defy the youthful Red Guards, creatures of the central party structure. In Japan, the party system and cliques within the Diet associated with business interests remain the primary actors. Voluntary and nonvoluntary groups in Japan are important and increasingly reflect an emerging broader base of legitimacy.

In each of the systems, the character of the political actors has remained generally the same. Thus, in the Soviet Union, we find that after 60 years, the top leadership of the Communist party is as entrenched as ever. Similar observations can be made about the other systems and their political actors. The political process and the general values of society retain their roots in the basic ideologies of the systems, perpetuating the power of existing political actors. Moreover, the general attitudes and values within the political system reinforce the legitimacy of each.

Table 16-2 shows the relative degrees of power of political actors in each of the systems as reflected in interest groups. The categorization of group activity is one way of showing relative importance as political actors. Obviously, there is not a clear delineation between these categories. Nevertheless, they do provide a picture of the nature of the political system and the character of the political actors. While the various categories appear self-explanatory, we should note that the degree of impact on the political system is identified by the following (in order of importance): Primary Actor, Major Actor, Actor, Minor Actor, Supportive, and Negligible. Primary Actor means that the group is the source and channel of power and legitimacy for all other political actors. Major Actor identifies an important group, but one that cannot rule by itself, nor is it the source of all power and legitimacy. Actor indicates that, while the group is overshadowed by the Primary Actor, it is by no means unimportant in the political

Figure 16-1: Relative Position Along the Ideological Spectrum

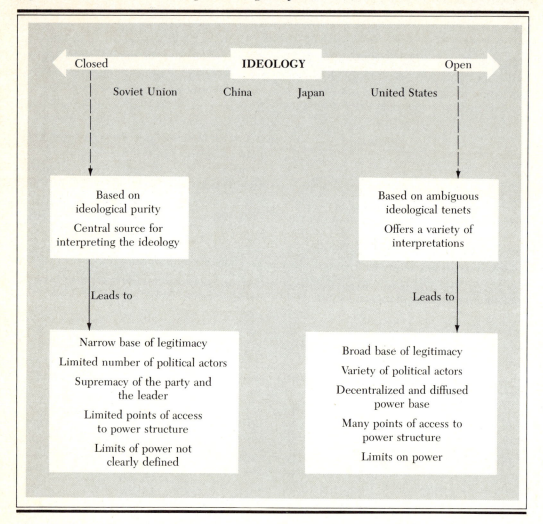

process. Its reference is the Major Actor, but the Actor has a freedom of action and impact to limit the Major Actor in exercising absolute power. Minor Actor is as the label indicates; it has a minor impact on the total political process. Supportive means that the group is controlled by the Primary Actor: it has no freedom of action except as dictated by the Primary Actor.

Power and Policy

As one would expect, the policy and the decision-making processes reflect the goals of the most powerful groups in society in each of the systems studied. While none of the systems has a consistent involvement of the people in the policy process, the American system is the most receptive in this regard.

Table 16–2: Groups as Political Actors

Types of Groups	United States	Japan	China	Soviet Union
Institutional	Major Actor	Major Actor	Primary Actor	Primary Actor
Voluntary	Major Actor	Actor	Supportive	Supportive
Nonvoluntary	Actor	Actor	Minor Actor	Minor Actor
Spontaneous	Minor Actor	Minor Actor	Supportive	Negligible

That is, as political actors, the people do have an impact on the policy process and the substance of policy when the issues are clear and when a crisis is perceived. Yet the fact remains that, in all the systems studied, the people and the individual citizen rarely have a direct input into the policy arena.

In the American system, the variety of political actors, the diffused nature of political power, and the multicentered decision-making process allow for a great deal of interaction among political actors, making the process vulnerable to external pressure. Similarly, compromise and bargaining among various political actors, characteristic of the American system, are reflected in the substance of policies: few ever get a whole loaf; rather, there is part of a loaf for a number of actors. Invariably policies emanating from Congress, for example, reflect agreements and compromises of powerful groups operating within that body. Similarly, presidential policies generally take account of the various demands made upon the office by political actors, both in and out of government. In sum, the relatively open process often precludes focused and clear policy goals, a reflection of the political system as a whole.

In the Soviet system, we find an almost opposite policy process with its parallel in the substance of policies. To be sure, the Soviet citizen no longer remains the terror-stricken subject of the Stalinist days. Nevertheless, the dominance of the Communist party, its character as an elite party, and the preoccupa-

tion with ideological relevance allows, at best, a narrow input to the process from outside the official institutions. The nature of the political actors and the fact that their power evolves from their linkages to the Communist party and the top echelons of the party leadership rarely allow an independent alternative to the proclaimed policy. Similarly, while the policy substance remains fixed in perpetuating a communist view of the state, some attention is being given to the individual needs and consumer demands, a concern generally ignored in the Stalinist period. In sum, the dominance of the party and state apparatus in the policy process remains the essential characteristic of the Soviet system.

In the Chinese system, institutionalization of the policy process is incomplete. Nevertheless, the general policy emanates, as in the Soviet system, from the top echelons of the party. The substance of policies appears to be focused on the problems generally associated with developing nations, that is, organizing the people, promoting economic growth, and institutionalizing the ideology and leadership. To be sure, the Chinese have come a long way since the early 1950s, but the fact remains that most of China's problems reflect the needs of development—to establish the basic infrastructure of a modern state system—and an almost xenophobic concern with security.

In Japan, while the constitution is democratic, the policy process remains generally hidden from public view or participation. The existence of a number of political actors has

Table 16–3: A Systems Perspective

Political Systems	Ideology	Political Actors	Policy Process and Substance
Soviet Union	Concern with ideological purity; central direction and interpretation	Limited; party is primary actor	Closed process based on central direction. Politics and process confined generally within elites.
China	Concern with ideological purity; central direction and interpretation	Limited; party is primary actor	Closed process based on central direction. Lack of complete institutionalization motivates politics and process within elite, and between elites and other groups on a very limited basis.
Japan	Ambiguity of ideological principles and some variety of interpretation	Semilimited; party and business groups are primary actors	Semiopen process where access is available to actors outside the party and business. Politics and process remain generally within party cliques and factions.
United States	Ambiguity of ideological principles and a variety of interpretations	Varied	Open process based on bargaining, compromise, negotiations. Politics and process generally within and among a variety of political actors.

not as yet been reflected in the policy process or, to a great extent, in the substance of policy. To be sure, policy substance increasingly reflects the demands and concerns of consumer groups and farmers. Yet it is clear that businessmen and industrialists are the major benefactors of policy. Thus, Japan's policy process and substance still resists the pressures from a variety of political actors that have emerged as a result of the democratic ideology and constitution. In light of Japan's increasingly open system, it is likely that such resistance will erode in a short span of years.

Table 16-3 shows the general associations among ideology, political actors, and power and policy.

The Future

There is no reason to suspect that the political systems we have analyzed here will change appreciably from their present character. The fact that each has remained in existence over a period of time and has been tested during some turbulent times suggests at least some minimum institutionalization of ideologies and relatively effective systems. It is the nature of the Chinese and Japanese ideologies that may cause some speculation. It can be argued that both are more or less transitory. This does not mean that the Maoist ideology, for example, is transient. Rather, it means that the Maoist ideology has yet to be interpreted by others than Mao, in an acceptable fashion. Moreover, the institutionalization of Maoism in the Chinese political system is not complete. In Japan, while the ideology appears to be institutionalized within the system, questions remain in its interpretation in terms of relevance to Japanese society. That is, the future role of the emperor, the status of traditional ideologies, and the continued function of an American-imposed democratic constitution have not been totally reconciled.

Summary: A Systems Perspective

In the final analysis, then, we have compared four countries using three major considerations as the basis for comparison. We have not identified countries according to moral criteria, that is, whether they are good or evil. Rather we have attempted to examine the evolution of ideology, political actors, power, and policy according to the uniqueness of each system, not necessarily as the basis for prognostication, but as a diagnostic intellectual exercise. Not only have we examined why the various political systems function as they do, but we have also identified three major areas common to each of the four systems assessing how they relate to each other, how they affect the operations of the system, and how they compare across the systems. Our conclusions are that the political systems we have studied generally reflect a dichotomy. On one side stand the United States and Japan; on the other, the Soviet Union and China. This does not necessarily mean that those in each group are allies or support one another. What it does suggest, however, is that the general orientation of the political systems seems to cluster these countries into two groups reflecting the following: individual versus collectivity orientation; participation versus nonparticipation; competition versus mobilization; pluralism versus elitism; and diffusion and decentralization versus monolithic orientation. Each country appears to be performing well enough to maintain the present character of the political system. Whether one system is good and the other evil, or whether one is good at times and evil at others, is left to the judgment of the individual student.

INDEX